Publishing Agreements

A Book of Precedents

Publishing Agreements

A Book of Precedents

Fifth Edition

General Editors
Charles Clark
Lynette Owen
Roger Palmer

Butterworths
London, Charlottesville, Dublin, Durban, Edinburgh,
Kuala Lumpur, Singapore, Sydney, Toronto, Wellington
1997

United Kingdom	Butterworths a Division of Reed Elsevier (UK) Ltd, Halsbury House, 35 Chancery Lane, LONDON WC2A 1EL and 4 Hill Street, EDINBURGH EH2 3JZ
Australia	Butterworths, SYDNEY, MELBOURNE, BRISBANE, ADELAIDE, PERTH, CANBERRA and HOBART
Canada	Butterworths Canada Ltd, TORONTO and VANCOUVER
Ireland	Butterworth (Ireland) Ltd, DUBLIN
Malaysia	Malayan Law Journal Sdn Bhd, KUALA LUMPUR
New Zealand	Butterworths of New Zealand Ltd, WELLINGTON and AUCKLAND
Singapore	Reed Elsevier (Singapore) Pte Ltd, SINGAPORE
South Africa	Butterworths Publishers (Pty) Ltd, DURBAN
USA	Michie, CHARLOTTESVILLE, Virginia

A CIP Catalogue record for this book is available from the British Library.

First Edition 1980
Second Edition 1984
    Reprinted 1986
Third Edition 1988
Fourth Edition 1993
    Reprinted 1995
Fifth Edition 1997

ISBN 0 406 00923 6

Printed and bound in Great Britain by Mackays of Chatham plc, Chatham, Kent

For Fiona
with all love
always

Introduction to the Fifth Edition

In 1988 the International Publishers Association held its four-yearly Congress in London. Copyright was, as usual, a key item. The agenda stays in the memory because simultaneously the UK delegation was explaining the beauties of the new 1988 UK Copyright, Designs and Patents Bill (then nearing the end of its passage through Parliament) and taking delivery though the front door of the Congress of a bulky document from the Commission of the European Community entitled *Green Paper on Copyright and the Challenge of Technology, a Communication from the Community.*

This Introduction incorporates and brings up to date from the Preface to the Fourth Edition a brief commentary on the 1988 Act, on the work of the World International Property Organisation (WIPO) which has culminated in December 1996 in the adoption of a WIPO Copyright Treaty, and a view of *Malcom v OUP* in the context of author/publisher contracts. New to this Fifth Edition is an account and review in this Introduction of the four main relevant European Copyright Directives adopted by the Council of Ministers during the years 1991–1996, and heralded by the Communication of June 1988. This review also glances forward to new European Commission initiatives, also heralded by a Communication, of November 1996, entitled *Follow up to the Green Paper on Copyright and Related Rights in the Information Society* (a document of July 1995).

The Copyright, Designs and Patents Act of 1988 performs the four 'bedrock' roles of modern copyright legislation: to establish the rights of authors of literary, dramatic, musical and artistic works; to establish the rights of those who invest, financially and creatively, in the works of authors; to balance the rights of such copyright owners with the needs of copyright users; and to protect the rights of copyright owners in both civil and criminal law.

The rights of authors are expressed in the familiar language of various 'acts restricted by copyright'. The rights of the cultural industries that invest in what authors have created are established in the world of book publishing in two ways: first, through the status given to exclusive licensees of rights acquired from authors; and secondly through an independent right of the publisher in the typographical arrangement of an edition which he/she has published. The balance between copyright owner and copyright user interests is maintained through the familiar concepts of fair dealing and of library privileges. And there is, fourthly, a welcome strengthening of civil and criminal law provisions against infringement of copyright.

Two features of the 1988 Act need special attention here. First, the Act incorporates specifically for the first time into UK copyright law moral rights. The reasoning behind this very important innovation is set out at Appendix D, and that Appendix also offers some drafts for the handling of the moral rights of paternity and integrity in contractual terms. What must be emphasised is that moral rights are here to stay, and that publishers must take care, as they make arrangements not only with book authors, but also and especially with the wide range of editors, re-writers, translators, graphic artists, catalogue producers, etc who work in the book trade, that those arrangements, right from the start of negotiations for them, address both the economic and the moral rights of copyright.

The second feature of the 1988 Act worth special attention here is the ways in which the Act grapples with new technology. As to computer programs, the Act is explicit. A program is a literary work (s. 3(1)(b)) and thus has the benefits of, and is also subject to, restrictions in the Act's provisions for literary works. Thus, copyright in a program will last for the life of its author plus 70 years (s. 12(2)). The copyright in a program made by an employee in the course of employment will, however, vest in the employer (s. 11(2)). An 'adaptation' of a work means, in relation to a computer program, an arrangement or altered version of the program or a translation of it (new s. 21(3)(ab)). Life since 1988 has become more, not less, complicated, and the Act of 1988 was revised, by statutory instrument, to take account in UK law of the EC Directive on the protection of computer programs, notably its provisions on interoperability, sometimes called 'reverse engineering'. See the new ss. 50A, 50B and 50C, together with new s. 296A, inserted into the text of the 1988 Act by CP 1992 regs. 8 and 11, which came into force on 1 January 1993.

As to the safeguarding of copyright works against unauthorised loading into, and subsequent downloading from, a database, s. 17(2) makes clear that storing of a copyright work 'in any medium by electronic means' is an act of reproduction, which is an act of copying, which is, of course, one of the fundamental acts restricted by the copyright in the work.

As with computer programs, the legal status of databases since 1988 has become more, not less, complicated. The very important problems, especially for the powerful British database industry, raised by the need to reconcile the different regimes for protection of databases within the single market of the EC have led to a Directive which will need intensive consultation before the due date for implementation.

* * * * *

Reference has been made twice now to the importance for UK law and practice of EC initiatives. It is important to grasp in some detail the initiatives which the EC has already processed or has in hand, with its eye set mainly on the need to create, in current jargon, a 'level playing-field' in the European single market.

The account which follows of the four most relevant European Copyright Directives and their impact on UK law and practice draws heavily (with her permission) on *Copyright, Designs and Patents Act 1988 – 8 Years On*, compiled and written by Vanessa Marsland of Clifford Chance and published by Clifford Chance for its clients and contacts. This very helpful work both reviews all the copyright Directives and also prints out most conveniently the text of the 1988 Act as revised by the implementation of the Directives, as at 1 January 1997. The four Directives surveyed here are:

Directive	*Due date for implementation*	*UK implementing legislation*
Software Protection	1 January 1993	The Copyright (Computer Programs) Regulations 1992 (SI 1992/3233): effective 1 January 1993
Rental and Lending	1 July 1994	The Copyright and Related Rights Regulations 1996 (SI 1996/2967): effective 1 December 1996
Copyright Duration	1 July 1995	The Duration of Copyright and Rights in Performance Regulations 1995 (SI 1995/3297): effective 1 January 1996
Databases	1 January 1998	Not yet implemented

Software Protection: Council Directive 91/250/EEC of 14 May 1991 on the legal protection of computer programs
This Directive confirms protection for computer programs as literary works, excludes protection for underlying ideas and principles, and defines the acts restricted by copyright in computer programs, and permitted derogations from these.

Rental and Lending: Council Directive 92/100/EEC of 19 November 1992 on rental right and lending right and on certain rights related to copyright in the field of intellectual property
This Directive requires member states to make rental and lending subject to the control of the copyright owner. It also requires them to enable performers and broadcasters to control the fixation and subsequent reproduction/broadcasting/distribution of their performances/broadcasts.

Copyright duration: Council Directive 93/98/EEC of 29 October 1993 harmonising the term of protection of copyright and certain related rights

This Directive harmonised duration of copyright to author's life plus 70 years for literary and other works – necessitating substantial reform of copyright term in the United Kingdom, and very complex transitional provisions dealing with restoration and extension of copyright on existing works. It also introduced a new 25-year copyright term for previously unpublished works in which copyright had already expired.

Databases: Directive 96/9/EC of the European Parliament and of the Council of 11 March 1996 on the legal protection of databases

This Directive is important to publishers because it contains a *sui generis* right (similar to copyright but not subject to all the same rules) in favour of the maker of a database, a form of publishers' right to protect investment in electronic and paper databases.

The Directive broadly requires member states to provide two different forms of protection which can exist in parallel, providing both copyright protection, conferred on the author (the creator) where the selection and arrangement of the database is sufficiently original to be an intellectual creation, and the *sui generis* right, conferred on the maker of the database:

– databases which are their authors' own intellectual creations, by reason of the selection or arrangement of their contents, are to be protected by copyright with traditional restricted acts broadly similar to those applied to copyright in literary works; and
– databases which reflect a sufficiently substantial level of investment, whether of labour, skill or financial resource, are additionally or alternatively to be protected by a new *sui generis* right, which will control the extraction and re-utilisation of the contents of protected databases. The protection is to be available both for databases which lack sufficient creativity to qualify for copyright protection and for those creative databases which do so qualify.

To deal with each Directive in turn:

Software Directive

The principal effect of this Directive has been on the drafting of software licences, with particular reference to the scope of the licence, and the permitted acts. The principal amendments to the legislation were to introduce provisions reflecting the 'permitted acts' introduced/confirmed by the Directive. These included the making of necessary back-up copies, acts incidental to lawful use (including debugging), and the limited reverse engineering defence. Although the Directive does not define 'computer program', the amendments also introduced language confirming that 'preparatory design materials' are to be protected as part of the program. Implementation is at new ss. 50A, 50B and 50C, together with new s. 296A.

Section 296A should be brought to the attention of any publisher who believes that 'contract is king'. The section renders void any condition in an agreement for the use of a computer program which aims to prohibit or restrict the making of a back-up copy or decompilation within the ambit of s. 50B.

Rental and Lending Directive

Rental and lending
The terms 'rental' and 'lending' are both defined as making a copy of the work available for use on terms that it will or may be returned. The distinction is that rental is making the work available for economic or commercial advantage, whereas lending is making the work available for no economic or commercial advantage (though operating costs may be covered) through an establishment which is accessible to the public.

The terms rental and lending do not include making works available for the purpose of exhibiting in public, making works available for on the spot reference use, or making works available for the purpose of public performance, playing or showing in public, broadcasting or inclusion in a cable programme service.

Rental
The Act already gave owners of copyright in computer programs, films and sound recordings the right to control rental, subject to provisions enabling compulsory licensing in prescribed circumstances. The right to control rental is now extended to cover all literary, dramatic and musical works, and all artistic works except buildings or models for buildings. The compulsory licensing provisions have now been repealed.

There are special provisions concerning deemed transfer and equitable remuneration in the case of rental of films, but terms for rental of books are left to author/publisher agreements. The relevant new provisions inserted in to the 1988 Act are to be found at ss. 16(1)(ba), 18A, 93A, 93B and 93C.

Copyright Duration Directive
Implementation of the Copyright Duration Directive has made a number of significant changes to UK law. The term of copyright in literary, dramatic, musical and artistic works originating from an EEA member state is extended from the previous author's life plus 50 years, to author's life plus 70 years. The terms for non-EEA works is the shorter of the EEA term and that in the country of origin. There are special provisions for works of unknown authorship, computer-generated works (a defined term), works of joint authorship, Crown and Parliamentary copyright material, and copyright material of certain international organisations.

This brief commentary concentrates on the *extension* and *revival* of copyright.

Extension

Literary, dramatic, musical and artistic works which had copyright protection under the former 'life plus 50 years' rule as at 31 December 1995 or which are made or first qualify for protection on or after 1 January 1996 are protected for life plus 70 years. The owner of the extended 20-year period of copyright will be the person who owned it on 31 December 1995 unless he/she owned it for a period of time less than the full term of copyright under the previous law. (It is thought that little difficulty will arise for the book business here. If an author had assigned his/her copyright to a publisher, it was highly likely that the period of assignment was for the full term of copyright.)

Revival

This 'windfall' provision is much more difficult and contentious than the extension provision. It states, in effect, that an author's copyright is revived if, despite its expiry in the UK before 31 December 1995, it was still protected in another EEA member state on 1 July 1995. The combination of long-established 'life plus 70 years' protection in Germany with the *Phil Collins* case in the European Court of Justice in 1993 means that copyright will revive for works of authors, artists and composers who died on or after 1 January 1926 but before 31 December 1944. The beneficiaries of many distinguished authors will be examining the small print in order to enjoy their windfalls! In some cases, eg Thomas Hardy who died in 1928, the extra period gained of 20 years will only take revival to the end of 1998 (1928 plus 70 years). In other cases, eg James Joyce who died in 1941, the estate will enjoy its windfall until the year end of 2011 (1941 plus 70 years).

The owner of copyright in the revised copyright period will be the person who owned it in the United Kingdom immediately before it expired, usually the author's personal representative. When copyright was assigned to a publisher which has ceased to exist, the revised copyright will belong to the personal representatives. (The personal representatives hold the copyright for the benefit of the person/s to whom the author's estate has devolved.)

There are two contentious issues as regards revived copyright:

First, there is a regime of 'licence of right' created in respect of a revived copyright work. Anyone, including obviously a publisher, can publish such a work subject only to payment of a reasonable royalty. The 'going rate' is likely to be below the rates long established for grants of exclusive licences, because, of course, the licence of right is in its nature non-exclusive. 'Ball-park' figures may emerge between 5% and 10% of price received, but negotiations between literary agents of major 'revived' estates and publishers continue.

Secondly, there is a provision that it will not be an infringement of revived copyright in a work to do anything after 1 January 1996 in pursuit of arrangements made before 1 January 1995 at any time when the work was in the public domain. Since exploitation resulting from such an arrangement will incur no payment, the meaning of 'arrangements made' is under close scrutiny by literary agents and publishers. Does the scope of the phrase encompass arrangements made for investment in film for one reprint of a revived copyright work to put the work on the market free of payment at the start of the revived copyright period? Or does the phrase encompass any subsequent printing from that film equally free of payment? The jury is still out.

Database Directive

The key elements of the Directive can be summarised as follows:

(i) A database is defined as a '*collection* of works, data or other independent materials arranged in a systematic or methodical way and capable of being *individually* accessed by electronic or *other means*'.

(a) The intention of 'collection' is to place the nature of a database firmly in the tradition of Art. 2(5) of the Berne Convention as affected by Art. 10 of TRIPS. That is, the items in the collection no longer themselves need to be copyright works for the collection to enjoy copyright protection: this 'Berne plus' approach is clearly essential for copyright protection of most databases, since they will usually consist of both copyright and non-copyright materials. It is suggested, however, that the high standard of criterion for originality in the Directive will make copyright protection thin. (See (ii) below.)

(b) The intention of 'individually accessed' is to exclude collective works such as films. This feature suggests that while some multimedia works will have features that *are* individually accessible, others, as sophistication of creative direction increases over time, will not. This Directive is *not* a multimedia directive.

(c) For publishers, the extension of this new regime to print-on-paper databases ('other means') will need careful thought as implementation into national laws approaches.

(ii)

(a) The text adopts the wording of the software directive on originality. Article 3.1 reads, 'databases which, by reason of the selection or arrangement of their contents, *constitutes the author's own intellectual creation*, shall be protected as such by copyright.'

(b) Article 3.1 is to be read together with Recital 15 – 'whereas such protection should cover the structure of the database'. The essential point is that the copyright protection offered by the text is only for 'intellectual creation' and only for 'the expression of the database which is protectable by copyright'. Some databases will pass the test of originality: many may not. It is very likely that the maker of a database will bypass the uncertainties of copyright protection and seek protection under the new *sui generis* regime (see (iii) below) which protects the *contents* of the database which the maker has put together, regardless of whether the *structure* qualifies for copyright protection or not.

(iii) The Directive creates an entirely new right based on investment, not creativity, by requiring member states, under Art. 7, to 'provide for a right for the maker of a database which shows that there has been qualatively and/or quantitatively a substantial investment in either the obtaining, verification or presentation of the contents, to prevent acts of extraction and/or re-utilisation of the whole or a substantial part, evaluated qualitively and/or quantitatively, of the contents of that database'.

Two comments:

(a) the Directive has left many issues on exceptions to the rights (eg fair dealing and library privilege, which could extensively corrode exploitation of a work in the electronic context) as options for member states. Given the traditional vigour of publisher/librarian exchanges in many member states, it seems possible that the legal regimes in Europe will end up on these critical issues less rather than more harmonised.

(b) the EU Directive's new *sui generis* right is setting the pace at international level. The European Commission and the US Government (which is considering introducing a similar right) have each tabled international versions of the right for consideration in the Berne agenda. Although the right was deferred in time at the Diplomatic Conference in Geneva in December 1996, the Conference adopted a Recommendation that an extraordinary session of WIPO Governing Bodies should be called in the first quarter of 1997 to decide on the schedule of further/preparatory work on a Treaty on Intellectual Property in Respect of Databases.

* * * * *

In the wide world beyond Europe, debate on the future of copyright and related interests has taken place over several years through successive sets of survey meetings, held under the expert guidance of the World Intellectual Property Organisation (WIPO). This series of meetings culminated in a Diplomatic Conference in December 1996, held in Geneva. The Conference adopted two treaties, the WIPO Copyright Treaty and the WIPO Performances and Phonograms Treaty. On the agenda of the Copyright Treaty, the market exclusivity of copyright licensing was of special interest to authors and publishers. The Berne Convention itself has been until 1996 silent on a right of publication or distribution, although such a right was often argued to be inherent in the right of reproduction in Art. 9(1) of the Convention. Indeed, it is difficult to see what sense Art. 16(2), which is directed against the importation into a member state of infringing reproductions, can possibly have unless 'distribution' is inherent in 'reproduction'.

In the Diplomatic Conference draft, the issue was framed in the form of an exclusive right to authorise importation. The matter is a live one for authors and publishers in the English language because of the Australian Copyright Law Amendment Act, which deals with the importation into

Australia of copies quite lawfully put on the market elsewhere. The Act enables importers to import into Australia such editions of books, which are legitimate but *not* licensed for Australia, in three circumstances—

- In the case of books published after the Act comes into force, if the book has not been published in Australia within 30 days of legitimate publication elsewhere.
- In the case of books published before or after the Act, and regardless of whether or not they have established territorial rights in Australia under the first provision (above), when the Australian copyright owner or licensee fails to confirm *within seven days* that he will fill an order from a bookseller within 90 days, or if in fact he fails to deliver within 90 days (though if territorial protection has been obtained under the first provision, it can be restored when stocks are again available, ie, the facility to import is on a one-off basis).

    In this case, the rule applies to hardback and paperback versions separately. So if the bookseller orders paperbacks which are not available in Australia when legitimate editions are available elsewhere, then, after seven days or 90 days, as appropriate, the bookseller will be able to import that other paperback edition.
- In the case of books published at any time, when the importer holds an order for a single copy of a book, and the purchaser has stated in writing that he needs the book only for private use. This could apply to single copy orders from libraries.

The copies that can be imported are only those produced in copyright convention countries in accordance with the copyright laws of those countries. They could, therefore, include cheap editions and advance or anti-piracy editions, produced in accordance with the copyright laws of the countries where they are made.

There is protection against importing of hardback copies when paperback copies are available in Australia, as the 90-day rule does not operate to permit the import of hardbacks when paperbacks are available. This is designed to prevent the importation of remaindered hardbacks to the detriment of the paperback edition.

But it does mean that if a publisher in the UK has not produced a paperback edition in Australia, but a paperback edition is available elsewhere, a bookseller will be able to import that other edition so long as the UK publisher has no paperback edition. So in effect, if a legitimate paperback is available anywhere, it must also be available in Australia, and it would seem that the bookseller can anticipate overseas availability by placing his order early.

The Australian Act clearly opens the door to parallel importation, and thus to the erosion of exclusive market rewards for authors. It is also certain that UK publishers' freight charges have already increased, and it is likely that these costs will work their way through to some high Australian book prices, and to a narrowing of the range of stocks held in Australia. The number of 'inadvertent' importations of books which *are* available within 30 days may increase, if publishers do not keep a vigilant eye on the bookshop market.

To return to the Berne Diplomatic Conference, it was unable to agree that a distribution right, which it *did* adopt into the WIPO Copyright Treaty, should be linked to an exclusive importation right, and the following language was adopted at Art. 6, entitled *Right to Distribution*:

> '(1) Authors of literary and artistic works shall enjoy the exclusive right of authorising the making available to the public of the original and copies of their works through sale or transfer of ownership.
>
> (2) Nothing in this Treaty shall affect the freedom of Contracting Parties to determine the conditions, if any, under which the exhaustion of the right in paragraph (1) applies after the first sale or other transfer of ownership of the original or a copy of the work with the authorisation of the author.'

Statements in Canada and New Zealand at the closing session of the Diplomatic Conference suggested that these countries, together with many developing countries, may in the future regard Art. 6(2) as an open door to the adoption of parallel importation through the doctrine of international exhaustion.

Fresh impetus to the copyright agenda will be given by the programme of activity set out in the European Commission's *Communication* of November 1996. This section of the Introduction opened with a *Communication* (of June 1988) and closes with one. The new Communication of November 1996 states that proposals will shortly be presented on four issues 'requiring immediate action'. They are:

- *Reproduction right*: Harmonised measures will be proposed in order to define the scope of the acts protected by the reproduction right, including the limitations to it, in so far as this has not yet been achieved in Community legislation. There will also need to be some differentiation between unlimited exclusive rights of reproduction, rights to remuneration (legal license), and certain acts of reproduction permitted without remuneration (fair use exception).
- *Communication to the public right*: Digital 'on-demand' transmissions will be protected on the basis of a further harmonised right of communication to the public as outlined in the submissions made by the Community and its member states during the present negotiations in WIPO. Harmonised measures will also set out the limitations to this right; such limitations will be similar to those for the harmonisation of the reproduction right.
- *Legal protection of the integrity of technical identification and protection schemes*: Legal protection of such schemes will be harmonised at Community level defining in particular the precise scope of protection, including the infringer's liability.

- *Distribution right*: The distribution right for authors as regards all categories of works will be harmonised so that only the first sale in the Community by or with the consent of the rightholder exhausts the distribution right. Harmonised legislation should also affirm that the principle of exhaustion applies to the distribution of goods only and not to the provision of services, including on-line services.

The importance to publishers of this initiative can hardly be exaggerated. The scope of reproduction in the digital environment failed to be enunciated in the WIPO Copyright Treaty: what 'the public' may mean will be critical to what 'private' may mean in a 'communication to the public' right: legal support for Electronic Copyright Management Systems is essential (a modified success in the text of the WIPO Copyright Treaty): the importance of exhaustion in the context of a distribution right has been demonstrated in the discussion above of parallel importation: and finally the place of limitations to and exceptions from the exclusive reproduction and communication rights as they operate in the digital environment will need to be most carefully thought through and drafted.

* * * * *

Let us return to the UK and to the context for author/publisher contracts. To update the Preface to the Third Edition in 1988:

'The contract bears, in the Anglo-Saxon tradition, a heavy burden, one might say, of responsibility. The law of copyright sets out the nature of the legal right of property that subsists in a literary work, but even with the advent of *droit moral* into the copyright law of the United Kingdom (see Appendix D), the law on the whole stands back from interfering in the contractual relationship between author and publisher in respect of that right. It is therefore important that the historical imbalance of bargaining power is being gradually evened up through the work of literary agents, of the authors' unions, the Society of Authors and the Writers Guild, and even of enlightened publishers. The unions' Minimum Terms Agreement is in the late 1990s a significant implementation of authors' determination to have more contractual say in how their works are published.'

To the work of literary agents, authors' unions and enlightened publishers must now be added the work of the judges — the decision in the Court of Appeal in *Malcolm v OUP* (1990). It is a classic instance of the maxim that 'hard cases make bad law'. The majority of the court seemed to wish to find for the plaintiff author, who had indeed been the victim of very inconsistent treatment by the publisher, and seized upon a letter from the author asking for 'a firm commitment' and a response in writing from the publisher's editor. This read 'I'm pleased that we are going to do your book', and followed a telephone conversation (carefully recorded by the plaintiff) in which the editor said: 'I mean what I think we should agree is that you have a fair royalty…'

The majority of the Court of Appeal held that this sequence of exchanges added up to a contract to publish the author's work. In a famous passage, Lord Justice Leggatt spoke strongly:

'when (the editor) used the expressions "commitment" and "a fair royalty" he did in fact mean what he said, and I venture to think that it would take a lawyer to arrive at any other conclusion'.

The Court of Appeal confirmed the view of its predecessor in 1922 that an agreement over reward alone (in 1922, 4d per copy and in 1990 not even a specific sum or percentage — 'what I *think* we *should* agree [emphasis added] is that you have a fair royalty') is sufficient to constitute an enforceable contract.

The decision is unsatisfactory, not on the ground of individual justice, but on the ground that in the 75 years that have passed between 1922 and 1997 contractual arrangements between author and publisher have become somewhat more complex, so that in general justice to authors (publishers must be deemed capable of looking after themselves) a rather more sophisticated view of what are essential terms for a contract to be created between author and publisher is needed. The following seven essential terms are proposed here:

1. The contract must be in writing.
2. It must grant either copyright itself or an exclusive licence in relation to specific languages.
3. The grant under 2 must state the duration in time of the grant.
4. The grant under 2 must state the territorial extent of the grant.
5. The nature and length of the material to be supplied by the author must be stated.
6. The delivery date for the material under 5 must be stated, together with provisions for the timing of the publication itself.
7. Sums of money due from publisher to author as consideration for the grant of specific rights under 2 must, whether royalty or lump sum or advance payments, be specified right by right, or else a procedure for agreeing such sums (eg 'mutual agreement') be stated.

This approach, it is suggested, would provide a floor of requirements, without which an author-publisher agreement would not come into being at all, or be voidable by the author. Certainty of terms, a key matter for mutual confidence between author and publisher, would be greatly encouraged.

* * * * *

The final task of this Introduction is to introduce the contents of the Fifth Edition. Precedent One has again been thoroughly reviewed and revised. New precedents have been added at Precedents Two and Three, so that the combination of Precedents Two, Three and Four will, it is hoped, strengthen the usefulness of the book for scientific, technical and medical (STM) publishers. Precedent Five reflects the increasing role of 'vertical publishing'. The difficult task of understanding and then applying the current rules and regulations for book club rights is tackled in a narrative, freshly revised for this Edition in the light of the virtual abandonment of the Net Book Agreement, as Precedent Six. Precedent Eight has been redrafted, and an Appendix has been brought as much up to date by Lynette Owen as the often confusing situations in the Commonwealth of Independent States and the Baltic States, in Central and Eastern Europe and in the People's Republic of China, allow. The fast-moving world of electronic publishing is represented for this Edition (heroically) by Roger Palmer by two drafts at Precedent Fourteen, one on the licensing of a literary work for inclusion in an off-line production, one for the licensing of a literary work for networking on site. Precedent Fifteen on Film, TV and Allied Rights has again been thoroughly revised. Appendix A reflects the enormous contribution of Gaye Poulton to the (still) ongoing negotiations between rightholders and the BBC. Moral rights are dealt with in some detail at Appendix D. Appendix E has been thoroughly revised by Richard Balkwill, while much attention will focus on Appendix H which offers some thoughts on the question 'what is Europe?', drafted by Stephen Aucutt, now a leading world authority on what *is* the world! Finally , Appendix I (a new appendix) sets out the countries of the world in membership of the Berne Convention and/or of the Universal Copyright Convention.

The astonishing pace of developments, both large and small, continues. Readers are warned that, beyond the main changes noted above, there are other innumerable detailed changes in the precedents, notes and appendices. These changes are a tribute to the vigilance and thoughtfulness of the team of contributors who have sifted through the fourth edition, offered new drafts and altogether made the editing of this Fifth Edition an education as well as a pleasure. They deserve every acknowledgment in the Acknowledgments which follow.

It is an important feature of *Publishing Agreements* that all of us who contribute do so 'in trust' for the trade. We hope that authors, authors' representatives, literary agents, publishers and legal advisers may all find something useful in these pages, if only something to disagree with. No royalties or fees earned are paid to any of us, as General Editors, contributor or adviser. All royalties and fees earned are donated by us to charity. For this Fifth Edition, half goes to Advance, the book trade's charity, and half goes to the Royal Literary Fund, the author's charity.

Finally, this Fifth Edition is the last to which I am, as retirement beckons, making my own contribution. I have been joined for this edition by Lynette Owen and Roger Palmer as joint General Editors. I want to thank them both most warmly for all their work on this Fifth Edition and for their confidence, in taking over the General Editorship of future editions, that *Publishing Agreements* will remain, in the new millennium, to quote a review of the Fourth Edition, 'a lasting companion of rare authority'. I thank them on my own, but much more importantly, on all our readers' behalf.

February 1997   CHARLES CLARK

Acknowledgments for the Fifth Edition

The drafting of *Publishing Agreements* is team work. The text of each previous edition is reviewed and revised by colleagues whose collective experience, Precedent by Precedent, clause by clause, is based on the day-to-day traffic in rights and contracts between author and publisher, between publisher and publisher, between publisher and producer. The role of the General Editors of this Fifth Edition, Charles Clark, Lynette Owen and Roger Palmer, has been that of agreeing with colleagues the tasks, sometimes minor, more often quite major, that must be undertaken for a new edition, then reading and reviewing drafts, discussing with (even, occasionally, disagreeing with) colleagues the final drafts, and then seeing the text into proof and the proofs, after much amendment, finally to press.

Very warm thanks are therefore offered by the retiring General Editor, in the sequence of Precedents and Appendices, as follows—

Precedent One Roger Palmer and Andrea Shallcross
Precedent Two Brenda Gvozdanoviz
Precedent Three Lynette Owen
Precedent Four Lynette Owen
Precedent Five Kevin Stewart
Precedent Eight Lynette Owen
Precedent Nine Lynette Owen
Precedent Ten Stephen Aucutt
Precedent Eleven Philip Clark for the Book Packagers Association
Precedent Twelve Lynette Owen
Precedent Thirteen Alan Williams and Catherine Bingham
Precedent Fourteen Roger Palmer
Precedent Fifteen Alan Williams
Appendix A Gaye Poulton
Appendix C Roger Palmer
Appendix E Richard Balkwill
Appendix H Stephen Aucutt

Beyond these specific acknowledgments (and behind which lie several mountains of work) may I thank for their commitment not only to *Publishing Agreements*, but, more broadly, to the ever-developing contexts — domestic, European and world-wide — within which contracts are forged, Clive Bradley, Hugh Jones, Lynette Owen, Roger Palmer, Gaye Poulton and Alan Williams. Their advice has been most generously given over many years, and it is their never-failing support and encouragement that drive *Publishing Agreements* forward to a new edition every four or five years.

For this edition David Lea and Siobhan Hughes have cast two pairs of very thorough eyes over the proofs and guided the General Editors away from error.

The General Editors are most grateful to Marian Donne for her constant goodwill over all matters that touch *Publishing Agreements*.

Finally, Butterworths commissioning staff has welcomed this Fifth Edition of *Publishing Agreements* with generous kindness, and the in-house editor at Butterworths has with patience, firmness and consistent courtesy seen the work through the press.

Contents

Introduction to the Fifth Edition vii
Acknowledgments for the Fifth Edition xxi

1   General Book Author — Publisher Agreement 1
2   Educational, Academic, Scientific and Professional Book Author—
    Publisher Agreements 41
3   Agreement for a General Editor of a Book 67
4   Agreement for a Contributor to a Book 93
5   Paperback Rights Agreement 101
6   Book Club Rights Agreements 115
7   Translator's Agreement 121
8   Agreement for Sale of Translation Rights 131
9   Same Language Low Price Reprint Agreement 155
10   Illustration and Artwork Agreement 165
11   Packaging Rights Agreement 177
12   International Co-Edition Agreement 205
13   Merchandising Rights Agreement 225
14   Electronic Media Rights Agreements 239
15   Film, Television and Allied Rights: Option and Assignment Agreements . 279

Appendix A   Permission Fees 303
Appendix B   Reversionary Provisions of the Copyright Act 1911 315
Appendix C   Non-Commercial Rights for the Print-Disabled 317
Appendix D   Moral Rights 323
Appendix E   Reprographic and Electronic Reproduction 331
Appendix F   The Publishers Association Code of Practice 339
Appendix G   Royalty Statements 347
Appendix H   Territories of the World 351
Appendix I   Member States of the Berne Convention and the UCC 363

Index 365

General Book Author – Publisher Agreement

The agreement between author and publisher is the cornerstone of their relationship. Care taken by them together to ensure that the contract really reflects in detail the nature of the book they are discussing pays off time and time again, not only in focusing early attention on the points of real substance, not only in avoiding subsequent unsettling disputes, but in giving the author the confidence needed to let the publisher get on in equal confidence with its job to their mutual advantage.

The detail of Precedent One and the variety of rights and dealings in those rights set out in the other Precedents, many of which stem from Precedent One, may appear at first sight daunting and confusing, but behind the detail in Precedent One lies a very simple structure. The author owns the copyright in what he/she writes. In return for various payments, he/she licenses to the publisher, exclusively at the publisher's own expense, the right to multiply in book form copies of what he/she has put on paper and the right to license further to others exploitation in both book and non-book forms. The author writes, the publisher invests, and from sales of the book they create together and from exploitation of rights, the author earns royalties and fees, and the publisher earns its profit. It is as simple — and as complicated — as that.

Preamble

(1) An agreement between author and publisher ideally sets out the rights and liabilities between them in the sequence of the events which lead up to and beyond the moment of publication. That principle is followed in this Precedent, and to help understanding headings have been given to each clause. Note however Clause 30.

(2) It is important, as take-overs and mergers continue through the 1990s, to distinguish between the assignment of a contract for an individual work held by a publisher and the selling by a publisher of his/her business to another company. In the latter situation there is no change in the authors' contractual relationships: the authors continue to have rights against and liabilities towards the same publishing company, provided it continues trading under its new ownership. There may be considerable uncertainties where, e.g., a publisher seeks to sell a part only of his/her business, possibly in the form of a publishing division or a subsidiary imprint, which is not itself a company at law, or where the acquiring publisher seeks not to continue the acquired business in its own name, but to transfer some of the works under contract with the acquired publisher to his/her own imprint/s. Legal advice should always be sought on this issue in advance by both acquiring and acquired publishers.

As to assignability of individual works, some authors may wish not to risk their work appearing under an imprint with which they do not want to be associated. A provision as a separate clause that 'the rights and licences hereby granted may not be assigned or transmitted by the Publishers without the prior written consent of the Author' is found in some contracts issued by literary agents. Such a clause should include a provision that such consent is not to be unreasonably withheld. Equally, the publisher who wishes to secure the benefit of assignability of the contract between him/herself and the author should probably have it written into the contract beyond the general wording of the preamble.

(3) Provision should always be made for the possible failure of the publishers' business, and a precedent is set out under Clause 23.

(4) In the case of a registered company it is important that signature of contracts should comply with the requirements of the articles of association. The person signing the contract is not entering into a personal contract, but is committing his/her firm.

(5) Publishers who trade through more than one imprint should be careful to allow for publication through the imprint which will give the book the best advantage and may find it sensible to include in the preamble wording such as: 'The expression "the Publishers" as used throughout this Agreement shall be deemed to include any imprint of the Publishing Group as aforesaid whether under its present or any future style and the benefit of this Agreement shall be transmissible accordingly' (but see also the caveat on behalf of authors made at (2) above).

(6) Where the author is shown on an agreement as a company, some publishers like the author him/herself to countersign a letter of inducement in which he/she undertakes to perform the author's obligations under the agreement. Such a letter is likely to be in the following terms:

Dear

Reference is made to the agreement (herein called 'the Agreement') which we are about to enter into with [the company] (herein called 'the Company') a copy of which is attached hereto and made part hereof, concerning a work provisionally entitled

In consideration of and as a further inducement to our entering into the Agreement you hereby warrant, guarantee and agree as follows:

1. That the Company has the full right and authority to enter into this Agreement, to furnish your services as therein provided and to grant the rights therein granted;

2. That you will be bound and will bind the Company by all the terms conditions and obligations of the Agreement and that you will look solely to the Company for any and all moneys, royalties or other consideration payable to you for your services under the Agreement;

3. That the Company will perform each and every provision of the Agreement and

MEMORANDUM OF AGREEMENT made this   day of
19   between   of
(hereinafter called 'the Author', which expression shall, where the context
admits, include the Author's executors and assigns) of the one part and
                of   (hereinafter called 'the
Publishers', which expression shall where the context admits include any
publishing imprint subsidiary to or associated with the Publishers, and the
Publishers' assigns or successors in business as the case may be) of the
other part
Whereby it is mutually agreed as follows concerning a work original to the
Author and provisionally entitled:

(hereinafter called 'the Work')

1. Rights Granted

In consideration of the payments hereinafter mentioned and subject to the
terms and conditions herein contained, the Author hereby grants to the

---

any changes and revisions in the Agreement as shall from time to time be agreed. This
guarantee shall be construed as absolute continuing and unlimited and shall be
enforceable against you your heirs and assigns without the obligation to first proceed
against the Company.

4. In the event that the Company shall for any reason fail or cease to perform or shall
not have the rights to your services required by the Agreement or herein you agree to
abide by and fulfil all said terms and conditions of the Agreement as if you had entered
into the Agreement directly with the [   ].

Yours sincerely

For and on behalf of

(7) Publishers' staff and authors should bear in mind that an agreement can be spelt out
from correspondence if the essential terms of such an agreement are present, e.g. length
of typescript, delivery date, duration of licence, royalty rate, advance and territory. Such
terms may be 'agreed' in preliminary correspondence between, for example, an editor and
the author. In this way, binding agreements could occasionally be unwittingly entered
into. It may be sensible to mark all pre-Memorandum of Agreement correspondence as
'Subject to Contract'. The Entire Agreement clause (31) in this Precedent also serves to
nullify any contractual effect that preliminary correspondence might have but does not, of
course, take effect until the contract is signed. See also the comments in the Introduction
on *Malcolm v OUP*.

1.   Rights Granted
(1) This clause secures all volume rights, but not non-volume rights, in English or in
any language. As to the extent of 'volume rights' see Clauses 12, 13 and 14 and the
introductory note to Clause 14. One overall effect of a good publishing contract should be
to place rights in the hands of those best able to exploit them in the interests both of the
wide availability of the work and also of income to the author and to those who work for
the author, e.g. publisher or literary agent. It follows that the publisher or literary agent
who asks in his/her contract for control of certain rights, e.g. electronic rights, has a

responsibility towards the author to carry the professional skills needed to exploit the rights and to be active in doing so. Many publishers now include a grant of 'electronic book' rights specifically in the following way:

> and as an electronic book, i.e. any means of distribution or transmission of the Work, whether now known or hereafter known or developed (including but not limited to electronic and machine-readable media and on-line and satellite-based transmission) intended to make the Work or any part thereof available for reading. See also the introductory note to Clause 14.

(2) The territories within which the publishers are to exercise their exclusive licence to publish need to be carefully negotiated and set out, with an equally clear understanding of the territories from which their editions of the work may be excluded, and the territories within which both British and US editions may be sold non-exclusively. Many publishers set out as a schedule to the agreement a printed list of territories with deletions and additions appropriate to the individual contract. Appendix H provides three schedules. Schedule 1 lists the nations of the world. Schedule 2 lists the territories outside the continent of Europe which are usually granted exclusively to a British publisher and Schedule 3 offers several approaches to dealing with the European Single Market.

Some US publishers seek, as a standard term of contract, to negotiate exclusivity for US bases throughout the world. There is no foundation in either territoriality or in US purchasing requirements for this provision, which is strongly and successfully resisted by both publishers and literary agents in the UK.

(3) Australian copyright legislation requires that, to maintain exclusivity of copyright in Australia, any new work is available there within 30 days of first lawful English language publication anywhere in the world. It is important therefore to ensure that where the UK publisher does not control US rights the author delivers the typescript simultaneously to each publisher. If the work has already been published in the US, Australia will be potentially a non-exclusive market. If this is the case, the UK publisher may well expect to pay a somewhat lower advance.

For a more detailed explanation, see Introduction.

(4) The traditional expectation of publishers to acquire a licence for the duration of copyright (i.e. for the life of the author plus 70 years — see Introduction) has been challenged in recent years. First, the licence has been increasingly restricted by strong requirements that the work should be kept in print (see Clause 24 of this Precedent and the notes to it); second, the Writers' Guild and the Society of Authors, as part of their concern to secure a 'flow of rights' for their members, have suggested through one version of their Minimum Terms Agreement that the publishers require only a 20 or 30 year licence from the date of publication, with provision for a review (at either party's request) after 10 years. Another form of the MTA leaves the licence term to be negotiated between the author and the publisher on each occasion and to be completed (or deleted as appropriate) in each contract. The 10-year review provision is retained, specifying particularly that, even if a paperback edition is in print with the publisher, the author will have the right to renegotiate paperback terms (including, possibly, a further advance); and in the absence of agreement the publisher, if requested to do so by the author, will offer paperback rights to other publishers including any specified by the author.

The MTAs have a number of other interesting features to which reference is made at separate points. In general, the more strenuously the publisher argues the importance of backlist income attainable through the holding of a full-term licence, the more convincingly he/she may seem to make the author's case at least for some kind of review during the term of the contract. Indeed, some publishers now include provision for a revision of terms in agreements that run for the full term of copyright, with wording such as the following: 'At any time after fifteen years from the date of signature of this Agreement either party shall give reasonable consideration to a request from the other to renegotiate such terms as are no longer in line with current publishing practice.'

(5) As to the relationship between duration of copyright and the limitation, under the Copyright Act 1911, on the author's power to assign or license an interest in his/her

Publishers the sole and exclusive right and licence to produce and publish and themselves further to license the production and publication of the Work or any adaptation or any abridgement of the Work or any substantial part of the Work in volume form in the English language/in all languages for the legal term of copyright and any and all extensions, renewals and revivals thereof throughout the world/the territories listed on the attached schedule(s): the rest of the world excluding the United States of America its territories and dependencies and the Philippine Islands [and Canada] shall be a non-exclusive market for the sale of the British and US editions of the Work.

2. Delivery of the Work

The Author has delivered/shall deliver material for the complete Work conforming to the specifications set out in the Appendix to this Agreement and by the date or dates specified therein.

The Author agrees to retain an additional copy of all material.

---

copyright beyond 25 years after his death, see Appendix B.

(6) Attention is drawn to the rights granted by the words 'any abridgement of the Work'. The opinion is sometimes held that, if the right to publish an abridgement or portion of the work is assigned to the publishers, then that right should not be exercised without the author's consent. Any abridgement would naturally be subject to the same restrictions of language and territory as apply to the complete work.

The words 'any substantial part of the Work' reflect the position at law that the publication by a third party of an insubstantial part of an author's work is not an infringement of the copyright in the work. What amounts to substantiality depends on the facts in any given instance, and quality as well as wordage comes into account. In very broad terms 'substantial' may appear to the layman as fairly insubstantial — as low a wordage as 5 per cent of the total may amount to substantiality, especially if quality is an issue. This tendency to set the marker low reflects the judges' concern to protect the author's rights in copyright.

2. Delivery of the Work

(1) A common source of disagreement between author and publisher is the question of exactly what is to be delivered. The placing of important items such as length, delivery date and illustrations in an Appendix is a useful signal to both author and publisher to get these items clear in their minds before ambiguities can create confusion. If, for example, price ceilings for a particular market make a maximum length important, then that length should be agreed and incorporated in the Appendix. Illustrations are a fertile source of misunderstanding: author and publisher should grasp the nettle before they sign the contract. (See Clause 8 for further details on illustrations.)

The Appendix will clearly vary in content from book to book in detail and in complexity. The common sense of setting out in an Appendix just what is being commissioned by publisher from author, and on what evidence, e.g. synopsis/specimen chapter, applies especially, but not only, to heavily illustrated works and to non-fiction. A possible form of Appendix is shown at the end of this Precedent. Authors are owed proper care and clarity by their editors, especially at a time when publishing staff move jobs frequently: neither author nor his/her new editor should have to rely on informal correspondence or memories of telephone or pub conversations.

(2) Delivery of material on disk is becoming a more common feature of author – publisher contracts. Sometimes there are savings of time and cost. Sometimes there are long delays and increased costs. The author and publisher must have early discussion and

agreement. If they do agree to delivery on disk, then variations of the following wording may be appropriate —

Submission of Text on Disk
If it is agreed that the Author shall supply the Work on disk, the following provisions shall apply:

1. The Author shall deliver one copy on disk as specified in the Appendix and a verbatim copy printed out on paper.
2. Any editorial changes proposed by the Publishers shall be clearly indicated to the Author either on a typescript copy or by marking up the alterations on the electronic version.
3. Before passing the disk(s) to the printers, the Publishers shall only include changes to the text that have been inserted by or agreed with the Author.
4. Except with the agreement of the Author, the Publishers shall not copy or sell the disk(s) other than for the purposes of typesetting the Work.

Publishers may also wish to include other specifications, such as the omission of formatting and may retain the right to charge to the author any costs incurred in converting on to a compatible disk (or in converting material – particularly artwork – into the correct format, such as making film of artwork so as to reduce it to the correct size).

(3) Since authors are very frequently late in delivering their typescripts, and since their publishers just as frequently simply make a note on the file and reschedule the work for a later season, it is the persistently overdue typescript at which the provisions are aimed. The alternatives follow the sense of item 7, *time*, of the Publishers Association Code of Practice (see Appendix F). In short, the publisher cannot have it both ways, i.e. both retain an option and reclaim any advance paid out.

In view of the above comment, a publisher who really does mean what his/her contract states should make explicit provision that 'time is of the essence'. 'Event' publishing requires rigid time scheduling (e.g. for books tied to sports events or to royal weddings).

Where publication is time-sensitive some publishers insert a penalty provision here. In such cases it should be made very clear when and why such a provision will be invoked. It should not, for instance, be invoked if delivery is delayed because the publisher has altered its requirements at a late stage.

3. Acceptance and Conditions of Acceptance and Approval

The publishers' commitment to publish depends on 'acceptance'. The publishers *shall* accept if the TS fulfils reasonably the author's intentions and the publishers' expectation at the time of contract. If the TS does not, then the publishers have a fall-back position which is explicitly stated and known to the author from the start. (It is, of course, hardly relevant to commissioned works of *fiction*.) This formula draws on several sources to try to resolve the most difficult issue in publishing contracts — the quality of the final TS in which the publishers are to invest very considerable direct and indirect costs and resources. The prime responsibility for minimising the risk of disagreement must lie with the publishers: they must not only through the Appendix define as closely as possible and in writing *before* contract the book which they would like to publish, they must also satisfy themselves at that stage that the author both understands and is capable of meeting their requirements.

The approval by the author of the final text of his/her work should be obtained before it goes to press in order to minimise any possible infringement of the author's moral right of integrity, described in the Copyright Act 1988 as the right to object to derogatory treatment of the author's work. See in general on moral rights Appendix D.

4. Competing Work

In the day of the 'book package', an author may well be invited to provide a text for such a work precisely because of a reputation established by a previous book (see also Precedent Eleven). This is only one example of a somewhat grey area. Authors must be able to maximise earnings, while publishers must be able to protect their investment in an

Should the Author fail to deliver material for the complete Work acceptable to the Publishers in accordance with Clause 3 by the due date or by such other date as may be agreed by the Publishers in writing, the Publishers shall be at liberty to decline to publish the Work. If the Publishers so decline in writing this Agreement shall terminate subject to the following alternative provisos the choice of which shall be in the sole discretion of the Publishers:

(a) that the Author shall not be at liberty to publish the Work elsewhere after its completion without having first offered it to the Publishers on the terms of this Agreement;
or
(b) that the Author shall refund any part of the advance already paid by the Publishers within thirty days of a request in writing from the Publishers to do so.

3. Acceptance and Conditions of Acceptance and Approval

The Publishers shall accept the Work provided that the material as delivered by the Author shall be technically competent and shall conform to a reasonable extent to the specifications set out in the Appendix hereto; and they shall have the right as a condition of acceptance of the Work to require amendments to ensure that the Work does so conform. The Publisher shall inform the Author in writing within   days after receipt of the complete material for the Work as to whether amendments are required or whether the Work is to be accepted as delivered or to be rejected. If the Author is unable or unwilling to undertake amendments required by the Publishers or arrange for them to be made within such reasonable period of time as shall have been agreed by the Publishers, then the Publishers shall have the right to employ a competent person or persons to make the amendments and any fees payable shall be deducted from any sums due to the Author under the terms of this Agreement. The Work, as finally amended and marked for press, shall be subject to the Author's approval and such approval shall not be unreasonably withheld or delayed.

4. Competing Work

The Author shall not during the continuance of this Agreement without the previous written consent of the Publishers prepare or publish (or collaborate in the preparation or publication of) any work of a nature which may be reasonably considered by the Publishers to be likely to compete with or to affect prejudicially the sales of the Work or the exploitation of any rights in the Work granted to the Publishers under this Agreement.

---

author's work from unreasonable competition. Any objections by the publishers must therefore be reasonable, and some authors may wish the clause to operate only while the publishers keep the original work in print.

Instead of restricting authors during the continuance of the agreement or while the work remains in print with the original publisher time limits on the restrictions are included by some publishers so as to allow expert authors to continue to write about their specialist subjects, while at the same time protecting the publisher during the all-important pre- and post- publication periods. Time limits can range from anything between one year before publication until two years after, to three months before until six months after.

Some publishers also include wording relating to derivative works, on the following lines:

> The Author hereby grants to the Publishers on terms to be agreed, such terms to be fair and reasonable, the sole and exclusive right throughout the world to publish any work or works written partly or wholly by the Author which in subject matter or style may clearly be deemed derivative from the Work. A 'derivative work' shall be understood to mean a work which clearly has been inspired by the Work and draws from its 'essence' but which also has its own independent identity. If, however, the Author makes a proposal to the Publishers for a derivative work and the Publishers do not within sixty days of receipt of a full written proposal therefor enter into negotiations with the Author with a view to agreeing fair and reasonable terms for publication of such work the Author may offer such proposal elsewhere but shall not accept from any third party terms less favourable than those offered by the Publishers; and furthermore the Author shall not publish or release or authorise publication or release of any such derivative work less than twelve months from the Publishers' first publication of the Work without the Publishers' prior written consent.

5. Warranties and Indemnities

Notes (3) and (4) to this clause in the First Edition of *Publishing Agreements* (1980) read as follows:

> (3) The most important warranty is that against publishing libels. The first and foremost responsibility must rest, in fiction and non-fiction alike, with the author. He/she alone commits to paper the words which the publishers pay to publish and there is no moral justification in moving the burden of care to the publishers, although, as the book goes through the press, the publishers will sometimes carry some of the financial burden of minimising the risk (e.g. through sharing the costs, which can be heavy, of libel readings and subsequent consultation with libel lawyers), and although, if a claim for libel is made after publication, the publishers will often help the author to meet his/her obligations.
>
> (4) Warranties and indemnities which include the phrase 'to the best of his/her knowledge' and/or which limit the author's liability to 'any breach of this warranty' only are of very little value. 'Knowledge' is easily denied, and in most instances a speedy settlement takes place under which it is not definitely established whether an actual 'breach' occurred or not.

These notes are still valid, but the situation is not satisfactory for either publisher or author. There is a growing concern to find some way, through insurance against libel, negligent misstatement, etc., to provide protection jointly to author and publisher so that the publisher is not put in the position of invoking remedies against his/her author, and so that the author is not faced with unforeseeable and escalating costs. An insurance policy may now be negotiated with a few underwriters through brokers by a publisher so as to include the author in the definition of 'the Insured' in the 'cover', which endures on behalf of all the publisher's publications during the term of the policy. In effect, a modest extra premium brings the author's liability (which is still expressed through stringent warranties and indemnities) into the publisher's insurance cover, save for a residual liability of the author. The value of such a scheme will depend on many factors: e.g. whether it covers only the publisher's own editions or whether it extends to editions licensed by him/her, especially to mass-market paperback editions so that licensees may be covered as 'additional insured'; whether it covers publication outside the UK especially in major markets such as Australia or Canada. The benefits, however, in relationships with authors (provided the extra premium is indeed modest) may attract publishers already insured and may persuade publishers who have preferred not to be insured to consider afresh seeking this new form of policy through discussions with their insurance brokers.

5. Warranties and Indemnities

The Author hereby warrants to the Publishers and their assignees, licensees printers and distributors that *he/she* has full power to make this Agreement, that *he/she* is the sole Author of the Work and is the owner of the rights herein granted, that the Work is original to *him/her*, and that it has not previously been published in any form in the territories covered by this Agreement and is in no way whatever a violation or infringement of any existing copyright or licence, or duty of confidentiality, or duty to respect privacy, or any other right of any person or party whatsoever, that it contains nothing libellous, that all statements contained therein purporting to be facts are true and that any recipe, formula or instruction contained therein will not, if followed accurately, cause any injury, illness or damage to the user.

The Author further warrants that the Work contains no obscene or improper or blasphemous material nor is in breach of Official Secrets Acts nor is in any other way unlawful.

The Author shall indemnify and keep the Publishers indemnified against all actions, suits, proceedings, claims, demands and costs (including any legal costs or expenses properly incurred and any compensation costs and disbursements paid by the Publishers on the advice of their legal advisers to compromise or settle any claim) occasioned to the Publishers in consequence of any breach of this warranty, or arising out of any claim alleging that the Work constitutes in any way a breach of this warranty.

The Publishers reserve the right having first notified the Author to alter, or to insist that the Author alter, the text of the Work as may appear to them appropriate for the purpose of modifying or removing any passage which in their absolute discretion or on the advice of their legal advisers may be considered objectionable or actionable at law, but any such alteration or removal shall be without prejudice to and shall not affect the Author's liability under this warranty and indemnity.

All warranties and indemnities herein contained shall survive the termination of this Agreement.

More publishers than in the past now have insurance policies, which have to be renegotiated annually; and despite a spate of high profile libel suits attracting huge damages over recent years since the fourth edition was published there has been a slight increase in the number of insurers offering policies. A policy is of limited reassurance if it does not include the author, the printer, the distributor and the publisher's licensees as 'additional insured'. Even so, the excess for which the author is liable can amount to a hefty sum, and is of small consolation to an author whose royalty account is in debit.

Warranty and Indemnity clauses may also include provisions —

(i) that, where appropriate, the Author has cleared or will clear copyright permissions and pay any fees as provided for in the agreement;

(ii) that photographs commissioned for private or domestic purposes and containing likenesses of living persons were either taken before 1 August 1989 or if taken after that date the author has obtained and will deliver to the publishers a written waiver of the right to privacy by the person entitled to such right (the commissioner of the photograph). For more details of the right to privacy see Appendix D.

6. Publishers' Responsibility to Publish

Increasingly publishers are including a specified time by which they will publish, which can range from a few weeks for highly topical books up to several years in rare cases, depending on the nature of the book and the amount of work that needs to be done on the material when it is delivered. For that reason it is prudent to refer back to Clause 3, although publishers should not delay the copy-editing and marking-up process unduly if this formula is adopted. See especially the final sentence of Clause 3 and the final paragraph of the note to Clause 3. Where other contributors (e.g. photographers) are to deliver key elements of the work the publication date may be set at X months after delivery and approval of all major components; and the contract may also provide for termination and rights reversion if the publisher is unable to publish because of the failure of contributors of other elements to deliver.

7. Textual Copyright Material

(1) The need for an author to obtain clearance from rights holders of copyright works for inclusion of extracts from those works in the author's work will only arise where the extent of the extract exceeds the limit which the law and practice allow for fair dealing for purposes of criticism or review. Fair dealing for such a purpose is not an infringement of copyright at all. See Appendix A for a detailed note of the limits of fair dealing.

(2) The need for care in clearing permissions of all kinds leads many editors to provide standard clearance letters for their authors to use and to insist that written evidence is produced that permission has been duly granted for the rights and territories specifically sought.

(3) This clause provides for the author to clear and pay for any extraneous material included in the work. But this practice, while very common (particularly for, say, biographies) is not invariable. The publisher may agree to bear the first, say, £100 and the author everything thereafter (or vice versa) or all fees may be jointly shared. In the case of anthologies the publisher may bear the cost of the contributions (although sometimes up to a figure carefully defined in the agreement with the author) and reduce the rate of royalty payable, as appropriate. See also note (2) to the following clause.

(4) Although the wording provides for authors to clear permissions for all territories, forms and editions licensed to the publisher (whether as primary or subsidiary rights) before first publication, in practice this may be impossible (because rights holders will often wish to know print runs, prices etc. before granting permission) and certainly may be more expensive than obtaining clearance only for known or envisaged uses. Publishers may therefore wish to limit initial clearance only to use of materials in their own editions and those which can reasonably be expected to be licensed to others, but to require the author to obtain further clearances as and when further editions or rights sales make it necessary to do so.

8. Illustrations

(1) The clause, as it applies to illustrations, is suitable for a text with illustrations in a supporting role. Books which consist equally of text and illustration or mainly of illustration with accompanying text will often need two contracts: one for the text and the other for the illustrations. As to ownership of original artwork, the licence to reproduce that artwork, etc., see Precedent Ten.

(2) It is important to clarify with the author the *extent*, in terms of geographical, chronological or other limitations, of the rights which are obtained by the author. Illustrations may be an important element in the book in the eyes of subsequent licensees of the publishers or of the author, e.g. foreign-language publishers, paperback publishers, book clubs and US publishers. Later expense in some instances, e.g. with the picture agencies who have granted the rights to reproduce their illustrations in one edition only, may make such further exploitation of the work impracticable. However, see note (4) to Clause 7, above; and see also Note (2) to Clause 7, above.

(3) In the case of diagrams and maps, it is sensible to form some view as early as possible on the number of them and the form in which they are to be provided. Increasingly, these matters are dealt with by professional technical illustrators and cartographers. The editor may need to bring in his/her production and design colleagues for an early meeting with the author. See also Precedent Ten.

6. Publishers' Responsibility to Publish

The Publishers shall unless otherwise mutually agreed or unless prevented by circumstances beyond their control, at their own expense produce and publish the Work within   months of approval by the Author of the Work as ready for press in accordance with Clause 3, or within months of the date of this Agreement, whichever shall be the later date.

7. Textual Copyright Material

Should the text of the Work contain extracts from other copyright works, the Author shall at *his/her* own expense (unless otherwise agreed) obtain from the owners of the respective copyrights written permission (which shall be forwarded to the Publishers on delivery of the material) to reproduce such extracts in the Work in all territories and editions and in all forms which are the subject of this Agreement.

8. Illustrations

The Author shall, on delivery of the Work, supply to the Publishers any photographs, pictures, maps, diagrams and other illustrative materials as set out in the Appendix.

In respect of any copyright illustrative materials the Author shall obtain from the owners of the respective copyrights written permission (which shall be forwarded to the Publishers on delivery of the material) to reproduce such materials in the Work and in all territories and editions and in all forms which are the subject of this Agreement.

All illustrations supplied by the Author shall be in a form acceptable to the Publishers, but the Publishers shall have the right to reject such material or to require of the Author such substitutions or amendments as may in the reasonable view of the Publishers be required on the grounds of poor quality, excessive cost or otherwise.

The cost of supplying illustrative material, including copyright fees, shall be borne *by the Author/by the Publishers*.

9. Index

If in the reasonable opinion of the Publishers an index is required it shall be supplied by the Author at *his/her* own expense ready for press within fourteen days of receipt by the Author of final page proofs. If the Author fails so to supply the index then the Publishers shall arrange for it to be supplied and the cost shall be debited to the Author's account unless such account shall contain insufficient funds, in which case the Author shall pay such cost within thirty days of receipt of the Publishers' invoice.

---

(4) See also note (ii) to Clause 5 above.

9. Index
The importance of a good index cannot be overrated. Not only should publisher and author agree in principle on whether or not an index is to be included, but they should agree, at final manuscript stage, on a clear briefing regarding its structure, density, etc. Minimum

Terms agreements and some other contracts provide for the expense of supplying an index to be shared equally between publisher and author if the author does not supply it.

11. Author's Corrections

(1) The period commonly allowed for the author's checking of proofs is 14 days, but a longer period may be required for a complex work.

(2) The author is generally expected to bear the amount by which the cost of his/her alterations exceeds 10 per cent of the cost of origination. Some publishers include a higher percentage (i.e. 12.5% or 15%) in this clause.

(3) All alteration in proofs is very expensive. Prevention is better than cure and editors should be especially meticulous over the approval by authors at draft stage of maps, charts etc.

12. Royalties and Fees Payable on Own Editions

(a) Home Hardbound Sales
A scale of royalties is often agreed, generally rising by steps of $2^1/2$ per cent geared to the number of copies sold, which may take the royalty rate from, for example, $7^1/2$ to $12^1/2$ per cent or from 10 to 15 per cent, depending on the nature of the work. The pressure on publishers to give high discounts to major booksellers in the home market has led increasingly to provision being made for four-fifths of the prevailing royalty to be paid on home sales at discounts of 50 per cent and over for hardback editions and increasingly for three-fifths for home sales at discounts of over 60 per cent; arrangements of this kind have been agreed in some Minimum Terms Agreements. The virtual collapse of the Net Book Agreement has caused some doubt about how royalties, previously expressed as being based on the British published price, should be expressed. For the moment reference to the

10. Production and Promotion Responsibility

All matters relating to the publication of the Work, including the paper, printing, design, binding and jacket or cover, the manner and extent of promotion and advertising, the number and distribution of free copies for the press or otherwise, the print number and the price and terms of sale of the first or any subsequent edition or impression of the Work shall be under the entire control of the Publishers but the Author shall be shown the artist's roughs (or, if that is impracticable, proofs) of the jacket/cover design and shall be consulted thereon and on the jacket/cover copy in good time before they are passed for press.

The Author shall endeavour to be available, if so requested in advance by the Publishers, to assist the Publishers in the promotion of the Work.

The Publishers undertake to set the name of the Author in its customary form with due prominence on the title page and on the binding, jacket *and/or* cover of every copy of the Work published by them and shall endeavour to ensure that a similar undertaking is made in respect of any editions of the Work licensed by them for publication in book form.

11. Author's Corrections

The Author undertakes to read, check and correct the proofs of the Work (and any finished artwork) and return them to the Publishers within fourteen days of their receipt, failing which the Publishers may consider the proofs and any artwork as passed for press by the Author. The cost of all alterations and corrections made by the Author in finished artwork and in the proofs (other than the correction of artist's, copy-editor's or typesetter's errors) in excess of 10 per cent of the cost of origination *and/or* origination of artwork shall be borne by the Author. Should any charge arise under this Clause the amount may be deducted from any sums due to the Author under the terms of this Agreement.

All materials for the Work supplied by the Author shall be returned to the Author after publication if *he/she* so requests in writing. The Publishers shall take due care of such materials while they are in the Publishers' possession but they shall not be responsible for any loss thereof or damage thereto.

12. Royalties and Fees Payable on Own Editions

Subject to the terms and conditions set out in this Agreement the Publishers shall make the following payments to the Author in respect of volume or sheet sales of the Work:

(a) *Home Hardbound Sales in Great Britain, Northern Ireland and the Irish Republic*

On the UK recommended retail price of all copies sold, excluding such copies as may by subsequent provisions of this Agreement, or as otherwise mutually agreed, be sold subject to a different royalty, a royalty of:

13

UK recommended retail price would seem appropriate, but if in the future it becomes the custom to omit printed prices on books a new formula for royalties may have to be found.

(b) Export Hardbound Sales

Export marketing is often conducted at high discounts of up to 60 per cent or even more off the British published price. Royalty payments can be expressed as either approximately one-half of the home royalty rate or approximately 10 per cent of the net price received per copy sold. Some publishers agree increased reward to authors as export sales build up: this increase can obviously be easily expressed under either method of payment. Publishers pressed by authors or their agents to pay royalties on the retail price of the work in export markets such as Australia or Canada should calculate carefully (a) whether they can afford to do so at all; and (b) if they can, the effect on published price of such an arrangement in the market concerned. There is little point in securing for the author a royalty of 10 per cent of the Australian retail price if the effect is to drive that price beyond the market ceiling and invite the importation to Australia of a competing American edition.

(c) Small Reprints

The 'small reprint' sub-clause is seen by the publisher as a necessary provision to enable him/her to keep the author's work in print, when the continuing demand is small yet the past demand has earned the author one of the higher royalty rates, e.g. 15 per cent. To the author, the point may seem reasonable, but not one which should be a pre-condition of the contract. Where this sub-clause is accepted the rate usually reverts to the starting royalty rate, and the print number on which it operates needs consideration book for book. It is important that an author is protected from abuse of this provision through frequent small-run reprints. The provision as a whole may become increasingly limited in scope. Literary agents, for example, may request that it should operate only after the first year following publication. The Minimum Terms Agreement states that the publishers 'may not invoke this provision more than once in twelve months without the prior agreement of the Author'.

(d) Hardbound Cheap Editions

The royalty rates on a cheap edition are usually the base rates under Clause 12(a) and (b) above for home and export sales respectively. The wording of the clause allows for agreement should it be necessary to distinguish between home and export sales.

(e) Publishers' Own Paperback Editions

(1) Since the publishers benefit from sharing in the profits of any paperback imprint wholly or partly owned by them, it is generally accepted that they should pay over to the author one hundred per cent of the royalty earned from sales of the author's book published by such an imprint. The royalties paid are usually lower than hardback rates, e.g. 7.5 per cent of the UK recommended retail price on home sales and 6 per cent (i.e. four-fifths) of the UK recommended retail price on export sales, possibly rising, for example to 10 per cent and 8 per cent respectively, after the sale of a stated number of copies. There is a move towards a net receipts-based royalty (e.g. 10%) for export sales. Provision can equally be made for rising royalty rates. See also the note to Clause 12(a) above concerning rates for high discount sales: the percentage in respect of paperback editions is commonly 52.5 per cent for a reduction to four-fifths and 62.5% to three-fifths.

(2) It has sometimes been difficult to decide whether to issue an 'own' paperback edition or license those rights, though few 'vertical' houses are now licensing paperback rights to others. With the increasing exploitation of smaller (and diverse) editions in the home market it is not unreasonable to explore the paperback market with different editions, each catering for a different readership. For example a trade paperback selling mainly in high-street retail outlets may or may not inhibit the sale of a mass-market paperback edition at a lower price mainly in confectionery, tobacco and newsagent outlets, supermarkets and at airports. Equally a book which may have had its day in the mass market may find a new lease of life in a more expensive trade paperback edition. Much will

(b) *Export Hardbound Sales*
On all copies sold for export, except as otherwise specified in this
Agreement, a royalty of   per cent *of the UK recommended retail
price./of the net amounts received by the Publishers.*

(c) *Small Reprints*
On reprints of   copies or less the royalties under (a) and (b) above shall
be reduced to   and   respectively *or* to the lowest rates
provided thereunder.

(d) *Hardbound Cheap Editions*
On any hardbound cheap edition of the Work issued by the Publishers at
two-thirds or less of the latest notified UK recommended retail price of the
latest edition, a royalty of   per cent of the UK recommended
retail price on home sales and   per cent of the net amounts received
by the Publishers from all copies sold for export, excluding such copies as
may by subsequent provisions of this Agreement, or as otherwise mutually
agreed be sold subject to a different royalty.

(e) *Publishers' Own Paperback Editions*
In the event of the publication of the Work in a paperback edition by the
Publishers or by their wholly or partly owned imprint a royalty of
per cent of the UK recommended retail price of all copies sold in the home
market and   per cent on all copies sold for export.

(f) *Non-Booktrade Sales*
On bulk sales in the home market of a special edition bearing the imprint
of a third party for promotional purposes or for sale outside the traditional
booktrade (including but not limited to mail order or coupon advertising)
a royalty of   per cent of the net amount received by the Publishers.

(g) *Premium Sales*
Should the Publishers with the consent of the Author, which shall not be
unreasonably withheld, sell copies of the Work to be given away in
connection with services or goods other than books, the sums payable to
the Author shall be subject to mutual agreement.

---

depend on how much markets diversify over the next few years. Meanwhile it will hardly
be surprising if the author, especially if represented by a literary agent, will want to be
consulted before a final judgment is made by the publishers.

(g) *Premium Sales*
Where copies of the book concerned are given away with other products or in exchange
for tokens collected from other products (the latter sometimes being called 'redemption'
sales) any deals should be agreed with authors before they are completed since authors
may have particular objection to the products with which their books are to be associated.
Discounts to purchasers of books to be used for premium purposes can be very high; on
the other hand very large quantities may be involved and an author's royalty of five to ten
per cent of the amount received is not unreasonable.

General Provisos
The second proviso reflects the great difficulties sometimes encountered by publishers in getting payment from certain countries in which 'central bank' problems take priority over proper trading. The proviso is only a proviso, should be used only in very serious cases of persistent non-payment and should never be used when the publisher has simply been guilty of overtrading.

13. Royalty-inclusive Sales
See Precedent Six for a full discussion of book club editions. This sub-clause (a) covers those transactions where copies are sold to the book club at a price inclusive of royalty. It is usual, where the book club manufactures, for a deal to be negotiated on an advance and royalty basis and this contingency is covered in the next clause. In some cases, either because the book is of minority or special interest or because it is being produced on a co-publication basis with editions in different languages or under different imprints being printed simultaneously by the originating publisher, sales will be made on a royalty-inclusive basis – i.e. the publisher will print copies for the book club or overseas publisher and will sell those copies at a price which includes royalty. From royalty-inclusive book club sales the author should normally expect to be paid 10% (sometimes with an escalator) of the total amount received by the publisher. Although the author will receive less money per copy than would be the case with a royalty sale, since the royalty is calculated on the price at which the copies are sold to the book club, the author does receive in one lump sum an amount which represents the royalties payable on *all* copies supplied – whether or not they are subsequently sold on by the book club. Such an arrangement facilitates sales of smaller quantities to book clubs and also often covers sales to small overseas publishers who would not otherwise be able to afford to take copies. Co-edition sales to American and other overseas publishers usually also work on this basis with varied royalties for copies produced for sale through different channels. For full price trade hardbound copies the author would usually be paid 7.5% to 10% of the publisher's receipts; for paperback or reduced-price copies the author's royalty is usually about 5%–6%. Again the sums received by the author are lower but the royalties due on *all* copies ordered are paid in full in advance.

14. Subsidiary Rights
This precedent sets out income to the author under three heads. Clauses 12, 13 and 14 cover the different volume forms in which the work may be published either by the publisher (Clause 12) or by other publishers licensed by him/her on a royalty-inclusive basis (Clause 13). Clause 14 covers the range of what many in the book trade think of as 'subsidiary rights'. This layout is convenient, but crosses the boundary from those subsidiary rights which are part of volume rights (e.g. paperback or book club rights, quotation and anthology rights, digest and digest book condensation rights, one-shot periodical rights) to those subsidiary rights which are not part of volume rights (e.g. first serial rights, film and TV rights). Hence the careful wording of the introduction to Clause 14.

In general, the point made in Clause 1, note (1) should be borne in mind especially by publishers' staff appointed to handle subsidiary rights. Once the publishers are satisfied, however, that they *have* the skills to handle various non-volume subsidiary rights effectively, they should negotiate forcefully, not least on their author's behalf, to secure those rights, retaining themselves only but not less than a fair percentage of the income from their exploitation. In all but exceptional cases the publishers, by the mere fact of contracting to publish a book, and apart from their services in its promotion and marketing all over the world, increase the value of these rights or may even bring them into existence. Furthermore the original advance for rights often takes into consideration the value of volume and non-volume subsidiary rights, especially serial and television rights.

16

General Provisos
Provided that no royalties shall be paid on copies of the Work given away to the Author or in the interests of the sale of the Work including review copies or on copies lost through theft or damaged or destroyed.

Provided that the Publishers reserve the right not to pay royalties or sums otherwise due to the Author in respect of copies sold until payment for the sale of such copies is received by the Publishers.

13. Royalty-inclusive Sales

Subject to the terms and conditions set out in this Agreement the Publishers shall make the following payments in respect of the following editions:

(a) *Royalty Inclusive Book Club Sales*
On all copies acquired at a price inclusive of royalty by book clubs or similar organisations for sale to their members at a special price   per cent of the net amount received by the Publishers.

(b) *Royalty Inclusive Overseas Sales*
Where a separate agreement is made for the publication in English or another language of the Work overseas under which copies are to be supplied bound or in sheets on a royalty-inclusive basis

(i) On all full price trade hardbound copies: per cent of the net amount received by the Publishers
(ii) On all full price paperback or reduced price copies (including cheap editions sold at no more than two-thirds of the overseas recommended retail price, premium editions, book club editions and editions sold through mail order or direct mail channels):   per cent of the net amount received by the Publishers.

14. Subsidiary Rights

In consideration of payment by the Publishers to the Author of the following percentages of all moneys received by them in respect of the undermentioned rights the Author hereby grants to the Publishers such rights in so far as they are not granted by Clause 1 to the Publishers within the territories specified in Clause 1 during the subsistence of this Agreement.

Consultation with the author over proposed major volume rights deals adopts the spirit of the Minimum Terms Agreement.

Some publishers include a provision, applicable to the whole of the subsidiary rights clause, allowing them to exploit any of the rights listed themselves. If such a provision is included any such proposed exploitation should be subject to prior consultation with the author and the royalty or other payment to the author should be subject to mutual agreement.

(a) and (b) Quotation and Extract Rights, and Anthology Rights
The publishers' interest does not usually exceed 50 per cent unless, in the case of a volume of verse, the contract specifically provides that some greater share of the anthology fees shall go to the publishers until costs of production have been covered. Where the author

has expressed a wish in writing for or against inclusion in an anthology, the publisher should as far as practicable give effect to it. As to scales of fees suitable for various circumstances, see Appendix A.

(c) Digest Rights
A share of 50 per cent to the author is normal.

(d) Digest Book Condensation Rights
A share of 50 per cent to the author is normal.

(e) One-Shot Periodical Rights
A share of 50 per cent to the author is normal. That this right is part of volume rights was established in *Jonathan Cape Ltd v. Consolidated Press Ltd* [1954] 1 WLR 1313: 3 All ER 253. There is no authority in the history of trade practice for regarding this right (exercised by a journal, periodical or newspaper which can, in each case, be properly so defined) as overlapping with or excluding the exercise of mass-market paperback rights, or vice versa. See also (f) and (g) below at note (3).

(f) and (g) Serialisation
(1) If the definitions are accepted, then sale of a serial right further to a first sale to take effect before publication will rank as a further sale of first serial rights and the author will be paid on that basis. The critical question is whether a serial right is to be exercised (i.e. whether the extracts are to be published) before or after publication date of the work. Whether a contract for second serial rights is signed before or after the publication date of the work is irrelevant to that issue.

(2) A share to the author of 90 per cent of receipts from sale of first serial rights is normal. Practice varies greatly on the share to the author from sale of second serial rights, from 50 per cent to as high as 75 per cent.

(3) Despite the apparent meaning of the word 'serial', it is now trade practice to treat one extract only published before publication as an exercise of a first serial right and the author is paid accordingly. Hence the scope of (e) above becomes restricted to publication of a complete (probably very short) work.

(h) Sub-Licensed Paperback Editions
Where the publishers license paperback rights to a third party they retain a percentage of the advance negotiated and of the royalty earned by the sales of such an edition, passing the balance on to the author. The percentage retained by the publisher is often between 40 and 50 per cent and may diminish (to 30 or even 25 per cent with a well established author) as sales increase. The increased return to the author may be 'triggered' either by the amount of money earned from paperback royalties or the number of copies sold.

Advance sums for paperback rights of works which have unanticipated success can be very high, sometimes well in excess of the advance sum paid by the original publisher under e.g. Clause 15 of this precedent. Literary agents will therefore negotiate very carefully over the dates for release of such sums to their author. In general, publishers should be sensitive to this issue and not appear to be hanging on to money arguably due to an author, especially in an industry which accounts to authors at the best twice per annum (see also note (1), Clause 16). In the particular, however, there may be some delicate issues. See note (5) to Clause 15 on payment of the author's share of subsidiary rights earnings prior to delivery of the work to the publishers.

(i) Hardcover reprint rights
Hardcover reprint rights may be 'library' reprint (typically of a book which has gone out of print in hardcover form but for which there is a continuing library demand) or intended for a more general sale. In the latter category are included titles which have been published as paperback originals, but for which a hardcover reprint publisher foresees a demand. If the licensing publisher has already issued the book in hard covers a greater percentage of the proceeds to the publisher (50 per cent or possibly 40 per cent) is

The negotiation of and final agreement to terms of exploitation of rights granted pursuant to this clause shall be in the control of the Publishers who shall wherever practicable consult the Author concerning the sale of US, translation, paperback, book club and first serial rights.

RIGHTS	PAYMENT DUE TO AUTHOR
(a) *Quotation and Extract Rights*	per cent
(b) *Anthology Rights*	per cent
(c) *Digest Rights* (i.e. the right to publish an abridgement of the complete Work in a single issue of a journal, periodical or newspaper)	per cent
(d) *Digest Book Condensation Rights* (i.e. the right to publish a shortened form of the Work in volume form)	per cent
(e) *One-Shot Periodical Rights* (i.e. the right to publish the complete Work in a single issue of a journal, periodical or newspaper)	per cent
(f) *Second and Subsequent Serial Rights* (i.e. the right to publish one or more extracts from the Work in successive issues of a periodical or newspaper beginning at or following publication of the Publishers' first edition of the Work)	per cent
(g) *First Serial Rights* (i.e. the right to publish one or more extracts from the Work in successive issues of a periodical or newspaper beginning before publication of the Publishers' first edition of the Work)	per cent
(h) *Sub-Licensed Paperback Editions*	per cent
(i) *Hardcover Reprint Rights* (i.e. the right to publish a straight reprint of the complete work, without notes or annotations, in hard covers)	per cent

justifiable. In the case of hardcover reprints of paperback originals the percentage to the publisher is likely to be lower – perhaps 20%.

(j)   Educational Reprint Rights: an equal division of proceeds is common.

(k)   There seems to be a growing consensus that a *large print* edition will be one where the print size is not less than 14 point. The author's share of proceeds is likely to be 50 or 60 per cent.

(l)   Book Club Rights on a Separate Royalty Basis: This covers deals where the book club manufactures its own copies and pays an advance against a flat royalty. Usually this edition appears at least six months after first trade publication. Sometimes the publisher will manufacture copies for the book club on this basis, for simultaneous publication with the trade edition. It is usual to divide royalties and advances equally between the author and the publishers although some authors command a share rising to 60 per cent.

(m)   US Rights
Where the publishers have negotiated for world rights, they have a particular responsibility to make as good a deal as they can for their author in the USA, since it comprises the world's largest single 'own language' market in the English language. Wherever possible the US publisher should pay a royalty on the US published price. The publishers act in effect as an agent, and their interest depends on whether they negotiate themselves or employ an US agent. For percentages and commission see note to 14(o) below.

For many books of minority interest, alas, the much less satisfactory deal of a sale of sheets or of bound books at a royalty-inclusive price may be the only realistic possibility. For that reason, most publishers insert a fall-back clause of the kind set out at Clause 13(b) above.

(n)   Strip Cartoon/Picturisation Book Rights
A share of 50 per cent to the author has been normal, but a share of 60–70 per cent is now often found. These rights, like translation rights, are specifically protected in copyright law as acts of adaptation of a literary or dramatic work.

(o)   Translation Rights
The author's share may vary from 75 per cent to 85 per cent according to the publishers' costs. Any commission due to an agent acting on the instructions of the publishers should be paid out of the publishers' share. Translation rights are specifically protected in copyright law (see note to item (n) above). Alternatively, they could be dealt with under Clause 13(b) above (and in the case of co-editions probably will be – though royalty exclusive co-editions may be negotiable for larger quantities).

(p)   Dramatisation and Documentary Rights
A share of 90 per cent to the author is normal. For the new Rental Right, see Introduction.

(q)   Single-Voice Readings
This provision covers radio, television and recorded and public performances in other media. No charge, however, is made for pieces chosen by the competitor for competition recital unless the work (e.g. a poem) is included in any prizewinners' performance at the end of the competition (often a festival), when a very modest fee might be charged. A share of 75 per cent to the author is normal. See also Appendix A, 3. Performance Fees.

(r)   Merchandising Rights
The share to the author may vary between 50 and 80 per cent. See Precedent Thirteen. If the publishers use a merchandising agent (whose commission is likely to be high) the cost should be deducted from the gross receipts before division with the author – and the publisher should expect its percentage to be at the lower end of this scale.

(s)   Mechanical Reproduction Rights
A share of between 50 and 75 per cent to the author is normal, the higher percentage being paid particularly in respect of audio recordings. For the new Rental Right, see Introduction.

(j) *Educational Reprint Rights* (i.e. the
right to publish an educational
edition of the work, with notes and/or
other educational apparatus, in hard
or limp covers)   per cent

(k) *Large Print Rights* (i.e. the right to
publish a straight reprint of the
complete work in large type,
primarily for readers with visual
handicaps, in hard or soft covers)   per cent

(l) *Book Club Rights on a Separate Royalty Basis*   per cent

(m) *Publication rights in the
United States of America*   per cent

(n) *Strip Cartoon Rights or Picturisation
Book Rights*   per cent

(o) *Translation Rights*   per cent

(p) *Dramatisation and Documentary
Rights* on stage, film, radio or television
and videograms thereof, including
transmission by cable, satellite or any
other medium   per cent

(q) *Single-Voice Readings* (i.e. the
right to read from the text of the Work)   per cent

(r) *Merchandising Rights* (i.e. the
right to exploit characters, movements,
representations, names, logos, artwork and
events in the Work through the manufacture,
licensing and/or sale of goods and services,
including but not limited to drawings, calendars,
toys, games, novelties, figures, souvenirs,
trinkets, fabrics, clothing, food
and drinks)   per cent

(s) *Mechanical Reproduction Rights*
(i.e. the right to produce or reproduce
the Work or to license the reproduction
of the Work or any part thereof by film
micrography, gramophone record,
compact disc, tape cassette, or by

(t) Film Strip Rights

This usually covers children's picture books where the book is photographed page by page on to a film strip or loop, usually with a recording of the story and possibly some sound effects or music. It is mainly for use in schools or libraries. A 50 per cent share to the author is normal.

(u) Electronic Book and Version Rights

The wording of these provisions are, of course, relevant only to the use of the work as a source for such publishing. The clause puts the publisher 'in the driving seat' and the publisher should nowadays be as vigilant in securing income from electronic publishers as it already is in pursuing, e.g., translation rights income if it handles them as one of the rights granted under the contract. See also Precedent 14.

If a publisher is by itself or as a joint venturer capable of exploiting electronic book rights (whether as electronic books or electronic versions or both) and intends to do so within the framework of a book publishing contract, provision should be made in Clause 1 for the necessary grant of rights and in Clause 12 for royalties to be paid to the author. If the publisher has such a capability but does not at the time of signing the book publishing contract know whether or not it will produce an electronic edition the matter can, subject to the agreement of the author or agent, be dealt with by including an option. See also note (1) to Clause 1 above. The definitions of electronic book and/or electronic version in the context of a grant or option of electronic rights to a book publisher will be as they are in Clause 14. As matters stand today, however, the vast majority of publishers do not have the capability of exploiting electronic rights themselves and for them licensing those rights to others is the only way in which to benefit from them.

(i) Electronic book rights – in which text in the form of print appears on the screen (and may be capable of being downloaded from a networked system, printed out etc.) – clearly has the potential to compete with and indeed in some instances to replace the printed edition in book form. Although hardly part of volume rights (see note to Clause 14, above) publishers understandably often seek to retain control of electronic book rights. In general agents and authors are sympathetic to that view, provided that there is a clear distinction (as there is in the wording of the two sub-clauses of Clause 14(u)) between electronic book and electronic version rights and provided also that the publisher builds into any licence or exploitation of electronic book rights such safeguards as are possible to protect the copyright and the author's moral rights in the work. See Precedent 14 for further information concerning the last point. The percentage of proceeds to be paid to the author can reasonably be expected to be 50 per cent.

For the new Rental Right, see Introduction.

(ii) In contrast with electronic book rights, the right to license electronic versions (of which multimedia is probably the most familiar example) will often be withheld from the publisher where the author has an agent since in many cases there is no verbatim reproduction of the contents of the published work. The relationship between the published work and a multimedia product is often akin to that between the book itself and a film. Where a publisher does control electronic version rights the percentage of proceeds to be paid to the author is often between 50 and 80 per cent. The note above concerning safeguards will be applicable to electronic version rights if the product is to use verbatim text or illustrations from the published work; otherwise the producer of an electronic version may well require a waiver of moral rights.

For the new Rental Right, see Introduction.

(v) Reprographic Reproduction Rights

Licensing bodies representing authors (ALCS) and publishers (PLS) have agreed terms on which copyright material can be licensed for photocopying by the Copyright Licensing Agency, which is the sole agent for ALCS and PLS. The photocopying is done under licence from CLA and moneys in respect of the photocopying of books are divided equally between author and publisher, with amounts calculated according to the degree of copying of individual works shown up on various sampling schemes, and distributed through ALCS and PLS twice yearly. Authors receive their money direct from ALCS. It is important to remember that publishers own the copyright in the typographical arrangement

means of any other contrivance whether
by sight or sound or a combination of
both, whether now in existence or hereafter
invented for purposes of mechanical
reproduction except in so far as
reproduction is for use as part of or
in conjunction with a commercial
cinematograph film or videogram
of such a film or in conjunction with
an electronic product)   per cent

(t) *Film Strip Rights* (i.e. the right to
reproduce the Work on a film strip
or loop)   per cent

(u) (i) *Electronic Book Rights* (i.e. any means
of distribution or transmission of the Work
whether now or hereafter known or developed,
including but not limited to electronic and machine-
readable media and on-line or satellite transmission,
intended to make the Work available to the public
for reading)   per cent

(ii) *Electronic Version Rights* (i.e. versions that
include the Work and any illustrations contained in
the Work, in complete or condensed or adapted or
abridged versions and in compilations, for performance
and display in any manner (whether sequentially or
non-sequentially and together with accompanying
sounds and images if any) by any electronic means,
method or device. 'Electronic means, method or
device' shall include but not be limited to digital
optical and magnetic information storage and retrieval
systems, on-line or satellite transmission and any other
device or medium for electronic reproduction, publication
or transmission whether now or hereafter known or
developed but excluding Electronic Book Rights)   per cent

(v) *Reprographic Reproduction Rights.* The
Author and the Publishers shall license
the Work non-exclusively to the Authors'
Licensing and Collecting Society and/or
to the Publishers Licensing Society
for the collective reprographic licences or
licensing schemes operated by the
Copyright Licensing Agency
as agent for such Societies and the
Author shall receive the Author's share

23

of their editions of works they publish (which lasts for twenty-five years from the end of the year of publication and is not to be confused with copyright in the text itself, which has its own copyright) so that they are fully entitled to insist on their participation in this scheme. The typographical copyright was established by the Copyright Act 1956 and is continued in the 1988 Act. See also Appendix E.

(w) Non-Commercial Rights for the Print-Handicapped
The wording for this provision has been approved jointly by the Society of Authors, the Association of Authors' Agents and the Publishers Association.

General Proviso
The Copyright, Designs and Patents Act 1988 gives the author the right to object to derogatory treatment of his/her work. This could affect the exercise of, say, digest rights (where the publisher of a condensed version may not be willing to allow a right to approve the condensed version) or film or electronic version rights (where the producer may require a waiver of moral rights as a matter of course). To enable the publishers to exercise such rights it is necessary for the author either to waive in writing his/her right of integrity or to give consent so as to cover specific rights. The right of integrity applies equally to authors and artists and photographers. (For a more detailed explanation see Appendix D.)

15. Advance Payments
(1) Payment of the advance, or more usually a part of the advance, on delivery of the typescript may amount to an acceptance that the typescript matches up to the publisher's expectation at the time he/she contracted the book. The wording set out under Clauses 2 and 3 tries to grapple with this issue explicitly and so to encourage, especially in non-fiction works, author and publishers to agree most carefully at the time of contract exactly what kind of book the author is to write. Where an advance payment schedule has many stages it may be easier to add it as a separate schedule.

(2) It should be noted that the advance is against all earnings due under the agreement and is not merely on royalties derived from sales of the publisher's own edition. If a clause specifies that an advance shall be 'in respect of all the above sums', particular care needs to be exercised to insert that clause after all clauses capable of earning money for the author.

(3) Publishers are under constant pressure to pay advances earlier and earlier. The prudent publisher will note the effect of such pressure on his/her cash flow and, especially in 'vertical' hardback/mass-market paperback deals, will try to spread advance payments forward to the date of paperback publication. He/she will in any event make sure that no earnings will be paid until their total exceeds the total advance (whether paid or in part still due under contract) or, at least, that any earnings paid, in excess of that portion of the advance already paid, are deducted from the balance of the advance still due.

(4) Most Minimum Terms Agreements include a formula for calculating the minimum advance sum to be paid, related to a percentage of the author's estimated earnings from the sale of the projected first printing. Where the publisher is to publish in hardcover only, 65 per cent is commonly specified; whereas for vertical contracts 55 per cent is the norm. For non-commissioned books MTAs often stipulate that half the total advance is due on signature and half on publication or within 12 months of signature if earlier, while for commissioned books the total advance is payable in three thirds, the extra stage being on delivery of the final revised typescript. In each case the stages for payment may be varied at the author's request, whilst some MTAs provide for payment of a portion of the advance on paperback publication if vertical publication is a contractual commitment.

of any proceeds from use of the Work
under such licences or licensing schemes
through the Authors' Licensing and
Collecting Society in accordance
with such Society's standard terms and
condition.   per cent

(w) *Non-Commercial Rights for the*
Print-Handicapped (i.e. the right to
convert the Work to Braille or to record
it for the sole use of the blind and
print-handicapped free of charge)   free of charge

General Proviso

The Author on written request from the Publishers undertakes to give consent in writing or to waive *his/her* right to object to derogatory treatment of *his/her* work as provided for in s. 80 of the Copyright, Designs and Patents Act 1988 when such consent or waiver is an essential condition of the exercise of any of the subsidiary rights set out in this Clause.

15. Advance Payments

The Publishers shall pay to the Author the sum of   in advance and on account of all royalty and other earnings accruing to the Author under this Agreement payable as follows:

---

(5) Given that most publishers account to authors at intervals of not less than six months, authors' agents may well ask for the author's share of subsidiary rights moneys, where that share is in excess of a certain sum, to be paid within 30 days of receipt (always provided that the original advance for the work has been earned) rather than at the next accounting. The sum in question will reflect the level at which it is economically viable for the publisher to draw a separate, often manual, statement and cheque (and may also relate to the viable economic level of the work in which the agent is involved in processing the payment); anything under £100 at the present time will probably not be possible for most publishers.

If the publishers agree to such a request, some other stipulations are prudent. First (and assuming the advance to be specified as on account of all earnings) such payments should not be made unless the total advance has been earned — or without deduction of any unearned balance of the advance before payment of the net amount, if that amount justifies payment. Secondly, although publishers should not appear to be hanging on to money arguably due to an author, there may be a problem in paying over the author's share of proceeds received prior to UK publication even if they exceed the UK publisher's advance. If for example the British publisher has contracted for world rights in an as yet unwritten work of non-fiction and has sold US rights on synopsis for a high advance, the British publisher may be wary of passing to the author his/her share of any such advance sums payable before delivery, in case the author is seriously late with delivery, in which event the US publisher may be entitled to rescind and to have his/her advance repaid. The cautious publisher may take the view that publication of his/her own edition of the book is the earliest moment at which the author's share of subsidiary rights advances should be paid.

16. Statement of Sales

(1) 'It is perhaps time for a forthright view of the frequency of accounting to authors. The entire book trade depends on authorship. The writers of books are the publishers' most important "suppliers" by far, and it is hardly tolerable that they should be paid on an annual basis — no supplier of other goods or services to the book trade would contract for such an interval of time.'

Since the above view was expressed in the Second Edition of 1984, there has been steady progress among general trade publishers towards accounting twice per year and it is now the norm in trade publishing and is becoming increasingly common among educational publishers. Clause 16 therefore offers as a precedent 'twice yearly' wording. It may even be that a general trade publisher who does not move to twice yearly accounting will find that the terms he/she offers to prospective authors are no longer competitive.

(2) The percentages retained as reserves against returns were, for some years, 10 per cent for hardbacks and 20 per cent for paperbacks; but the increasing returns percentages suffered by publishers (and the far wider incidence — formal or otherwise — of the supply of books to booksellers on a sale or return basis) made it necessary for those percentages to be re-examined. Between 15 and 20 per cent has become widespread for the hardback reserve while paperback reserves are now generally in the range of 25 per cent to 30 per cent. It is of course possible to apply such percentages selectively; children's books, for example, tend to suffer comparatively low returns so it may be reasonable to reduce the reserve percentages for them. It has been suggested that reserves should be held only in respect of royalties on non-firm sales; and if a publisher's accounting system is capable of handling that then clearly it is equitable to do so. Crediting the reserve at the fourth account is of course, only acceptable to authors if accounting is twice yearly.

Another approach, common in the US and sometimes encountered in the UK, is to make a deduction for reserves at the first account and credit the amount deducted at the second account, whilst making a new deduction from earnings at that account and crediting it at the third account and so on. The US method often involves deducting a percentage from the sales figures (rather than the earnings); often the percentage is not quantified in the contract but is merely stated as to be 'reasonable' and frequently the publisher is entitled to continue to deduct (and credit) throughout the life of the book. Whilst the last facet sometimes applies when such a system is used in the UK, the percentage is generally stipulated in the contract.

(3) Payments are not normally made where the sum is less than £50.

(4) What information a good royalty account should contain has been the subject of much discussion in recent years. See Appendix G.

(5) Some publishers, in allowing access to their accounts for the purpose of sub-clause (c), stipulate an acceptable margin of error as, e.g., £10 or £25. Such a sum may however be a trivial sum in relation to a high-earning author with a major title in dispute. To express an acceptable margin as a percentage of error (here 2.5 per cent) may be more prudent.

17. VAT

The second sentence should, of course, be included if HM Customs and Excise *have* agreed a self-billing system for the publisher.

16. Statement of Sales

(a) The Publishers shall prepare accounts for the Work twice yearly to 30 June and 31 December following publication and the said accounts shall be delivered to the Author and settled within three months thereafter, provided however that no payment need be made in respect of any period in which the sum due is less than £50 in which case the amounts shall be carried forward to the next accounting date.

(b) The Publishers shall at their discretion have the right to set aside as a reserve against returns a sum representing in the case of a hardback edition   per cent and in the case of a paperback edition per cent of the royalties earned under Clause 12 at the first accounting after publication or re-issue of any edition of the Work, and to withhold this sum for a period up to and including the third royalty statement following publication or reissue, after which all moneys due shall be paid in full at the time of the next royalty statement.

(c) Upon reasonable written notice and during the Publishers' normal business hours the Author or the Author's appointed representative shall have the right to examine the Publishers' records of account at the place at which they are normally kept, in so far as such records relate to sales and receipts in respect of the Work. Such examination shall be at the cost of the Author unless errors shall be found, to the disadvantage of the Author, in excess of 2.5 per cent of the amount due to the Author in respect of the last preceding accounting period, in which case the cost of such examination shall be borne by the Publishers. Any amount thereby shown to be due to the Author shall be paid to the Author on receipt by the Publishers of the Author's account relating thereto. No more than one such inspection shall be made in any twelve-month period.

(d) Any overpayment (which shall exclude any unearned balance of the advance paid to the Author in respect of the Work but without further limitation shall include any debit royalties caused by returns of copies of the Work for which the Author shall previously have received royalty payments from the Publishers) made by the Publishers to the Author in respect of the Work may be deducted from any sums due subsequently to the Author from the Publishers in respect of the Work.

17. VAT

All moneys due under the terms of this Agreement are exclusive of any VAT due thereupon. The Publishers operate a self-billing system for the payment of royalties and to account for Value Added Tax. The Publishers therefore require details of the Author's VAT registration number where applicable which shall be supplied upon signature of this Agreement. Should the Author fail to supply a VAT registration number the Publishers shall not pay VAT on any sums due under the terms of this Agreement.

18. Copyright

(1) Although the author under Clause 1 clearly grants only an exclusive licence to the publisher, it is desirable, not least in order to combat piracy in certain overseas markets, to make crystal clear in the contract's wording that copyright is retained by the author (see also, however, Precedent Two, note 2(a)).

(2) The sign ©, printed on all copies of the work and accompanied by the name of the copyright owner and the first year of publication, is the only formality required to ensure protection for the work under the Universal Copyright Convention (signed at Geneva in 1952 under UNESCO auspices), irrespective of whether the work was published inside or outside the territory of a contracting state. The United Kingdom is a contracting state. The main intention of the UCC was to bring the USA into the family of international copyright relationships in the hope that eventually the USA might join the Berne Convention, which, indeed, it did in 1989.

(3) International copyright is a minefield and professional advice should always be sought. Relationships between countries will vary according to membership (or otherwise) of Berne and/or UCC, according to ratification (or otherwise) by Berne member states of numerous amending conventions from 1896 to 1971, and/or according to any direct bilateral agreements between individual states.

19. Infringement of Copyright

(1) *Piracy.* Piracy is an international crime. Both developed and developing countries recognise the need to pursue piracy vigorously and relentlessly. The interests at stake are not only those of authors and publishers in developed countries whose intellectual property is seized through plain theft, but also of authors and publishers in developing countries: they see *their* authorship, *their* publishing, the development of *their* national culture being swept aside in a flood of imported or even locally manufactured pirate editions of foreign works.

Clause 19 therefore places the initiative and the responsibility for fighting piracy in the hands of the publishers. The clause requires, indeed, the total co-operation of the author (not least for reasons of copyright law) but does equally offer to the author a 50 per cent share of any net profit or damages received as a result of enforcement action, which will have been funded at high cost by the publishers alone. Publishers may also give the author the opportunity to join with them as equal parties to an action for infringement, bearing half of all costs and expenses.

(2) *Market infringement.* Publishers in the main overseas markets, e.g. Australia and New Zealand, who act as importing agents for or who are subsidiaries of United Kingdom publishers may seek protection from market infringement through the transfer of an interest in copyright sufficient to enable them to take quick action on the spot in their own right. The transfer may be on the following lines (a New Zealand example is offered):

> agrees to transfer the copyright or assign the exclusive licence to publish (as the case may be) in respect of all their titles to the   Group (NZ) Ltd in respect of New Zealand and all associated territories for the duration of the current agency agreement and accepts   Group (NZ) Ltd's right to act on their behalf in any action against copyright infringement taken under the terms of the New Zealand Copyright Act 1962 and its subsequent amendments.

The importing publisher should also have printed on forms used for ordering books from the United Kingdom publisher from whom he/she acquires such a transfer letter wording such as:

> The placing and acceptance of this order constitutes the transfer of copyright or the assignation of the exclusive licence to publish (as the case may be) in respect of New Zealand and its associated territories for these titles to this Company for the duration of our current agency agreement.

18. Copyright

The copyright in the Work shall remain the property of the Author and the copyright notice to be printed in every copy of the Work published by the Publishers shall be in the Author's name, with the year of first publication. The Publishers shall use all reasonable endeavours to include in any contract with any licensee concerning any edition of the Work an undertaking that the same notice shall be printed in every edition published or further licensed by the licensee.

19. Infringement of Copyright

If the Publishers consider that the copyright in the Work has been or is likely to be infringed they shall on giving notice to the Author of such infringement be at liberty to take such steps as they may consider necessary for dealing with the matter and if they desire to take proceedings they shall, on giving the Author an undertaking in writing to pay all costs and expenses and to indemnify the Author against all liability for costs, be entitled to use the Author's name as a party to such proceedings, but at the same time to control, settle or compromise as they see fit. The Publishers shall further be entitled to take urgent proceedings in their own sole name for interlocutory relief without prior notice to the Author. Any profits or damages which may be received in respect of any infringement of the copyright shall after deduction of all costs and expenses be divided equally between the Author and the Publishers. The provisions of this Clause are intended to apply only in the case of an infringement of the copyright in the Work affecting the interest in the same granted to the Publishers under this Agreement.

20. Author's Copies

The Author shall be entitled to receive on publication ten presentation copies of the hardback and twenty presentation copies of any paperback edition and shall be entitled to purchase further copies at trade terms for personal use but not for resale and shall pay for such copies within thirty days of invoice. The Author shall receive two copies of any sub-licensed edition on receipt by the Publishers from the sub-licensed publishers.

21. Revision of the Work

(a) Should the Author and the Publishers agree that a revision of the Work is necessary, the Author shall, without charge to the Publishers, edit

---

20. Author's Copies
When ordering copies of their books some authors ask for the amount to be debited to their accounts. If the account is already in debit there is often little chance of the publisher recouping his/her money. Thus, as an inducement, some publishers will offer a greater discount (usually 50 per cent) for cash with order or for advance payment by credit card.

21. Revision of the Work
The clause reflects the contention on behalf of authors in general trade publishing that until the author's death the author and publishers should jointly decide whether the work

requires revision. The matter is, of course, of central importance in certain kinds of educational publishing, as is the death of the author. On each point see Clause 18 of Precedent Two. Where re-writing constitutes a reasonable proportion (e.g. over 10%) of the total length of a work the publisher may be willing to pay a further advance – possibly based on a proportion of the original advance – if the original advance has been earned.

As to the meaning of 'substantially to reoriginate' production of the Work, see Precedent Two, note 3.1.2 ('substantially reset the work for a new edition'). Some publishers, if substantial reorigination is required, prefer to negotiate with the author a new agreement altogether, and will therefore build this option into the wording of Clause 21 (b). If the work is extensively revised or re-written by someone other than the original author the royalties to the original author may need to be reduced below the lowest rate provided in the agreement: it may, for instance, be necessary to pay the reviser a royalty rather than an outright fee, in which case the percentage due to the original author will be shared between him/her and the reviser.

22. Remainders/Disposal of Surplus Stock

(1) What is the difference between a remainder at more than cost and a cheap edition at less than two-thirds of the original edition's published price (Clause 12(d))? It is suggested that if the latest notified price of an original edition is reduced by more than 60 per cent, then copies so sold should be treated for royalty purposes as 'remainders' and not 'cheaps'. The question is usually academic since most remainders are disposed of at well below cost.

(2) There has been much debate in recent years over whether the author should receive *something*, however small, in respect of proceeds from remainders sold off at cost price or below. Many publishers have stood firm on paying 10 per cent of net receipts only if the remaindered copies are sold at above cost price. Others have indicated some sympathy for the author's argument by agreeing to pay, e.g., 5 per cent of net receipts on copies sold at cost price or below.

(3) Authors must be notified of an impending remainder sale or destruction of remaining stocks and given the opportunity to acquire all or some of the remaining copies at the best remainder price, but the sale of the remainder or destruction should not be left contingent on the author's approval.

(4) Some, but by no means all, contracts drafted by literary agents include a specific provision to the effect that the exercise by the publishers of the right to remainder amounts to a repudiation of the contract, so that publishing rights revert to the author forthwith. The issue is not made any easier by the practice of 'part-remaindering'. Whether such a provision is accepted in principle or not, reversion of the publisher's rights should not be permitted to take place if the book is in print in any other edition published by the publisher — or, some will argue, under current licence from the publisher to a sub-licensee (at least in book form). See Clause 24 below and the relevant note.

23. Termination of Contract

See Preamble, note (3).

Some publishers may find Clause 23(b) wider in scope than they would like. The appointment of a receiver is not the end of the road for a limited company. However, the receiver may well 'freeze' any earnings due to the company's authors as assets of the ailing company, as are, of course, the company's contracts with its authors. This precedent, on balance, puts the authors' interests first.

and revise the Work during the currency of this agreement and shall supply any new matter that may be needed to keep the Work up to date within a reasonable period. In the event of the Author neglecting or being unable for any reason to revise or edit the work or supply new matter where needed within a reasonable period the Publishers may procure some other person to revise the Work, or supply new matter, and may deduct the expense thereof from royalties or other sums payable to the Author under this Agreement.

(b) Should the revisions to the Work make it necessary in the opinion of the Publishers substantially to reoriginate production of the Work for the issue of a revised or new edition then the royalties payable on all copies sold of the first impression of such revised edition shall be at the lowest rates of royalty as provided under the terms of this Agreement.

22. Remainders/Disposal of Surplus Stock

If, after a period of one year from the date of first publication, the Work shall in the opinion of the Publishers have ceased to have a remunerative sale, the Publishers shall be at liberty to dispose of any copies remaining on hand as a remainder or overstock or to destroy them. The Publishers shall inform the Author of their decision to remainder or to destroy the remaining copies and shall give *him/her* the opportunity of purchasing copies at the remainder price on offer or of taking copies intended for destruction free of charge except for carriage. The Author shall inform the Publishers whether *he/she* wishes to acquire part or all of the stock and, if *he/she* fails to so inform the Publishers within three weeks of posting, they may remainder or destroy the Work forthwith. If the price obtained is more than the cost of production the Publishers shall pay to the Author 10 per cent of the net amounts received by the Publishers. On disposal of stock at or below cost of production, no royalty shall be payable.

23. Termination of Contract

(a) The Author may terminate this Agreement by summary notice in writing to the Publishers if the Publishers are in material breach of any of the provisions of this Agreement and have failed to remedy such breach within one month of notice to them from the Author of such breach.

(b) This Agreement shall automatically terminate if and when a manager, receiver, or other encumbrancer takes possession of, or is appointed over the whole or any substantial part of, the Publishers' assets; or if and when the Publishers enter into any arrangement or composition with or for the benefit of their creditors (including any voluntary arrangement under the Insolvency Act, 1986); or if and when a petition is presented or a meeting is convened for the purpose of considering a resolution for the making of an administrative order, the winding up or dissolution of the Publishers (otherwise than a voluntary liquidation for the purpose of reconstruction).

24. Reversion of Rights

(1) The provision makes it clear that if the original publisher does not have the work available in any edition then the author can give notice to reprint and, if the publisher fails to do so within the time stipulated, reclaim the rights. This does not seem unreasonable for a 'vertical' publisher which has the facilities to publish in hardcover and paperback form. For publishers which do not produce paperbacks themselves and indeed for publishers a substantial part of whose business may be overseas licensed editions it may be reasonable for rights to be retained on the basis of existing sub-licences, even though the work is out of print with the original publisher. Publishers will have to decide where they stand on this point: some publishers decline to revert rights where the book is available in English in an American or other full-length edition sub-leased by the publishers. Others consider that any sub-licensed edition should be capable of keeping the work in print.

(2) The clause, if invoked, should not terminate any option clause on future work which may be part of the same agreement. It is therefore advisable to make this explicit by the wording in parentheses in the draft.

(3) If the contract grants the publisher the right to exploit the work in more than one medium (e.g. as a book, an audio recording and an electronic product) it is only reasonable for this provision to allow for the rights to revert in each medium separately – without, of course, affecting the publisher's rights in any other medium in which the work is available.

25. Moneys Owing

Invoices for authors' purchases of books, excess corrections and so on are often charged against their royalty account. If the account is in debit (because the advance is not earned, or for any other reason) the amounts owing are unable to be recovered from authors' earnings; and authors are seldom inclined to send publishers cheques for the outstanding invoices. The sums involved are generally too small to make it worth the publishers' while to spend much time or money on collecting them by conventional means. The clause is, frankly, a blunt instrument: there is no direct relationship between such sums owing to publishers and the reversion of rights to authors. But some publishers include it and report that it often results in payment of long-outstanding invoices when authors (or their agents) are anxious to revert rights.

26. Option on Future Work

(1) This option clause can be adapted to cover the author's 'next full-length work', 'next full-length work of non-fiction', etc. If the option is for more than one work it is advisable to add: 'If, however, the Publishers decline the first of these works, the Author shall not be bound to offer them the second.'

(2) Some publishers require the author to offer the same rights and territories in the option work as those covered in the agreement. This is not popular with authors' organisations or agents and can work against a publisher whose rights and/or territories in the agreement contains such option clause wording.

(3) The publishers should not generally undertake to exercise their option in less than six weeks.

(4) It will, of course, be realised from Clause 24, note (2), that the option secured by this clause is not lost upon the termination of the agreement for causes other than bankruptcy or wilful failure to implement the agreement.

(5) It is necessary in negotiations over an author who is published also in America to ensure that the option can be exercised at the same time as and not after the equivalent option clause is being exercised by the American publisher. Otherwise, the British publisher may be faced with a *fait accompli* over aspects of territory, release dates in open markets, etc. which would seriously affect the prospects for the British edition of the work under option.

27. Moral Rights

For this very important provision of statutory copyright law, see Appendix D.

(c) Upon termination of this Agreement under (a) or (b) above, but subject to the terms of Clauses 25 and 26, all rights granted herein shall revert to the Author without further notice, without prejudice to any rights of the Publishers or of third parties in respect of contracts or negotiations properly entered into by them with any such third party prior to the date of such reversion, and without prejudice to any moneys already paid or then due to the Author from the Publishers.

24. Reversion of Rights

If the Work shall become out of print and unavailable in all editions issued by the Publishers then the Author may give notice in writing to the Publishers to reprint or reissue the Work within nine months. In the event of the Publishers' failure to do so, all the Publishers' rights in the Work (but not those deriving from the option in Clause 26 and subject to Clause 25) shall terminate upon the expiration of the said notice, without prejudice to all rights of the Publishers and any third party in respect of any agreement previously entered into by the Publishers hereunder with any such party. Except nevertheless that no rights shall revert if it is not possible to reprint or reissue the Work for reasons connected with any war, strikes, lock-outs or other circumstances beyond the Publishers' control.

25. Moneys Owing

Notwithstanding the foregoing provisions of this Agreement the rights hereby granted to the Publishers shall not revert unless any moneys owing by the Author to the Publishers shall have been paid and always providing that any unearned balance of the advance shall not be deemed to constitute moneys so owing.

26. Option on Future Work

The Publishers shall have the first opportunity to read and consider for publication either the complete typescript or a synopsis and specimen chapter for the Author's next work suitable for publication in volume form. Such work shall be the subject of a fresh agreement between the Author and the Publishers, on terms which shall be fair and reasonable. If the Publishers and Author are unable to agree terms for its publication the Author shall be at liberty to enter into an agreement with another publisher provided that the Author shall not subsequently accept from anyone else terms less favourable than are offered by the Publishers. The Publishers shall exercise this option within six weeks of receipt of complete typescript or detailed outline.

27. Moral Rights

The Author hereby asserts *his/her* right to be identified as the Author of the Work and the Publishers undertake

28. Agency
If a contract is offered by an agent, this clause is usually in his/her standard form of words.

29. Arbitration
The Informal Disputes Settlement Scheme offers fast, informal, inexpensive settlement of disputes between authors and publishers which even under arbitration rules may cost thousands of pounds to resolve where the amount of money in dispute may amount only to hundreds.

31. Entire Agreement
This provision, if included, does of course require both publisher and author to commit agreed changes to the signed contract to writing – a discipline which some may feel to be unduly onerous. However it may be highly unwise to rely on oral agreement to changes: see comments in the Introduction on *Malcolm v OUP* and note (7) to Preamble.

(i) to print on every edition of the Work published by them the words: '[The Author] has asserted *his/her* right under the Copyright, Designs and Patents Act, 1988, to be identified as Author of this Work';

(ii) to use all reasonable endeavours to include in any contract for volume rights with any licensee concerning any edition of the Work to be published in the United Kingdom an undertaking that a notice of assertion in the same terms shall be printed in every edition published or further licensed by such licensee.

28. Agency

The Author hereby authorises and empowers *his/her* Agents,
, to collect and receive all sums of money payable to the Author under the terms of this Agreement and declares that
receipt shall be a good and valid discharge to all persons paying such moneys to them and that they shall be empowered to act in all matters arising out of this Agreement unless the Publishers are notified in writing otherwise by the Author.

29. Arbitration

If any difference shall arise between the Author and the Publishers touching the meaning of this Agreement or the rights and liabilities of the parties thereto, the same shall in the first instance be referred to the Informal Disputes Settlement Scheme of the Publishers Association and, failing agreed submission by both parties to such Scheme, shall be referred to the arbitration of two persons (one to be named by each party) or to a mutually agreed umpire in accordance with the provisions of the Arbitration Act 1996, or any amending or substitute statute for the time being in force.

30. Interpretation

The headings in this Agreement are for convenience only and shall not affect its interpretation. References to Clauses are to clauses of this Agreement.

31. Entire Agreement

This Agreement is the entire and only agreement between the Author and the Publishers concerning its subject matter and supersedes any and all prior agreements, arrangements and understandings (whether written or oral) relating thereto. No addition to or modification of any provision of this Agreement shall be binding upon the parties unless it is in writing and signed on behalf of the Author and the Publishers.

32. Governing Law

This Agreement shall be deemed to be a contract made in England and shall be construed and applied in all respects in accordance with English law and the parties hereto submit and agree to the jurisdiction of the English courts.

AS WITNESS THE HANDS OF THE PARTIES

For and on behalf of the Publishers:

— — — — — — — — — — — —

Director

For and on behalf of the Author:

— — — — — — — — — — — —

Author

APPENDIX

Author	James Bridges
Title (provisional)	A LITTLE FLUSHED
Nature of work	a history of the water waste preventer, for general readers

---

TEXT

Length	between 80,000 and 100,000 words
Medium for delivery	3.5 inch IBM PC-compatible floppy disk and one hard copy printed from such disk with no alterations
Date by which to be delivered to the Publishers	31st December 199x

---

ILLUSTRATIVE MATERIAL

Type	Black and white photographs and line drawings
Extent	8 pages of photographs; up to 50 line drawings, to be integrated with text
Date by which to be delivered to the Publishers	Photographs: by 31st March 199x Diagrams: with text

Otherwise in accordance with Clause 8

INDEX

Extent	6 pages (approx)
Date by which to be delivered to the Publishers	within 21 days of receipt of final page proofs by Author

Otherwise in accordance with Clause 9

OTHER MATERIALS

Introduction by Sir George Jennings. 3 typescript pages. Already in Author's possession. To be delivered to Publishers with text. Otherwise in accordance with Clause 2.

Educational, Academic, Scientific and Professional Book Author – Publisher Agreements

An agreement between author and publisher for a school, university, college or professional book does not differ in essence from that for a general trade book. However, editors of books for schools and for the tertiary and professional markets will lay particular emphasis on some aspects of the agreement. Precedent Two, therefore, deals with those matters where the emphasis differs and which may require special wording. In respect of those issues where the Notes on Precedent One apply equally to educational (that is in broad terms, schools, tertiary, scientific, technical, medical and professional) publishing agreements, the reader is referred to the appropriate section of those Notes.

Although both the Publishers Association's Code of Practice and the Minimum Terms Agreement draft offered jointly by the Society of Authors and the Writers' Guild tend to regard educational publishing as a special occupation, nevertheless editors in educational companies will increasingly recognise that some aspects of authors' rights have a proper place in their company's dealings with educational authors.

Preamble
For general commentary please refer to the Note to Precedent One.

(1) *Joint and multiple authorship* are common in educational books.

Joint authorship takes place where the authors act as one author; it is not possible to, and it is not intended that the reader, distinguish the contribution of each author to the final work. The authors carry joint responsibility and the publishers should emphasise this feature strongly to the authors in writing before contract.

Experience, alas, suggests that, possibly through a note signed by each joint author and to be read as part of the contract, provision should be made from the start for any falling out among the joint authors. Young lecturers A and B jointly and enthusiastically write up their lectures on a new topic into a best-selling text. Fifteen years and three editions later, distinguished professors A and B have one of those violent academic disputes which so enliven the pages of academic journals. The publishers have on their hands a best-selling, internationally marketed textbook into which many publishing resources have been invested. Rival textbooks are on the scene: the publishers need urgently a new edition to keep competitive edge and are faced with two authors who are no longer on academic speaking terms with each other.

What is to be done? The answer must depend on the infinite delicacies of each situation, but a contractual note on file of the kind suggested above may turn out to have been a very useful investment in the interest of all parties.

In some cases each author only takes responsibility for what he/she has written. Here the question at issue is often the varying qualities of the contributions (works of 20 and more multiple authors are not uncommon in, e.g., medical publishing). See Precedent Four, Clause and note 5.

(2) *Institutional/corporate authorship.* Increasingly educational and academic publishers find themselves entering into agreements not with individuals but with institutions (such as a local education authority or a college). In essence, the rules of authorship do not change, but the following points should be borne in mind:

(a) It is important to establish, before contract, whether it is the institution that holds copyright — either by virtue of the work having been written by its employees or by virtue of separate contracts; if so the contract should be entered into with the institution (as the proprietors) and the following recital should be inserted into the Preamble to Precedent Two immediately following the definitions of the parties, namely:

WHEREAS the Proprietors are the proprietors of a work by [*name of author*] at present entitled: [*name of work*] (hereinafter termed 'the Work'), NOW IT IS HEREBY MUTUALLY AGREED AS FOLLOWS:

(b) In royalty payments, a distinction may need to be made between the copyright holder as in (a) above, and the author(s). They may sometimes be paid employees of that institution, and it must be made clear not only with whom the agreement is to be made, but whether or not the individual authors are entitled to separate payment (often the institution regards the writing done as part of their contractual commitment to that institution).

(c) The terms under which the institution receives copies of the work can sometimes form part of the agreement, e.g. bulk supply at no cost to the institution, but in lieu of royalty. The terms under which the institution receives further copies of the work need to be agreed in advance. Alternatively, the institution may prefer to purchase a specified number of copies of the work on publication at a substantial discount off the publishers' list price; such an arrangement should also form part of the agreement, as should the terms of supply of any re-order.

(d) It is obviously important that bulk copies supplied under (c) above do not attract royalty earnings to the same institution. Contract and Accounts departments need to be warned of any 'royalty-free' supplies such as these.

THIS AGREEMENT is made this   day of   19
BETWEEN:
[*name*]
of [*address*]
   (hereinafter termed 'the Author', which expression shall, where the context admits, include the Author's executors, administrators and assigns) of the one part, and [*name of company*] of [*address*] (hereinafter termed 'the Publishers', which expression shall, where the context admits, include the Publishers' successors in business and assigns) of the other part,
WHEREBY it is agreed as follows concerning a work by the Author at present entitled: [*name of work*] (hereinafter termed 'the Work')

1. Delivery and Acceptance of the Work

1.1 The Author undertakes to deliver to the Publishers by the [*date*] day of [*month*]   19[   ]:

 1.1.1 the complete manuscript of the Work consisting of not more than [*number*] and not less than [*number*] words on a word processor disk in [*specify word processing package to be used*] format together with two identical hard copies printed out from the said disk in double line spacing;

 1.1.2 artwork or roughs for a maximum of [*number*] line drawings (the finished artwork for which shall be prepared by the Publishers);

---

1. Delivery and Acceptance of the Work

1.1 The manuscript delivery date will clearly be of importance where the work is required to be available to coincide with the publishers' main selling season, or with a new syllabus or course or examination requirements, and the production schedule is tight. However, it is often the case when syllabus changes occur that these changes will not have been published in final form when the author starts writing, and the work in progress will have to be amended to take account of such changes as they occur. The inevitable result is that deadlines may slip through no fault of the author or the publishers and it is sensible to provide in the agreement for an extension to the manuscript delivery date. See Clause 1.4 and note to Precedent One Clause 2 (Delivery of the Work).

1.1.1 Both parties should be clear from the outset as to the proposed extent of the work being commissioned as this may well reflect market expectations or requirements, and the publishers' production estimate and other costings will have been based on what has been agreed. If the author is to submit the manuscript on disk, as is becoming the norm rather than the exception, then it is important to agree the word processing package which is to be used and the style in which the text is to be laid out, more especially if the disk is to be used in typesetting and other production processes, and time is of the essence. For further comment on submission of text on disk see the note to Precedent One Clause 2 (Delivery of the Work).

 The publishers may require the author to submit one or more hard copy print-outs together with the disk for mark-up and estimating purposes.

1.1.2 Care about illustrations is especially needed in educational works and publishers of, for example, primary schoolbooks or medical texts or technical manuals may consider using or adapting Precedent Ten.

However, the costs of originating and producing full-colour highly illustrated school textbooks without the benefit of trade prices may make the need to pay the fee without a recurring royalty a condition of publishing the book. Most illustrators understand this, but it is particularly important that the terms of the assignment of copyright, and of any waiver of moral rights (see Appendix D), are clearly understood and that any agreement to return artwork to the artist for personal reasons does not entitle him/her to re-use it in reproduced form.

Sometimes, however, the cost of originating the artwork will not be borne entirely by the publishers. Specialist artwork, for example, may be prepared under the auspices of the authors within their own university department in return for which the publishers will pay a reasonable fee.

Where artwork is submitted by the author in the form of roughs it is wise to stipulate in the agreement who is to redraw the artwork and at whose cost.

Where valuable or irreplaceable transparencies are submitted by the author, arrangements should be made for their safe-keeping and eventual return to the author, and the issue of insurance should also be discussed.

1.1.3 If the author is to prepare additional material such as exercises, answers or an index for inclusion in the work at no additional cost to the publishers, then this should be made clear at the outset. If the index (or any other additional material) is not to be supplied by the author, this should likewise be stated in the agreement, together with details of who is responsible for the preparation of such material and for bearing any associated costs.

1.1.4 Where material taken from third party sources has been included in the work, the publishers will need to be aware of precisely what material has been used and from where it has been taken. If the publishers are to obtain permission for the use of such material on the author's behalf, then their in-house editorial staff will need to set the wheels in motion when the manuscript is delivered, in order to ensure that all the relevant permissions are obtained and appropriate acknowledgement copy prepared in advance of publication. This is particularly important in respect of 'fast-track' textbooks with a very short production lead time.

1.2 More detailed guidance to authors in the preparation of their manuscripts is sometimes available in the form of the publishers' 'Guide for Authors', often a short booklet, produced in-house, giving broad guidelines on manuscript formatting and presentation. Where such a document exists and it is expected that authors will follow the guidance it offers, it is wise to make reference to the fact in the agreement.

1.3 Lest the unthinkable happen, it is prudent for the publishers to suggest that the author retain for safe-keeping a copy of all the material he/she has submitted to the publishers.

1.4 Whilst the majority of manuscripts appear (more or less) on time, inevitably some do not despite numerous extensions to deadlines and coaxing and cajoling on the part of editors. In such circumstances the publishers may exercise one of two options: either to require the author to repay any advance payments made to him/her; or, alternatively, to require the author to give the publishers first option on publishing the manuscript if the author does subsequently complete it. In the case of educational books where syllabus changes and topicality of subject matter are of great importance, the publishers may often elect to do the former. For further comment on late delivery see the note to Precedent One Clause 2 (Delivery of the Work).

1.5, 1.6 and 1.7 See the note to Precedent One Clause 3 (Acceptance and Conditions of Acceptance and Approval).

1.8 The publishers will wish to seek to minimise their risk in respect of claims for libel, negligent misstatement, breach of copyright and the like. See the note to Precedent One Clause 5 (Warranties and Indemnities) for further discussion of this issue.

a maximum of [*number*] transparencies; a maximum of [*number*] charts/maps/diagrams ready for reproduction/to be redrawn by the Publishers;

1.1.3 any additional matter for inclusion in the Work such as notes/ appendices/exercises/answers and an index, if so required by the Publishers;

1.1.4 a complete list of all material taken by the Author from other sources for inclusion in the Work.

1.2 The Work shall be prepared in accordance with the Publishers' 'Guide for Authors' or in any other form agreed with the Publishers.

1.3 The Author shall retain a duplicate copy of the complete manuscript of the Work and all other material supplied by the Author to the Publishers for inclusion therein.

1.4 Should the Author neglect to deliver the complete manuscript, together with any illustrative and/or additional matter by the prescribed date (or by any extension thereto mutually agreed in writing) the Publishers may, if they so wish, decline to publish the Work in which case this Agreement shall terminate forthwith, subject as the Publishers in their sole discretion shall elect one or other of the following:

EITHER:

1.4.1 the Author shall not be at liberty to arrange for the publication of the Work elsewhere without first offering the complete manuscript to the Publishers on the terms of this Agreement;

OR:

1.4.2 the Author shall, upon the Publishers' written request, repay to the Publishers any monies which have been paid to the Author under this Agreement.

1.5 The Publishers shall accept the Work provided that the complete manuscript and any illustrative and/or additional matter as delivered by the Author conforms in nature, scope, length and style to the specifications agreed in writing between the parties hereto.

1.6 Should the manuscript not so conform the Publishers shall have the right either to decline to publish the Work in which case this Agreement shall terminate forthwith, or as a condition of acceptance of the Work require the Author to make amendments to the Work to ensure that it does so conform.

1.7 If the Author is unable or unwilling to make such amendments, or to arrange for them to be made, within such reasonable period of time as shall have been agreed with the Publishers then the Publishers, after consultation with the Author, shall have the right to employ a competent person or persons to make such amendments and to deduct the cost thereof from any sum which may become due to the Author under this Agreement. The Work, as finally amended and marked for press, shall be subject to the Author's approval, such approval not to be unreasonably withheld or delayed.

1.8 The Publishers reserve the right to alter or to insist that the Author alters the text of the Work in such a way as may appear to the Publishers appropriate for the purpose of removing or amending any passage

1.9 See the note to Precedent One Clause 6 (Publishers' Responsibility to Publish).

2. Rights Granted to the Publishers

2.1 Traditionally, educational publishers have sought to obtain assignments of copyright from their authors. Where copyright is not assigned, the publishers may seek to acquire the exclusive right of publication of the work throughout the world in all forms and in all languages for the full legal term of copyright and all renewals and extensions thereof. Where electronic form rights are to be acquired as part of such a licence this should be clearly stipulated in the agreement. For further commentary on the acquisition of rights, see the note to Precedent One Clause 1 (Rights Granted).

3. Payments to the Author

3.1.1 Advance payments to the author are not *sine qua non* in educational or academic publishing, and may indeed prove the exception rather than the rule. Where advance payments are made they are, by trade publishing standards, modest and rarely are large amounts paid on signature of the agreement. Whilst a token amount or 'carrot' may be paid on signature, the more substantial balance is likely to be paid on receipt and approval by (not delivery to) the publishers of the complete manuscript or on publication of the work, or alternatively on evidence of progress, or delivery of a given portion, e.g. half, of the manuscript. Payment of the entire advance on signature of the agreement with the author is most unwise unless the manuscript has been received and approved. See the note to Precedent One Clause 15 (Advance Payments) for further comment.

3.1.2 In recent years the trend in educational publishing has been away from payment of royalties based on the British published price, to payment of royalties on the net sums received by the publishers. As a result, home and export sales are usually paid at the same rate and no particular provision need be made in the agreement for high discount export sales, as was previously the case. Royalties may be paid on a 'flat rate' or on a 'stepped' basis depending on the prevailing market conditions for the book and whether the publishers can afford it. The base rate for school textbook royalties is usually lower than for general trade works and the break-point for royalty rate rises tends to be higher. This is because such classroom textbooks depend on high print runs and low prices. (The argument is analogous to that which justifies the low opening royalty rate for mass market paperbacks). Where a 'stepped' royalty is agreed, it is usual for the rate of royalty to revert to the lower 'step' when the book is substantially reset for the issue of a new edition, the reason being that the publishers' origination costs for such an edition are often on a par with those for a new book. To maintain royalty payments to the author at the higher rate could endanger the price competitiveness of the work. The publishers will cut their costs and margins and can reasonably expect the author to accept a cut in royalty rates in order, to their mutual advantage, to maintain the work's success. For this reason many educational publishers insert in the royalty clause of their contracts a proviso of the kind offered here following 3.1.2 (b). As to what the words 'substantially reset the Work for the issue of a new edition' in this formula mean, the publishers will come to a reasonable view in the circumstances of each work: a rough and ready view would be that 'substan-

which on the advice of the Publishers' legal advisers may be considered objectionable or likely to be actionable at law without affecting the Author's liability under Clause 14 hereof in respect of any passage not so removed or amended.

1.9 Unless prevented by circumstances beyond their control, or unless otherwise mutually agreed, the Publishers undertake to publish the Work by the [*date*] day of [*month*]   19[   ], provided that the Author delivers to the Publishers an acceptable manuscript by the date (or by any extension thereto mutually agreed in writing) provided for herein. The Publishers shall publish the Work at their own expense.

2. Rights Granted to the Publishers

2.1 In consideration of the sums payable to the Author hereunder, the Author hereby assigns where relevant by way of present assignment of future copyright to the Publishers the entire copyright and all other rights of a like nature in and to the Work throughout the world for the full legal term of copyright and all renewals and extensions thereof.

3. Payments to the Author

The Publishers shall make the following payments to the Author, namely:

3.1 *Publication of the Work by the Publishers in book form:*

3.1.1 The sum of £   [   ] in advance and on account of any sums which may become due to the Author under this Agreement, payable in the following manner, namely:

   (a) The sum of £   [   ] on signature of this Agreement.

   (b) The sum of £   [   ] on the receipt and approval by the Publishers of the complete manuscript of the Work as prescribed in Clause 1 hereof.

   (c) The sum of £   [   ] on publication of the Work.

3.1.2 A royalty based on the Net Sum Received by the Publishers on all copies of the Work sold by the Publishers, wherever sold:

   (a) A royalty of [*number*] per cent on the first [*number*] [thousand] copies sold.

   (b) A royalty of [*number*] per cent on all copies sold beyond the first [*number*] [thousand].

   Provided that should the revisions to a printing of the Work make it necessary in the opinion of the Publishers to substantially reset the Work for the issue of a new edition then the royalties payable on the sales of each such new edition shall commence at the original rate of [*number*] per cent based on the Net Sum Received by the Publishers on the first [*number*] [thousand] copies sold rising to [*number*] per cent based on the Net Sum Received by the Publishers on all copies sold thereafter, subject to the general terms and conditions of this Agreement.

tially' means a cost for corrections to text and illustrations of not less than one-third of the original cost of composition and origination.

For further comment on royalties and fees to the author, including provision for 'small reprint' royalties, see the note to Precedent One Clause 12 (Royalties and Fees Payable on Own Editions).

3.2 Although the rate of royalty payable to the author is provided for in the case of publication by the publishers of the work in adapted or abridged form, see the note to Precedent One Clause 1 (Rights Granted, point 6).

3.3.1 Whilst the number of educational publishers with substantial experience of publication of their authors' works in electronic form remains relatively small, there are no clear norms or standards for the payment of royalties on electronic products. A cautious 'guesstimate' may be preferable to an agreement to agree and avoids a situation where the publishers are prevented from exercising their electronic rights due to inability to agree an appropriate royalty to the author, as will wording such as that in Clause 3.3.4. Clause 3.3.3 suggests a mechanism for review if, with the benefit of hindsight, the suggested percentage should prove to be particularly disadvantageous from the author's or the publishers' point of view.

3.3.2 Where the author's work is to be combined with the works of other authors in electronic form, a formula has to be agreed for sharing out the total royalty payable on the combined work between the authors of its constituent parts. In such cases, a pro rata arrangement seems sensible, although inevitably issues such as the relative eminence of the authors and the importance of the individual contributions to the work, may come into play.

4. Subsidiary Rights

Unlike trade publications, educational books are not written primarily with a view to their subsidiary rights earning potential. By their very nature, they are closely tied to school or university courses, examination syllabuses and other statutory requirements of the education system in the United Kingdom. Nevertheless, medicine, the 'hard' sciences, mathematics, computer science and history at undergraduate level travel reasonably well, school textbooks, as a general rule, less so. Bearing this in mind, any additional income generated for the author through the efforts of the publishers' subsidiary rights team is a

3.2 *Publication of the Work by the Publishers in adapted or abridged form (other than as provided for in Clause 3.3 hereof)*:

A royalty of [*number*] per cent based on the Net Sum Received by the Publishers on all such copies of the Work sold by the Publishers, wherever sold.

PROVIDED THAT:

No royalties shall be payable on copies of the Work sold at cost or less than cost, destroyed in transit or otherwise, presented to the Author, or distributed as specimen or inspection copies, the number and destination of such copies so distributed being left to the judgement and sole discretion of the Publishers.

3.3 *Publication of the Work (or any part thereof) or any adaptation or abridgement of the Work, by the Publishers in Electronic Form*:

3.3.1 Should the Publishers publish the Work (or any part thereof), or any adaptation or abridgement of the Work, by exercising their Electronic Publishing Rights, the Publishers shall pay to the Author a royalty of [*number*] per cent based on the Net Sum Received by the Publishers in respect of sales of the Work in whole or in part in Electronic Form, subject to Clause 3.3.2 hereof.

3.3.2 If the Work (or any part thereof), or any adaptation or abridgement of the Work, is combined in an Electronic Form together with other works published by the Publishers the rate of royalty payable to the Author shall be the same proportion of [*number*] per cent as the Work (or any part thereof) or any adaptation or abridgement of the Work constitutes of the total combined works in Electronic Form.

3.3.3 On the date falling [*number*] years from the date of first publication of the Work in Electronic Form and every [*number*] years thereafter either party may serve notice on the other for a review of the rates of royalty provided for in this Clause 3.3 in which case the rates of royalty shall be considered in the light of comparable terms then prevailing in the trade and shall be altered with effect from the date of the notice to an extent that shall be fair and reasonable.

3.3.4 The existence of a dispute over the royalties shall not prevent the Publishers continuing to exploit the rights granted under this Agreement.

4. Subsidiary Rights

4.1 In consideration of the payment to the Author of the applicable percentages of the Publishers' receipts listed below, the Author grants to the Publishers the sole and exclusive right during the period of this Agreement to exercise and/or to license others to exercise all of the Subsidiary Rights hereinafter following:

plus. The subsidiary rights listed are those which an educational publisher is most likely to exploit on behalf of the author. A 50:50 share of the income from the exploitation of such rights between author and publisher is usually the norm in the case of educational books, except in the case of electronic form rights, where no norms have yet emerged. For a fuller list of subsidiary rights and further commentary, please see the note to Precedent One Clause 14 (Subsidiary Rights).

5. Copyright Licensing Agency

The majority of educational publishers have mandated the Copyright Licensing Agency to license users to photocopy extracts from their copyright material, e.g. books, journals and periodicals. Authors whose works are copied under a licence granted by CLA are entitled to a half share of the income (fees) collected by CLA in respect of such copying; the balance being paid to the publishers. Please refer to Appendix E for details on the functions and operation of CLA.

Rights	*Payments due to the Author*
4.1.1 Anthology and Quotation Rights, being the right to authorise the reproduction in other publications of extracts and quotations from the Work, including any original maps, charts, diagrams, or other illustrations provided by the Author.	Fifty per cent
4.1.2 Translation Rights, being the right to license the exploitation of the Work in languages other than English.	Fifty per cent
4.1.3 Book Club Rights, being the right to license the Work to book clubs and similar organisations on a separate royalty basis.	Fifty per cent
4.1.4 Reprint Rights, being the right to license a reprint of the Work to another publisher.	Fifty per cent
4.1.5 Adaptation Rights, being the right to license the right to adapt the Work to another publisher.	Fifty per cent
4.1.6 Electronic Publishing Rights, being the right to license the use of the Work in Electronic Form.	[ ] per cent
4.1.7 Paperback Rights, being the right to license the Work in paperback format to another publisher.	Fifty per cent
4.1.8 Non-commercial Rights for the Print Handicapped, being the right to transcribe the Work into Braille or to record the Work for the sole use of the blind and print-handicapped free of charge.	No payments to the Author
4.1.9 Any other Rights which are or may become vested in the Publishers under this Agreement.	Payments to be agreed

5. Copyright Licensing Agency

5.1 The Publishers have empowered the Copyright Licensing Agency (CLA) to grant non-exclusive licences to reproduce by photocopying and other reprographic means literary works published by the Publishers.

5.2 The Work is accordingly deemed to be included with such literary works and CLA shall divide the proceeds from reprographic reproduction of the Work authorised by CLA equally between the Author and the Publishers.

5.3 The Author shall receive the Author's share of such proceeds through the Authors' Licensing and Collecting Society (ALCS) in accordance with ALCS standard terms and conditions.

6. Accounts

Recently there have been moves by several major educational publishers away from a policy of accounting to authors annually, to six monthly accounting. Pressure to remain competitive and the influence of the authors' organisations have undoubtedly been instrumental in bringing about this change. For further discussion of good accounting practice, author access to the publishers' accounts, and reserves against returns, refer to the Note to Precedent One Clause 16 (Statement of Sales).

7. Tax

Under certain circumstances publishers may be required to deduct withholding or other taxes from royalties and this clause makes provision for such eventuality.

9. Copyright Material from Other Sources

9.1 and 9.2 The publishers will require details of any material taken by the author from third party sources. The reasons for this are several. Firstly, the publishers will want to ensure that what they are getting is an original work, which does not draw excessively on material written by others. Secondly, the publishers will wish to ensure that, wherever necessary either they, or the author, obtain permission for the use of any third party material and that appropriate acknowledgment is made in their own publication. Finally, the publishers will not wish to incur the cost of permissions fees unnecessarily, i.e. if the author could write original material instead.

9.3 Where heavy use of third party material is unavoidable, e.g. in course readers or anthologies, the publishers may agree to pay the cost of including such material in the work up to an agreed maximum amount but, in such circumstances, the publishers may also wish to consider reducing the rate of royalty payable to the author. The publishers may further wish to reserve the right to require the author to substitute alternative material which is available at a more acceptable cost. See also the note to Precedent One Clause 7 (Textual Copyright Material) re authors obtaining their own permissions.

5.4 The foregoing provisions shall survive the termination of this Agreement.

6. Accounts

6.1 The Publishers shall make up accounts for the sale of the Work twice yearly to [*date, month*] and [*date, month*] and the said accounts shall be sent to the Author together with any payment due within [*number*] months of each accounting date.

6.2 No account need be submitted unless specifically demanded nor payment made in respect of any period in which the sum due is less than £50.00 (fifty pounds) in which case the sum will be carried forward to the next accounting date.

7. Tax

7.1 The Publishers may deduct from any amount due to the Author under this Agreement, any sum that the Publishers are or may be under statutory obligation to deduct in respect of any tax, duty, or other similar levy.

8. Value Added Tax

8.1 All sums due to the Author hereunder are exclusive of Value Added Tax (VAT), which shall, where applicable, be paid in addition at the rate in force at the time of payment.

8.2 Should the Author neglect to provide details of the Author's VAT registration number, the Publishers shall not pay VAT on any sums due to the Author under this Agreement.

9. Copyright Material from Other Sources

9.1 The Work shall not contain any textual or illustrative material taken from other sources, except with the prior written consent of the Publishers and the copyright holders of such material.

9.2 The Author shall advise the Publishers of the quotation or inclusion in the Work of any textual or illustrative material from any source and the Publishers shall obtain, wherever necessary, written permission from the copyright holders for the inclusion of such material and shall ensure that appropriate acknowledgement is made in the Work.

9.3 The Publishers shall bear the cost of any necessary fees for permission to include such material in the Work up to a maximum of £　　[　　]. Should the permissions fees payable exceed £　　[　　] the Publishers shall after consultation with the Author exercise one of the following options:

　　9.3.1 require the Author to substitute alternative materials which are available at a cost acceptable to the Publishers;

　　9.3.2 after first informing the Author in writing of the amount of the excess, deduct the same from any sum which may become due to the Author under this Agreement.

10. Control of Publication

10.1 The Publishers shall have the entire control of the production,

12. Moral Rights
See Appendix D.

13. Copyright Notice
See note to Precedent One Clause 18 (Copyright).

14. Warranties and Indemnity
See note to Precedent One Clause 5 (Warranties and Indemnities).

publication, pricing, reprinting and sale of the Work, including by way of example and not limitation the design, format, paper, print run, binding, cover, jacket (if any), advertising and distribution of free copies for the press or otherwise. The right to reproduce the typography and design of the Work is reserved by the Publishers.

11. Inclusion of Author's Name

11.1 The Publishers shall include the name of the Author with due prominence on the cover, jacket (if any) and title page of every copy of the Work published by the Publishers and in all appropriate publicity material for the Work and shall impose a similar obligation in respect of any editions of the Work licensed by them.

12. Moral Rights

12.1 The Author hereby asserts to the Publishers *his/her* moral right to be identified as the Author of the Work in accordance with sections 77 and 78 of the Copyright, Designs and Patents Act 1988.

12.2 The Publishers undertake:

12.2.1 to print the following notice with due prominence on every copy of the Work published by them in the United Kingdom: 'The right of [*name of author*] to be identified as author of this Work has been asserted by him/her in accordance with sections 77 and 78 of the Copyright, Designs and Patents Act 1988'

12.2.2 to require the Publishers' licensees to include an identical notice on any edition of the Work to be published by such licensees in the United Kingdom.

12.3 No accidental or inadvertent failure by the Publishers or by any third party to include such a notice shall constitute a breach of this Agreement or the Author's rights.

13. Copyright Notice

13.1 All copies of the Work published by the Publishers shall bear on the title verso a copyright notice comprising the copyright symbol, the name of the copyright holder and the year of first publication.

14. Warranties and Indemnity

14.1 The Author hereby warrants to the Publishers that:

14.1.1 the Author is the sole legal owner of the copyright in the Work, and has the right and power to make this Agreement;

14.1.2 the Work is an original Work and will in no way whatever give rise to a violation of any existing copyright or a breach of any existing agreement;

14.1.3 the Work contains nothing defamatory or libellous and all statements contained therein purporting to be facts are true;

14.1.4 any recipe, formula or instruction contained in the Work will not, if followed accurately, be injurious to or damage the user.

14.2 The Author will indemnify the Publishers against any loss, injury or damage (including any legal costs or expenses and any compensation costs and disbursements paid by the Publishers on the advice of the

15. Proof Correction

See note to Precedent One Clause 11 (Author's Corrections). All alteration in proofs is very expensive: many texts for technical markets, for example, need not only careful but formal signed approval by the author at a very early stage of, for example, the accuracy of technical drawings, of the cropping of photographs, or of the positioning of colour illustrations. If this is not done, costs of alteration multiply and any formal contractual liability of the author may be quite without value.

More generally, printers in the final account for a book itemise all corrections simply as 'corrections' — as indeed from their point of view they are. In the making of a book, page for page, there are however many elements contributed by the author and the publishing staff and corrections to film of a complex textbook will often be a mixture of author's errors not previously noticed, of 'house' editorial second, and third, thoughts on some vital point, of design adjustment, etc. No contractual formula can really deal with this vexed point and editors must be on the watch in order to settle apportionment at the final stages of production. Otherwise, after the printer's bill has come in, and when the first royalty account goes out, the unfortunate author may find his/her opening royalties virtually wiped out by a massive 'corrections' charge which is only partly his/her liability. Clause 15.2 suggests a formula to pre-empt unanticipated costs.

16. Author's Copies

See note to Precedent Two — Preamble (2)(c) and also note to Precedent One Clause 20 (Author's Copies).

18. Revision of the Work

(a) Many successful educational books need bringing up to date at regular intervals, and the control of the decision about the need for the author to start work on a revised or completely new edition should be the publishers' (cf. the view offered at Precedent One, Clause 21 and note), since they are in most cases very much closer to the needs of the market than perhaps the author is, and also have to juggle with the practicalities of stock rates, small 'bridging' reprints, etc.

(b) For professional works, e.g. in law and medicine where a work of authority may command the market for several generations with updates, some very vexed questions may

Publishers' legal advisers to compromise or settle any claim) arising out of any breach or alleged breach of the foregoing warranties.

14.3 The foregoing warranties and indemnity shall survive the termination of this Agreement.

15. Proof Correction

15.1 The Author undertakes to read, check, and correct the proofs of the Work and return them to the Publishers within such period of time as shall have been mutually agreed, failing which the Publishers shall consider the proofs passed for press.

15.2 Costs of all corrections and alterations made by the Author in the finished artwork and the proofs (artists', copy-editors' and printers' errors and those alterations made necessary by changes in professional practice excepted) in excess of 10 per cent of the cost of origination of the Work shall be borne by the Author provided that:

15.2.1 before passing proofs for press the Publishers shall advise the Author in writing of the amount of the excess;

15.2.2 the Author shall have the opportunity exercisable within 14 days of receipt of written notice from the Publishers to remove or reduce such corrections and alterations.

15.3 Should any charge arise under this Clause the amount may be deducted from any sums which may become due to the Author under this Agreement.

16. Author's Copies

16.1 The Author shall be entitled to receive on publication six free copies of the first and any new edition of the Work and to purchase on normal domestic trade terms further copies for personal use but not for resale.

17. Remaindering

17.1 The Publishers shall be entitled not less than two years from the date of first publication of the Work to dispose of copies thereof as a remainder at a reduced price and shall pay to the Author the rate of royalty provided for in Clause 3.1.2 hereof on such sales, except that where copies are sold at cost or less than cost, no royalty shall be payable.

17.2 The Publishers shall give the Author six free copies of the Work under this Clause and the first option for a period of six weeks to purchase copies at the said reduced price.

18. Revision of the Work

18.1 If in the opinion of the Publishers a new edition of the Work is desirable or necessary, they shall so notify the Author in writing.

18.2 The Author undertakes to revise and edit the Work and to supply to the Publishers by such time as shall be mutually agreed any new matter that may be needed to keep the Work up to date, such new matter to be supplied at no cost to the Publishers.

arise unless the educational publisher grapples categorically with the consequences of the author's death. The precedent tries to balance the right of the author's estate to continue to draw income from his/her authorship with the need of the publishers to find a new contributor to the work without either overloading the royalty costs or damaging heavily the market power of the work through having to withdraw the original author's name.

19. Infringement of Copyright
See note to Precedent One Clause 19 (Infringement of Copyright).

20. Out of Print
See note to Precedent One Clause 24 (Reversion of Rights).

18.3 Should the Author neglect or be unable or unwilling to supply such new matter or to revise or edit the Work, the Publishers may after written notice to the Author arrange for a competent person or persons to do so and may deduct the expense thereof from any sums which may become payable to the Author or the Author's representatives under this Agreement.

18.4 In the event of the death of the Author the following provisions shall apply:

18.4.1 all sums payable under the terms of this Agreement shall be paid to the deceased Author's representatives on any edition in print at the time of *his/her* death and on any reprints of such an edition.

18.4.2 all sums payable under the terms of this Agreement shall be paid to the deceased Author's representatives on the next edition subsequent to the Author's death including any reprints thereof, less any fees and/or royalties payable to an editor or reviser in the course of preparing such edition for press.

18.4.3 the deceased Author's representatives shall then cease to participate financially in any further editions or substantially revised reprints of the Work.

18.5 The Publishers may display in the revised Work and in all appropriate publicity material for the revised Work, the name of the person or persons who revised the Work together with the name of the Author. Should the Author or the Author's representatives object to having the Author's name acknowledged in connection with the revised Work, the Author or the Author's representatives shall so notify the Publishers in writing upon receipt of the written notice from the Publishers provided for in Clause 18.3 hereof.

19. Infringement of Copyright

19.1 It is agreed that if at any time during the continuance of this Agreement the Publishers consider that the copyright in the Work has been infringed they shall be at liberty to take such steps as they may consider necessary in their sole discretion for dealing with the matter and if they desire to take legal proceedings they shall on giving the Author an undertaking to pay all costs and expenses and to indemnify the Author against all liability for costs, be entitled to use the Author's name as a party to such proceedings but at the same time to control, settle or compromise as they think fit.

19.2 Any profits or damages which may be recovered in respect of any infringement of the copyright shall after deduction of all costs and expenses be divided equally between the parties hereto.

20. Out of Print

20.1 If the Work shall be allowed to go out of print and not be available in any English language edition published by the Publishers or licensed by them, the Author may give nine months' notice in writing to the Publishers to put in hand a reprint or a new edition.

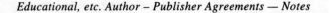

21. Termination
See note to Precedent One Clause 23 (Termination of Contract).

22. Competing Works
Scientific, technical, medical and professional publishers may want a competing works clause which suits the specific needs of their authors, the precedent offers one such formula.

For the purpose of this Clause 20.1 'out of print' shall mean when fewer than [*number*] copies of the Work remain in the Publishers' warehouse and the Publishers have no plans for a reissue or a new edition.

20.2 The Author's requirements that the Work be reprinted shall be regarded as satisfied if at the time of the Author giving notice the Publishers have sub-licensed rights for an English language edition of the Work scheduled for publication within 12 months of such notice being given.

20.3 Should the Publishers fail to comply with such notice, other than through circumstances beyond their control, all rights in the Work granted to the Publishers herein shall upon expiration of the said notice revert to the Author without prejudice to all rights of the Publishers and any third party in respect of any agreement properly entered into by the Publishers with such third party prior to the date of such reversion and without prejudice to any claim which the Author may have for monies due and/or damages and/or otherwise.

21. Termination

21.1 This Agreement shall automatically terminate if the Publishers go into liquidation other than voluntary liquidation for the purpose of reconstruction, or have a receiver or an administrative receiver appointed over the whole or any substantial part of the Publishers' assets.

21.2 The Author may terminate this Agreement by summary notice in writing to the Publishers if the Publishers wilfully fail to fulfil or comply with any of the provisions of this Agreement within three months after written notification from the Author of such failure.

21.3 Upon termination of this Agreement under Clause 21.1 or 21.2 hereof, all rights in the Work granted to the Publishers herein shall revert to the Author without prejudice to all rights of the Publishers and any third party in respect of any agreement properly entered into by the Publishers with such third party prior to the date of such termination and without prejudice to any claim which the Author may have for monies due and/or damages and/or otherwise.

22. Competing Works

22.1 While the Work is in course of preparation or in current publication:

22.1.1 the Author shall be entitled to use material written or compiled by him for the purposes of the Work in articles submitted to learned or professional journals, in papers presented at professional conferences and for the Author's professional purposes generally, provided that the Author so advises the Publishers in advance and makes appropriate acknowledgement to the Work and the Publishers, but

22.1.2 the Author shall not without the written consent of the Publishers write, edit or contribute, jointly or severally, to any work which may reasonably be considered by the Publishers to com-

23. Arbitration
For details of the Publishers Association's Informal Disputes Settlement Scheme see note
to Precedent One Clause 29 (Arbitration).

pete with or prejudice sales of the Work or the exploitation of any of the rights granted to the Publishers under this Agreement.

23. Arbitration
23.1 If any difference shall arise between the Author and the Publishers touching the meaning of this Agreement or the rights and liabilities of the parties hereto, the same shall be referred to the arbitration of two persons (one to be named by each party) or their umpire in accordance with the provisions of the Arbitration Act 1996 or any amending or substituted statute for the time being in force.

24. Entire Agreement
24.1 This Agreement sets forth the entire agreement between the parties at the date hereof and supersedes any prior written or oral agreement between them with respect to the subject matter hereof.
24.2 This Agreement shall be governed by and construed in accordance with the laws of England.
24.3 Any amendment of or variation to this Agreement must be in writing and signed by both parties.

25. Headings
25.1 Headings to the clauses hereof are for guidance only and are not to be taken into account in the construction of this Agreement which has been prepared in [*number*] copies.

26. Definitions
26.1 In this Agreement the following words and expressions shall have the following meanings unless the context requires otherwise:

'Associated Company' shall have the meaning attributed to that term in section 416 (et seq) of the Income and Corporation Taxes Act 1988, as amended;

'Electronic Form' shall include but shall not be limited to off-line electronic storage and information retrieval systems of a digital, optical or magnetic nature including (by way of example and not limitation) floppy disk, CD-ROM, CD-I, ROM-card, compact disc, video, integrated circuit; on-line transmission by satellite and other means of telecommunication; and any other electronic means of reproduction, publication, dissemination and transmission whether now in existence or hereafter invented;

27. Assignment
See note to Precedent One Preamble.

'Electronic Publishing Rights'	means the right to produce, copy, publish and sell, perform, display, broadcast and transmit the Work whether in whole or in part, adapted or abridged, on its own or in combination with another work or works, together with any accompanying sounds and images, in any Electronic Form and to license the foregoing rights in electronic versions of the Work;
'Net Sum Received by the Publishers'	means the amount received by the Publishers and any amounts receivable by the Publishers after deducting any discounts granted by the Publishers and any sales or other similar taxes or duties (excluding marketing and distribution costs) incurred by the Publishers in respect of sales of copies of the Work;
'Subsidiary Rights'	means in relation to the Work the rights specified in Clause 4 hereof;
'Work'	means the Work (and any new editions thereof) written by the Author under this Agreement together with any abridgements, adaptations, or electronic versions thereof;
'[*insert name*] Group'	means any associated company of [*insert name*] Limited.

27. Assignment

27.1 The Publishers may assign any benefit or transfer, delegate or subcontract any of their duties or obligations under this Agreement to any company within the [*insert name*] Group without the prior written consent of the Author.

AS WITNESS THE HANDS OF THE PARTIES

Signed by ....

[*author*]

Signed by ....

For and on behalf of [*name of publishers*] Limited

Agreement for a General Editor of a Book

Many academic and professional books are works with many contributors, compiled under the direction of a general editor, a specialist in the subject concerned. The general editor is responsible for briefing and dealing with individual contributors, overseeing progress on the work and acting as a contact point between the contributors and the publishing house. The general editor will normally provide an introduction to the book and may in addition contribute one or more chapters or articles to the book.

The general editor will normally receive an advance payment and modest royalty percentage on sales, whilst individual contributions are normally paid for on a lump sum basis (see Precedent Four).

Many of the general provisions of this model parallel those in Precedent Two.

1. This clause sets out the responsibilities of the general editor during the preparation stages of the work.

The contributions written by the general editor personally will depend on what has been agreed with the publishers; this precedent covers provision of an overall introduction and for one or more sections of the work (1.1.5).

Because of the complexity of multi-author works, the general editor is responsible for ensuring that each contribution is submitted promptly and in suitable form (1.1.3).

In this precedent, responsibility for arrangements for assignment of copyright from individual contributors rests with the publishers, who would then draw up a separate letter of agreement with each contributor (see Precedent Four). An alternative would be for that responsibility to lie with the general editor, in which case alternative wording here might be:

'The General Editor shall be responsible for securing from the Contributors written confirmation of assignment of copyright in each contribution to the Publishers.'

THIS AGREEMENT is made this   day of   19
BETWEEN   [*name*]   of   [*address*]
(hereinafter termed the General Editor, which expression shall, where the
context admits, include the General Editor's executors, administrators or
assigns) of the one part and   [*name of company*] (registered
number [*number*]) of [*address*] (hereinafter termed the Publishers, which
expression shall, where the context admits, include the Publishers' successors in business and assigns) of the other part,

WHEREBY it is agreed as follows concerning a work to be edited by the
General Editor at present entitled: [*name of work*] (hereinafter termed the
Work)

1. Responsibilities of the General Editor in Preparation of the Work

The responsibilities of the General Editor shall be as follows:

1.1 The General Editor shall be responsible for commissioning contributions to the Work from appropriately qualified third parties (hereinafter termed the Contributors) on terms to be agreed with the Publishers.
The final choice of Contributors is subject to the written approval of
the Publishers (such approval not to be unreasonably withheld).

1.2 The General Editor shall be responsible for briefing each Contributor
on the nature and length of his/her contribution and for ensuring that
the content of each contribution meets the designated requirements of
the Publishers for the Work.

1.3 The General Editor shall be responsible for ensuring that each Contributor delivers his/her contribution in appropriate form and in due
time to enable the General Editor to meet the Publishers' required
schedule as specified in Clause 2.1 hereof.

1.4 The General Editor shall be responsible for the overall checking and
editing of each contribution and (where appropriate) for arranging for
reviews of individual contributions by appropriate external advisers.

1.5 The General Editor shall be responsible for writing an Introduction to
the Work of no less than [*number*] and no more than [*number*] words
and also for writing [*number*] contribution/s to the work (hereinafter
termed the General Editor's part in the Work).

1.6 The General Editor shall, if so required by the Publishers, supply an
index for inclusion in the Work. If the General Editor is unable for any
reason to supply the said index, the Publishers may make appropriate
arrangements for the supply of the said index and may deduct the
expense thereof from any sum which may become payable to the
General Editor under the terms of this Agreement.

1.7 The Publishers undertake to be responsible for arranging separate
letters of agreement to each Contributor to cover assignment of
copyright in each contribution to the Publishers and also to cover
separate payment to each Contributor.

2. This clause covers the general editor's responsibility for the delivery of the complete text of the work in a form acceptable to the publishers. The general editor's responsibilities for briefing and vetting contributions under the terms of Clause 1 should ideally mean that no radical amendments or replacement of contributors is required at this stage.

2. Delivery and Acceptance of the Work

2.1 The General Editor agrees to deliver to the Publishers by the [*date*] day of [*month*] 19 :

  2.1.1 the complete manuscript of the Work consisting of not more than [*number*] and not less than [*number*] words on a word processor disk in [*specify word processing package to be used*] format together with two identical hard copies printed out from the said disk in double line spacing;

  2.1.2 artwork or roughs for a maximum of [*number*] line drawings (the finished artwork for which shall be prepared by the Publishers); a maximum of [*number*] half-tones/colour transparencies; a maximum of [*number*] charts/maps/diagrams ready for reproduction/to be redrawn by the Publishers;

  2.1.3 any additional matter for inclusion in the Work such as notes/appendices/exercises/answers and an index, if so required by the Publishers;

  2.1.4 a complete list of all copyright material taken by the General Editor and the Contributors from other sources for inclusion in the Work.

2.2 The Work shall be prepared in accordance with the Publishers' 'Guide for Authors' or in any other form agreed with the Publishers.

2.3 The General Editor shall retain a duplicated copy of the complete manuscript of the Work and all other material supplied by the General Editor to the Publishers for inclusion therein.

2.4 Should the General Editor neglect to deliver the complete manuscript, together with any illustrative and/or additional matter by the prescribed date (or by any extension thereto mutually agreed in writing) the Publishers may, if they so wish, decline to publish the Work in which case this Agreement shall terminate forthwith, subject as the Publishers in their sole discretion shall elect to one or other of the following:

either:

  2.4.1 The General Editor shall not be at liberty to arrange for the publication of the Work elsewhere without first offering the complete manuscript to the Publishers on the terms of this Agreement;

or:

  2.4.2 The General Editor shall, upon the Publishers' written request, repay to the Publishers any monies which have been paid to the General Editor under this Agreement.

2.5 The Publishers shall accept the Work provided that the complete manuscript and any illustrative and/or additional matter as delivered by the General Editor conforms in nature, scope, length and style to the specifications agreed in writing between the parties hereto.

2.6 Should the manuscript not so conform the Publishers shall have the right either to decline to publish the Work in which case this Agreement shall terminate forthwith, or as a condition of acceptance of the

71

3. Here the general editor assigns copyright in his or her own part in the work.

4. This clause outlines payments to the general editor; an advance payable in instalments and a modest royalty on sales (the percentage is likely to be less than 5 per cent). Since the demise of the UK Net Book Agreement, payment will almost certainly be based on the publishers' net receipts, as publishers are no longer able to set a fixed retail price.

Work require the General Editor to make amendments to the Work to ensure that it does so conform.

2.7 If the General Editor is unable or unwilling to make such amendments, or to arrange for them to be made within such reasonable period of time as shall have been agreed with the Publishers, then the Publishers after consultation with the General Editor shall have the right to employ a competent person or persons to make such amendments and to deduct the cost thereof from any sum which may become due to the General Editor under this Agreement. The Work, as finally amended and marked for press, shall be subject to the General Editor's approval, such approval not to be unreasonably withheld or delayed.

2.8 The Publishers reserve the right to alter or to insist that the General Editor alters the text of the Work in such a way as may appear to the Publishers appropriate for the purpose of removing or amending any passage which on the advice of the Publishers' legal advisers may be considered objectionable or likely to be actionable at law without affecting the General Editor's liability under Clause 15 hereof in respect of any passage not to removed or amended.

2.9 Unless prevented by circumstances beyond their control, or unless otherwise mutually agreed, the Publishers undertake to publish the Work at their own expense by the [*date*] day of [*month*] 19 , provided that the General Editor delivers an acceptable manuscript by the date (or by any extension thereto mutually agreed in writing) provided for herein.

3. Rights Granted to the Publishers

In consideration of the sums payable to the General Editor hereunder, the General Editor hereby assigns where relevant by way of present assignment of future copyright to the Publishers the entire copyright in the General Editor's part in the Work inclusive of *his/her* contribution/s written for inclusion therein and all other rights of a like nature in and to the General Editor's part in the Work inclusive of *his/her* contribution/s written for inclusion therein throughout the world for the full legal term of copyright and all renewals and extensions thereof.

4. Payments to the General Editor

The Publishers shall make the following payments to the General Editor, namely:

4.1 Publication of the Work by the Publishers in book form

4.1.1 The sum of £ in advance and on account of any sums which may become due to the General Editor under this Agreement, payable in the following manner, namely:

(a) The sum of on signature of this Agreement

(b) The sum of on the receipt and approval by the Publishers of the complete manuscript as prescribed in Clause 2 hereof.

(c) The sum of on publication of the Work.

4.1.2 A royalty based on the Net Sum Received by the Publishers on all copies of the Work sold by the Publishers, wherever sold:

(a)   A royalty of   per cent on the first [*number*] thousand copies sold.

(b)   A royalty of   per cent on all copies sold beyond the first [*number*] thousand.

Provided that should the revisions to a printing of the Work make it necessary in the opinion of the Publishers to substantially reset the Work for the issue of a new edition then the royalties payable on the sales of each such new edition shall commence at the original rate of   per cent based on the Net Sum Received by the Publishers on the first [*number*] thousand copies sold rising to   per cent based on the Net Sum Received by the Publishers on all copies sold thereafter, subject to the general terms and conditions of this Agreement.

4.2 Publication of the Work by the Publishers in adapated or abridged form (other than as provided for in Clause 4.3 hereof):

A royalty of   per cent based on the Net Sum Received by the Publishers on all such copies of the Work sold by the Publishers, wherever sold

PROVIDED THAT:

No royalties shall be payable on copies of the Work sold at cost or less than cost, destroyed in transit or otherwise, presented to the General Editor and the Contributors, or distributed as specimen or inspection copies, the number and destination of such copies so distributed being left to the judgment and sole discretion of the Publishers.

4.3 Publication of the Work (or any part thereof) or any adaptation or abridgement of the Work by the Publishers in Electronic Form:

4.3.1 Should the Publishers publish the Work (or any part thereof) or any adaptation of the Work by exercising their Electronic Publishing Rights, the Publishers shall pay to the General Editor a royalty of   per cent based on the Net Sum Received by the Publishers in respect of sales of the Work in whole or in part in Electronic Form, subject to Clause 4.3.2 hereof

4.3.2 If the Work (or any part thereof), or any adaptation or abridgement of the Work, is combined in an Electronic Form together with other works published by the Publishers the rate of royalty payable to the General Editor shall be the same proportion of   per cent as the Work (or any part thereof) or any adaptation or abridgement of the Work constitutes of the total combined works in Electronic Form.

4.3.3 On the date falling [*number*] years from the date of first publication of the Work in Electronic Form and every [*number*] years thereafter either party may serve notice on the other for a review of the rates of royalty provided for in this Clause 4.3 in which case the rates of royalty shall be considered in the light of comparable terms then prevailing in the trade and shall be altered with effect from the date of the notice to an extent that shall be fair and reasonable.

5. This precedent provides for the sale of a range of subsidiary rights in the work, with a share of the proceeds to be divided between the general editor and individual contributors. If however the contributors were to be paid an outright fee for their work with no provision for any share of rights income, a smaller percentage of the proceeds would be payable to the general editor alone.

5. Subsidiary Rights

5.1 The General Editor grants to the Publishers the sole and exclusive right during the period of this Agreement to exercise and/or to license others to exercise all of the Subsidiary Rights hereinafter following. The applicable percentages of the Publishers' receipts listed shall be divided equally between the General Editor of the one part and the Contributors, including the General Editor acting as a contributor, of the other part, except when any contribution is sold separately, quoted from exclusively or translated exclusively in whole or in part, in which case all monies due in respect thereof shall only be paid to the Contributor who wrote the contribution concerned.

Rights	*Payments due to the General Editor/Contributors*
5.1.1 Anthology and quotation rights, being the right to authorise the reproduction in other publications of extracts and quotations from the Work, including any maps, charts, diagrams, or other illustrations original to the General Editor or the Contributors	Fifty per cent
5.1.2 Translation rights, being the right to license the exploitation of the Work in languages other than English	Fifty per cent
5.1.3 Book club rights, being the right to license the Work to book clubs and similar organisations on a separate royalty basis	Fifty per cent
5.1.4 Reprint rights, being the right to license a reprint of the Work to another Publisher	Fifty per cent
5.1.5 Adaptation rights, being the right to license the right to adapt the Work to another publisher	Fifty per cent
5.1.6 Electronic Publishing Rights, being the right to license the use of the Work in Electronic Form	[ ] per cent
5.1.7 Paperback rights, being the right to license the use of the Work in paperback format	Fifty per cent
5.1.8 Non-commercial rights for the print-handicapped, being the right to transcribe the Work into Braille or to record the Work for the sole use of the blind and print-handicapped free of charge	No payment
5.1.9 Any other rights which are or may become vested in the Publishers under this Agreement	Fifty per cent

6. Copyright Licensing Agency

6.1 The Publishers have empowered the Copyright Licensing Agency (CLA) to grant non-exclusive licences to reproduce by photocopying and other reprographic means literary works published by the Publishers.

6.2 The Work is accordingly deemed to be included with such literary works and CLA shall divide the proceeds from reprographic

10. As with a single author work, it is vital that the publishers are alerted to the use of external textual or illustrative material. The question of responsibility for clearance of such permissions and payment of any fees to the external copyright owners will depend on what has been agreed between the publishers, the general editor and the contributors themselves. This precedent assumes that the contributors will be responsible (see Precedent Four, Clause 2) and that the general editor will have overall responsibility for ensuring that clearance has been obtained.

In some cases, the publishers may be prepared to reimburse the cost of permissions clearance up to an agreed amount. In such cases a further sub-clause could be added as follows:

'10.3 The Publishers agree to reimburse the cost of any necessary fees for permission to include such material in the Work up to a maximum of £[   ]. Should the permissions fees payable exceed £[   ] the Publishers shall after consultation with the General Editor exercise one of the following options:

10.3.1 require the General Editor to substitute alternative materials which are acceptable to the Publishers;

10.3.2 after first informing the General Editor in writing of the amount of the excess, deduct the same from any sums which may become due to the General Editor and/or the individual Contributors under this Agreement as appropriate.'

reproduction of the Work authorised by CLA equally between the General Editor and the Publishers.

6.3 The General Editor shall receive the General Editor's share of such proceeds through the Authors' Licensing and Collecting Society (ALCS) in accordance with ALCS standard terms and conditions.

6.4 The foregoing provisions shall survive the termination of this Agreement.

7. Accounts

7.1 The Publishers shall make up accounts for the sale of the Work twice yearly to [*date, month*] and [*date, month*] and the said accounts shall be sent to the General Editor together with any payment due within [*number*] months of each accounting date.

7.2 No account need be submitted unless specifically demanded nor payment made in respect of any period in which the sum due is less than £50.00 (fifty pounds) in which case the sum will be carried forward to the next accounting date.

8. Tax

8.1 The Publishers may deduct from any amount due to the General Editor under this Agreement, any sum that the Publishers are or may be under statutory obligation to deduct in respect of any tax, duty, or other similar levy.

9. Value Added Tax

9.1 All sums due to the General Editor hereunder are exclusive of Value Added Tax, which shall, where applicable, be paid in addition at the rate in force at the time of payment.

9.2 Should the General Editor neglect to provide details of the General Editor's VAT registration number, the Publishers shall not pay Value Added Tax on any sums due to the General Editor under this Agreement.

10. Copyright Material from Other Sources

10.1 The Work shall not contain any textual or illustrative material taken from other sources, except with the prior written consent of the Publishers and copyright holders of such material.

10.2 The General Editor shall advise the Publishers of the quotation or inclusion in the Work of any textual or illustrative material from any source and shall ensure that written permission has been secured from and fees paid to the copyright holders for the inclusion of such material. The Publishers shall ensure that appropriate acknowledgment is made in the Work.

11. Control of Publication

11.1 The Publishers shall have the entire control of the production, publication, pricing, reprinting and sale of the Work, including by way of example and not limitation the design, format, paper, print

13. The general editor can assert moral rights only for his/her own contribution to the work.

15. The general editor can only provide warranties and an indemnity relating to his/her own contribution to the work.

16. This precedent provides for the general editor to have overall responsibility for the checking of proofs. If the individual contributors are required to check proofs of their own contributions (see Precedent Four, Clauses 6 and 7) there will need to be an adjustment to the correction limits permitted.

run, binding, cover, jacket (if any), advertising and distribution of free copies for the press or otherwise.

12. Inclusion of General Editor's Name
12.1 The Publishers shall include the name of the General Editor with due prominence on the cover, jacket (if any) and title page of every copy of the Work published by the Publishers and in all publicity material for the Work and shall impose a similar obligation in respect of any editions licensed by them.

13. Moral Rights
13.1 The General Editor hereby asserts to the Publishers *his/her* moral right to be identified as the Author of the General Editor's part in the Work in accordance with Sections 77 and 78 of the Copyright, Designs and Patents Act 1988.

14. Copyright Notice
14.1 All copies of the Work published by the Publishers shall bear on the title verso a copyright notice comprising the copyright symbol, the name of the copyright holder and the year of first publication.

15. Warranties and Indemnity
15.1 The General Editor hereby warrants to the Publishers that:
    15.1.1 the General Editor has the right and power to make this Agreement;
    15.1.2 the General Editor's part in the Work will in no way whatever give rise to a violation of any existing copyright or a breach of any existing agreement;
    15.1.3 the General Editor's part in the Work contains nothing defamatory or libellous and all statements contained therein purporting to be facts are true;
    15.1.4 any recipe, formula or instruction contained in the General Editor's part in the Work will not, if followed accurately, be injurious to or damage the user
15.2 The General Editor will indemnity the Publishers against any loss, injury or damage (including any legal costs or expenses and any compensation costs or disbursements paid by the Publishers on the advice of the Publishers' legal advisers to compromise or settle any claim) arising out of any breach or alleged breach of the foregoing warranties.
15.3 The foregoing warranties and indemnity shall survive the termination of this Agreement.

16. Proof Correction
16.1 The General Editor undertakes to read, check and correct the proofs of the Work and return them to the Publishers within such period of time as shall have been mutually agreed, failing which the Publishers shall consider the proofs passed for press.

19. In the case of revised edition, the publishers would be responsible for paying existing or replacement contributors for revised material included in the work (see Precedent Four, Clause 5).

16.2 Costs of all corrections and alterations made by the General Editor in the finished artwork and the proofs (artists', copy-editors' and printers' errors and those alterations made necessary by changes in professional practice excepted) in excess of ten per cent of the cost of origination of the Work shall be borne by the General Editor provided that:

16.2.1 before passing proofs for press the Publishers shall advise the General Editor of the amount of the excess;

16.2.2 the General Editor shall have the opportunity exercisable within 14 days of receipt of written notice from the Publishers to remove or reduce such corrections and alterations.

16.3 Should any charge arise under this clause the amount may be deducted from any sums which may become due to the General Editor under this Agreement.

17. Remaindering

17.1 The Publishers shall be entitled not less than two years from the date of first publication of the Work to dispose of copies thereof as a remainder at a reduced price and shall pay the General Editor the rate of royalty provided for in Clause 4.1.2 hereof on such sales, except that where copies are sold at cost or less than cost, no royalty shall be payable.

17.2 The Publishers shall give the General Editor [*number*] free copies of the Work under this clause and the first option for a period of six weeks to purchase copies at the said reduced price.

18. General Editor's Copies

18.1 The General Editor shall be entitled to receive on publication six free copies of the first and any new edition of the Work and to purchase on normal domestic trade terms further copies for personal use but not for resale.

19. Revision of the Work

19.1 If in the opinion of the Publishers a new edition of the Work is desirable or necessary, they shall so notify the General Editor in writing.

19.2 The General Editor undertakes to make arrangements for the revision of and to edit the Work and to supply to the Publishers at no additional cost by such time as shall be mutually agreed any new matter that may be needed to keep the Work up to date.

19.3 Should the General Editor neglect or be unable or unwilling to supply such new matter or to arrange for the revision of or to edit the Work, the Publishers may after written notice to the General Editor arrange for a competent person or persons to do so and may deduct the expense thereof from any sums which may become payable to the General Editor or the General Editor's representatives under this Agreement.

20. Since this contract covers a multi-author work, any profits or damages resulting from a successful action against infringement of copyright will be divided in proportions to be agreed.

19.4 In the event of the death of the General Editor the following provisions shall apply:

19.4.1 all sums payable under the terms of this Agreement shall be paid to the representatives of the deceased General Editor on any edition in print at the time of *his/her* death and on any reprints of such an edition.

19.4.2 the representatives of the deceased General Editor shall then cease to participate financially in any new editions or substantially revised reprints of the Work.

20. Infringement of Copyright

20.1 It is agreed that if at any time during the continuance of this Agreement the Publishers consider that the copyright in the Work has been infringed they shall be at liberty to take such steps as they may consider necessary at their sole discretion for dealing with the matter and if they desire to take legal proceedings they shall on giving the General Editor an undertaking to pay all costs and expenses and to indemnify the General Editor against all liability for costs, be entitled to use the General Editor's name as a party to such proceedings but at the same time to control, settle or compromise as they think fit.

20.2 Any profits or damages which may be recovered in respect of any infringement of the copyright shall after deduction of all costs and expenses be divided between the parties hereto in proportions to be mutually agreed.

21. Out of Print

21.1 If the Work is allowed to go out of print and not be available in any English language edition published by the Publishers or licensed by them, the General Editor may give nine months' notice in writing to the Publishers to put in hand a reprint or a new edition.
For the purposes of this Clause 21.1 'out of print' shall mean when fewer than [*number*] copies of the Work remain in the Publishers' warehouse and the Publishers have no plans for a reissue or a new edition.

21.2 The General Editor's requirements that the Work be reprinted shall be regarded as satisfied if at the time of the General Editor's giving notice the Publishers have sub-licensed rights for an English language edition of the Work scheduled for publication within 12 months of such notice being given.

21.3 Should the Publishers fail to comply with such notice, other than through circumstances beyond their control, all rights in the General Editor's part in the Work granted to the Publishers herein shall upon expiration of the said notice revert to the General Editor without prejudice to all rights of the Publishers and any third party in respect of any agreement properly entered into by the Publishers with such third party prior to the date of such reversion and without prejudice to any claim which the General Editor may have for monies due and/or damages and/or otherwise.

22. Termination

22.1 This Agreement shall automatically terminate if the Publishers go into liquidation other than voluntary liquidation for the purpose of reconstruction, or have a receiver or an administrative receiver appointed over the whole or any substantial part of the Publishers' assets.

22.2 The General Editor may terminate this Agreement by summary notice in writing to the Publishers if the Publishers wilfully fail to fulfil or comply with any of the provisions of this Agreement within three months after written notification from the General Editor of such failure.

22.3 Upon termination of this Agreement under Clause 22.1 or 22.2 hereof, all rights in the Work granted to the Publishers herein shall revert to the General Editor without prejudice to all rights of the Publishers and any third party in respect of any agreement properly entered into by the Publishers with such party prior to the date of termination and without prejudice to any claim which the General Editor may have for monies due and/or damages and/or otherwise.

23. Competing Works

23.1 While the Work is in course of preparation or in current publication:

23.1.1 the General Editor shall be entitled to use material written by *him/her* for the purposes of the Work in articles submitted to learned or professional journals, in papers presented at professional conferences and for the General Editor's professional purposes generally, provided that the General Editor shall make appropriate acknowledgment to the Work and the Publishers, but

23.1.2 the General Editor shall not without the written consent of the Publishers write, edit or contribute, jointly or severally, to any work which may reasonably be considered by the Publishers to compete with or prejudice sales of the Work or the exploitation of any of the rights granted to the Publishers under this Agreement.

24. Arbitration

24.1 If any difference shall arise between the General Editor and the Publishers touching the meaning of this Agreement or the rights and liabilities of the parties hereto, the same shall be referred to the arbitration of two persons (one to be named by each party) or their umpire in accordance with the provisions of the Arbitration Act 1996 or any amending or substituted statute for the time being in force.

25. Entire Agreement

25.1 This Agreement sets forth the entire agreement between the parties at the date hereof and supersedes any prior written or oral agreement between them with respect to the subject matter hereof.

25.2 This Agreement shall be governed by and construed in accordance with the laws of England.

25.3 Any amendment of or variation to this Agreement must be in writing and signed by both parties.

26. Headings

26.1 Headings to the clauses hereof are for guidance only and are not to be taken into account in the construction of this Agreement which has been prepared in [*number*] copies.

27. Definitions

27.1 In this Agreement the following words and expressions shall have the following meanings unless the context requires otherwise:

'Associated Company' shall have the meaning attributed to that term in section 416 (et seq) of the Income and Corporation Taxes Act 1988, as amended;

'Electronic Form' shall include but shall not be limited to off-line electronic storage and information retrieval systems of a digital, optical or magnetic nature including (by way of example and not limitation) floppy disk, CD-ROM, CD-I, ROM-card, compact disc, video, integrated circuit; on-line transmission by satellite and other means of telecommunication; and any other electronic means of reproduction, publication, dissemination and transmission whether now in existence or hereafter invented;

'Electronic Publishing Rights' means the right to produce, copy, publish and sell, perform, display, broadcast and transmit the Work whether in whole or in part, adapted or abridged on its own or in combination with another work or works, together with any accompanying sounds and

	images, in any Electronic Form and to license the foregoing rights in electronic versions of the Work;
'Net Sum Received by the Publishers'	means the amount received by the Publishers and any amounts receivable by the Publishers after deducting any discounts granted by the Publishers and any sales or other similar taxes or duties incurred by the Publishers in respect of sales of copies of the Work;
'Subsidiary Rights'	means in relation to the Work the rights specified in Clause 5 hereof;
'Work'	means the Work (and any new editions thereof) edited by the General Editor under this Agreement together with any abridgements, adaptations, or electronic versions thereof;
'[*Insert name*] Group'	means any associated company of [*insert name*] Limited.

28. Assignment

28.1 The Publishers may assign any benefit or transfer, delegate or sub-contract any of their duties or obligations under this Agreement to any company within the [*insert name*] Group without the prior written consent of the General Editor.

AS WITNESS THE HANDS OF THE PARTIES

Signed by ....

(GENERAL EDITOR)

Signed by ....

For and on behalf of [*name of publishers*] LIMITED

Agreement for a Contributor to a Book

As indicated in Precedent Two, multiple authorship is often necessary, especially for the publication of texts for specialist readers. It is not uncommon to find as many as/more than 25 specialist authorities each writing a specialist chapter (each with its own copyright implications) to make up a definitive text or reference work for scientific or medical readership. In this Precedent, which is set out (as such agreements often are) in letter form, that is the context which is assumed.

1. In the case of a multi-author work, failure to deliver on time by one contributor may wreck publication plans, particularly in the case of textbooks with tight publication time limits. It may sometimes be preferable to cancel a commissioned chapter which is running late and to recommission, rather than to hang on indefinitely to the increasing irritation of those contributors who have delivered on time and who may threaten to withdraw from the project.

Delivery in disk form is now very common, but it is important to ensure that contributors have been properly briefed on the publishers' requirements from the very beginning.

2. As for single-author books, it is vital that the contributor alerts the publishers to any textual or illustrative material quoted from outside sources and provides evidence that permission has been properly sought and obtained. The publishers may wish to provide a sample clearance letter, particularly if they wish to ensure that clearance includes the right to reuse the quoted material in any sublicensed editions of the collective work, e.g. translations.

3. As with many other publications, publication and reproduction of a specialist multi-author work may be in print-on-paper form, but will increasingly take place via electronic media; STM (scientific, technical and medical) works are increasingly taking advantage of CD-ROM and on-line forms of publication. It is therefore vital that the publishers secure control of such rights, either to exploit them directly or via licensing. The question of whether publication in part and in electronic form (perhaps as part of a work containing other material and allowing for interactivity) constitutes a breach of the contributor's moral rights of integrity has yet to be tested (see also notes to Clause 5 and Clause 10).

Dear
We are happy to learn that you have agreed to contribute to our publication:
(the Work)
Edited by: (the General Editor)
Your contribution will be published on the following terms:

1. You will contribute the chapter on (the Contribution)
which will consist of not more than words and not less than
words on a word processor disk in [*specify word processing package to be used*] format together with two identical hard copies printed out from the said disk in double line spacing, retaining a further hard copy for your own files. The Contribution will be delivered to the General Editor no later than together with any illustrations, photographs, drawings, charts or graphs in a form suitable for reproduction as agreed with the Publishers.

Should you fail to deliver the Contribution by this date or by such other date as may have been agreed in writing by the Publishers, or should you fail to deliver the Contribution in the form specified, then the Publishers shall be at liberty to decline to publish the Contribution, in which case the sum specified in Clause 8 hereof shall not be payable to you.

2. You as the Author of the Contribution warrant to us (hereinafter called the Publishers) that the Contribution is original to yourself, that it has not hitherto been published in any form, and is not a violation or infringement of any existing copyright or licence or of any other right of any other person or party whatsoever. You undertake to indemnify the Publishers against any claims, any loss, damage or costs, including any legal costs properly incurred, occasioned to the Publishers in consequence of any breach of this warranty or arising out of any claim alleging that your Contribution constitutes a breach of this warranty.

You accept responsibility for obtaining permission for publication in the Contribution at your expense of any textual and/or illustrative material in which copyright vests in any other person or party and will deliver to the Publishers for safe keeping any documents relating to the granting of such permissions.

3. For the consideration mentioned in Clause 8, you, by way of assignment of present or future copyright, hereby assign to the Publishers the entire copyright and all other rights of a like nature in and to the Contribution throughout the world for the full legal term of copyright and all renewals and extensions thereof, and the Publishers shall have the exclusive right during such period to publish, and to license for publication, the Contribution in whole and in part in all editions forms and media in the English language and in any translations without limitation.

4. You may republish the Contribution in whole or in part at no charge with the Publishers' prior written permission, such permission not to be unreasonably withheld, provided that proper acknowledgment is given to the Publishers in such republication.

5. The prudent publisher will, under the guidance of the general editor, commission contributions for the first edition only. If then the book succeeds, and a second edition is called for, any less satisfactory contributions can be quietly dropped with minimal embarrassment, and new/replacement contributors can be commissioned.

Whether heavy revisions by a general editor may or may not infringe the moral rights of integrity of a contributor has yet to be extensively tested under the provisions of the 1988 Copyright Act.

8. If it has been agreed that the individual contributors should receive a share of any subsidiary rights income resulting from exploitation of the whole work or in an individual contribution, this clause would need to be amended.

'You will receive a share of any income generated from the sale of any subsidiary right in the Work involving the use of your contribution, such share to be agreed with the Publishers.'

10. Those publishers who fear that exploitation of the work, particularly in electronic form, could be restricted by the adherence of every contributor to their moral rights of

5. The Contribution will be offered by you and subject to the decision of the General Editor (see below) and the terms of Clause 1 (above) will be accepted for publication in the first edition of the Work only and the Publishers shall have the right to include the Contribution in any subsequent revised edition or editions of the Work on the terms set out below.

The General Editor shall have the right to make any revision to the Contribution which he may deem desirable in the interests of uniformity and style of the Work. The General Editor shall have the final decision on the inclusion or omission of the Contribution in or from the first and any subsequent editions of the Work.

You will, if so required by the General Editor, revise the Contribution for any new edition of the Work and you agree that such revised Contribution shall be subject to the terms and conditions herein generally stated except that the payment for such revised Contribution shall be mutually agreed between yourself and the Publishers.

6. To reduce the length and expense of production time, the Publishers may agree with the General Editor to dispense with proof corrections by you in which event the Publishers and their printers will ensure the correction of any typographical errors, and you will see the artwork of all redrawn illustrations before their reproduction in the Work. Accordingly the Publishers request your co-operation in making all reasonable efforts to ensure that all required amendments and corrections are incorporated in the final completed text before it is submitted in the required form to the Publishers.

Should proofs of the Contribution (and finished artwork) be provided to you, you undertake to read, check and correct them and return them to the Publishers within 14 days of their receipt, failing which the Publishers may consider the proofs and artwork passed for press by you.

7. The Publishers will absorb the cost of your corrections up to but not exceeding an amount equal to 10 per cent of the cost of origination of the Contribution but any cost incurred in excess of that amount will be charged against payment to you referred to in Clause 8.

8. As full consideration for the copyright and all other rights in the Contribution assigned to the Publishers in Clause 3 and subject to the terms of Clause 5 as regards any revised Contribution the Publishers will pay you on publication the sum of   and in the event that there is more than one author of the Contribution payment will be divided equally between each of you unless the Publishers are authorised to the contrary in writing signed by each of you.

9. The Publishers shall include your name with due prominence on the title page of the Contribution or elsewhere as determined by the Publishers as the author (or co-author as the case may be) of the Contribution.

10. You hereby assert to the Publishers and to our licensees your moral right to be identified in the Work as the Author (or co-author as the case

integrity, could take advantage of the fact that (unusually in Europe) the 1988 UK Copyright Act permits for waiver of moral rights. Wording to cover a full waiver might read as follows:

> 'You hereby irrevocably and unconditionally waive all moral rights under section 80 and pursuant to section 87 of the Copyright, Designs and Patents Act 1988.'

It should be remembered that the copyright laws of most other countries supporting the concept of moral rights do not permit waiver and hence any attempt to extend the waiver beyond the United Kingdom is unlikely to be valid.

It is likely that contributors will need to be carefully persuaded of the reasons for seeking such a waiver, particularly in subject areas where manipulation of content could be held to be dangerous (e.g. in medical publications).

Some publishers have sought to obtain a partial waiver of the right of integrity for publication in electronic form only.

may be) of your Contribution, in accordance with the Copyright, Designs and Patents Act 1988.

11. All sums payable to you under this letter are exclusive of UK Value Added Tax which shall, where applicable, be paid in addition at the rate in force at the time of payment, provided you have supplied the Publishers with a current and valid UK VAT registration number.

12. The Publishers may deduct from any sum due to you under this letter of agreement any sum that we are or may be under an obligation to deduct or withhold in respect of any tax, duty or other similar levy.

13. You will receive one free copy of the Work on publication. In addition you are entitled to purchase further copies directly from the Publishers at normal trade discount off the recommended retail price. You are also entitled to purchase from the Publishers at a discount of   per cent other publications published by us.

14. Any dispute or difference of any kind whatsoever which arises between you and the Publishers in relation to any matter in connection with this letter of agreement shall be referred to arbitration under the Arbitration Rules of the Chartered Institute of Arbitrators.

15. This letter of agreement shall be governed by and construed in accordance with the laws of England.

16. Also enclosed is a contributor card for your completion to be returned to the General Editor together with the material for your Contribution. It is most important that this document is completed as fully as possible. If your Contribution is being co-authored please photocopy the card, as appropriate, for completion by your co-author/authors.

Would you please sign and return to us, the Publishers, the enclosed duplicate copy of this letter to confirm your agreement to the terms of this letter. Where more than one author is involved, please all sign and return the duplicate copy.

I/We confirm our agreement to the above terms.

Yours sincerely

(for the Publishers)

Date:

Paperback Rights Agreement

A paperback edition is for many books the most important source of income for hardback publishers and authors alike. Mass-market paperback publishing is a separate trade with its own professional skills of book selection, production, sales and marketing.

This Precedent accordingly looks at the world through the eyes of the mass-market paperback publisher who negotiates with the hardback publisher at arm's length. It should however be noted that there has been a decline in the number of 'arm's length' paperback licences over the last few years. Hardback publishers with their own mass-market paperback imprints are able to offer authors a commitment to paperback publication on acquisition together with 'full' royalties on their paperback sales. In return the paperback imprint acquires its rights for the full term of copyright without the need to renew its licences or pay refresher advances. This practice of 'vertical publishing', under which a book is published in hardback and paperback by one group of companies, is reflected in the royalty provisions of Precedent One, Clause 12(e).

In an effort to compete with the terms offered to authors by vertical publishers, independent hardcover publishers will sometimes jointly acquire volume rights on a profit-sharing basis with paperback publishers. These 'joint ventures' vary in detail but all contain an element of shared investment (advance, royalties, production costs, marketing, etc.), an overhead deduction and profit sharing. Usually a separate joint venture document is prepared itemising costs and accounting procedures, together with a paperback rights agreement (see this Precedent) often however for the full period of copyright. Alternatively the paperback publisher may be a joint signatory to a volume rights agreement, as provided by Precedent One.

The mass-market paperback publisher may, or may not, be also in the business of issuing trade paperbacks. This Precedent considers the issue under the scope of the grant of paperback rights within Clause 1, and then under the royalty provisions of Clause 10.

1. (1) It is important to define, contract for contract, exactly what rights are being licensed. The critical point, of course, is that the publisher, in this precedent, must know from the start the real extent of the rights for which he/she is negotiating. Firstly, books may be issued by the grantor not only in hardback editions but also in trade paperback editions, or even licensed for paperback book club editions. The wording of Clause 1 should put the grantor on notice. Either he/she grants 'all paperback editions' knowing that he/she is thus forfeiting the issue subsequently of a trade paperback edition; or he/she grants rights subject to the existence, notified to the paperback publisher in advance, of a trade paperback issued or to be issued by him/herself or by another trade paperback publisher. In the latter case some modification to the wording of Clause 1 will be needed. Secondly, there is an apparent conflict with educational editions of, for example, contemporary novels issued in limp bindings; the paperback publisher will need to know the grantor's position on educational editions of all kinds. A proposed definition of an educational edition is as follows:

> An educational edition, whatever its format or binding, is one to which the following two criteria apply:
> (a) The book is sold at normal school book or educational terms and is promoted solely by educational sales methods (e.g. through educational representatives and educational catalogues, by advertising in the educational press and not the literary press, and by inspection copies being sent to teachers) and not through trade bookshop display
> (b) The book contains, in addition to the original text, direct editorial apparatus to an extent which forms not less than 20% of the original text, measured either by wordage or by printed area.

Finally the other effects of granting 'all paperback editions' should be considered. Should the grantor be expected to license large print paperback rights to the publisher to sub-license? What are the perils of the publisher not controlling digest book condensation rights in paperback format? In the case of the former it is common for the grantor to withhold these rights. For the latter, see Clause 14. Perhaps there is the possibility of an anti-piracy paperback edition which the grantor may feel is vital they issue; should the paperback publisher cede this right to the grantor without condition? It is also useful to consider the matter of omnibus paperback editions. The necessity of obtaining the consent of the grantor to the inclusion of the title in an omnibus on terms which are subject to agreement (and, therefore, an additional, possibly separate advance and royalty) is not an uncommon solution.

(2) The territories covered by the agreement need to be carefully set out (see Precedent One, Clause 1, note (2), and Appendix H). It is vital only to grant exclusive rights in the territories the grantor controls exclusively. Cognisance of any American or other English language licences should be taken when presented with the publisher's required list of territories.

2. (1) Currently, most licences are signed for a period of eight years — short enough to allow renegotiation and long enough to allow the paperback publisher to establish the work in the trade in home and overseas markets. It is advisable to state that the licence begins from the date of the agreement in order to ensure that there is no possibility of an alternative short licence being given to cover the period before the publisher publishes. Due and careful consideration of this should be given if the publisher is purchasing rights to a previously published paperback edition where the previous publisher has the right to sell-off existing stock on expiry (see Clause 18).

(2) A mechanism for the renewal of the licence could usefully be included. For example:

> 'The Publishers may only seek the renewal of the licence by giving written notice to the Grantors of their wish to do so not earlier than 6 months prior to the expiry of the licence and not later than 3 months prior to the expiry of the licence. The parties shall

MEMORANDUM OF AGREEMENT made this day of 19 between of (hereinafter called 'the Grantors', which expression shall, where the context admits, include the Grantors' assigns or successors in business as the case may be) of the one part and of (hereinafter called 'the Publishers', which expression shall, where the context admits, include any publishing imprint subsidiary to or associated with the Publishers, and the Publishers' assigns or successors in business as the case may be) of the other part Whereby it is mutually agreed as follows concerning a work at present entitled
by (hereinafter called 'the Work'):

1. In consideration of the payments hereinafter mentioned the Grantors hereby grant to the Publishers the exclusive right and licence to produce and publish the Work in all paperback editions in the English language throughout

2. The Licence herein granted shall endure from the date hereof and for a period of years from the date of first publication of the Publishers' edition

---

then negotiate a renewal on reasonable terms (including the payment of an additional advance) in good faith but if they are unable to agree terms within 30 days of receipt of the notice of desire to renew the Grantors may offer the rights elsewhere or proceed to publish themselves at their discretion.'

(3) The date of publication, as is emphasised by the cross-reference to Clause 19, is often of great importance to both sides in a negotiation. To the grantors, the paperback edition is only one (if often the most important one) in a series of rights they are deploying on the author's behalf and the relationship in time of the rights is part of their strategy (see in particular Clause 14 and note). To the publishers, the paperback edition is their entire business and they will be especially alert to ensuring early release for the open market and/or for film, TV or stage 'tie-ins', sometimes seeking to oblige the grantors to use their reasonable endeavours to keep the publishers fully up to date on opening dates and to assist in obtaining the right to use 'tie-in' materials on the paperback edition. Both grantors and publishers should consider very carefully contracts offered by some American publishers which require that no British paperback edition should be published until a number of months after publication of an American paperback edition. To accept this condition (or one with similar intent) may be to throw away the open market in paperback and to put in peril many exclusive overseas markets in paperback. Some paperback publishers specify that they should have the right:

(a) to issue early export editions in the open market to coincide with known shipment dates of competing American paperback editions;
(b) to issue early home and/or export editions some weeks before release of film, TV or dramatic versions of the work;
(c) to issue paperback editions for the Australian market to protect the publishers' exclusivity in Australia;
(d) to require the grantors to publish their edition in Australia in sufficient time to protect their respective exclusive Australian markets;
(e) to require the grantors to keep the publishers comprehensively informed of the American publishers' plans for publication in the open market and the American publishers' exclusive territories.

As to the particular issues of publication in the Australian market, see Introduction.
(4) Two additional points concerning early release should be made:

(a) Such release will certainly constitute an act of publication, so that payment of part of an advance may be triggered, unless careful provision otherwise is made. See, for example, note to Clause 22.

(b) Such release may jeopardise income to the author in respect of countries in which English is virtually a second language, e.g. the Netherlands, much of Scandinavia and, increasingly, Germany. An author who is well established in those countries, e.g. a leading crime novelist, may lose significant income from foreign language edition royalties through release of an English-language paperback edition (whether from the UK or USA) earlier than it is physically possible for a translated edition to be put on the market. The foreign language publisher may in such circumstances become increasingly unwilling to support British authors.

3. It is not advisable for the grantors to offer any warranties or indemnity wider than those offered to them by the author in the head contract. If there are separate author and artist Contracts the lowest common denominator should be applied.

4. The revision of the work can cause anxiety to the grantor and author. For the latter see the section on the 'moral right of integrity' in Appendix D. The grantor may reasonably ask that the Author be given the chance to revise the offending matter but that if this is not possible the agreement may be terminated which should be acceptable only on repayment of all monies paid in connection with the Work. In addition, the grantor may reasonably require that the last sentence of the Clause apply only to revisions made with the agreement of the grantor.

5. The grantor may insist that all revisions are included in the next reprint. The publishers should ensure they retain the right to sell previously printed copies. It is also worth remembering that for paperback editions which include specially written additional material (e.g. an autobiography) that the contractual position for that material should be clarified. It will often be necessary to prepare a short form of agreement with the author to ensure the publishers have the rights and suitable warranties and indemnity for that material.

and shall be subject to renewal by mutual agreement. The Publishers shall publish the Work not earlier than   and not later than
. Should the Publishers fail to comply with these dates (save as hereinafter provided or unless the Publishers are prevented from doing so by circumstances beyond the Publishers' control) the Grantors shall be at liberty to terminate the Agreement under the provisions of Clause 19 hereof.

3. The Grantors hereby warrant to the Publishers that they have full power to make this Agreement, that the Work has not previously been published in any paperback form in the territories covered by this Agreement, and is in no way whatever a violation or infringement of any existing copyright or licence, or any other right of any person or party whatsoever, that it contains nothing libellous or unlawful, that all statements contained therein purporting to be facts are true and that any recipe, formula or instruction contained therein will not, if followed accurately, cause any injury, illness or damage to the user.

The Grantors further warrant that the Work contains no obscene or improper material.

The Grantors shall indemnify and keep the Publishers indemnified against all actions, suits, proceedings, claims, demands and costs (including any legal costs or expenses properly incurred and any compensation costs and disbursements paid by the Publishers on the advice of their legal advisers to compromise or settle any claim) occasioned to the Publishers in consequence of any breach of this warranty, or arising out of any claim alleging that the Work constitutes in any way a breach of this warranty.

All warranties and indemnities herein contained shall survive the termination of this Agreement.

4. The Publishers reserve the right having first notified the Grantors to alter the text of the Work as may appear to them appropriate for the purpose of modifying or removing any passage which in their absolute discretion or on the advice of their lawyers may be considered objectionable or actionable at law, but any such alteration or removal shall be without prejudice to and shall not affect the Grantors' liability under any warranties and indemnities herein contained.

5. The Grantors will on request deliver to the Publishers ten printed copies of the Work together with all corrections, revisions, additions and other amendments which have been notified by the author or editor of the Work, and will keep the Publishers informed of all further amendments which may be proposed from time to time. All costs of further alterations made in the proofs by the Grantors (other than the correction of artists', copy editors' and printers' errors) shall be paid by the Grantors unless otherwise mutually agreed between the parties hereto.

6. The paper, printing, binding, covers and embellishments, the promotion, the manner and extent of advertisement, the number and distribution of free copies for the Press or otherwise, the reprinting, pricing and terms of

7. Frequently, the grantors will supply film of illustrations for a loan fee, or the publisher will offset from the grantors' edition for a fee at a per-page rate. The loan fee basis is particularly used for children's picture books.

It is worth remembering that if no provision is made in the contract for the use of the grantors' typographical arrangement that it is an infringement of the copyright in that arrangement if it is copied by the publishers without the grantors' consent. A note on copyright in the typographical arrangement will be found in the note to Clause 14 (v) of Precedent One.

8. The undertaking here may be enlarged to include the proper display of the title of the work also. With works which have more than one author a problem may arise of the relative prominence of the names. The paperback publisher will want to 'play up' the best-known of the authors. The other authors may have views on this issue, and the grantor should be consulted well in advance if any layout is intended which alters the sequence or relative prominence of the grantor's original layout.

9. It would seem reasonable that if 10 copies are supplied under Clause 5 then the same should be supplied here.

10. (1) Royalty rates on paperback editions generally start at $7\frac{1}{2}$ per cent on home market sales and 6 per cent on export sales, and rise separately in respect of home and export sales at intervals of $2\frac{1}{2}$ and 2 per cent respectively by targets of thousands of copies sold (all these royalties being paid on the recommended retail price). Some trade and children's paperback publishers continue to calculate export royalties on receipts, the percentage being that offered for home sales. For a full discussion of high discount royalty rules see page 12.

The question of aggregation of home and export sales to achieve the higher royalty rates should be expressed clearly in the contract. The inclusion of the phrase 'Home sales and export sales will be aggregated to achieve the change points set out above' should be sufficient.

With the increase of book/tape packs being published by the publishers of children's books it may sometimes be necessary to cover this aspect in a paperback licence. The wording should carefully explain that the book element is to be accounted for only under the book/tape royalty rate provision.

(2) The publisher in this precedent acquires, as is made clear in Clause 1 and the notes to it, the right to issue the work in both trade and mass-market paperback editions. Some paperback publishers may therefore reflect this point in setting out separate royalty clauses, with separate royalty rates. Whether a trade paperback deserves a higher, or lower, or roughly the same, rate of royalty as a mass-market paperback is not at all clear. The mass-market paperback publisher, in this precedent, may well be considering a

sale of the first and any subsequent edition of the Work issued by the Publishers shall be in the sole discretion of the Publishers, who shall in all other respects (except only as herein provided) have the entire control of the publication.

7. The Grantors shall supply to the Publishers originals or prints of any illustrations, charts, maps, diagrams or other artwork which the Grantors include in their edition of the Work, and the Grantors hereby grant to the Publishers permission to reproduce such material free of charge and hereby warrant to the Publishers that they have full power to grant such permission throughout the territory covered by this Agreement.

After use by the Publishers such material shall be returned to the Grantors, but while proper care will be taken of such material supplied by the Grantors, the Publishers shall not be responsible for any loss of or damage to it while it is in the Publishers' possession or in the course of production or in transit.

8. The Publishers undertake that the name of the Author will appear in its customary form with due prominence on the title page and on the binding of every copy of the Work published by them and that the copyright notice shall appear in exactly the same form as in the Grantors' edition, together with the words 'First published by   '.

The Author has asserted to the Grantors *his/her* right to be identified as the author of the Work and a notice to that effect shall be printed in every copy of the Work published or licensed by the Publishers.

9. The Publishers shall send to the Grantors on publication   complimentary copies of each edition of the Work issued by the Publishers. The Grantors shall have the right to purchase at normal trade terms further copies for personal use but not for resale.

10. The Publishers shall prepare accounts of sales of the Work half-yearly to the   and   each year and deliver and settle these (subject to a minimum sum of   being due to the Grantors under this Agreement) within three months thereafter respectively, paying the Grantors, except as otherwise provided, as follows:

calculated on the United Kingdom recommended retail price.

The Publishers shall at the first accounting after first publication or reissue of their edition of the Work be entitled to deduct from royalties due to the Grantors a sum as a reserve against returns of   per cent, and to withhold this sum for a period up to and including the third royalty statement after such first publication or reissue, following which all moneys due shall be paid in full at the time of the next royalty statement.

The Grantors or their authorised representative shall have the right upon written request to examine the records of accounts of the Publishers in so far as they relate to the sales and receipts in respect of the Work, which examination shall be at the cost of the Grantors unless errors exceeding

lavishly illustrated trade paperback edition, followed by a more cost-conscious mass-market paperback, and the costs of reproduction fees and of production in general may lead him/her to seek a lower set of royalty rates than for the mass-market paperback edition. The case may be quite different where, as in Precedent One, Clause 12(e), the original hardback publisher considers the issue of a trade paperback edition.

(3) A provision against returns is now standard practice. The reserve percentage requested is between 20 and 30 per cent: the flow of returns is usually known within 18 months of effective first publication, whether at home or in a major overseas market, so retention of the reserve until after the third accounting date (i.e. at the fourth accounting date) after first publication is reasonable, where accounting is twice yearly. It is not unreasonable to request a reserve be taken at the first account after reissue though some grantors will require that the reissue qualifies only if it entails resubscription.

(4) The arguments which lead the grantor to insist on a small reprint clause in his/her agreement with the author may lead the paperback publisher to seek an analogous clause in his/her agreement with the grantor. Note, however, the common pitfall of including wording like 'The Publishers may not reprint the work more than once in any 12 month period' when the intention is really to prohibit the reduction of the royalty on more than one occasion in the period! See in general note (c) to Clause 12 of Precedent One.

(5) The precedent assumes earnings to come from sales made through the retail trade. 'Special sales', however, are on the increase in both hardback and paperback publishing. The paperback publisher may therefore wish to include in his/her standard agreement provision for a royalty payment as follows: ' . . . on copies sold outside normal trade channels such as but not limited to mail order, premiums and subscriptions, a percentage calculated on the net sums received by the Publishers'. It is not unusual for the grantors to seek a full explanation of what the publisher considers to be 'a special sale' and to seek prior approval over both them and premium sales. The grantors must be aware of the publishers' need to recognise that the former do require quick responses in order for the deal to be struck. Some of the larger paperback publishers run 'promotional reprint operations' and, again, a definition should be sought and consent can often be a contractual condition.

11. The licensing of paperback book club editions in the same format as hardcovers is a less contentious issue today than it was at the time of writing the last edition. However, the question as to who should license such rights and the division of income therefrom still needs careful consideration. The timing of publication of such editions is of much concern to the paperback publisher, and there are strong arguments for the paperback house to receive some share of the income, whoever issues the licence or manufactures the books.

13. The royalty on paperbacks remaindered at above cost is usually lower than the equivalent royalty in respect of hardback remainders, e.g. 5 per cent of receipts. See also in general Precedent One, Clause 22, and notes.

14. See in general the note to Clause 2. The impact on each other of paperbacks, 'cheaps', book club and remaindered editions is often contentious, each publisher fervently believing that his/her edition is suffering from the ill-timed release of some other edition. Clause 14 sets out the currently accepted period of limitation on the grantors' powers of disposal and of grant of rights. Following the collapse of the Net Book Agreement the grantors should look very carefully at any wording prohibiting sales at a reduced price and, therefore, their ability to monitor performance. On the other side, the publishers have to consider the impact of heavily discounted hardbacks as they near and follow through the date of paperback publication.

15. This clause is aimed at the problem of 'library binding-up'. The proportion of a paperback edition bound up in hard covers for library use is so small as not to affect the paperback publisher. The author, however, may (in so far as a copy of the hardback edition is not bought by the library) suffer considerably in royalty earnings. Hence the stringent notice printed on the reverse of the title pages of most paperback editions of books first published by hardback publishers.

per cent of such sales and receipts in respect of the last preceding accounting period to their disadvantage shall be found, in which case the cost shall be paid by the Publishers.

11. In the event of the sale by the Publishers with the prior consent of the Grantors (such consent not to be unreasonably withheld or delayed) of paperback book club rights within the territory covered by this Agreement, the payment to be made to the Grantors on copies so sold shall be arranged mutually between the Grantors and Publishers.

12. The Publishers shall not abridge, expand or otherwise alter the Work, including illustrations where applicable, in any way without the written consent of the Grantors.

13. If, after a period of 12 months from the date of first publication hereunder, the Work shall in the opinion of the Publishers have ceased to have a remunerative sale, the Publishers shall be at liberty to dispose of any copies remaining on hand as a remainder or overstock and shall pay the Grantors on such copies   per cent of the net amounts received by the Publishers, except that on any copies sold at cost price or less no royalty shall be payable.

14. The Grantors shall not before or within six months of the date of first publication of the Publishers' edition dispose of any copies of their edition of the Work as a remainder or at a reduced price without the agreement of the Publishers, and such agreement shall not be unreasonably withheld. Nor shall the Grantors allow publication of any edition of the Work other than a book club edition at a recommended retail price less than one-third of that of the Grantors' edition before or within six months of the date of first publication of the Publishers' edition without the agreement of the Publishers, and such agreement shall not be unreasonably withheld. The Grantors shall not permit the publication of the whole or a substantial part of the Work in condensed form without the prior written consent of the Publishers.

15. The Publishers shall not wittingly sell copies of the Work to be bound in hardback form by any company or person whatsoever without the consent of the Grantors, and the Publishers shall print a notice to that effect on the reverse of the title page of every copy of the Work published by them.

16. No royalties shall be paid on any copies of the Work sold at cost or less, presented to the Grantors, presented in the interests of the sale of the Work, lost through theft or damage or destroyed by fire, water, in transit or otherwise.

17. If at any time during the period of licence or any extension thereof the Publishers allow the Work to go out of print, and if they have failed to

18. Paperback publishing is highly competitive, and rights to backlist best-selling authors may change hands for high advance payments. The publishers should have the reasonable right to sell off existing stock after the termination of their licence in competition with an edition from a new paperback publisher. If the grantors are prepared to allow an exclusive sell-off period it is likely to be for a shorter period than noted here. The right to sell-off may be permitted only if the agreement expires by virtue of the licence not being renewed or under Clause 17 if there is a minimum stock level imposed. The argument to have this right under any other circumstances is difficult to sustain.

A restriction on reprinting within 3 months of expiry is sometimes required to prevent the paperback publisher 'flooding' the market on termination or during the sell-off period.

19. As with Clause 18 it is difficult to sustain an argument that the publishers' right to continue to participate should be available if termination is under this clause. See note to Precedent One, Clause 23.

21. (1) Some hardback publishers are reluctant to sign option clauses for paperback rights, preferring to assure the paperback publishers that they will receive 'first sight' of the author's next work.

publish a new edition within 12 months of having received a written request from the Grantors to do so, then all rights granted under this Agreement shall revert to the Grantors forthwith and without further notice, without prejudice to all rights of the Publishers in respect of any contracts or negotiations properly entered into by them with any third party prior to the date of such reversion and without prejudice to any moneys already paid or then due to the Grantors from the Publishers.

18. The Publishers shall have the right for a period of   months from the expiry of this Agreement or   months from the date of notification of reversion of rights from the Grantors (whichever is the greater period) to sell or otherwise dispose of any copies of the Work which they may have in stock.

19. (a) The Grantors may terminate this agreement by summary notice in writing to the Publishers if the Publishers are in material breach of any of the provisions of this agreement and have failed to remedy such breach within one month of notice to them from the Grantors of such breach.

(b) This Agreement shall automatically terminate if and when a manager, receiver, or other encumbrancer takes possession of or is appointed over the whole or any substantial part of the Publishers' assets; or if and when the Publishers enter into any arrangement or composition with or for the benefit of their creditors (including any voluntary arrangement under the Insolvency Act 1986); or if and when a petition is presented or a meeting is convened for the purpose of considering a resolution for the making of an administrative order, the winding up or dissolution of the Publishers (otherwise than a voluntary liquidation for the purpose of reconstruction).

(c) Upon termination of this Agreement howsoever occurring all rights granted herein shall revert to the Grantors without further notice, without prejudice to any rights of the Publishers in respect of contracts or negotiations properly entered into by them with a third party prior to the date of such reversion and without prejudice to any moneys already paid or then due to the Grantors from the Publishers.

20. If any difference shall arise between the Grantors and the Publishers touching the meaning of this Agreement or the rights and liabilities of the parties thereto, the same shall in the first instance be referred to the Informal Disputes Settlement Scheme of the Publishers Association, or, failing agreed submission to that Scheme, shall be referred to the arbitration of two persons (one to be named by each party) or their mutually agreed umpire, in accordance with the provisions of the Arbitration Act 1996 or any amending or substituted statute for the time being in force.

21. The Grantors shall give the Publishers the first offer of at least the same rights as are hereby granted in the first full-length work which   may write and the paperback rights of which the Grantors

(2) Paperback publishers need to watch carefully the placing of contracts for volume rights by authors and their agents. It is possible to invest heavily in marketing and promoting the paperback editions of several books by an author and then find that the author has moved to a fresh hardback publishing house, at which moment any option clause with the previous publisher is, of course, valueless.

(3) In these days of increasing vertical publishing the retention of an option on the paperback rights is of increasing importance to a paperback publisher. It should be made clear that the option survives termination but the reservations expressed in the notes on Clauses 18 and 19 apply.

22. Modest advances will in general be paid half on signature of the contract and half on the United Kingdom publication. Payment of large advances is likely to be spread over a longer period and/or in more stages. A proportion will be paid on signature, a proportion on publication and a final part being payable up to one year after publication. If there is a film or TV tie-in, then part of the advance will be payable on release of the film or on broadcast of the TV programme. When the paperback publisher has supported the hardback publisher in the purchase of their rights it is common for the paperback publisher to pay a portion of their advance on hardback publication, subject to the provision of notice and proof of the event by the grantors.

control, on terms to be mutually agreed. The Publishers undertake to decide within   weeks of receipt of the book in final typescript or proof or bound form whether they will make an offer for its publication. If within a further period of one month no agreement as to the terms of publication shall have been reached, then the Grantors shall be at liberty to negotiate for its publication in paperbound form elsewhere, provided that they shall not subsequently accept from any other publishers terms less favourable than those offered by the Publishers.

22. The Publishers shall pay to the Grantors in advance and on account of all sums that may become due to the Grantors under the provisions of this Agreement the sum of   , payable

23. It is understood and agreed that the Publishers have empowered the Copyright Licensing Agency (CLA) to grant non-exclusive licences to reproduce by photocopying and other reprographic means material from literary works published by the Publishers. The Work is accordingly deemed to be included with such literary works and the CLA shall divide the proceeds from reprographic reproduction of the Work authorised by the CLA equally between the Author and the Publisher. The Author shall receive the Author's share of such proceeds through the Authors' Licensing and Collecting Society (ALCS) in accordance with ALCS' standard terms and conditions.

24. All rights in the Work other than those expressly granted herein are reserved by the Grantors.

25. This Agreement shall be governed by and interpreted in all respects in accordance with the laws of England and any actions shall be brought before the courts of England.

26. This Agreement is the entire and only agreement between the Grantors and the Publishers concerning its subject matter and supersedes any and all prior agreements, arrangements and understandings (whether written or oral) relating thereto. No addition to or modification of any provision of this Agreement shall be binding upon the parties unless it is in writing and signed on behalf of the Grantors and the Publishers.

Book Club Rights Agreements

Book clubs are an important means of making books available to consumers, but, perhaps more than any other part of the consumer book market, their position has been affected by the effective ending of the Net Book Agreement, and with it the ending of the *Book Club Regulations*, which governed the relationship between the trade supplies of a title, sold through bookshops (formerly at a net or minimum price), and the book club edition, which could be sold at a lower price to members. Now, instead of the BCRs spelling out the status of the book club editions when a book was published as net (as most trade books were), and imposing various conditions to keep the two principal supplies separate, the limits on the use of a title through a book club need to be a matter of individual contract, as interpreted, no doubt, by the custom and practice of the trade.

It should be noted, however, that a second major document governing book clubs, the so-called *Book Club Concordat*, which seeks to limit how far a book club may enjoy exclusive 'book club rights' to a title, is not limited to net books, and so is not affected by the ending of the NBA. In essence, book clubs signing the Concordat (which all significant book clubs have done) agree not to take exclusive book club rights to a title for a period of longer than three years, not to renew such an exclusive agreement, not to take exclusive rights when its order is for 3,500 copies or less, and to publish exclusive editions in a different format from the trade edition. The objective behind the Concordat, which was agreed after intervention by the Office of Fair Trading, is to ensure that one book club is not able to obtain an unduly dominant position in the book club market by depriving other clubs of access to titles for which it has long-term exclusive book club rights. Further details are set out later in this narrative.

The distinguishing characteristic of a book club is that it sells titles only to its registered members, who are customers who commit themselves to buying books selected by the club on a regular basis, and who benefit from the lower prices that firm quantity orders can provide.

Initially, when book clubs first came on the scene, book club editions were exclusively hardback reprint editions published nine months after the first trade edition; some time later, simultaneous but separate hardback editions were introduced; now, when a publisher agrees, it may supply copies of the trade edition, usually as a top-up to provide extra supplies, but fairly commonly also for smaller non-exclusive book club orders. Paperback clubs have now also been formed.

In the early days, too, a club would usually offer only one main choice in each monthly (or other periodical) offer to members, with a small number of alternate choices, but the number of alternates has now increased considerably, supplemented by very low price 'premiums' offered to new members, so that a club may now offer a sizeable catalogue and indeed, within one group, offer the same title to members of a number of different clubs within the group. This may require definition within the contract.

Usually, a book club sells its offers only by mail, though in recent years attempts have been made to establish retail book club outlets, with access limited to members making a minimum purchase commitment, leading to considerable resentment from bookshops which alleged, particularly when the NBA was in operation, that such book club outlets enjoy advantageous trade terms without having the bookshops' stockholding commitment.

A publisher wanting to license book club rights may therefore have a number of contractual issues to deal with if it wishes to ensure that a title being exploited through different outlets is used effectively, without intruding on separate markets in which different trading conditions may apply. The whole of this area, involving the imposition or acceptance of restrictions on trading opportunities by the parties, is governed by UK restrictive practices law (and, if inter-state trade is involved in the European Union, by EU law as well). In the case of the United Kingdom, there are limited exceptions where i) the agreement containing restrictions confers rights in copyright, or ii) the restrictions relate only to goods (copies) supplied under the contract. EU law, which applies when trade between member states is affected, is broader in its prohibitions, and the parties to licences and contracts for the supply of goods are well advised to seek careful legal advice when drafting their agreements.

In general, a licensor publisher (or a licensee book club) may want some or all of the provisions previously covered by the BCRs set out in the licence or contract for supply of copies. Under UK law, he would seem well advised to do this (especially when supplying trade copies to the club) within each separate contract or licence, rather than in a general trading agreement which may not be limited in its extent to the goods supplied under each different contract or licence.

Alternatively, it might presumably be possible to build the former BCRs into the contract but, as the BCRs applied only to net books, they would need to be amended to broaden out their application, and there could also be difficulties (especially should the NBA and its instruments, such as the BCRs, as is likely, lose their special legal exemption and become prohibited as unapproved restrictive agreements) in what might be seen as attempted concerted continuance.

Some of the issues which may be relevant include:

1. **Exclusivity**   As noted above, the terms of the Concordat (below) may limit the circumstances in which a club can obtain exclusive book club rights, and it should be noted that, even when the criteria for exclusive rights have been met, this does not impose an obligation on a publisher to

grant exclusive book club rights if he does not wish to: only that exclusivity is not prohibited. This is an issue which a publisher must determine on commercial criteria, taking account of the benefits of the better promotion that usually accompanies the granting of exclusivity in a market against other opportunities for exploitation in that market.

It is a slightly arcane point of copyright law as to whether book club rights are properly rights in copyright, so benefiting from the various special treatments afforded to rights – particularly exclusive rights – in copyright, or are merely convenient forms of commercial exploitation. Clearly they fall within the rights to make copies and to issue copies to the public which are the essence of copyright law, but the extent to which such rights may be subdivided in separate exclusive copyright agreements is not clear. Would a book club, as the licensee of exclusive book club rights, have the right to sue another trader purporting to offer copies to its own book club as a breach of copyright, or would the only remedy be against the publisher-licensor under the agreement for failure to deliver the promised exclusive book club rights? The issue could well be relevant should a bookshop, for example, decide to set up a book club offering privileged prices amongst its own regular customers. Again, a publisher granting an exclusive book club licence may well seek legal advice as to how far the exclusivity can be delivered, and what the consequences of failure might be.

A similar issue arises under EU law where the exclusivity is limited to the UK or perhaps the UK and Ireland. In such a case, it is increasingly established law that the import of copies put on the market in another EU state with the consent of the copyright owner cannot be prevented as infringing importation in breach of a UK (or Irish) exclusive right in copyright, or by the operation of the terms of the contract. Thus, a book club in the United Kingdom may have difficulty in seeking to prevent a book club operating legitimately in another EU state from making available titles to which the UK club purportedly has exclusive UK book club rights to its own book club customers in the UK. The best solution would seem to be that rights agreements should not divide the European Single Market, and that exclusive rights in particular should be negotiated for the whole EU and other territories subject to the same requirements.

2. **Supply to club members only**   The BCRs clearly restricted sales of book club titles sold to the trade as net titles to members of the book club only, and defined such members as being persons who had made a commitment to buy at least three choices from the club within the first period of membership (not less than six months), by definition from three different periodical offers (this is known as a 'positive option': the member must buy at least three different book club choices). An alternative formula, applied only to reprint book club editions and subject to other criteria, including a publication delay, was for a minimum number of 'negative options' – the member must agree to the choices being supplied over a minimum period of time unless he or she specifically refuses them.

A publisher granting book club rights may now want to establish some definition of what a book club member is, and the status of lapsed members, in its book club contracts.

3. **Requirement for separate book club edition**   The BCRs required book clubs to publish in a separate book club edition, specifying exceptions when copies of the trade edition might be used. The Concordat continues to provide that, subject to similar small exceptions, an exclusive book club edition must be in a separate edition. If therefore a publisher needs to provide for separation of the book club from the trade market by use of separate editions, this will now need to be done by the contract, taking account of legal considerations.

4. **Limitation on use as premium offer**   Premiums are used as a means of winning new members. A publisher may not want a title still selling well in other outlets to be used as a book club premium until later in the sales life of the title. The BCRs provided a time restraint of six months from original publication.

5. **Limitation of disposal as remainders**   A publisher (and author) may want to prevent a book club from disposing of surplus copies on the retail market as remainders without permission while the title has an active sales life.

6. **Sale through book club retail outlets**   A publisher may want to limit book club sales to mail order, excluding retail sales.

7. **Provisions re advertising of book club editions to avoid disadvantaging the trade**

The Concordat
The purpose of the Concordat is to ensure that one or more clubs do not take advantage of a dominant position to acquire exclusive rights in a large number of titles, or in all the important titles of a particular category, and so prevent other clubs from competing effectively. The Concordat is supported by a recommendation of the PA Council that publishers should not license book club rights to clubs which are not signatories.
   The Concordat provides as follows:

* Book clubs will not obtain exclusive book club rights for a term of more than three years, and will not seek to renew those rights. They may however negotiate for continuing non-exclusive rights at the time they negotiate the exclusive rights or thereafter. Bona fide new editions attracting a new copyright qualify as new titles, except that automatic rights to acquire new editions of a title are not allowed.
* When book clubs share rights to a title, the Concordat applies to the joint arrangement on the same basis as for a sole licence.

- Book clubs will not obtain exclusive rights for any title to be supplied to or produced by the book club in less than 3,500 copies, or 50 per cent of the publisher's print run, whichever is lower.
- Exclusive book club editions are required to have their own imprint, crest or legend indicating that the book is a book club edition on the title page and on the jacket, and on the binding, in such place as to be visible in any advertising or display, except that in exceptional cases where there proves to be an inadequate supply of copies of the book club edition, the hardbound trade edition may be used in quantities not exceeding 20 per cent of the order for the book club edition.
- One book club will not obtain the grant of exclusive book club rights at any time over all titles in a specific category (e.g. atlases, dictionaries, year books) to the total exclusion of other separately controlled clubs.
- When a 'general' book club enjoys exclusive book club rights to a title, it will release the licensing publisher from that exclusivity if a specialist book club which has 'a legitimate interest in a title which is essential to its list' is seeking a non-exclusive licence for that title, which will not take effect until at least two months after the general book club's edition.

[*Readers are advised to consult the actual terms of the Concordat, obtainable from the Publishers Association, for more precise statements of these requirements.*]

The recent introduction of paperback book clubs has caused a further problem, in that a book club may seek to obtain both hardback and paperback book club rights to a title, without necessarily having the intention of offering both, but to protect itself from competition from another book club offering a competing edition in the different format. In general, this is a legitimate exercise of copyright, and it would obviously be a serious limitation on the exclusive rights, themselves limited to three years, if they did not offer protection against other book club editions competing in similar circumstances. This must therefore be a matter for individual negotiation. However, the practice could be open to attack as being anti-competitive if it was used extensively as a means of eliminating competition. Book clubs may be prepared to allow unused rights to revert after the marketing of their edition.

Translator's Agreement

At the General Conference of UNESCO in Nairobi in 1976, twenty years of campaigning by FIT (Fédération Internationale des Traducteurs) culminated in the adoption of a Recommendation, dated 28 October. This Recommendation sought to assimilate the status of translators to that of authors. The United Kingdom, together with 49 other states, has approved the Recommendation, which if not an international convention must yet carry considerable force.

The problem of holding a fair balance of reward for author, foreign publisher and translator, while preserving the necessary margin of profit for the original publisher, is not easy. The precedent and notes which follow here, for this Fifth Edition, take careful account of the specimen publishing contract drawn up by the Translators Association in its latest revised version of 1994.

If the translator is to be assimilated to the author in some respects, then his/her status needs to be spelt out as in the comparable preamble to an author's contract. The statement of the publishers' rights in the work goes some way to meeting UNESCO Recommendation III 5(e).

The assumption of the words 'of which the Publishers hold the English-language translation rights' is that the publishers do indeed hold those rights throughout the world for the duration of the copyright in the work in all media. That might, or might not, be so: it is the publishers' responsibility to check very carefully the extent of the translation rights they hold, and to draft accordingly.

1. If we follow the 'Nairobi principles', it is not necessary to require from the translator a grant of copyright. The publishers have, as exclusive licensees of all rights in the translation, all the powers they need to make subsidiary deals on behalf of the work. Since, however, scientific, technical and medical (STM) works are frequently translated into the English language, some STM publishers request a grant of copyright so that they are in the strongest position to take fast action against pirate editions.

2. See also the comment on delivery in disc form at Precedent One, note (2) to Clause 2.

2. and 3. The fitness of the translation for the market envisaged by the publishers is often a delicate question. Early and thorough discussion should avoid later recriminations. Given the sad circumstances contemplated under Clause 3, an arbitration clause is included in this precedent.

5, 6 and **7.** (1) The aim of Clause 5 is to find some point in the success of the work which represents an equitable 'trigger' after which the translator, as in effect a secondary author, is entitled to a continuing reward. That reward is bound to be modest and calculations will have to be made book for book. Clauses 6 and 7 contemplate that for some works, the bulk of income reward may come from editions other than the 'original edition', e.g. from a home paperback edition or from an academic book club edition in the USA.

(2) For a note about the royalty on special discount sales, see the note to Precedent One, Clause 12 (b).

MEMORANDUM OF AGREEMENT made this   day of   19 between   of   (hereinafter called 'the Translator', which expression shall, where the context admits, include the Translator's executors and assigns as the case may be) of the one part and   of   (hereinafter called 'the Publishers', which expression shall, where the context admits, include any publishing imprint subsidiary to or associated with the Publishers, and the Publishers' assigns or successors in business as the case may be) of the other part
Whereby it is mutually agreed as follows concerning the translation into the English language from the   language (hereinafter called 'the Translation') of a work at present entitled   by   (hereinafter called 'the Work') of which the Publishers hold the English-language translation rights:

1. In consideration of the payments hereinafter mentioned the Translator grants to the Publishers during the legal term of copyright the exclusive right to produce and publish and further to license the production and publication of the Translation or any abridgement or substantial part of it in all editions, forms and media throughout the world.

2. The Translator shall deliver to the Publishers, not later than   , copies of the Translation which shall be faithful to the Work and rendered into good and accurate English.

3. The Publishers will not make any alterations to the Translation without the prior consent of the Translator, such consent not to be unreasonably withheld. If consent is unreasonably withheld, the Publishers may make such changes as they think fit and the Translator may withdraw *his/her* name from the Translation with such amendment to the terms of this Agreement as shall be mutually agreed.

4. The Publishers shall pay the Translator the sum of   which represents payment for   words at the rate of   per thousand words in the   language, and this sum shall be payable

5. On all copies sold at home and abroad of the Publishers' original edition of the Translation over and above   copies the Publishers shall pay the Translator a royalty of   per cent of the published price of copies sold, except that on all copies sold at a discount of more than   per cent, whether overseas or for export or for bulk sales at home or overseas the royalty shall be   per cent of the *British published price/net amounts received by the Publishers*.

No royalties shall be paid on copies of the Translation sold at cost or less, presented to the Translator, presented in the interests of the sale of the Translation, lost through theft or damaged or destroyed by fire, water, in transit or otherwise.

8. See also in general Precedent One, notes to Clause 16.

9. Acknowledgement of the translator's contribution follows acceptance of his/her status as a secondary author. The good intentions concerning copyright follow UNESCO Recommendation III (5(i)).

The translator, under UK law, now has the moral rights of paternity and of integrity in his/her translation. See in general Appendix D. The first sentence of Clause 9 meets the requirement of UK law that the right of paternity must be asserted.

10. This clause expresses the view of the Translators Association that translators should be held harmless against action in respect of anything not introduced into the translation by their own work. The intent, it is suggested, is reasonable, but see the mild caveat in the note to Clause 17.

Some publishers may wish to secure from the translator full warranty and indemnity provisions of the kind set out in Precedent One at Clause 5.

11. The period to be inserted here is that specified in the publishers' agreement for the English-language translation rights. If no such period is specified in the agreement between the original language publisher and the publishers, then a 'reasonable time' clause should be inserted. The translator, who may have spent a great deal of time, energy and creativity in completing the translation is surely entitled to a time-clause, and to proceed under Clause 16 against the publishers if they turn out to be in material breach of it.

6. In the event of a sale by the Publishers of publication rights in the Translation to the USA, the Translator shall receive   per cent of all net amounts received.

7. In the event of a sale by the Publishers of book club rights, paperback rights, serial rights, dramatic broadcasting rights or any other rights whatsoever, payment to the Translator shall be by mutual agreement.

8. The Publishers shall make up accounts of sales of the Translation to   and   following the date of first publication and the said accounts shall be delivered to the Translator and settled within three months thereafter respectively, provided however that no account need be submitted to the Translator unless specifically demanded nor payment made in respect of any period in which the sum due is less than   in which case the amount will be carried forward to the next accounting date.

The Translator or *his/her* authorised representative shall have the right upon written request to examine the records of account of the Publishers in so far as they relate to the sales and receipts in respect of the Translation, which examination shall be at the cost of the Translator unless errors exceeding   per cent in the last preceding accounting period to *his/her* disadvantage shall be found, in which case the cost shall be paid by the Publishers.

9. The Translator asserts *his/her* moral right to be identified as the Translator the Work. The Publishers undertake that the Translator's name shall appear on the title page and jacket/cover of their edition of the Translation and in all publicity material (catalogues, advertisements and similar materials), and shall use their best endeavours to ensure that this undertaking is adhered to also in other editions of the Translation. The Publishers shall print the following copyright notice on the Translation: 'English language translation ©   19 ' and other such notices as are necessary to comply with copyright formalities in those countries in which it might reasonably be expected to be used.

10. The Translator guarantees to the Publishers that *he/she* will not introduce into the Translation any matter of an objectionable or libellous character which was not present in the original Work. In reliance on such a guarantee the Publishers undertake to hold the Translator harmless from all suits and all manner of claims and proceedings or expenses which may be taken against or incurred by them on the grounds that the Translation contains anything objectionable or libellous.

11. The Publishers shall publish the Translation within   unless they shall be prevented from so publishing by circumstances beyond their control.

12. The Publishers shall send to the Translator on publication   complimentary copies of the Translation. The Translator

15. The importance of rights in the translation of a work as well as rights in the work itself must always be kept in mind. If the publishers are unwilling or unable (possibly because they cannot renegotiate a contract with the original foreign-language publishers) to keep the work in print in the translation which they themselves arranged, then it is reasonable for the translator to be entitled to have rights in the translation returned to him/her. But see also note to Clause 16 below and, of course, the clause may be irrelevant if the translator of an STM work has assigned the copyright itself to the publishers.

16. The return of rights in the translation to the translator under Clause 15 or 16 or otherwise does not in itself, of course, allow him/her to authorise its publication by another publisher. Such a third party would have to acquire translation rights de novo from the original foreign-language publishers or by assignment from the original English-language publishers.

17. The status of 'secondary author' may raise some unforeseen points. What is to happen if the publisher and the original language publisher fall out so that there is a breach of the agreement between them? What is to happen if the manuscript is acceptable to the UK publisher but not to the original foreign publisher, who has a difficult author on his/her hands anxious to approve the translation of his/her work under a clause between him/

shall have the right to purchase at normal trade terms further copies for personal use but not for resale.

13. The Translator undertakes to read, check and correct the proofs of the Translation and to return them to the Publishers within   days of their receipt, failing which the Publishers may consider the proofs as passed for press. The cost of translation alterations and corrections made by the Translator in the proofs (other than the correction of artists', copy-editors' and printers' errors) above   per cent of the original cost of composition shall be paid by the Translator.

14. While proper care will be taken of the Translation, the Publishers shall not be responsible for any loss of or damage to it while it is in the Publishers' possession or in the course of production or in transit.

15. If at any time the Publishers allow the Translation to go out of print or off the market in all editions issued by the Publishers or authorised by them, and if within   months after receiving written notice from the Translator to do so they have not reprinted and placed on the market a new edition, then all rights granted under this Agreement shall forthwith and without further notice revert to the Translator without prejudice to all rights of the Publishers in respect of any contracts or negotiations properly entered into by them with any third party prior to the date of such reversion and without prejudice to any moneys already paid or then due to the Translator from the Publishers.

16. (a) Should the Publishers at any time by themselves or anyone acting on their behalf be in material breach of any of the clauses or conditions set forth in this Agreement within   months after written notice from the Translator to rectify such breach,

(b) should a petition be presented or a meeting be convened for the purpose of considering a resolution for the making of an administrative order, the winding up or dissolution of the Publishers (otherwise than a voluntary liquidation for the purpose of reconstruction)

then in either event all rights granted under this Agreement shall revert to the Translator forthwith and without further notice, without prejudice to all rights of the Publishers in respect of any contracts or negotiations properly entered into by them with any third party prior to the date of such reversion, without prejudice to any claim which the Translator may have for damages or otherwise and without prejudice to any moneys already paid or then due to the Translator from the Publishers.

17. If any difference shall arise between the Translator and the Publishers touching the meaning of this Agreement or the rights and liabilities of the parties thereto, the same shall be referred in the first instance to the Informal Disputes Settlement Scheme of the Publishers Association, or,

herself and the original publisher only? What is to happen if the translator, following the publisher's instruction (agreed with the foreign publisher and author) in changing some names and the milieu, commits in such changes a libel on some real person? The guarantee contained in Clause 10 may look somewhat unclear in such circumstances. The status of an author carries rights *and* responsibilities, and it seems best to have a broadly drafted arbitration clause in reserve.

failing agreed submission to the terms of that Scheme, to the arbitration of two persons (one to be named by each party) or their mutually agreed umpire, in accordance with the provisions of the Arbitration Act 1996 or any amending or substituted statute for the time being in force.

18. The Publishers operate a self-billing system for the payment of royalties and to account for Value Added Tax. The Publishers therefore require details of the Translator's VAT registration number where applicable. Where the Translator fails to provide a VAT registration number the Publishers shall not pay VAT on any sums due under the terms of this Agreement.

19. This Agreement shall be deemed to be a contract made in England and shall be governed by and interpreted in all respects in accordance with the laws of England.

Agreement for Sale of Translation Rights

The negotiation of translation rights is the daily bread-and-butter work of rights and contracts departments in many publishing houses. Correspondence tends to be lengthy, if not voluble, and it is therefore very much in publishers' interests to keep down the overhead expenses of this service to authors by having a good standard contract. Precedent Eight provides a contract on an advance and royalty basis, probably the most common form of arrangement for translation licences. Alternative clauses are provided in the notes to cover arrangements on the basis of a lump sum for a designated print run, which can sometimes be a preferable arrangement for licences involving very modest sums, or for countries where remittance of payment abroad is problematic.

Although the majority of licences may be covered by standard agreements, special contracts may still need to be devised to reflect different publishing, payment or legislative practice in some markets. The Appendix to Precedent Eight seeks to provide an overview of licensing conditions in central and eastern Europe and the countries which once formed part of the Soviet Union – markets still in a state of transition from a command to a market economy – and the People's Republic of China, a market which is still relatively new to authorised licensing arrangements and where Western publishers must take into account the implications of the transfer of rule of Hong Kong to China from 1 July 1997, and also China's troubled relationship with Taiwan.

Preamble

Automatic transfer of the contract to the successors and assigns of the licensee may not always be desirable in countries where the publishing industry is in a volatile state.

If the work is not yet delivered to the proprietors in the original language in typescript or disk form, it may be necessary to add a description of the material, delivery date etc.

1. This clause defines the rights granted to the licensee. This precedent covers an advance and royalty arrangement deal with no specific limit on the number of copies of the translation which may be printed. In some cases, a lump sum payment to cover a designated print run may be preferable in which case the words ' [*number*] copies only of' should be inserted after the words 'the exclusive licence to translate, produce and publish' in this clause.

In the case of languages confined to limited markets, it may be advisable to grant world rights in that language to cover the core market and some expatriate sales. However, for languages such as English, Portuguese, Spanish and French, which are the national languages in more than one market, it may be advisable to limit the licence territorially – for example, granting separate licences for Portugal and Brazil.

Some foreign language publishers are content to acquire only volume rights or perhaps only volume rights in a designated binding; however, to license hardback and paperback translation rights separately to different publishers in the same market is problematic, and raises too the question of access to the translated text. If the book in question has potential for publication in both forms, it is best handled by a single licence which then permits the licensee to sublicense within his designated territory (see note to Clause 11).

If the proprietors do not wish to allow the licensee to reproduce the artwork, typography or design of the original jacket or cover of the work, the following words should be added to this clause:

'The right to reproduce the artwork, typography or design of the Proprietors' jacket/ cover is not included in this Agreement.'

2. The duration of the licence may be for the full term of copyright or (more commonly) for an agreed number of years as specified here; in either case there should be subsequent provision for termination of the contract if the translation is allowed to go out of print and is not being exploited via any authorised sublicences.

It is preferable that the term of the contract should run from a fixed date given at the commencement of the contract, rather than by a less precise date such as 'the date of signature of the Agreement' as there could well be a delay between signature of the contract by each party.

Publishers of non-fiction works, in particular textbooks which are likely to be regularly updated, may find it advisable to restrict the duration of the contract not by a period of years but by the life of the edition which is being licensed. This can be covered by omitting Clause 2, inserting the number of the edition after the title in the preamble (e.g. Second Edition) and adding to the end of Clause 1 the words 'This Agreement does not grant any rights with respect to subsequent editions of the Work.' Although in practice it is usually preferable to continue to license subsequent editions to the same licensee, this limitation

MEMORANDUM OF AGREEMENT made this   day of
19   Between: of   (hereinafter termed the
Proprietors which expression shall, where the context admits, include the
Proprietors' successors and assigns in business) of the one part,
and   of   (hereinafter termed the Publishers which
expression shall, where the context admits, include the Publishers'
successors and assigns in business) of the other part

WHEREAS the Proprietors are the proprietors of a work by
(hereinafter termed the Author), entitled:
(hereinafter termed the Work),

NOW IT IS HEREBY MUTUALLY AGREED AS FOLLOWS:

1. Subject to the terms detailed in this Agreement, the Proprietors hereby
grant to the Publishers the exclusive licence to translate, produce and
publish the Work in hardback/paperback volume form in the
language under the Publishers' imprint (hereinafter termed
the Translation) for sale throughout the following territories:

2. Subject to the terms of Clauses 4, 10, 12 and 17 hereof, the licence herein
granted shall last for a period of   years from the date of this Agreement
and may thereafter be renewed by mutual agreement between the parties.

3. The Publishers shall make the following payments to the Proprietors, in
accordance with the terms of Clause 19 hereof, namely:

(a) The sum of   payable on signature of this Agreement in
    advance and on account of any sums which may become due to the
    Proprietors under this Agreement from sales of the Translation.

---

does enable alternative arrangements to be made for a new edition if the original licensee
proves unsatisfactory. For additional safety, the following clause could also be inserted:

'The Proprietors shall be free to license the rights in any subsequent revised edition
of the Work to a third party at their discretion but on the understanding that publication
by a third party shall not take place unless sales of the Translation have fallen below
50 copies per annum in which case the Publishers shall not unreasonably retain the
rights, subject to satisfactory arrangements being made for the remaining stock of the
Translation.'

It should however be remembered that the acquisition of translation rights in a large and
complex work (such as a major medical textbook) involves considerable investment and
labour on the part of the licensee, who may be employing large teams of translators. In such
cases the licensee may well be reluctant to accept such limitations and may instead seek
to acquire an option to publish the next edition. The decision of the proprietors must then
depend on the circumstances (see note on option clause at the end of these notes).

3. The advance payment and royalty rates are to be inserted. If the advance is to be paid
in instalments rather than in full on signature of the contract, it is normally advisable to

specify that each instalment shall be paid by a designated calendar date rather than by dates which may be unpredictable, e.g. 'on publication of the Translation' or 'six months after publication of the Translation'. A compromise might be to specify that an instalment is payable 'on publication of the Translation or by [*date*], whichever is earlier'.

Royalty rates for translations normally take into account the fact that the licensee has additional costs for the translation work, either in the form of a royalty or an outright fee payable to the translator. It is customary for the royalty rates to escalate after an agreed level of sales has been reached. The royalty percentages and the level and number of the escalation points are of course open to negotiation between the parties. It is customary for different royalty rates to apply to hardback and paperback editions.

The wording 'catalogue retail price' is intended to allow for either the fixed retail price in countries where this is permitted or the publisher's recommended retail price. In some countries the price should be specified as less sales tax.

If the royalties are to be calculated on a basis other than on the catalogue retail price (e.g. on the wholesale price in countries where market circumstances make it impossible to set either a fixed or a recommended retail price) Clause 3(b) would have to be modified accordingly. In such cases it would be advisable to negotiate higher percentage royalty rates to allow for the lower price on which the calculation will be based.

When entering into agreements with French publishers, it should be remembered that it is sometimes their practice to insist on the inclusion of their *clause de passe* whereby royalties are payable on only 90 per cent of the number printed. The remaining 10 per cent is considered to be necessary to cover review copies, damaged copies and the practice of French booksellers expecting 'bakers' dozens', i.e. one free copy for every 12 ordered. This 10 per cent of royalties applies not only to the first printing (where an allowance for review copies, etc. would be expected) but to all printings.

If the contract is to be based on a lump sum for a designated printing rather than on an advance and royalty basis, Clause 3 should be amended to read:

'For the right to produce the aforesaid [*number*] copies of the Translation, the Publishers shall make the following payments to the Proprietors in accordance with the terms of Clause 19 hereof, namely:
A lump sum of   payable   on signature of this Agreement and   on publication of the Translation or by   [*date*] whichever is earlier.'

It is also highly advisable to add to this alternative clause some protection against inflation, since the lump sum will be calculated on the estimated price of the Translation at the time of the negotiations and the final price could well be significantly higher. Wording to cover this might read:

'Should the Translation be issued at a price higher than the estimated price of   the total payment due to the Proprietors shall be increased on publication of the Translation by a percentage equivalent to the increase in the price of the Translation.'

4. The contract is only valid when the proprietors have received the sum due on signature of the contract.

5. Since any proposed changes to the work in translation will almost certainly require consultation with the author, this clause provides for details of any changes or additions to be supplied in English. There is also provision for full approval of the translated text prior to the licensee commencing production, although in practice only a small number of manuscripts are likely to be vetted in this way. In such cases, approval should not be unreasonably withheld, and a response should be given within a reasonable time of receipt of the text of the translation (e.g. 60 days).

6. This clause is intended to alert both parties before they sign the contract to the need to agree which party will undertake any necessary reclearance for the reuse of copyright

The said payment in advance is not recoverable in the event of any default by the Publishers in carrying out the terms of this Agreement.

(b) On the catalogue retail price of all copies of the Translation sold by the Publishers:

    (i)   A royalty of   per cent on the first   thousand copies sold.

    (ii)   A royalty of   per cent on all copies sold between thousand and   thousand.

    (iii)   A royalty of   per cent on all copies sold beyond the first thousand.

(c) No royalty shall be payable on copies of the Translation presented in the interests of sale of the Translation, lost through theft or damaged or destroyed by fire, water, in transit or otherwise.

(d) On remainder copies of the Translation sold by the Publishers at or below cost no royalty shall be payable to the Proprietors but no such remainder copies shall be sold within a period of two years from the date of first publication of the Translation.

4. Should the Publishers fail to sign this Agreement within 60 days of signature by the Proprietors, or should the Proprietors not have received from the Publishers the sum by way of advance provided for herein within 60 days of signature of this Agreement by the Publishers, then this Agreement shall be deemed not to have come into effect, and all rights granted herein may at the sole option of the Proprietors and on notice in writing from the Proprietors to the Publishers revert to the Proprietors, without prejudice to any claim which the Proprietors may have for sums due, for damages or otherwise.

5. The Publishers shall arrange for the translation of the Work to be made at their own expense faithfully and accurately by a qualified and competent translator, whose name and qualifications shall be sent to the Proprietors. Abbreviations, alterations and/or additions shall only be made with the proper written consent of the Proprietors. Where such changes are agreed, details thereof are to be supplied by the Publishers in English if so requested by the Proprietors. The Publishers agree to include if requested by the Proprietors any new manuscript and/or illustrations supplied during the preparation of the Translation, such new manuscript and/or illustrations remaining the copyright of the Proprietors/Author. The Proprietors reserve the right to request the Publishers to submit the text of the Translation to the Proprietors for their prior written approval before commencing production of the Translation.

6. The Proprietors and the Publishers shall mutually agree responsibility for obtaining, wherever necessary, permission for the use in the Translation of copyright literary or artistic material incorporated in the Work and belonging to third parties, and shall also agree upon responsibility for paying any fees required for such permissions and for ensuring that

material controlled by external owners if the proprietors did not preclear rights for sublicensed editions; also who will pay any attendant fees. The circumstances of each book vary so much that it may be best to finalise the exact details by separate correspondence. A sharing of costs may at times be appropriate.

The proprietors reserve the right not to supply duplicate film of the illustrations in the work to the licensee until full reclearance has been obtained, as to do so earlier may place them in breach of their own contracts with the external copyright holders, such as picture agencies or museums.

7. It is recognised that in some countries it may not be possible to produce the licensed edition to standards comparable with that of the original edition.

8. It is advisable to spell out in detail the obligations of the licensee to credit the author properly; in some countries there can be a danger that the translator is credited more prominently, particularly if the translator is better known as an academic or educator in the market concerned.

It is also wise to spell out in full detail the exact text of the copyright notice relating to the original edition, to the original title (and edition number if appropriate) and the form in which acknowledgement should be made to the proprietors as the original publishers. The licensee should also add a copyright notice relating to the translated text. It is a favourite tendency of some publishers who are tardy in publishing a translation of a scientific book to omit the year of first publication from the copyright notice relating to the original edition, thus making the book appear more recent.

Since the introduction of moral rights in the UK Copyright, Designs and Patents Act 1988, some head contracts with British authors place a requirement on the British publisher to ensure that any editions published under licence reproduce the statement in the original work in which the author asserts his or her right of paternity. If this is the case, this obligation should be included in this clause, clearly specifying the required words of the statement.

9. This clause allows for provision of the required number of finished copies of the translation to be sent to the proprietors; a larger number will be required if there are several authors involved. There is an additional requirement to confirm details of the publication date and final price; the latter may indicate a rise in the estimated price which may necessitate calculation of a pro-rata increase if a lump sum arrangement has been negotiated (see note to Clause 3).

If any subsidiary rights have been granted under the terms of Clause 11, provision should also be made here for the supply of an agreed quantity of any sublicensed editions.

10. (a) The publication time limit will depend on the length and complexity of the book, but may also be affected if the content of the book is time sensitive; this might mean a short time limit for a highly newsworthy topic, or for computer books which have a short lifespan and are often licensed to appear in translation virtually simultaneously with the original edition. If the licensee subsequently has a valid reason for delay (e.g. the death of a specialised translator) the time limit can be extended by an addendum to the contract.

(b) The contract can be terminated if the translation goes out of print or off the market; it is important to have a clear understanding between the parties on what this means, and some publishers may choose to insert a definition e.g. if sales have fallen to less than x copies per year. It should however be remembered that if any subsidiary rights are permitted under the terms of Clause 11 it may be necessary to adjust this clause to permit any properly negotiated sublicences to continue to run their term.

For licences negotiated on the basis of a lump sum for a designated print run, the following wording should be substituted:

'The Publishers shall inform the Proprietors when the Translation goes out of print, whereupon all rights shall revert to the Proprietors, but the Publishers shall have the

appropriate acknowledgement is made in the Translation. The Proprietors reserve the right not to supply the Publishers with duplicate production material for any illustrations contained in the Work until such permission has been obtained.

7. The paper, printing, binding, jackets or covers, the promotion, the manner and extent of advertisement, the number and distribution of free copies for the press or otherwise, the pricing and terms of sale of the Translation shall be in the sole discretion of the Publishers who undertake to ensure that, wherever possible, the printing, paper and binding of the Translation shall be of the highest quality.

8. The Publishers undertake that the name of the Author shall appear in its customary form with due prominence on the title page, binding and jacket/cover of every copy of the Translation issued and on the reverse side of the title page shall appear the following copyright notice: '©   ' together with the following acknowledgement: 'This translation of   is published by arrangement with   '. The Publishers shall also include an appropriate copyright notice to cover the text of the Translation.

9. The Publishers shall supply the Proprietors with   free copies of the Translation on publication, together with details of the actual date of publication and the catalogue retail price of the Translation. The Proprietors shall have the right to purchase at normal trade terms further copies for personal use but not for resale.

10. (a)   In the event of the Publishers failing to issue the Translation within   months from the date of this Agreement all rights granted hereunder shall revert to the Proprietors without prejudice to any claim which the Proprietors may have for monies due, for damages or otherwise.

(b)   In the event of the Translation going out of print or off the market the Proprietors shall be at liberty to terminate this Agreement on giving to the Publishers six months' notice in writing to reprint the Translation and on the expiration of such period of six months should such reprint not have been made all rights granted under this Agreement shall revert to the Proprietors without prejudice to any claim which the Proprietors may have for monies due.

---

first option of producing and publishing a further printing of the Translation on terms to be agreed between the parties hereto and shall not proceed with publication of such further printing until written permission has been obtained from the Proprietors and terms have been agreed.'

Some licences may provide for ownership of the translated text to be transferred to the proprietors on termination of the contract.

11. This precedent confines the rights granted to volume rights only in the designated language; many specialist works licensed for translation do not have potential for the exploitation of sublicences.

For trade titles, the situation may well be different. If the licensee wishes to acquire a range of additional rights in the language and territories granted, these should be discussed at the negotiation stage and a division of the proceeds between the licensee and the proprietors should be agreed. In such cases, Clause 11 might be replaced by the following:

'In addition to the rights granted under Clause 1 hereof, the Proprietors hereby grant to the Publishers the following rights, subject to payment of the designated percentages of all monies received from the sale of such rights:

Reprint rights licensed to another publisher:	per cent
Book club rights licensed on a royalty basis:	per cent
First serial rights:	per cent
Second serial rights:	per cent
Digest and anthology rights:	per cent
Single voice reading rights for radio:	per cent

All such licences shall be subject to the prior written approval of the Proprietors, such approval not to be unreasonably withheld. All sums due to the Proprietors from such sales shall be paid to the Proprietors within six weeks of receipt by the Publishers.'

The inclusion of subsidiary rights in a translation licence assumes that the proprietors have themselves the authority to grant such rights (e.g. the literary agent representing the author may have held back first serial rights, film and television rights etc.). Each contract must be carefully negotiated according to the specific bundle of rights held by the proprietors.

It is normally unwise to include any form of electronic rights in a licence to a foreign publisher even if these are held by the proprietors, as this may jeopardise chances for an overall licence of electronic rights by the proprietors.

In some Scandinavian countries, broadcasting organisations are allowed to use extracts without permission from the copyright holder. Fees are paid for such use to an equivalent to the Performing Right Society and can be recovered only by someone whose business is registered in the Scandinavian country concerned. For such countries, therefore, it is important to allow control of broadcasting rights to be in the hands of local publishers.

It should also be remembered that the legislation of many communist or ex-communist countries permits very broad use of copyright material, often without permission or payment. This includes the right to quote from copyright works extensively 'provided the use is justified'; some countries also permit extracts from copyright works to be broadcast without permission or payment provided that the source is acknowledged.

The division of proceeds from sublicences between the foreign publisher and the proprietors may vary from 50/50 for all rights (common in the case of academic works) to 75/25 for sublicensed paperback rights and 80/20 in the case of first serial rights. Care should be taken that the proprietors receive a higher proportion of the receipts in the case of arrangements for paperback editions or book club editions produced by a publishing operation within the same publishing group as the licensee, i.e. a form of 'vertical publishing'. In such a case it may be possible to negotiate for the proprietors to receive the full royalty on the sublicensed edition and an additional advance.

12. Accounting is commonly half-yearly in the Anglo-American tradition, and yearly in the Continental tradition; the clause offers alternative wording. Some countries (in particular in Scandinavia) ask for three months in which to render statements and a further six months in which to render any monies due. This practice should be resisted; a further three months may be acceptable.

NB this clause covers accounting for royalties on the licensee's own edition of the book; if subsidiary rights are granted under the terms of Clause 11, provision is made for

11. The Publishers shall not dispose of any subsidiary rights in the Translation without obtaining the prior written consent of the Proprietors.

12. Accounts for the sale of the Translation shall be made up twice annually/annually by the Publishers to [30 June and] 31 December and the account rendered together with any sums payable for such sales within three months of the accounting date/s. Accounts will show:

(a) the number of copies in stock if any, at the beginning of the accounting period
(b) the number of copies printed if any, during the accounting period
(c) the number of copies sold during the accounting period
(d) the number of copies presented during the accounting period and
(e) the number of copies remaining in stock at the end of the accounting period

and accounts and royalties shall be paid in accordance with the provisions of Clause 19 hereof.

Should any of the payments detailed in this Agreement be three months overdue the licence herein granted shall forthwith lapse and all rights conveyed by it shall, without further notice, revert to the Proprietors without prejudice to any claim the Proprietors may have for monies due, for damages or otherwise.

The Proprietors or their authorised representative shall have the right upon written request to examine the records of accounts of the Publishers in so far as they relate to sales and receipts in respect of the Translation, which examination shall be at the cost of the Proprietors unless errors exceeding   per cent of such sales and receipts in the last two preceding accounting periods to their disadvantage shall be found, in which case the cost shall be paid by the Publishers.

13. The Publishers undertake not to reprint the Translation without first informing the Proprietors and obtaining their consent in writing.

---

the proprietors' share of such income to be remitted within 60 days of receipt from the sublicensees.

If the licence has been granted on a lump sum basis, it will be sufficient to retain for Clause 12 only the penultimate paragraph of the precedent, 'Should any of the payments detailed in this Agreement …'.

13. This clause appears even in the advance and royalty agreement as a safeguard against the licensee continuing to print copies of an edition which may have been found to be unsatisfactory, either in terms of translation or production quality. Clearance for further printings can be obtained swiftly by fax or e-mail.

14. The proprietors provide warranties and indemnities to the licensee under English law since they cannot be expected to be familiar with the exact details of legislation in the country of the licensee. Care should be taken to ensure that the warranties and indemnities match those given to the proprietors by the author. If the licensee requires further warranties (e.g. against libel or obscenity) these can be granted under English law provided that the author has provided such warranties to the proprietors.

15. If subsidiary rights have been granted to the licensees under the terms of Clause 11, this clause should be amended to read:

'The licence hereby granted to the Publishers shall not be transferred to or extended to include any other party other than in connection with sublicences properly granted under the terms of Clause 11 hereof; nor shall the Translation appear under any imprint other than that of the Publishers or their duly authorised sublicensees, except with the prior written consent of the Proprietors.'

18. Whilst arbitration under the terms of the country of the proprietors may be preferable, publishers in some communist or ex-communist countries may not accept this. A compromise might be to substitute the following wording providing for arbitration in a neutral territory:

'If any difference shall arise between the Publishers and the Proprietors touching the meaning of this Agreement and the rights and liabilities of the parties hereto, the same shall be referred to arbitration via the Chamber of Commerce in Stockholm, Sweden.'

19. If the accounting department of the proprietors is located at a different address from the main address given at the commencement of the contract, details should be inserted into this clause.

Licensees in some countries (e.g. Latin America, central and eastern Europe, the former Soviet Union and mainland China) may find it easier to remit payment in US dollars and this point should therefore be discussed at the negotiation stage. It may then be preferable to specify all payments in Clause 3 in dollars.

Documentation on any tax deductions is required for those British publishers who are entitled to set such deductions against corporation tax.

14. The Proprietors hereby warrant to the Publishers that they have the right and power to make this Agreement and that according to English law the Work will in no way whatever give rise to a violation of any existing copyright, or a breach of any existing agreement and that nothing in the Work is liable to give rise to a criminal prosecution or to a civil action for damages or any other remedy and the Proprietors will indemnify the Publishers against any loss, injury or expense arising out of any breach of this warranty. If in the opinion of the Publishers and on the advice of their legal advisers the Work contains any passage that may reasonably be considered actionable at law in the territories granted to the Publishers under this Agreement, the Publishers shall have the right upon prior written notice to the Proprietors to modify or to remove such passage from the Translation.

15. The licence hereby granted to the Publishers shall not be transferred to or extended to include any other party; nor shall the Translation appear under any imprint other than that of the Publishers, except with the prior written consent of the Proprietors.

16. All rights in the Work, other than those specifically granted to the Publishers under this Agreement, are reserved by the Proprietors.

17. In the event of the Publishers being declared bankrupt or should they fail to comply with any of the provisions of this Agreement and not rectify such failure within one month of having received written notice from the Proprietors to do so by a registered letter sent to the Publishers at their address given at the commencement of this Agreement, then in either event this Agreement automatically becomes null and void and the licence granted to the Publishers herein shall revert to the Proprietors without prejudice to any monies paid or due to the Proprietors.

18. If any difference shall arise between the Publishers and the Proprietors touching the meaning of this Agreement or the rights and liabilities of the parties hereto, the same shall be referred to the arbitration of two persons (one to be named by each party) or their umpire, in accordance with the provisions of the Arbitration Act 1996 or any subsisting statutory modification or re-enactment thereof, provided that any dispute between the parties hereto not resolved by arbitration or agreement shall be submitted to the jurisdiction of the English courts.

19. All sums which may become due to the Proprietors under this Agreement shall be paid by the Publishers in sterling without any deduction in respect of exchange or commission. Payment may be remitted either by cheque or bank draft sent by post to the Royalty Department of the Proprietors or by direct bank transfer to the Proprietors' bank account number at   .
    Should the Publishers be obliged by law to deduct tax they shall send a declaration to this effect with the relevant statement of account showing the amount deducted.

21. In the Anglo-American tradition, it is the proprietors' jurisdiction that is usually stated as applicable (although American publishers increasingly insist on their own jurisdiction whether they are buying or selling rights). The issue must be faced and settled before signature of the contract, otherwise it may actually be unlawful from the start, especially if the law chosen is that of one of the Continental countries which limit the transfer of rights in publishing contracts, e.g. Switzerland, Germany, France or Italy. An excellent note in the Contract Column of Rights, Vol. 4, No. 1, by Andre Bertrand on the subject concludes:

'The choice of applicable law is therefore the first question to be resolved in the transnational contract. Once this choice has been made by the parties they can proceed to write a publishing contract which is in conformity with this law. If the parties do not respect this rule, they risk drawing up a contract that will not be legal with regard to the stipulations of the law to which the contract will be submitted in the event of a dispute.'

It should be noted that some communist or ex-communist countries may not be prepared to accept a contract which is operable under the law of the proprietors. Compromise wording might be:

'Any dispute between the parties not resolved by arbitration or agreement shall be decided by the court of the summoned party.'

22. Some countries have formal registration procedures in order to secure copyright protection. This clause places the obligation on the licensee to fulfil any such procedures and also to take action against any infringement within the market granted.

Agency arrangements: if the deal has been arranged via a sub-agent in the country concerned, it will be necessary to cover this in the contract:

'All payments due under this Agreement are to be made via [*name and address of agent*] and will be subject to   per cent agency commission.'

Option clause: some licensees may seek to acquire an option either on the next edition of the work (see note to Clause 1) or on the next book to be written by the author. If the proprietors agree to this, the following clause could be inserted:

'The Proprietors agree to grant to the Publishers the first option on the [*language*] translation rights for the next edition of the Work/the next work by the Author providing rights in such work are controlled by the Proprietors. The Publishers shall reach a decision within 60 days of receipt of suitable material from the Proprietors and any licence arrangements will then be covered by a separate agreement on terms to be agreed between the parties.'

20. Any and all notices given hereunder shall be in writing and sent by telex, fax, e-mail or registered mail to the parties at their respective addresses herein specified. The parties undertake to notify each other of any change of address within 30 days of such change.

21. This Agreement shall be governed by and interpreted and construed in accordance with the laws of England.

22. The Publishers agree to take any necessary steps to register the title of the Work in the name of the Proprietors/Author under local copyright laws at the sole expense of the Publishers. The Publishers also agree to protect such copyright and to prosecute at their own expense any person who infringes such copyright in the territories granted to them under this Agreement.

APPENDIX

Markets in Transition: The People's Republic of China, Central and Eastern Europe and the former Soviet Union

In previous editions of *Publishing Agreements*, the appendices to Precedent Eight have dealt with the sale of rights to the Soviet Union and its successor states and the People's Republic of China. These markets still merit some special treatment and coverage has been combined in this edition into a single appendix which also deals with the markets of central and eastern Europe.

The People's Republic of China

Introduction

For many years the People's Republic of China was the largest country in the world remaining outside membership of the Berne Convention and the Universal Copyright Convention; foreign books and journals were reprinted and translated in China on a vast scale, usually without permission from or payment to the original publisher and the author. Foreign recorded music, video tapes, computer software and CD-ROMs have also been reproduced on a huge scale with consequent losses to the industries concerned.

Domestic copyright legislation was finally introduced on 1 June 1991, at which point the authorities reiterated their intention to seek membership of both conventions. Although the domestic legislation contained a number of welcome features, including a term of copyright protection of fifty years *post mortem auctoris*, a number of other areas including very broad provisions for fair dealing, the blanket use of copyright works by the state, and lack of automatic protection for foreign works except through membership of an international convention, gave cause for concern and at the time of writing the legislation is under review; it is likely to deal amongst other items with the issues of photocopying and electrocopying which were not covered in the 1991 legislation.

Following strong trade pressure from the west (in particular from the United States) China finally acceded to the Berne Convention on 15 October 1992, to the Universal Copyright Convention on 30 October 1992 and to the Geneva Phonogram Convention on 1 June 1993. In the case of Berne and UCC, China ratified the Paris texts of 1971, although as yet there has been no evidence of its seeking access to compulsory licences. China also agreed to provide retrospective protection to all US works created before the signing date of a bilateral accord between the two countries provided that those works were still protected by copyright under US domestic legislation. Following a 'period of grace' until 15 October 1993 to allow Chinese publishers to dispose of unauthorised stock, British works published from the October 1992 dates onwards are protected through mutual membership of the conventions.

Despite membership of the conventions, piracy continues in China although the music, video and software industries are now probably more seriously affected than the book industry. A number of successful prosecutions have been brought on behalf of foreign copyright holders with the assistance of the National Copyright Administration of China, and there are special intellectual property divisions in the regional courts. It is however likely to be some time before western copyright holders can be sure of better compliance.

Method of payment

Until 1980 Chinese authors were salaried, regardless of the size or frequency of their output. In April 1980 the National Publishing Administration of China formulated *Provisional Regulations on Remunerations for Book Writing* which were applied to domestic authors on an experimental basis. The regulations were updated and payment rates revised in 1983. The system was socialist in concept and was in many ways similar to that introduced in the former Soviet Union in 1973. Payment was linked primarily to the length of the book, with basic rates on a scale per 1000 characters, with the possibility of higher rates for works of exceptional quality. An additional 'print remuneration' was allowed, calculated as a percentage of the basic rate for the book in question, and diminishing as the print run increased.

Although the Chinese publishing industry is still state-controlled, Chinese publishers are now able to negotiate payment to their own authors without the use of the old scales. The main problem for foreign publishers wishing to license to China is still the shortage of direct access to hard currency.

There is also still much to learn in terms of applying for rights from the west, and even the larger publishing houses can still behave in an unorthodox manner. It is still a common scenario for a western author to be approached by an individual Chinese translator, who has either already translated a book by that author or is intending to do so. Usually there is no mention of payment or even the name of the publishing house concerned. The author is often asked to confirm that he or she has no objection to the translation going ahead free of charge, and in some cases the author may also be asked to provide revisions or a special preface to the Chinese edition. It has unfortunately been the case that many authors – most of them unaware of the copyright history of China – have gladly endorsed such translations, even in cases where the copyright has been assigned to the British publishing house or where rights are within the control of the publisher.

Such endorsements make it extremely difficult to enter into negotiations with the translator and the Chinese publisher at a later stage.

Where an approach is first received from an individual translator, it is usually advisable to respond by explaining that negotiations must be undertaken with the publishing house or academic institute concerned. Care can be taken to explain that whilst the British publisher is aware of factors such as the relatively new recognition of copyright, low book prices in China, and the shortage of hard currency available, a book represents a major investment of expertise, time and money by the author and the original publishing house, and these factors should be recognised if the book is to be used in China. Any commercial negotiation should be conducted with the Chinese publishing house or institute rather than with the individual translator; however, in the area of academic publishing it has become apparent that many individual translators are actually paying Chinese publishers to subsidise the cost of publication of the translation. It is important to stress that there is now a legal obligation to pay for the rights but that this should not be the responsibility of the individual translator. There have been cases of individual translators offering several months of their salary for the rights or of Chinese publishers threatening to withdraw from publication (to the distress of the translator) if the foreign copyright holder or his representative requires payment. It is vital to continue to reinforce the principle of copyright recognition and avoid waiving copyright fees, whilst recognising the economic reality of the individual situation.

Before China's accession to the conventions in October 1992, it was recommended that western publishers should explore alternative avenues to transferable royalty payments, such as payment in blocked currency, sponsorship of an author's visit to China or some modest gifts for the author. Some form of payment should now be negotiated; it should however be remembered that book prices are still very low by comparison with western standards and print runs for specialised academic books can be very modest. Since the beginning of 1994 it is easier for Chinese publishers to remit modest sums of hard currency abroad on production of a valid licence contract to their bank. For larger sums (for example, for reprint licences of English language teaching materials or dictionaries where licensed printings can be substantial) some publishers may still offer part payment in blocked currency. This is now more easily used for expenses within China since the abolition of the Foreign Exchange Certificate (FEC) system, and may be attractive to western publishers who visit the market regularly.

Whatever the mode of payment, it is still preferable to negotiate for a lump sum equivalent to an agreed royalty percentage of the local price for a designated print run, and to renew the licence for further printings if appropriate. This corresponds with the existing Chinese system of payment for their own authors and has the added advantage that licensing policy can be regularly reviewed. Some Chinese publishers may be prepared to pay the whole lump sum on signature of the contract; others may wish to make the total payment within three months of completion of printing of the designated quantity.

Contracts

When contracting with China a number of points are worth bearing in mind.

The sales territory for the licensed edition (whether it is a translation or a local reprint edition) should be limited to the mainland territory of the People's Republic of China only, and a clear market restriction notice to this effect should appear both on the cover and on the title verso of the licensed edition. If the work is to be translated rather than reprinted in the original language, the licence should be for the Chinese language in simplified character form.

It should of course be remembered that the PRC is not the only Chinese language market where rights can be licensed: Hong Kong, Singapore and Taiwan all have strong local publishing industries and higher customer purchasing power than the mainland, despite their smaller populations. The markets differ linguistically, economically and politically and these differences may affect licensing strategy and should certainly be reflected in contractual arrangements with the different markets. Chinese editions published for the PRC or Singapore will utilise simplified characters, whilst Hong Kong and Taiwan use traditional characters. It must however be remembered that the PRC views Taiwan as a province rather than as an independent country; trade between the two markets has been increasing in recent years despite the continuing ideological divide and the rise in political tensions in 1996 and there is therefore a need to make a clear geographical as well as a linguistic distinction when defining licences to the two markets. The fact that many western publishers and literary agents have chosen to allow world Chinese rights to be handled via Taiwanese publishers or sub-agents such as the Big Apple-Tuttle Mori Agency and the Bardon Chinese Media Agency in Taipei is a source of considerable annoyance to mainland publishers, although it was understandable when there were more barriers to remitting hard currency from the mainland that payment via Taiwan was attractive to some western copyright holders.

From 1 July 1997 political rule of Hong Kong will be transferred to China. It may therefore be advisable to consider carefully the duration of any Chinese licences granted to publishers in the region and whether Hong Kong should specifically be excluded from the territory granted to a mainland publisher. It is as yet unclear whether China may seek to introduce the use of simplified characters in Hong Kong, which would then remove another means of distinguishing between licences to what are currently separate markets.

The following clause should be included as an obligation on the licensee:

'The Publishers have already reported the details of the Translation/ Licensed Edition to the China National Copyright Administration and

147

have received approval to use all endeavours to protect the copyright in the Translation/Licensed Edition within the People's Republic of China according to the appropriate regulations of that country. The Publishers further agree to prosecute at their own expense any person or organisation who infringes such copyright.'

It is unlikely that the Chinese authorities will agree that the contract should be operable under UK law. The following wording is considered acceptable:

'This Agreement is made subject to the laws of the People's Republic of China and any disputes or differences arising between the parties in respect of the construction or otherwise of this Agreement shall be referred to the Chinese International Economic and Trade Arbitration Committee and the decision of the Committee shall be final and binding upon both parties hereto.'

Literary agents
There are no private literary agencies operating in mainland China. The Copyright Agency of China in Beijing is a state-owned organisation operating from the same offices as the National Copyright Administration of China. There are also a number of small regional agencies in the individual provinces which can provide assistance to Chinese publishers seeking to make contact with western copyright holders.

Central and Eastern Europe

Introduction
Depending on the pace of political change in the individual countries, it has been possible to establish private publishing houses in the region from the late 1980s following many years of publishing industries which were totally controlled by the state. The initial result was a surge in private publishing enterprises; at the same time, a number of state houses sought to diversify from their monopoly subject areas as a means of survival, and some sought to privatise either with the help of foreign investment or through partial or total staff buy-outs.

All these developments led to a boom in rights purchases from the west, in particular of mass market titles in areas such as romance, crime and science fiction and titles which had hitherto been unavailable for political reasons. The euphoria was short lived. Many private publishers went out of business in less than a year, in some cases leaving substantial debts to western publishers in the form of unpaid licence royalties or invoices for co-editions. In some cases this was due to simple over-optimism combined with inexperience and unrealistic expectations of the market. Others were out to make a fast buck and move on the other forms of entrepreneurship. The more serious private publishing houses have survived, although they are now forced to be more realistic about print runs in competitive markets.

Because of the huge desire to learn English in all countries in the region (English is often the passport to a better job with a western company) there was a visible increase in the number of applications for local English language reprint licences for English language teaching materials and dictionaries. Here the licensing policy must depend on the individual market and the British publisher's plans for that market; for example, in Poland the licensing arrangements which had started in the 1960s and 1970s as the only means of accessing the ELT market have tended to be reduced if not terminated completely as British publishers were able to set up distribution arrangements, agents or subsidiary companies. As local manufacturing costs and purchasing power increased, it made little sense to license rights in key projects as the Polish licensee would have difficulty in producing an edition more cheaply than that of the original publisher. For some markets however (Albania and Romania in particular) it may still make sense to operate a careful licensing policy.

At the time of writing, the upheaval in the publishing industry has settled down somewhat although there are still variations from country to country. The boom in translating western mass market titles has started to slow down as the novelty wears off and in some cases there is a perceptible backlash against the flood of western goods which have appeared in the markets. It is to be hoped that this may encourage a return to the publication of more upmarket fiction by both domestic and foreign authors as well as better circumstances for the publication of specialist academic literature. In all countries in the region, the state publishers have been the hardest hit; without the subsidised paper costs, printing facilities and guaranteed sales to state outlets which they enjoyed for so many years, they have been forced to make radical cuts to their publishing programmes, their print runs and their staff, and have been forced to diversify their publishing programmes in order to survive. They have also had to face competition in the marketplace, something unknown in the time of state-controlled publishing programmes. They face the particular problem that paper and production costs are now at world levels, whilst their target readership – academics, professionals and the intelligentsia – are often on salaries of less than US $100 a month. Many publishers are only able to continue to publish specialised foreign literature with the help of translation subsidy programmes such as those run by the French, German and US governments (the United Kingdom unfortunately has no official scheme) or organisations such as the Soros Foundation.

The picture in the private sector varies from country to country. Poland and the Czech Republic have developed relatively healthy private publishing industries alongside the remaining state houses, whilst in countries such as Romania and Albania private publishing is conducted in very difficult circumstances. Publishers in some countries such as Bulgaria started with high hopes which have increasingly been eroded by factors such as inflation and stringent government regulations which threaten to stifle private enterprise. In all countries in the region the huge interest rates charged for business loans make it difficult to rely on borrowing to start or to expand a business.

Copyright
With the exception of Albania, all of the former eastern bloc countries belonged to one or both of the two international copyright conventions in communist times. Those who acquired new status (e.g. the Czech and Slovak Republics) introduced new domestic copyright legislation as a prelude to seeking convention membership as independent states. Albania finally acceded to the Berne Convention in 1994. Almost all countries in the region have introduced new domestic copyright legislation since 1990 in order to deal with new technological developments and also to reflect movement from a command to a market economy. It is however apparent that some vestiges of socialist copyright philosophy remain in the new legislations, in particular in the area of the very wide 'fair dealing' permitted for educational, academic and research purposes which is likely to be detrimental to the interests of local authors and publishers as well as to foreign copyright holders. Most of the legislations also contain quite stringent restrictions on the form of contract between creator and user, and in some cases impose very short terms on contracts between authors and publishers.

One of the penalties of the opening up of these markets was the arrival of full-scale piracy, a phenomenon which had not existed when both the publishing and the printing industries were controlled by the state. The prime targets were translations of western best-sellers and this was often extremely damaging not only to the foreign copyright holder but also to the legitimate licensee who often saw pirated editions on the streets before the authorised edition had reached the market. Although the new bodies of domestic legislation provide for the first time for penalties against infringement, the severity of punishment varies from country to country with relatively few imposing prison sentences on offenders. The real problem is the lack of an effective enforcement mechanism, combined with the fact that the rise in violent crime throughout the region can be a very real deterrent to taking official action.

Method of payment
Relatively few publishers in the region are yet in a position to monitor sales and returns accurately enough to be able to administer a western-style advance and royalty system; there are now a few exceptions to this in Poland. For the time being, it is still preferable to work on the basis of a lump sum to cover an agreed print run, although the old communist system of paying a proportion (usually 25 per cent of the total) on signature of the contract and the full balance on publication may now be unrealistic given the cash flows faced by small private publishers in all these markets, even though they aim to dispose of their print run within weeks or a few months of publication. A compromise might be to formulate a lump sum payable in instalments: perhaps 25 per cent on signature of the contract, 25 per cent

on publication or by an agreed 'latest date', 25 per cent six months later and 25 per cent 12 months later.

A key point of which western publishers should be aware is that very few publishers in the region are able to set reliable retail prices for their books and indeed in all these markets the same book may be seen at wildly differing prices from bookshop to bookshop or from stall to stall. The preferred unit for calculating the royalty percentage on which any lump sum is based is therefore the wholesale price, i.e. the price received by the publisher from their distributors; this could be anything from 25 per cent to 50 per cent less than the price at which the book is on sale to the end customer. The wholesale price is often referred to by local publishers as the 'publisher's price' which can mislead western publishers unused to the market into assuming it is the retail price. It is therefore wise to obtain a definition of the price from each licensee and to negotiate a higher royalty percentage to allow for the discounted price.

Since inflation is rife in all these markets it is also wise to include in any lump sum contract a provision to increase later instalments of the lump sum once the final price is known (see note to Clause 3 of Precedent Eight).

The preferred hard currency in the region remains the US dollar and it is usually advisable to specify all amounts in this currency. Publishers in some countries may require signed and stamped invoices for all amounts due in addition to the licence contract itself, and this should be checked with the licensee.

Most publishers in the region now seem prepared to accept licence contracts which are governed by the law of the country of the western publisher.

It is still recommended that if copies are being manufactured by the western publisher for a publisher in central and eastern Europe as part of a co-edition, extra care is employed to take up references on new contacts. Prepayment of a significant proportion of the total prior to commencement of manufacture can be a partial safeguard and payment against a letter of credit can also be wise.

Literary agents
The monopolies of the state literary agencies which operated in most countries in the region have long been abolished, although some of them still exist in the form of collecting societies for areas such as performing rights.

Whereas western educational and academic publishers have long travelled to the region, many trade publishers have chosen instead to delegate licensing to specialist agents. The agencies of Gerd Plessl and Jovan Milankovic entered the markets early and secured a wide range of lists containing many major western authors.

On the whole, publishers in the region would far prefer to work direct for reasons of speed and efficiency, but many of the larger western trade publishers continue to rely on intermediaries in markets which they still regard as volatile. A number of local agents have now been established in the individual markets, and the UK agent Andrew Nurnberg has recently established offices in Bulgaria, Latvia, Poland, the Czech Republic, Hungary and Romania.

The former Soviet Union

Introduction

Much of what has been covered above applies also to the territories of the former Soviet Union: now 15 independent states (the Russian Federation, Ukraine, Belarus, Georgia, Moldova, Armenia, Azerbaijan, Uzbekhistan, Kazakhstan, Kirghizstan, Tadzhikistan, Turkmenistan and the three Baltic states of Estonia, Latvia and Lithuania). At the time of writing, all belong to the Commonwealth of Independent States (CIS) with the exception of the Baltic states.

All of the state publishing houses continue to exist (although at the time of writing the activities of Nauka, the publishing arm of the Russian Academy of Sciences, had been temporarily suspended). All have been forced to cut their staff, print runs and publishing programmes. Some have adapted better than others to the new circumstances; the most successful have diversified in order to survive and to subsidise their traditional publishing fields, whilst others appear to be in a state of paralysis. Many are only able to publish academic works with the help of occasional funding from the federal subsidy programme.

A host of private publishing houses were established as soon as this was legally possible, some of which disappeared virtually overnight and some of which have survived. Those which have flourished have tended to start their programmes by publishing translations of western bestsellers, but some have gone on to invest the profits in publishing more serious literature.

Both state and private publishers face similar problems; the massive increase in the cost of paper and printing, the withdrawal of most state assistance either in the form of paper allocation or in guaranteed sales through the state distribution system, and the total collapse of that distribution system. In Russia in particular, publishers are often only able to guarantee distribution of their books in the Moscow and St Petersburg regions; the cost and practicalities of distributing effectively through such a vast geographical region are daunting. Some of the more enterprising and successful private publishers have invested in their own vans and trucks. This situation should be taken into account when dealing with licences to the region; it makes little sense to grant Russian translation rights to one publisher for the whole of the CIS or even for a substantial number of the constituent states if the publisher has no means of covering those territories. Russian is of course still widely spoken throughout the former Republics and some publishers have been able to set up distribution arrangements in a small number of key states such as Ukraine, Belarus, Kazakhstan and the Baltics as well as the Russian Federation itself. The question of defining licences by both language and geographical territory therefore needs careful thought.

There is increasing interest in the learning of English and hence an increasing number of licence requests for English language reprint rights or bilingual rights for English language teaching materials and dictionaries. Here much will depend on the overall policy of the British publisher for the region; if representation, agencies or distribution arrangements have already been set up for ELT materials then licensing may not be attractive. There is also a considerable danger of leakage of licensed editions over borders, not just within the territory of the former Soviet Union but also into markets such as Poland and other central and eastern European countries where distribution of the original edition may be better established.

Copyright

The Soviet Union acceded to the Universal Copyright Convention on 27 May 1973. Copyright legislation within the Soviet Union was covered by a section of the Civil Code of each Republic. Since independence, it is necessary for each newly-formed state to introduce its own domestic copyright legislation and decide whether to join one or both of the conventions. At the time of writing, Russia, Ukraine, Belarus, Kazakhstan, Armenia and the Baltic states have all introduced new domestic legislation and new laws are in preparation in other states. In particular, the extension of the period of copyright protection in Russia from 25 to 50 years *post-mortem auctoris* enabled that country to accede to the Berne Convention on 13 March 1995, albeit with the proviso that foreign works first published before 27 May 1973 remain in the public domain in Russia. At the time of writing, Russia, Estonia, Georgia, Latvia, Lithuania, Moldova and Ukraine have acceded to the Berne Convention, whilst Russia, Belarus, Kazakhstan, Tadzhikistan and Ukraine retain their membership of the Universal Copyright Convention.

The discrepancies in the levels of domestic copyright protection and international copyright recognition between individual states means that piracies can take place in one market with copies then transported across the border to larger markets such as the Russian Federation.

Piracy of books, music tapes, audio-visual tapes and CDs is endemic in Russia and in many of the other former Republics. The new Russian domestic copyright law of 1993 introduced penalties for copyright infringement under both civil and criminal law but relatively few successful actions have been brought because of the high cost of a court case and the very real danger of violence from mafia connections.

Method of payment

The monopoly of the old Soviet copyright agency, VAAP, was abolished on 1 January 1991 although it still exists in much reduced form as a Russian authors' organisation, initially RAIS and currently RAO. It continues to administer collective arrangements such as performing rights. There is still a substantial debt to foreign copyright holders for licences arranged through VAAP during the Soviet period; this has remained unpaid since the Russian government froze the agency's hard currency account.

Whilst in principle the removal of state controls on licensing is to be welcomed, it has had a major effect on the availability of hard currency for the purchase of rights. In the past, Soviet publishers made payment to VAAP in roubles and VAAP then remitted hard currency to foreign copyright holders from its own hard currency earnings (in particular from the rights in the works of Russian composers). Now that facility has been removed and publishers must rely on their own resources to buy rights. Technically hard currency can be remitted abroad and the favoured currency remains the US dollar. The exchange rate has stabilised in the last two years but the future is unpredictable and most of the debts to foreign copyright holders frozen through VAAP were negotiated at a time when one rouble was equivalent to one pound sterling. It is therefore still a market where caution is advisable; it is preferable to structure licence deals in the form of a lump sum to cover a designated number of copies, with as much of the total as possible payable on signature of the contract. With new publishers still appearing and disappearing overnight, it is wise to take up as many references as possible when dealing with a new contact, and to work on letters of credit or substantial prepayment if supplying printed copies or expensive printing film. A number of western publishers now refuse to supply film to publishers in the region because of the danger of piracy or overproduction of copies beyond the terms of the contract which are then not accounted for. Abuse of this kind has been undertaken by some publishers but also by their printers. Mafia pressure (and indeed involvement) is not unknown in both the publishing and the printing sectors.

Literary agents

As outlined above, RAO is no longer a channel for individual licence deals. Two western literary agents have specialised in selling rights to the region; the Andrew Nurnberg agency has offices in Moscow, whilst David Matlock operates out of St Petersburg.

PRECEDENT NINE
Same-Language Low Price Reprint Agreement

The Revised 1971 Paris Texts of the Berne Convention and of the Universal Copyright Convention established new rules to facilitate the access of the developing countries to compulsory licences for translations, reprints of works in the original languages and audio-visual materials. The rules cover 'world', 'local' and other languages. Since English is, together with Spanish and French, a 'world' language, there is clearly some incentive among British publishers and authors to arrange voluntary licences whose terms can be negotiated, rather than to become subject to compulsory licences over which they have no control. For this reason, large-scale compulsory licensing has on the whole been avoided to date. Nevertheless, British publishers owe it to themselves and to their authors to remember that the word 'voluntary' conceals the granting of economic and cultural aid to developing countries not out of the British Government's aid programme but out of the pockets of authors and publishers.

It is perhaps worth pointing out here that a same-language compulsory licence can only be granted if the work is not available in the country concerned at a price considered sufficiently low for the market. The availability of the work in an ELBS edition produced with the aid of a British government subsidy or a special cheap edition produced by the original publisher for sale in developing countries could be held to preclude the granting of a compulsory licence, and certainly these avenues should be fully explored before agreeing to grant a reprint licence. It should be noted that it has been a condition of the ELBS scheme that any title included in the programme must not be licensed for translation or local reprinting in the designated ELBS territories.

Under the compulsory licence rules, same-language reprints must be of works used in connection with 'systematic instructional activities'. The needs of the developing countries are predominantly in applied science, although there are also many applications for such works as dictionaries and books for the teaching of English as a foreign language. The period from first publication after which a compulsory licence can be enforced is for the natural and physical sciences and technical works only three years; for fiction, poetry, drama and art, it is seven years; for all other types of work, five years. Scientific and technical publishers therefore need to be especially alert to making arrangements for low-cost editions of their books soon after first publication, either under their own imprints or through the medium of carefully controlled voluntary licences to reliable partners. The pressure from developing countries will not lessen and at the time of writing the ELBS scheme is destined to end in April 1997; if no alternative scheme is introduced, this may lead to an increased number of applications for licences and indeed to the granting of compulsory licences.

Since the late 1980s there has been a significant increase in licence requests for the newly independent countries of central and eastern Europe and the former Soviet Union; many requests tend to be for reprint rights in English language teaching materials and dictionaries, with books in other categories more likely to be translated into the local language. Whilst there is undoubtedly a demand for foreign books as these countries have gained better access to the west, the price gap which has justified licensing is now narrowing in many of the countries concerned; the removal of most government subsidies and the requirement to purchase paper at world prices makes it difficult for local publishers in some countries to undercut western prices. Direct sales of the original publisher's own edition or of a special low-cost edition such as those introduced for certain subject areas in 1991 under the British government Know-How Fund Low Price British Books Scheme (LPBB) may be preferable to granting a licence if local distribution can be assured. Books subsidised under the LPBB scheme are also precluded from being licensed for translation or reprinting in the designated LPBB territories. British publishers may still choose to license non-subsidised titles to some countries if publication under a local imprint is perceived to give better access to the market concerned.

MEMORANDUM OF AGREEMENT made this day
of   19
Between   of   (hereinafter termed the Publishers) of
the one part, and   of   (hereinafter termed the
Proprietors) of the other part

WHEREAS the Proprietors are the proprietors of a work by
(hereinafter termed the Author), entitled: [no. of]
Edition   (hereinafter termed the Work),

NOW IT IS HEREBY MUTUALLY AGREED AS FOLLOWS:

1. Subject to the terms detailed in this Agreement, the Proprietors hereby
grant to the Publishers the exclusive licence to produce and publish a single
printing of   copies only of the Work in hardback/paperback volume
form in the English language under the Publishers' own imprint (hereinafter
termed the Licensed Edition) for sale throughout   only. This
restricted circulation is to be clearly indicated on the outside of the cover
and on the reverse of the title page of the Licensed Edition by the following
words: 'Licensed for sale in   only; not for export.'

2. The Publishers shall make the following payment/s to the Proprietors in
accordance with the provisions of Clause 12 hereof:

Preamble
The licence should be specifically limited to the current edition of the book in question.
This is particularly important since the majority of requests for such licences will be for
educational and academic titles which will be regularly revised by the original publishers.

1. As this is a voluntary licence, the right is exclusive but is limited to a single printing of
a specified number of copies in the country concerned. No subsidiary rights of any kind
are conveyed and are specifically reserved by Clause 10. The work must appear under the
imprint of the licensee; this is stressed here as there have been cases of publishers in the
developing countries deliberately producing reprints which externally appear to have been
published by the proprietors; in other cases the reprints have been reproduced under a joint
imprint without permission from the proprietors. The sales territory granted must be
clearly defined and a market restriction notice must appear clearly on both the cover and
title verso of the reprint; this will facilitate legal action if copies appear outside the
specified territory.

2. The method of payment chosen will depend very much on the individual circumstances
of each licence application, and may also be influenced by copyright or exchange control
regulations in the country concerned. Ideally, it would be preferable to specify that a single
lump sum should be paid for the right to produce the printing specified in Clause 1, and
that the entire amount should be payable on signature of the agreement; an alternative
might be half payable on signature of the agreement and the balance on publication of the
licensed edition or by an agreed 'latest date' as an incentive to prompt publication.

Publishers in the countries of central and eastern Europe, the former Soviet Union and
the People's Republic of China have traditionally worked on the basis of a lump sum
payment for a designated print run quantity, usually with an advance payment on signature
of the contract and the balance on publication. This stemmed from the fact that many titles

sold out immediately or within a few months of publication, making yearly or twice-yearly royalty accounting inappropriate. As these countries move towards a market economy with higher prices and sales no longer guaranteed through the state system, it is likely that publishers there may wish to move over to a western-style advance and royalty system; however, this is only really practical where there is firm evidence that the publisher concerned has the facilities to track sales and returns accurately. It may therefore still be wise to work on a lump sum basis. See also the Appendix to Precedent Eight.

A lump sum arrangement is particularly desirable when licensing to countries where remitting payment abroad may be notoriously complicated or slow. However, the amount payable for some licences (particularly if the print run is large) may exceed the maximum amount which can be remitted at any one time, and in such cases payment in instalments or an advance and royalty arrangement may be the only alternative. Again, local restrictions may apply; for example, in India (a major applicant for reprint licences) the maximum advance payment which can be remitted without special dispensation from the Reserve Bank of India is US $500; similarly, the maximum royalty rate is 15 per cent of the local published price. The choice of method of payment will also affect the wording of Clause 11.

As a general guide, the initial royalty rate of same-language reprint licences should not be less than 10 per cent of the local published price, and in a number of countries considerably higher rates can be negotiated. It should be remembered that the licensee is normally acquiring rights in a well-established work; there will be no editorial expenses, minimal promotion expenses and the royalty represents compensation to the proprietors and the author for the total loss of sales of the original edition in the territory once the licensed edition appears.

3. The word 'advance' and '(a)' would be omitted if a single lump sum arrangement has been negotiated.

4. It may be necessary for third party permissions to be recleared for the re-use of copyright material in the licensed edition if the copyright owners concerned have restricted the original permission granted to use in the proprietors' edition only. It would be administratively safer for the proprietors to undertake such clearance and to recharge the cost to the publishers in addition to the terms of the reprint licence.

6. Production quality in developing countries can still be very poor and this clause seeks to impose the best standards possible in view of the local circumstances prevailing. Production standards in central and eastern Europe are improving; some publishers in the region are now undertaking some manufacturing in the west or the Far East to achieve higher standards.

7. The exact wording of the required copyright notice should be inserted here, together with details of the title and the name of the original publisher and/or copyright holder.

(NB. the following are alternative methods of payment)

(Lump sum arrangement)
The sum of   for the right to produce the aforesaid printing of copies of the Licensed Edition, which sum shall be payable in its entirety on signature of this Agreement. The said payment is not recoverable in the event of any default by the Publishers in carrying out the terms of this Agreement.

(Advance/Royalty arrangement)
  (a) The sum of   payable on signature of this Agreement in advance and on account of any sums which may become due to the Proprietors under this Agreement. The said payment in advance is not recoverable in the event of any default by the Publishers in carrying out the terms of this Agreement.

  (b) On the   published price of all copies of the Licensed Edition issued by the Publishers   :

(i) A royalty of   per cent on the first   thousand copies sold
(ii) A royalty of   per cent on all copies sold beyond the first
      thousand.

  (c) On remainder copies of the Licensed Edition sold by the Publishers at or below cost no royalty shall be payable to the Proprietors but no such remainder copies shall be sold within a period of   years from the date of first publication of the Licensed Edition.

3. This Agreement shall not come into effect until the Proprietors have received the [advance] payment detailed in Clause 2[or 2(a)] hereof.

4. The Proprietors shall be responsible for obtaining permission wherever necessary for the use in the Licensed Edition of copyright material included in the Work belonging to third parties and will advise the Publishers of any additional fees due for such permissions. The Publishers agree to reimburse the Proprietors promptly for any fees so incurred.

5. The Publishers shall produce the Licensed Edition at their own expense. They shall cause it to be reproduced faithfully and accurately and shall not abridge, expand or otherwise alter the Work, including illustrations where applicable, without the prior written consent of the Proprietors.

6. The Publishers undertake to ensure that, wherever possible, the printing, paper and binding of the Licensed Edition shall be of the highest quality.

7. The name of the Author shall appear prominently displayed on the cover, jacket (if any) and title page of every copy of the Licensed Edition issued

9. (a) The publication time limit for a straightforward reprint edition might reasonably be expected to be short, since no editorial or translation work is involved.

(b) This sub-clause provides for the termination of the contract when the designated print run is exhausted; however, if the licensing arrangements have been satisfactory, the contract could be extended for a further designated print run by an addendum to the contract; this provides an opportunity for a review of the financial terms.

11. The exact wording of this clause will be affected by the type of payment arrangement selected in Clause 2. If an advance and royalty arrangement has been chosen, regular royalties will be payable once sales have justified the initial advance payment. These may be specified as payable once or perhaps twice yearly, with appropriate accounting dates to be inserted. The details required in the sales statement are listed.

If a single lump sum arrangement has been chosen, no further payments will be due, but it may well be of interest to the proprietors to receive the same detailed sales statements which will enable them to monitor the publishers' performance.

12. An increasing number of countries are obliged by law to deduct tax at source from licence payments remitted abroad. If adequate documentation is provided and a double taxation exemption treaty is in force between the United Kingdom and the country concerned, it should be possible to reclaim the tax deducted.

Publishers in some markets (e.g. central and eastern Europe and the People's Republic of China) may find it easier to remit payment in hard currency if the financial terms are expressed in US dollars.

and on the reverse of the title page shall appear the following copyright notice: '© ' together with the following acknowledgement: 'This edition of is published by arrangement with ,

8. The Publishers shall send free copies of the Licensed Edition to the Proprietors on publication, together with details of the actual date of publication and the price of the Licensed Edition.

9. (a) Should the Publishers fail to issue the Licensed Edition within months from the date of this Agreement all rights granted under this Agreement shall revert to the Proprietors without prejudice to any monies paid or due to the Proprietors.

(b) Should the Licensed Edition go out of print or off the market the rights granted under this Agreement shall forthwith revert to the Proprietors without prejudice to any monies paid or due to the Proprietors.

10. The Publishers shall not dispose of any subsidiary rights in the Licensed Edition without obtaining the prior written consent of the Proprietors.

11. Accounts/Statements for the sale of the Licensed Edition shall be made up yearly by the Publishers to and the account/statement rendered (together with any sums payable under this Agreement) within three months of the accounting date. Accounts/Statements will show:

(a) the number of copies in stock at the beginning of the accounting period
(b) the number of copies sold during the accounting period
(c) the number of copies presented free of charge during the accounting period
(d) the number of copies remaining in stock at the end of the accounting period

Should any of the payments detailed in this Agreement be three months overdue the licence herein granted shall forthwith lapse and all rights conveyed by it shall without further notice revert to the Proprietors.

12. All sums which may become due to the Proprietors under this Agreement shall be paid by the Publishers in sterling, without any deduction in respect of exchange or commission. Should the Publishers be required by law to deduct tax they shall send a declaration to this effect with the relevant statement of account showing the amount deducted.

13. The Proprietors hereby warrant to the Publishers that they have the right and power to make this Agreement and that according to English law the Work will in no way whatever give rise to a violation of any existing copyright, or a breach of any existing agreement and that nothing in the

16. The duration of the licence should not, it is suggested, be shorter than two years or longer than five years. When setting the period, the size of the print run, the status of the licensee and the nature of the work should be taken into account. In principle it is usually preferable to specify a short period, with a provision for renewal if the publishers' performance is satisfactory.

18 and **19.** Ideally, the contract should be specified as operable under English law with English arbitration provisions prevailing. In practice, local legislation in the country of the publishers may preclude this; if so, the following alternative wording could be considered:

'If any difference shall arise between the Proprietors and the Publishers touching the meaning of this Agreement or the rights and liabilities of the parties thereto, the same shall be referred to the arbitration of two persons (one to be named by each party) or their mutually agreed arbitrator in accordance with the provisions of the arbitration legislation for the time being in force in [*country of Publishers*]. Any dispute between the parties not resolved by arbitration or agreement shall be submitted to the jurisdiction of the courts of [*country of Publishers*].

20. This places an obligation on the publishers to protect the work in the territory they have been granted at their own expense; this would include any copyright registration procedure required under local laws.

Work is liable to give rise to a civil prosecution or to a civil action for damages or any other remedy and the Proprietors will indemnify the Publishers against any loss, injury or expense arising out of any breach of this warranty.

14. The Licence hereby granted to the Publishers shall not be transferred in whole or in part or extended to include any other party nor shall the Licensed Edition appear under any imprint other than that of the Publishers, except with the prior written consent of the Proprietors.

15. All rights in the Work, other than those specifically granted to the Publishers herein, are reserved by the Proprietors.

16. The licence herein granted shall continue for a period of   years from the date of first publication by the Publishers of the Licensed Edition and thereafter may be subject to renewal by mutual agreement between the parties hereto.

17. In the event of the Publishers being declared bankrupt or should they or anyone acting on their behalf fail to comply with any of the provisions of this Agreement and not rectify such failure within one month of having received notice from the Proprietors to do so by a registered letter sent to the Publishers at their address given at the commencement of this Agreement, then in either event this Agreement automatically becomes null and void and the licence granted to the Publishers herein shall revert to the Proprietors without prejudice to any claim which the Proprietors may have for damages or otherwise and without prejudice to any monies paid or due to the Proprietors.

18. If any difference shall arise between the Proprietors and the Publishers touching the meaning of this Agreement or the rights and liabilities of the parties hereto, the same shall be referred to the arbitration of two persons (one to be named by each party) or their umpire, in accordance with the provisions of the Arbitration Act 1996 or any subsisting statutory modification or re-enactment thereof, provided that any dispute between the parties hereto not resolved by arbitration or agreement shall be submitted to the jurisdiction of the English courts.

19. This Agreement shall be governed by and interpreted in all respects in accordance with the laws of England.

20. The Publishers agree to take any necessary steps to register the title of the Work in the name of the Proprietors/Author under local copyright laws at the sole expense of the Publishers. The Publishers also agree to protect such copyright and to prosecute at their own expense any person who infringes such copyright.

Illustration and Artwork Agreement

There remains some confusion about the nature of agreements with illustrators. Briefing of illustrators is still done orally and informally, with no clear idea of exactly what rights are being acquired or retained. The mistaken belief which derived from section 4(3) of the Copyright Act 1956, that the publisher when commissioning artwork automatically owned it and the copyright stemming from it, still prevails in many quarters.

The true position, which has existed since the Copyright, Designs and Patents Act 1988 came into effect, can be set out in four propositions:

1. When an illustration is drawn or painted, copyright automatically exists and is owned by the illustrator, regardless of whether it is commissioned or not.
2. If the commissioner wishes to have the copyright, the illustrator has to agree to assign it to the commissioner in writing and signed by the illustrator.
3. Unless the illustrator agrees to give the original to the commissioner it remains the illustrator's property. The fact that someone has purchased the copyright does not entitle that person to own the original artwork.
4. Moral rights apply under the Act to artistic works as they apply to literary works.

In any contract it is always important to clarify the following:

(a) ownership of the original artwork;
(b) possession of or access to the original artwork for varying purposes, e.g. art exhibitions, or promotional use or further publication in a foreign language edition of which the artwork is a part;
(c) copyright, that is, the right to grant or refuse reproduction of the artwork;
(d) exploitation of that right both for and beyond the initial publication, through the grant to the publisher of an exclusive licence from the copyright holder.

Publishers acquiring ownership of original artwork will now need to bear in mind a directive proposed by the European Commission which seeks to ensure that illustrators are paid when their works are resold by public auction or through an agent (e.g. a gallery or dealer); the first sale of the work by the illustrator and sales between private individuals will be excluded. Such artists' resale rights or *droit de suite* are envisaged as an integral part of copyright and will apply exclusively to 20th century works. The directive proposes the payment to an illustrator of a percentage of the sale price net of tax ranging from 4 per cent to 2 per cent, though sales below 1,000 ECU are likely to be excluded.

The assumption of this precedent is that there is a direct relationship between the publisher and the illustrator. This is not always so. In some branches of publishing, e.g. in medical books, a specialist illustrator may well be recruited by a specialist author, and in educational publishing, the publisher may require the overall designer of a book to recruit the illustrators. In these situations it may be appropriate for the publisher to supply the necessary contractual documentation for the purpose of ensuring that the details with respect to ownership of artwork and grant of rights are correct.

The Association of Illustrators continues to express concern at the practice of some publishers in requiring an assignment both of copyright in and also ownership of the artwork. In the majority of cases there is no reason why the publisher, which in almost all cases is in the position of obtaining rights through the grant of an exclusive licence from the author, needs to acquire either the copyright itself or ownership of the artwork from the illustrator. Ownership of artwork for the purposes of re-use in book or other form is becoming increasingly unnecessary due to advances in digital storage technology, though the introduction of artists' resale rights may result in fewer objections to the transfer of ownership. Whatever is agreed with respect to ownership of artwork and the grant of rights, re-use of artwork in another book must in equity entitle the illustrator to further fees. There do, however, remain areas of publishing, e.g. character-based publishing, where the publisher may be obliged to acquire the copyright and ownership of artwork for subsequent transfer to the owner of the rights in the character.

Throughout the precedent, the word 'artwork' is used. Many of the points are equally relevant to the work of a photographer, as the alternative wording of Clause 1 implies; the words 'photographs' or 'transparencies' can be easily substituted throughout for artwork. Photographs are treated under the Copyright, etc. Act 1988 as artistic works, and ownership and duration of copyright in them are therefore treated exactly as ownership and duration of other artistic works.

This precedent is not intended for use when the illustrator is to be paid on a royalty basis. In those cases Precedent One is more suitable, with appropriate amendment and inclusion of promotional use and other artwork specific provisions of this precedent.

MEMORANDUM OF AGREEMENT made this   day of
19

Between   of   (hereinafter called 'the Illustrator', which expression shall, where the context admits, include the Illustrator's executors and assigns) of the one part and   of   (hereinafter called 'the Publishers', which expression shall, where the context admits, include any publishing imprint subsidiary to or associated with the Publishers, and the Publishers' assigns or successors in business as the case may be) of the other part

Whereby it is mutually agreed as follows concerning the Illustrator's *artwork/transparencies/photographs* for a work at present entitled   by   (hereinafter called 'the Work'):

1. The Illustrator shall provide *artwork/transparencies/photographs* (hereinafter called 'the Artwork') for the Work in a form suitable for reproduction and subject to the approval of the Publishers (which approval shall not be unreasonably withheld) as provided for in the Schedule to this Agreement.

2. The Illustrator shall provide roughs not later than   and the finished Artwork not later than

3. The Illustrator hereby warrants to the Publishers and their assigns and licensees that *he/she* has full power to make this Agreement, that *he/she* is the sole author of the Artwork and is the owner of the rights herein granted, that the Artwork is original to *him/her* and has not previously been published in volume form in the territories covered by this Agreement, that the Artwork is in no way whatever a violation or an infringement of any existing copyright or licence, and that it contains nothing obscene, libellous or defamatory. The Illustrator will indemnify and keep the Publishers indemnified against all actions, suits, proceedings, claims, demands, damages and costs (including any legal costs or expenses properly incurred and any compensation costs and disbursements paid by the Publishers on the advice of their legal advisers to compromise or settle any claim) occasioned to the Publishers in consequence of any breach of this warranty or arising out of any claim alleging that the Artwork constitutes in any way a breach of this warranty. The Publishers reserve the right to insist that the Illustrator alter the Artwork in such a way as may appear to them appropriate for the purpose of removing any feature which on the advice of the

---

1 and 2. Full details of what precisely is required from the illustrator and the form in which it is to be delivered should always be spelled out and agreement recorded for delivery dates for both roughs and finished artwork.

3. It may be important to ensure that the artwork is original and/or has not been published before in volume form; indeed some publishers prefer that it has not before been published in any form.

4. See the notes to Clause 10 which refer to subsidiary rights.

5. It is important that the publisher has access to the original artwork or transparencies or the artwork in digitial form: this is particularly important because the illustrator, unless otherwise agreed, owns the original artwork and can dispose of it as he/she wishes. Practice varies from publisher to publisher but it should be borne in mind that artwork in a form suitable for reproduction may be needed for exhibitions, publicity, paperback, or foreign editions – and also that production film deteriorates with time.

It is one thing for the publisher to reproduce an artist's work in order to promote the book in which the work appears. It is quite another thing for a publisher to reproduce an artist's work in order to promote other books as well. The use of a leading illustrator's work on the cover of, e.g., a catalogue of children's books for the Christmas market is the kind of use which will need separate agreement.

6. Insurance against loss of or damage to artwork is a vexed problem. Illustrators sometimes have difficulty in getting cover for their own work so it is not always feasible to ask them to insure it. Some publishers may have a general insurance policy which covers them, but the conditions for secure storage required by insurers may be too stringent for other publishers. Some publishers will undertake responsibility but limit their liability contractually to a sum equal to the original fee (i.e. the fee expressed in this precedent under Clause 9). One formula reads as follows:

> 'The Publishers shall be responsible for the Artwork while it is in their custody always provided that the Illustrator shall upon delivery to the Publishers of the final Artwork state in writing the value that he/she places upon each piece of Artwork which valuation shall be mutually agreed between the parties hereto.'

8. This clause is particularly important for photographic sessions with models needed for paperback covers, where print runs can be very high and damages sought for improper exploitation correspondingly so.

9. If the agreement is for jacket artwork only, or one piece of artwork as opposed to a complete book, a single fee is in order, payable usually at a specified time, e.g. within six weeks, from receipt of the invoice submitted by the illustrator after delivery of the final artwork.

10. Clause 4 gives the publishers the sole and exclusive right to exploit any subsidiary rights. These may include:

paperback
book club
condensed book
first and second serial and syndication rights
anthology rights
strip cartoon rights

Publishers' legal advisers may be considered objectionable or likely to be actionable by law, but any such alteration or removal shall be without prejudice to and shall not affect the Illustrator's liability under this warranty and indemnity.

All warranties and indemnities herein contained shall survive the termination of this Agreement.

4. In consideration of the payments hereinafter mentioned the Illustrator hereby grants to the Publishers the sole and exclusive right and licence to produce, publish and themselves further to license the Artwork or any part of it in any and all forms and media for the legal term of copyright and any and all extensions, renewals and revivals thereof throughout the world.

5. The Illustrator shall permit the Publishers free of charge to use the Artwork to promote the Work in catalogues, advertisements and other promotional material. If the Artwork shall have been returned by the Publishers to the Illustrator, the Illustrator shall endeavour to ensure that the Artwork or good quality transparencies thereof are available to the Publishers without charge for any subsequent publishing or promotional purposes.

6. While proper care will be taken of the Artwork, the Publishers shall not be responsible for any loss or damage to it while it is in the Publishers' possession or in the course of production or in transit.

7. The Illustrator shall ensure that any exhibition of the Artwork shall make full acknowledgement to the Work, its author and to the Publishers.

8. Should the Artwork contain a recognisable likeness of any person the Illustrator undertakes to explain to such person the use to which the Artwork will be put and to obtain from each such person a form of release and to deliver the same to the Publishers in a form satisfactory to them.

9. The Publishers shall pay to the Illustrator a fee of   payable as to   on signature of this Agreement,   on delivery and approval of roughs of the Artwork and   on delivery and approval of finished Artwork as provided for in Clauses 1 and 2 hereof.

10. The Publishers shall further pay to the Illustrator a proportion to be mutually agreed of any net sums received by the Publishers in respect of

---

American hardback/paperback and book club rights
translation rights
merchandising rights
electronic rights
film and television rights

Equal division of moneys for reproduction in volume or serial form is general, but must be negotiable in the circumstances of each work. Illustration fees for any of the rights should, where possible, be negotiated separately from fees for the use of the author's text.

169

In the case of merchandising, film, electronic and strip cartoon rights it is not always easy to determine the contribution to these of, respectively, author and illustrator and here any moneys could be divided three ways (as between author, illustrator and publisher).

11. The nearer to completion the illustrations are when the publishers cancel the commission, the greater should be the proportion of the total fee payable to the illustrator. As an indication, the following pro forma might be helpful:

Between signature of the agreement and approval of the roughs: per cent of the total fee. Between approval of roughs and approval of finished artwork: per cent of the total fee. After approval of finished artwork: per cent of total fee.

12. For Public Lending Right purposes, it is particularly important to decide whether the illustrator's part in creating the total work merits the printing of his/her name on the title page. Unless it is so printed, the illustrator is likely not to be eligible to register for his/her share in PLR.

the Artwork sub-licensed by them to a third party for reproduction in volume form or in newspapers or magazines or otherwise.

11. Should the Publishers for any reason cancel the commission, they shall pay to the Illustrator a cancellation fee to be agreed and proportional to the degree of completion. The Publishers shall have no rights in any Artwork so cancelled.

12. The Illustrator's name shall be printed either on the title page of the Work or prominently on the half-title or the reverse of the title page at the discretion of the Publishers and the Publishers shall use their best endeavours to ensure that *he/she* is given full acknowledgement in any edition of the Work sub-licensed by the Publishers to a third party.

13. The Illustrator shall retain ownership of and copyright in the Artwork and the Publishers shall print the following line on the reverse of the title page of the Work: 'Illustrations ©

14. The Publishers shall send to the Illustrator on publication complimentary copies of the Work. The Illustrator shall have the right to purchase at normal trade terms further copies for personal use but not for resale. The Illustrator shall receive   complimentary copies of any sub-licensed edition of the Work which includes the Artwork on receipt by the Publishers from the sub-licensed publishers of their edition of the Work.

15. If at any time the Publishers allow the Work to become out of print and not available in any edition and if the Publishers return to the author of the text all rights granted to them under the terms of the agreement between them and the author the Publishers shall at the same time return to the Illustrator all rights in the Artwork granted under this Agreement without prejudice to all rights of the Publishers in respect of any contracts or negotiations properly entered into by them with any third party prior to the date of such reversion.

16. Should the Publishers fail to fulfil or comply with any of the conditions accepted by the Publishers in this Agreement within 30 days' notice of such failure from the Illustrator, or if a manager, receiver, or other encumbrancer takes possession of or is appointed over, the whole or any substantial part of the Publishers' assets, or if the Publishers enter into any arrangement or composition with or for the benefit of their creditors (including any voluntary arrangement under the Insolvency Act 1986), or if a petition is presented or a meeting convened for the purposes of considering a resolution for the making of an administrative order, the winding up or dissolution of the Publishers (other than voluntary liquidation for the purpose of reconstruction) then, in any of the foregoing events, this Agreement shall thereupon terminate and all rights granted under this Agreement shall revert to the Illustrator, without prejudice to all rights of the Publishers in respect of any contracts or negotiations properly entered

171

into with any third party prior to the date of such termination and without prejudice to any monies already paid or then due to the Illustrator from the Publishers.

17. All monies accruing to the Illustrator under this Agreement shall be exclusive of Value Added Tax (VAT). If the Illustrator is at any time registered for the purposes of VAT the Publishers shall, after notification of the Illustrator's VAT registration number, add VAT to payments made to the Illustrator in accordance with statutory regulations. The Publishers shall be notified of any change in the Illustrator's VAT status, including any alteration to the Illustrator's VAT registration number.

18. If any difference shall arise between the Illustrator and the Publishers touching the meaning of this Agreement or the rights and liabilities of the parties thereto, the same shall be referred in the first place to the Publishers Association's Informal Disputes Settlement Scheme, and failing agreed submission to that Scheme, to the arbitration of two person (one to be named by each party) or their mutually agreed umpire, in accordance with the provisions of the Arbitration Act 1996 or any amending or substituted statute for the time being in force.

19. This Agreement shall be governed by and interpreted in all respects in accordance with the law of England and the parties hereto submit and agree to the jurisdiction of the English courts.

20. This Agreement is the entire and only agreement between the Illustrator and the Publishers concerning its subject matter and supersedes any and all prior agreements, arrangements and understandings (whether written or oral) relating thereto. No addition to or modification of any provision of this Agreement shall be binding upon the parties unless it is in writing and signed on behalf of the Illustrator and the Publishers.

21. The Illustrator hereby asserts *his/her* right to be identified as the Illustrator of the Work and the Publishers undertake

(i) to print on every edition of the Work published by them the words: '[The Illustrator] has asserted *his/her* right under the Copyright, Designs and Patents Act 1988, to be identified as Illustrator of this Work';
(ii) to use all reasonable endeavours to include in any contract for volume rights with any licensee concerning any edition of the Work to be published in the United Kingdom an undertaking that a notice of assertion in the same terms shall be printed in every edition published or further licensed by such licensee.

The Illustrator on written request from the Publishers undertakes to give consent or to waive in writing the right to object to derogatory treatment of the Artwork as provided for in s. 80 of the Copyright, Designs and Patents Act 1988 when such consent or waiver is an essential condition of

the exercise of any of the rights granted to the Publishers under this Agreement.

Schedule
The Artwork referred to in Clause 1 hereof shall consist of:
      illustrations in black and white
    illustrations in   colours
A *jacket/cover* (*front only/wrap-around*) for printing in colours
Medium:
Method of reproduction:
Size/proportion:

Packaging Rights Agreement

This document, the Book Packagers Association's Standard Agreement between Book Packager and UK Publisher (Eleventh Draft, April 1996), includes a form of contract with provisions covering the most common kind of packaging deal — the sale of finished copies of an illustrated book to a publisher in the UK.

The recommendations included in this document are given in good faith by the Contracts Committee of the Book Packagers Association, no members of which shall accept responsibility for the consequences of following them, or for the reproduction of the contract for the purpose of any transaction.

2. The appropriate staging of payments will vary according to the book and the circumstances, but the following points should be borne in mind:

(a) too many stages are administratively tiresome, since each requires invoicing and chasing; (b) the final stage, coinciding with the payment of the printer, should be large enough to meet that payment; and (c) the appropriate stages may include some of the following: signature of the agreement; delivery of the typescript; galley proofs; page proofs; illustration proofs; complete ozalid; advance bound copies; complete delivery. As the pattern of expenditure varies from project to project, it is a good idea to draw up a cash-flow before finalising stage payments.

The percentage of overs or unders given here is standard in the British book printing industry, but higher or lower percentages may be agreed.

Practices differ over the inclusion in the price of such elements as royalty, and delivery to the publisher's warehouse as opposed to 'cif a United Kingdom port' or 'ex printing works'.

Some publishers' delivery and packing requirements may be abnormal and involve expenditure in excess of what was allowed for when the unit price was calculated and

AGREEMENT made this [*date*] day of 199

BETWEEN

(1)   [*Publisher*]
of   [*address*]
('the Publishers', which expression shall where the context admits include
the Publishers' assigns or successors in business as the case may be)

AND

(2)   [*Packager*]

of   [*address*]
('the Proprietors', which expression shall where the context admits include
the Proprietors' assigns or successors in business as the case may be)

BACKGROUND

The Proprietors control the rights in a work provisionally entitled
          [*title of work*] ('the Work') [to be] written/edited by
          [*author's name*] ('the Author') of which the Proprietors have
the sole and exclusive rights of manufacture and disposal of the licence to
publish and have agreed to grant certain rights in the Work to the Publishers
under the terms of this Agreement.

IT IS AGREED AS FOLLOWS

1. Sale and Purchase of Copies
The Proprietors agree to sell and the Publishers agree to purchase [*x*]
copies of the Work ('the Order') in accordance with the specification set
out in Appendix 1 attached to and forming part of this Agreement and
subject to the terms and conditions set out in this Agreement.

2. Price per Copy and Date of Delivery
2.1 The Publishers shall pay the Proprietors the sum of £ [*x*] per copy ('the
    Price') and shall make such payment in the following instalments:
    £   on signature of this Agreement;
    £   on
    £   on
    £   on
    £   on delivery to the Publishers of the Order.
2.2 The Price is inclusive of royalty and the costs of bulk packing, shipping
    and insurance for delivery to the Publishers' warehouse, which delivery
    shall be made, unless prevented by circumstances beyond the
    Proprietors' control, on or before   [*date*] 199 , in
    accordance with the Publishers' delivery and packing requirements set
    out in Appendix 2 attached to and forming part of this Agreement. A

179

agreed. In this event the extra cost of such special packing should be charged to the Publisher.

3.   The packager may wish to grant less than 'volume' rights or to provide that, for example, paperback rights should revert to it if after a certain period (e.g. 18 months) the publisher has taken no steps to exploit them.

4.   If the publisher has also bought US rights, this clause should require the filing of an application for registration within three months of publication of the work in the United States in the Copyright Office, Library of Congress.

variation of 5 per cent over or under the quantity of copies shall constitute full delivery of the Order.

2.3 The Publishers may by giving notice to the Proprietors in adequate time to enable the Proprietors to notify the printer of the Work order additional run-on copies of the Work at the price of £ [*x*] per copy and such copies shall be subject to the terms of this Agreement.

3. Rights and Territory

The Proprietors hereby grant to the Publishers during the term of this Agreement the sole and exclusive licence to publish, distribute and sell the Work in [*hardback*] volume form in the English language in the Territory as defined in Appendix 3 of this Agreement. All rights in the Work other than those expressly granted to the Publishers under the terms of this Agreement are retained by the Proprietors.

4. Copyright

4.1 The Proprietors shall ensure that all copies of the Work delivered to the Publishers by the Proprietors bear the following copyright notice: '©   [*name of copyright owner*], 199*   [* *represents year of first publication*]'.

4.2 The Publishers shall ensure that all copies of the Work published by them and licensed in the United Kingdom and in any other part of the Territory to which the Copyright, Designs and Patents Act 1988 extends shall include the above copyright notice on the reverse of the title page.

4.3 (i) If at any time during the term of this Agreement the copyright of the Work shall in the reasonable opinion of the Publishers be infringed by a third party the Publishers shall at their own expense be entitled to take such steps as they consider necessary to deal with the matter, including but not restricted to proceedings in the joint name of the Publishers and the Proprietors on giving the Proprietors a sufficient and reasonable indemnity against all liability for costs and expenses (whether of the Proprietors or of the defendants in any such proceedings) and the Proprietors shall give the Publishers all reasonable co-operation in such proceedings.

(ii) The Publishers shall be entitled to nominate the solicitors through whom such proceedings may be carried on and shall have full power to abandon compromise or settle such proceedings at their own discretion but will first consult fully with the Proprietors.

(iii) Any sum recovered by way of damages and costs shall be applied first towards repayment of the costs incurred in such proceedings and any balance shall be divided equally between the parties.

(iv) Notwithstanding any other provisions of this Agreement the Publishers and their sub-licensees shall if they reasonably consider it necessary for the protection of the Work be entitled to take urgent proceedings in their sole name in any country of the world for interlocutory relief without prior notice to the Proprietors provided

6. (d) If the indemnity given to the publisher in this clause is felt to be too much of a catch-all, it can be left out. However, some publishers may insist on a clause of this kind. At least providing a form of words gives the packager some degree of control over settlement. If packagers wish to protect themselves further, they can require publishers to print a disclaimer. Appropriate wording might be:

'No responsibility for loss occasioned to any person acting or refraining from action as a result of the material in this publication can be accepted by the Author, the Proprietors or the Publishers.'

7. British publishers have varying practices as regards the checking of progress on books bought in; and book packagers have different attitudes as well. It should be borne in mind that there are advantages in securing the publisher's approval of the book at various stages of preparation, in addition to the obvious disadvantages.

that the Publishers shall as soon as reasonably practicable afterwards give to the Proprietors notice of such proceedings.

(v) The provisions of this clause apply only to an infringement of the copyright in the Work which affects the interest in it granted to the Publishers under the terms of this Agreement.

5. Author's Moral Right to be Identified

5.1 The Author has asserted the Author's moral right to be identified as the Author of the Work. The Proprietors shall ensure that all copies of the Work manufactured by the Proprietors [*and the Publishers undertake to ensure that every copy of the Work licensed by the Publishers*] shall include the words 'The right of the Author to be identified as the Author of this work has been asserted by the Author in accordance with the Copyright Designs and Patents Act 1988';]

5.2 The Proprietors shall ensure that on every copy of the Work produced by the Proprietors or under licence from them [*and the Publishers undertake to ensure that on every copy of the Work licensed by the Publishers*] the name of the Author shall appear in its customary form with due prominence on the title page and on the binding.

6. Proprietors' Warranties

The Proprietors warrant to the Publishers:

(a) The Proprietors are the sole owners of the rights granted under this Agreement and have full power to enter into this Agreement and to give the warranties and indemnity contained in the Agreement.

(b) To the best of the Proprietors' knowledge and belief the Work contains nothing obscene, blasphemous, libellous or in breach of the Official Secrets Act or otherwise unlawful and the exploitation of the rights granted under this Agreement will not infringe the copyright or any other rights of any third party.

(c) To the best of the Proprietors' knowledge and belief all statements in the Work purporting to be facts are true and any recipe, formula or instruction contained in it will not if followed accurately cause any injury, illness or damage to the user.

(d) The Proprietors shall keep the Publishers fully indemnified against all losses and all actions, claims, proceedings, costs and damages, including any damages or compensation paid by the Publishers after written approval by the Proprietors on the advice of their legal advisers to compromise or settle any claim and all legal costs or other expenses arising out of any breach of any of the above warranties.

7. Approval of Material

The Publishers shall approve the typescript and proofs of the Work within a reasonable time to be specified by the Proprietors, such approval not to be unreasonably withheld or delayed. Any costs incurred as a consequence of changes required to material previously approved shall be borne by the Publishers.

It is probably best to avoid a specific time limit for checking proofs because there may be occasions when a particularly fast turn-around is required to meet the publisher's own delivery date.

8. The revised wording of this clause is intended to provide the packager with the following safeguards:

(1) Even if the printers accept that copies of the work are defective, they are highly unlikely to credit the packager with more than the price received.

By way of example, and to keep the figures simple, consider the case of a reprint with no editorial or other plant costs.

Suppose that a packager pays the printers of the work £2.00 per copy for a printing of 10,000 copies and charges the publishers £3.00 per copy. Suppose further that all parties agree that 1000 copies are defective. Under the previous wording of this clause, the publishers could expect to be credited automatically by the packager, who would in turn be credited by the printers. The packager would consequently lose £1000 of gross profit as a result of the printers' errors.

(2) The revised wording should help indemnify the packager against claims by publishers for consequential loss, and go some way to make it harder for publishers to claim for tiny or imagined blemishes.

(3) Sub-clause 8(ii) is designed to prevent the packager from becoming liable in a situation where the publisher discovers two or three defective copies, immediately orders a stock check, and subsequently tries to pass the cost of this exercise on to the packager.

It is important that the packager also has a written agreement with the printers setting out what happens when copies are found to be defective, and obliging the printers to repair or replace copies where more than (say) three per cent of the total are found to be defective.

8. Imperfect Copies

8.1 The Publishers shall notify the Proprietors in writing within 30 days of delivery of the Order of any defects in such copies of the Work attributable to faulty materials or faulty workmanship being copies which in the reasonable view of the Publishers are unacceptable ('the Imperfect Copies'). The parties shall forthwith attempt in good faith to agree the number of Imperfect Copies or failing such agreement the number shall be determined under Clause 8.4. Where the number so agreed or determined is less than 3 per cent of the Order the Proprietors shall credit the Publishers with the Price of the agreed number of Imperfect Copies. Where the number so agreed is more than 3 per cent of the Order, the Proprietors shall at their option re-cover, repair or replace the Imperfect Copies or credit the Publishers the Price of the Imperfect Copies. The total liability of the Proprietors shall be limited to the Price of the Imperfect Copies, and the Proprietors shall be under no liability whatsoever for any claims for loss of profits or contracts or indirect or consequential loss or damage arising in respect of the Imperfect Copies whether by reason of negligence, breach of contract, or any other cause of action arising out of the Imperfect Copies, except as expressly provided in this Agreement.

8.2 The Proprietors shall not be liable for the cost of checking stocks of the Work in the Publishers' warehouse unless the aggregate of the Imperfect Copies is more than 100 copies of the Work or 1 per cent of the Order, whichever is the greater, and in the event of such liability the cost of the stock check must first be agreed by the parties, such agreement not to be unreasonably withheld or delayed.

8.3 The Proprietors do not exclude liability for death or personal injury caused by the Publishers' negligence.

8.4 If the parties are unable to agree the number of Imperfect Copies within 7 days the matter may be referred by either party for resolution by an independent arbitrator to be nominated by the parties, and, failing agreement on such nomination within a further 7 days, to such person as is appointed on the application of either party by the President for the time being of the British Printing Industries Federation. The independent arbitrator shall be deemed to act as an expert and not as an arbitrator; the independent arbitrator shall take into account the written representations of the parties; and the independent arbitrator's determination shall (in the absence of manifest error) be conclusive and binding upon the parties, and the costs of any such determination shall be borne as the independent arbitrator shall direct, or failing such direction, equally by the parties.

8.5 The express terms of this Agreement are in lieu of all warranties, conditions, terms, undertakings and obligations implied by statute, common law, custom, trade usage, course of dealing or otherwise, all of which are hereby excluded to the fullest extent permitted by law.

10. This clause is mainly designed to ensure that the packager is kept informed on promotion plans, and to avoid inaccuracies in advertising copy. It may occasionally be possible to include an undertaking by the publisher to spend a specific sum on advertising and promotion.

11.1. The following subsidiary rights are normally or often granted to British publishers under this clause: anthology, digest and quotation; first serial; second and subsequent serial; syndication; readings on radio and television; advertising; strip cartoon; digest book condensation. Trade paperback rights are also frequently granted. It is common to reserve: mass market paperback; cheap edition/reprint; film, video and television; and merchandising. The percentages payable may vary between 50% (for most rights) and 90% (for first serial rights).

As regards the disposition of book club rights, which insofar as they involve manufacture are often vitally important to the packager, there are wide variations in practice. They are frequently retained wholly by the packager; often granted to the publisher; and sometimes dealt with on a profit-sharing basis between the parties.

11.2. This sub-clause provides for the circumstances where illustration rights have been cleared for volume publication but not for further exploitation. It obliges the publisher to obtain the packager's agreement to such exploitation, which can be withheld if the additional fee payable does not make the sale worthwhile.

12. Since most packaged books are sold inclusive of royalty, and hence normal procedures regarding royalty statements are not automatically followed, it often proves difficult to obtain from publishers any information on the sales performance of the books sold to them. This clause at least makes such information a contractual obligation.

9. Undertaking to Publish
The Publishers shall publish the Work at their own risk and expense, unless prevented by circumstances beyond their control, within six months of the delivery to them of copies of the Work.

10. Undertaking to Advertise and Promote
The Publishers agree actively to advertise and to promote the sales of the Work in accordance with the best commercial practice, to ensure its circulation and availability throughout the Territory, to discuss their plans for promotion with the Proprietors and to provide the Proprietors with [*a reasonable opportunity to check advertising and promotional copy for accuracy* or *all advertising and promotional copy for written approval, such approval not to be unreasonably withheld or delayed.*]

11. Licences Granted by the Publishers
11.1 The Publishers shall pay to the Proprietors the following percentages of all monies received by the Publishers in respect of sub-licensing the rights set out below:
   [x] per cent
   [y] per cent
   [z] per cent
11.2 The Publishers shall consult the Proprietors over any sale of rights under this clause. No agreement for the disposal of rights including illustrations contained in the Work shall be entered into by the Publishers without the Proprietors' prior agreement in writing. In the event that in respect of such rights additional fees are payable to sources of illustrations contained in the Work such fees shall be paid by the Publishers.
11.3 The Publishers agree to supply the Proprietors with photocopies of all sub-licences and agreements in connection with the sale of rights within 30 days of signature of such documents by the Publishers and copies of all statements received by them in connection with all such sales when accounting for such sales to the Proprietors. The Publishers shall pay to the Proprietors their share of any advance payments received by the Publishers in respect of sales of rights within 28 days of their receipt by the Publishers.

12. Accounting for sales
12.1 The Publishers shall keep accurate, detailed and up-to-date accounts of sales and income from sales of copies of and exploitation of rights in the Work.
12.2 Within 90 days of each six month accounting period ending on [*date*] and [*date*] following first publication the Publishers shall submit to the Proprietors a statement showing the sales of copies and editions of the Work and of payments received under sub-licences referred to in Clause 11 during the relevant period and the relevant percentage

13. If delivery has been made but the publisher fails to pay, the packager can cancel the contract and the rights granted under it revert. But since 'possession is nine points of the law', the actual ownership of the copies (as distinct from the right to sell or exploit them) may remain vested in the publisher. This clause seeks to avoid this difficulty by including a sub-clause defining precisely the point at which ownership in the goods is transferred.

    NB This clause has been drafted to meet specific legal requirements, and should not be changed without professional legal advice.

applicable thereto and shall forthwith pay to the Proprietors such sums as are then due.

12.3 The Publishers shall allow the Proprietors (or a firm of chartered accountants appointed to act on the Proprietors' behalf) to examine the accounting records of the Publishers insofar as they relate to the Work and to take copies and extracts of the relevant parts of such accounting records. Any inspection shall take place by appointment during normal office hours after reasonable notice has been given and shall not be carried out more than twice in any calendar year. Such inspection shall be at the Proprietors' expense unless it reveals an underpayment to the Proprietors of more than 5% in which event the Publishers shall bear the cost of such inspection.

13. Retention of Title

13.1 The legal and beneficial ownership of all copies of the Work ('the Goods') supplied to the Publishers shall remain vested in the Proprietors until either:

(a) all sums owed to the Proprietors by the Publishers have been paid, or

(b) (if for any reason the provision in sub-clause 13.1 (a) is held to be invalid) the Publishers have paid to the Proprietors all sums due to the Proprietors in respect of the Goods.

13.2 Until the ownership of the Goods passes to the Publishers under the provisions of Clause 13.1 the Publishers shall hold the Goods as agent for the Proprietors and shall deal with the Goods only in accordance with such instructions as the Proprietors may give from time to time and in particular:

(i) The Publishers shall store the Goods in such a manner that they are separate and identifiable from all other goods and shall notify the Proprietors of the place of storage.

(ii) The Publishers shall insure the Goods against all normal insurable risks and such other items as the Proprietors may require and shall on request provide the Proprietors with details of the insurance policy.

(iii) The Publishers may dispose of the Goods as the agent of the Proprietors PROVIDED THAT:

(a) the Proprietors shall be informed in advance of the terms of any disposal and shall have approved the same in writing;

(b) the proceeds of sale of any disposal together with proceeds of any insurance claim relating to the Goods shall be held by the Publishers as trustee for the Proprietors until ownership of the Goods would have been transferred to the Publishers under Clause 13.1 and such proceeds shall be placed by the Publishers in a separate bank account which is clearly marked as a trust account;

14. The contract as drafted is terminable only by default of either party or if (after due process) the book goes out of print. In the absence of those events it will survive the full term of copyright. However, it is not uncommon to limit such contracts to a fixed term – such as five or eight years. A time limit is a useful way of clearing the ground in advance for a promotional reprint, for example.

    (c)   the Publishers shall on request assign to the Proprietors all the Publishers' rights against any person who purchases the Goods from the Publishers.

14. Term of Agreement

This Agreement, unless previously terminated under Clause 15, shall commence on [*the date hereof*] and continue for a period of [*x*] years after the date of first publication of the Work by the Publishers. This Agreement may be extended on the same terms by a period of a further [*y*] years upon written agreement by the parties, such agreement not to be unreasonably withheld.

15. Termination

15.1 The Proprietors may terminate this Agreement forthwith by notice in writing to the Publishers:

    (a)   if the Publishers fail to publish the Work within the time stipulated in Clause 9;

    (b)   if the Publishers are in breach of any of their other obligations under this Agreement and in the case of a breach capable of being remedied fail to remedy such breach within one month of being requested in writing by the Proprietors to do so;

    (c)   if the Publishers purport to assign the benefit of this Agreement without the prior written consent of the Proprietors;

    (d)   if the Publishers go into liquidation either compulsorily or voluntarily (except for the purpose of and immediately followed by a solvent reconstruction or amalgamation) or if a receiver, administrative receiver, receiver and manager or administrator is appointed in respect of the whole or any part of their assets or if the Publishers make an assignment for the benefit of or composition with their creditors generally or threaten to do any of these things;

    (e)   if the Publishers remainder the Work under the terms of Clause 18;

    (f)   if the Publishers put the Work out of print so that it is not available in the Territory in the English language unless within [*x*] months of receipt of notice in writing from the Proprietors the Publishers agree to publish in the Territory a reprint of not less than [*y*] copies or notify the Proprietors that they have licensed another publisher to publish such a reprint which will be published within that period time being of the essence.

15.2 (i)   On the expiry or termination of this Agreement all rights granted to the Publishers under its terms shall automatically and immediately revert to the Proprietors absolutely;

    (ii)   The Publishers may for a period of six months on a non-exclusive basis continue to sell any copies of the Work that are on hand as at the date of expiry or termination of this Agreement;

    (iii)   Termination shall not affect:

16. This clause deals with the important question of the penalties applicable in the case of (a) late payment and (b) late delivery of books. Book packagers should consider carefully whether to press for its inclusion. If late payment is penalised, it will be hard to resist the publisher's request for equally severe penalties for late delivery of books or other defaults. On the other hand, prompt settlement is not a common virtue among publishers. Even if the clause is omitted, it is nonetheless possible to obtain agreement for settlement of at least the final instalment by bill of exchange, which gives some protection; or even to obtain irrevocable letters of credit.

     (a)   the subsidiary rights (if any) of any third party under a sub-licence validly entered into by the Publishers prior to termination;

     (b)   the rights of the Proprietors to money accrued due to the Proprietors in respect of the Publishers' sales and exploitation of the Work up to the date of termination;

     (c)   any claim which either party may have against the other for damages or otherwise.

15.3 After termination or expiry of this Agreement the Publishers shall from time to time when so requested do all such things and sign and execute such documents and deeds as the Proprietors may reasonably require in order to confirm the reversion of rights to the Proprietors under the terms of this Agreement and in particular (but not by way of limitation) the Publishers shall give notice in the form specified by the Proprietors to all (if any) of the Publishers' sub-licensees of the termination of this Agreement and requesting such sub-licensees as from the date of termination to account to the Proprietors or as the Proprietors shall direct for money payable by such sub-licensees in respect of the Work.

16. Penalties

16.1 If the Publishers fail to pay to the Proprietors sums due under this Agreement within the times specified in this Agreement the Publishers agree to pay to the Proprietors interest on such sums overdue equal to [x] per cent above the current base rate at [*Bank*] from the due date until such payment is made.

16.2 If delivery of the Work is delayed by more than four weeks after the date provided for in Clause 2.2 unless the parties have agreed in writing upon a revised date of delivery the Publishers shall be entitled to postpone publication by a maximum of 16 weeks and the settlement of the final instalment of the purchase price herein provided for shall be postponed by an equivalent period. If delivery of the Work is delayed by more than 24 weeks after the date provided for in Clause 2.2 the Publishers shall be entitled forthwith by notice in writing to the Proprietors to cancel this Agreement and to be repaid all sums advanced to the Proprietors hereunder together with interest on such sums equal to [x] per cent above the current base rate at [*Bank*] from [*date*] up to the date of cancellation.

17. Proprietors' Copies

17.1 The Proprietors shall retain twelve copies of the Work, of which six copies shall be presented to the Author.

17.2 The Proprietors shall additionally be entitled to repurchase not more than 250 copies of the Work from the Publishers at the Price and additional copies at the best UK trade discount for promotional purposes only and not for resale.

18.1. The period of two years is common, but other periods can be agreed.

18.2 The reason for the inclusion of this sub-clause is to avoid a situation whereby remaindered copies of the UK edition of the work find their way into, for example, the USA, thus potentially damaging sales of any US edition.

19. It may be unnecessary to include this undertaking to supply materials free of charge; but if such materials as proofs and extra jackets are to be supplied, it should be clear in the agreement whether they are free, at cost, or at cost plus a handling charge.

20. Packagers may wish to relate the unit price of any reprint to the cover price, in which case a sentence can be added to say that the price paid to the packager for any reprint shall not be less than (eg 25%) of the publisher's cover price.

7.3 The Publishers shall supply to the Proprietors free of charge six copies of each and every edition of the Work sub-licensed by them to third parties under the terms of this Agreement.

8. Remainders

8.1 The Publishers shall be entitled no earlier than [*24*] calendar months after first publication of their edition of the Work to dispose of surplus copies of that edition only as a remainder after first making an offer in writing to the Proprietors to sell such copies to the Proprietors at a price equal to the best written offer from any potential purchaser, such offer to be accepted within three months of its receipt.

8.2 The Publishers may not dispose of stocks of the Work under the provisions of this clause outside the Territory nor permit their disposal by any third party outside the Territory without the prior written permission of the Proprietors.

9. Provision of Advance Material

The Proprietors shall provide the Publishers with the advance information and material specified in Appendix 4 attached to and forming part of this Agreement and shall at the Publishers' request supply additional sales material at cost price subject to reasonable notice from the Publishers.

10. Reprints

The price of any future reprint or new edition of the Work shall be the subject of a separate agreement between the Publishers and the Proprietors.

11. *Force Majeure*

No failure or delay in performance of the obligations of either party to this Agreement shall be deemed a breach if such failure or delay is caused by or is due to any cause beyond the reasonable control of such party.

12. Assignment

12.1 The Proprietors may not assign the benefit of this Agreement (or any interest in the Agreement) without the prior written consent of the Publishers except to any person as part of the transfer of the relevant part of the Proprietors' business, and provided that the Proprietors procure the assignee to enter into a direct covenant with the Publishers to observe and perform all of the obligations of the Proprietors as set out in this Agreement.

12.2 The Publishers may not assign or dispose of the Publishers' rights or obligations under this Agreement without the prior written consent of the Proprietors.

13. Notices

13.1 Any notice, consent or the like ('the Notice') required or permitted to be given under this Agreement shall not be binding unless in writing. It may be sent to a party to this Agreement by hand delivery, pre-paid first class post [*addressed to the Company Secretary or by electronic*

mail transmission] at the address set out in this Agreement or as otherwise notified.

23.2 Any Notice sent by post shall be deemed received on the second business day following posting.

23.3 Any Notice sent by electronic mail shall be deemed given 24 hours after the time of its actual transmission.

24. Miscellaneous

24.1 This Agreement shall be binding upon and inure to the benefit of the parties, and their permitted assigns.

24.2 This Agreement contains the full and complete understanding between the parties and supersedes all prior arrangements and understandings whether written or oral relating to the subject matter of this Agreement.

24.3 This Agreement shall not be modified except in writing and signed by both parties or their duly authorised representatives.

24.4 The failure by either party to enforce at any time or for any period any one or more of the terms or conditions of this Agreement shall not constitute a waiver of any such term or of that party's right at any time subsequently to enforce any and all terms and conditions of this Agreement.

24.5 The warranties and indemnities contained in this Agreement and the provisions for payment of and accounting in respect of royalties and other monies due to the Proprietors under the terms of this Agreement shall survive the termination or expiry of this Agreement.

24.6 The headings in this Agreement are for convenience only and shall not affect its interpretation.

24.7 References to clauses, sub-clauses and schedules are to clauses, sub-clauses and schedules of this Agreement.

24.8 Nothing contained in this Agreement shall constitute or be construed as constituting a partnership or the relationship of principal and agent between the parties.

25. Jurisdiction

This Agreement shall be governed by the law of England and the parties hereby submit to the jurisdiction of the English courts.

AS WITNESS

the hands of authorised representatives of the parties on the date first above written

....

for and on behalf of the Publishers

....

for and on behalf of the Proprietors

Appendix 1. It is advisable to make the description of specifications clear enough to define accurately what the publisher is buying, but not so detailed as to limit the packager's freedom to make reasonable adjustments in the course of production.

APPENDIX 1

Specification

Title:

Author:

Order No:

Quantity:

Price per copy: fob/cif

Royalty:

Price:

Delivery date:

Extent:

Approximate number of words:

Trimmed page size:

Illustrations:

Printing:

Binding:

Jacket:

Text paper:

Date for supply of Publishers' ISBN, barcode, etc:

Appendix 3.   There are many ways of defining the territory, including a complete listing of territories world-wide. The appropriate form will depend on the circumstances. See especially Appendix H.

UK publishers still often ask for exclusive UK and Commonwealth rights, in which case Canadian rights at least should be retained in order to facilitate selling rights in the USA.

The question here for packagers to ask themselves is, who will sell the various rights more effectively — publisher or packager? There is no point in the packager selling rights that the publisher will not exploit. From the packager's point of view, there is an argument for starting off with the territory as suggested in the draft agreement, and asking the publisher to increase the total print quantity in exchange for concessions. It also makes sense for the packager to include a time limit in the case of at least the most important overseas markets, so that if, for example, Australian rights are licensed to the publisher, they automatically revert to the packager if after a reasonable period of time the work has not been made available, or ceases to be available, on the Australian market.

An increasingly important set of right that packagers may prefer to retain is that of English-language sales in Europe. It is sometimes possible for a packager to deal direct with European distributors, but among the factors to consider is the possibility of competing with co-editions in other languages.

APPENDIX 2

Publishers' Delivery and Packing Requirements

APPENDIX 3

Territory

Exclusive in the Commonwealth as constituted at the date of this Agreement excluding Canada, Australia and New Zealand; non-exclusive throughout the rest of the world excluding the United States of America and its dependencies and the Philippine Islands.

APPENDIX 4

Advance Information and Material

1. Not less than [x] days before delivery: full title; author's name; description of contents and illustrations; biographical details of author; jacket copy.
2. Not less than [x] days before delivery: [y] sets of complete proofs of the text.
3. Not less than [x] days before delivery: [y] advance jackets.
4. Not less than [x] days before delivery: [y] advance sets of sewn sheets with jackets/advance bound and jacketed copies.

Additional Clauses
A number of other items can be dealt with in the contract. Among the additional matters which can arise are:

Prices
It may happen that a price is agreed between packager and publisher based on a percentage of a notional retail price. In theory the publisher can make a last-minute decision to raise the cover price, while the per copy price to the packager remains unchanged. If this is perceived as a possible difficulty, it can be guarded against by using the following clause:

'The Price assumes a UK retail price per copy for the Work of not more than £ [x]. Should the Publishers increase the said retail price (except by reason of the addition of VAT or other tax) then the Price shall also be increased to a sum not less than [y] per cent of the final retail price.'

Inflation
It is not uncommon, particularly with books on a long production schedule, for provisions to be included in the agreement to protect the packager against the effects of inflation, cost increases in materials and labour, and fluctuating rates of currency exchange. Such protection is usually limited to a fixed percentage of the contract price. A possible wording is as follows:

'The Price is based upon rates of exchange and costs of labour and manufacture prevailing at the date of this Agreement and is subject to variation in the event of rises or falls in such rates and costs at the date of delivery. The Price shall be increased or reduced by a maximum of [x] per cent in proportion to such rises or falls and the Proprietors shall notify the Publishers of such increases or reductions as soon as practicable and not later than [y] days before the date of delivery.'

Publisher's Right to Manufacture
Publishers sometimes seek to acquire the right, in certain circumstances, to obtain from the packager original or duplicate film from which to reprint the book. Such a request should usually be resisted.

Changes to the Jacket Design
The publisher may wish to make changes to the jacket design after approval of the original dummy; but such matters are better dealt with outside the context of the contract.

Prohibition on the Production of Competing Works
Some publishers attempt to prohibit the packager from producing books for other publishers which might compete with the book concerned. This should obviously be resisted.

Option on the Author's Next Work
Sometimes the publisher seeks to obtain an option on the next work by the same author in which rights are controlled by the packager. There may be a case for this. It should be remembered that options are in practice difficult to enforce.

New Edition
A situation can arise when a packager wishes to produce a new edition of a book, perhaps for an overseas customer. If the original publisher does not want to produce a new edition, it is useful for the packager to have the right to offer the new edition to a different publisher. Here is a suggested form of words:

'In the event of either (a) the rate of sale of the Work declining below 250 copies in a year, or (b) stocks of the Publishers' edition of the Work totalling less than 250 copies, the Proprietors shall have the right to offer the Publishers the first option to consider the acquisition of rights in a revised and amended edition of the Work on terms similar to those provided herein having due regard to prices of manufacture and like factors, such option to be exercised within three months of notification by the Proprietors of details of the revision and the price thereof. Should the parties fail to enter into an agreement concerning the new edition within six months of notification by the Proprietors, the Publishers' rights under this Agreement shall terminate forthwith, and any stock held by the Publishers shall be remaindered in accordance with the provisions of this Agreement, whereupon the Proprietors shall be entitled to enter into agreement with a third party to publish the new edition.'

Reprints
The same point can be made with regard to reprints:

'The price of any future reprint or new edition of the Work shall be the subject of a separate agreement between the Proprietors and the Publishers, except that the unit price paid by the Publishers to the Proprietors shall not be less than 25% of the Publishers' retail price.'

The Sale of the Publisher's Stock to Book Clubs
For obvious reasons publishers sometimes wish to sell off surplus stock to book clubs, and if the quantities involved are moderate this procedure may be acceptable. But an open-ended provision to this effect in the contract should be resisted.

Arbitration
A clause providing for arbitration is sometimes included, although rarely invoked:

'Any question or difference arising between the parties concerning the meaning of this Agreement or the rights and liabilities of the parties shall be referred to a single arbitrator in London to be agreed between the parties. Failing such agreement within 30 days of the request by one party to the other such reference shall be to an arbitrator appointed by the Chief Executive for the time being of the Publishers Association. The decision of such arbitrator shall be final and binding upon the parties. Any reference under this Clause shall be deemed to be a reference to arbitration in accordance with the provisions of the Arbitration Act 1996 or any statutory modification or re-enactment thereof.'

It should be borne in mind that arbitration is costly. The arbitrators require high fees and in practice, frequently owing to other commitments, take a considerable time to determine any case referred to them. The courts have set time limits, and there are several judges experienced in publishing/copyright matters to whom publishing cases are normally referred. It is always possible for the parties to agree to arbitration where it is appropriate, but the legal advice the BPA has been given is to resist the inclusion of a general arbitration clause in the agreement.

International Co-Edition Agreement

A co-edition is normally a project where a book is conceived by one publisher who then approaches one or more overseas partners with a view to licensing the work to them and organising the simultaneous printing of editions for all the co-edition partners in order to achieve economy of scale. A simple co-edition could consist of a British publisher co-printing the English edition for an American partner, or a more complex arrangement whereby the original publisher prints for several partners, perhaps including American and foreign language licensees. The following contract covers a co-edition produced for a foreign language partner.

The originating publisher makes a substantial investment in developing the project and will carry responsibility for payment for the combined printing; it will therefore be crucial to consider carefully at what stage payment will be received from the various co-edition partners (see note to Clause 9).

If the work is not yet delivered to the proprietors in the original language in typescript form, it may be necessary to add a description of the material, including details of illustrations since these will be crucial to a co-edition.

Publishers may find it advisable to reinforce the fact that the licence is limited to a specific edition of the book in question. Although in practice it is usually preferable to continue to license subsequent editions to the same licensee, this limitation does enable alternative arrangements to be made for a new edition in the case of any book which is likely to need regular revision or updating, if the original licensee proves unsatisfactory.

1. Form

As the proprietors will be providing the publishers with printed copies under the terms of Clause 7, the form of volume rights (hardback with or without jacket, or paperback) can be specified here. The publishers do not have the facilities to manufacture copies in volume form for any sublicensees (see Clause 19).

Territory

In the case of languages such as Portuguese and Spanish which are national languages in more than one country (e.g. Portugal and Brazil, Spain and Argentina, etc.), it may be advisable to limit the licence territorially, as provided for in the wording. If more extensive rights are granted, it is worth noting that in the case of co-editions of heavily illustrated books for the general reader, the publishers as licensees may attempt to require the proprietors not to export their own edition of the work into the publishers' market. As this may be a crucial element in the negotiations, the proprietors as sellers must clearly establish the publishers' requirements on sales territories at a sufficiently early stage of the negotiations to avoid misunderstandings or conflict at a later stage. It should also be remembered that to require the imposition of a market bar in an EU territory will bring the contract into conflict with EU legislation. (See also Appendix J)

2. Licence Period

The aim of the contract is to enable the proprietors to supply the publishers with physical copies, and to continue to resupply further copies if required provided that agreement can be reached on timing and price. The life of the licence is therefore tied to the availability of copies provided by the proprietors; it would be unrealistic to grant a licence for the full term of copyright under these circumstances, although the term might perhaps be extended if a reprint licence is subsequently granted to the publishers under the terms of Clause 11 to enable them to manufacture themselves. In practice, allowing the manufacturing control of a book of this kind to pass from the proprietors to the publishers is not desirable, although it may sometimes be a means of continuing the life of the book if agreement on the timing and pricing of manufacture by the proprietors cannot be reached (see note to Clause 11).

The licence term will run from the date inserted by the proprietors on submission of the agreement to the publishers.

3. Integrity of Text

No changes should be made without the prior permission of the proprietors.

Approval of Text

In certain cases it may be advisable to reserve the right to approve the text of the translation in manuscript form prior to the proprietors commencing production of copies for the publishers, although it is not every author who is the best judge of the quality of translation of his/her work. Such approval should not be unreasonably withheld and should be given within a reasonable time, e.g. 60 days of receipt of the text of the translation. It should be established at an early stage of the negotiations whether the proprietors require such approval, as any delay may affect the co-edition production schedule for this and perhaps for other editions which are being co-ordinated with this printing.

MEMORANDUM OF AGREEMENT made this   day of
    19   between   of   (hereinafter called 'the
Proprietors', which expression shall, where the context admits, include the
Proprietors' administrators and assigns or successors in business as the
case may be) of the one part and   of   (hereinafter
called 'the Publishers', which expression shall, where the context admits,
include any publishing imprint subsidiary to or associated with the
Publishers and the Publishers' administrators and assigns or successors in
business as the case may be) of the other part

Whereby it is mutually agreed as follows concerning a translation which
the Publishers wish to issue in the   language (hereinafter
called 'the Translation') of a work at present entitled
[*title*]   [*number*] Edition (hereinafter called 'the Work') by
        (hereinafter called 'the Author') which is/is to be published in the
        language by the Proprietors.

1. In consideration of the payments herein mentioned the Proprietors grant
to the Publishers the exclusive right and licence to publish the Translation
in   form and to sell copies of the Translation throughout the
following territories:

2. Subject to the terms of Clauses 11 and 18 hereof, the licence herein
granted shall last for a period of   years from the date of this Agreement.
The Agreement may be renewable thereafter subject to the mutual agreement
of terms between the parties.

3. The Publishers shall arrange for the translation of the Work to be made
at their own expense faithfully and accurately by a qualified and competent
translator, whose name and qualifications shall be sent to the Proprietors.
The Publishers undertake that no abbreviations of, alterations and/or
additions to the Work shall be made without the prior written consent of the
Proprietors. If in the opinion of the Publishers and on the advice of their
legal advisers the Work contains any passage that may be reasonably
considered actionable at law in the territories granted to the Publishers
under this Agreement, the Publishers shall have the right upon prior written
notice to the Proprietors to modify or to remove such passage from the
Translation.

The Publishers, if requested to do so, shall submit the text of the
Translation to the Proprietors for approval prior to the commencement of
production of the Translation.

Changes for Legal Reasons
This clause also makes provision for the publishers to make changes to the work for their
translation if the content is deemed likely to lead to legal action in their own country,
subject to notifying the proprietors (see also warranty in Clause 23 plus note).

4. External Permissions Clearance

This clause is intended to alert both parties before they sign the contract to the need to agree which party is to obtain permission from and pay any required permissions fees due to third parties, and indeed to remind them in the first place that such costs may have to be paid. Given the time constraints of the production schedule for a heavily-illustrated co-edition project where other foreign publishers may also be involved, it would seem advisable for the proprietors to be responsible for the work of all permissions clearance required, rather than to be dependent on each licensee undertaking the clearance work for his own market. However, the proprietors must then decide whether the full cost for clearance for each market should be quoted to the licensees in each country as a separate item, or whether it should be included in the unit cost quoted to each customer in Clause 7.

5. Acknowledgment and Copyright Details

While the proprietors will be manufacturing copies for the publishers, the correct form of acknowledgment to the author and the proprietors plus a correct copyright line should be spelled out for inclusion in the text film which the publishers will supply to the proprietors under the terms of Clause 6.

6. Production Requirements

The proprietors will need to brief the publishers carefully on the exact form in which film of the text of the translation is to be supplied; it is likely that the exact details for this will be agreed separately from the contract. The publishers will need to be supplied with a grid of the layout of each page of the book so that the translated text is typeset to fit round the existing imposition of the illustrations. The question of whether items such as black rules are to be included in the illustration or the text film must be discussed well in advance. The proprietors will also need to specify whether the text film supplied by the publishers should be in sheet or page form and positive or negative, right or wrong reading, emulsion side up or down. The deadline for the supply of film to the proprietors should be a contractual matter since the late supply of film from one foreign partner could jeopardise the whole schedule for a multi-language co-edition.

The proprietors should supply the publishers with ozalid proofs of the translation by an agreed date and the publishers must in turn approve those ozalids or identify any errors within an agreed period from their receipt so that final production may go ahead on time.

7. Supply of Copies

This clause details the product which will be supplied by the proprietors to the publishers, together with the agreed price. Exact physical specifications for the translation will be appended in a schedule to the contract, giving details of format, extent, paper, binding, packing etc. In some cases the proprietors may agree to supply an additional quantity free of charge, for promotional use by the publishers.

The exact terms of supply are crucial and must be clearly agreed between the parties: whether the price is royalty inclusive or exclusive (an exclusive deal will necessitate the inclusion of Clause 12 and modifications to several other clauses); whether export packing is included; whether the price is ex-works (if so the printing location must be specified); FOB (free on board) a designated port in the country of manufacture, in which case the proprietors' responsibility will end half-way over the rail of the vessel; or CIF (cost, insurance and freight) a designated port in the country of the publishers, who will then be responsible for the cost of offloading, customs clearance and onward transport into their own warehouse. It is perhaps less usual for the proprietors to quote a price delivered into the publishers' warehouse since the publishers would be expected to have greater familiarity with local procedures and services.

It is vital that if there is any decision by the proprietors to alter the printing location all the co-edition partners should be warned immediately, since it may adversely affect shipping costs.

It is also vital that before a price per copy is agreed any specific requirements by the publishers which would not normally be provided (e.g. a different jacket design,

4. The Proprietors and the Publishers shall mutually agree responsibility for obtaining, wherever necessary, permission for the use in the Translation of copyright literary or artistic material incorporated in the Work, and shall also agree upon responsibility for paying any fees required for such permissions and for ensuring that appropriate acknowledgment is made in the Translation.

5. The Publishers undertake that the name of the Author shall appear in its customary form with due prominence on the title page and on the binding and jacket/cover of every copy of the Translation. On the reverse of the title page shall appear the following copyright notice: '©   ' together with the following acknowledgment: 'This translation of   [*title*] [*number*] Edition is published by arrangement with   [*name of Proprietors*]'.

6. The Publishers shall supply the Proprietors with imposed film of the text and jacket/cover of the Translation to the Proprietors' required specifications no later than   . The Proprietors shall supply the Publishers with ozalids of the Translation for their approval on or about   . The Publishers shall confirm their approval to the Proprietors by telex fax or e-mail within   days of the receipt of the ozalids.

7. The Proprietors undertake to supply to the Publishers   copies of the Translation in *hardback jacketed/paperback* form with the Publishers' imprint at a royalty *inclusive/exclusive* price of   per copy/ *plus a further*   *copies free of charge/* all such copies to conform to the

---

shrinkwrapping or individual cartoning if this is not standard) are discussed since they will affect the price. Any variations of this kind should be covered in this clause.

It is important for the proprietors to qualify here the duration of the price quoted; if the publishers fail to deliver the film or approve ozalids of the translation by the required deadlines, their order may not be included in the co-edition and any reduction in the total print run may affect the price quoted to all participants. A licensee who fails to meet required deadlines cannot expect the proprietors to hold to the same unit price if he is to supply the copies at a later date.

However, this clause may include a provision for the publishers to increase their order provided that this is confirmed before the paper cut-off date. Such copies may be supplied at a run-on price which would facilitate the onward sale of copies to a book club by the publishers.

Over- or Under-Supply
Since the final print run for the translation may be over or under the exact quantity ordered, provision is here made for the acceptance of up to an agreed percentage variance. A variance of 5 per cent is generally considered acceptable, although German publishers may accept up to 10 per cent. It is important to note that a distinction should be drawn between an additional allowance of 'free' copies (usually provided to cover review copies or a small number of damaged copies) and a true over- or under-supply by the proprietors' printers.

The question of including provision for a fluctuation in the exchange rate is a vexed one. In principle, the safest way for the proprietors to ensure that they are able to pay their printers is to quote the unit price in the currency of the country in which the translation is being printed, but this may not always be practical. The range of printing locations used today may mean that in any single co-edition deal three currencies are involved: that of the proprietors, that of the publishers, and that of the printing location. A fluctuation of more than 5 per cent in either direction would seem an appropriate point for the parties to share the differential.

8. Delivery

(a) Provision should be included here for the supply of an agreed number of advance copies and the parties should agree on whether these will be standard copies as they come off the production line or early handbound copies if the production schedule is particularly tight. The method of despatch of these copies should be agreed and the publishers required to inform the proprietors of their approval or of any problems immediately on receipt of the advance copies and before the bulk shipment date outlined in (b).

(b) A realistic schedule for bulk shipment must be agreed between the parties, although the proprietors would be unwise to agree to a date 'not later than . . .', particularly if several partners are involved in the co-edition. A firm deadline should however be imposed for the provision of shipping and documentation instructions by the publishers.

9. Payment

This clause should specify the schedule for payment for the copies supplied. These terms may vary greatly according to the title in question, the level of investment by the proprietors, and the relationship between the parties. An arrangement might be one-third of the total amount on signature of the contract, one-third on commencement of production, on completion of the colour separations or by an agreed calendar date, and one-third on shipment of the copies. An alternative might be half on signature of the contract and half an agreed number of days after shipment. Some proprietors may be prepared to agree to accept full payment an agreed number of days after receipt of the copies by the publishers. However, as considerable investment is often involved on the part of the proprietors, in origination costs, paper purchase and printing costs, it would seem reasonable for the publishers to offset some of those costs by paying a proportion as they are incurred by the proprietors. It is always wise to obtain both bank and trade references when dealing with a new licensee; if there is any doubt, payment could be required against an irrevocable letter of credit drawn on a bank in the country of the proprietors.

10. Quality

While it is hoped that the publishers will have reported any problems on quality as soon as the advance copies are received, it is nevertheless essential that any problems with the bulk consignment, e.g. of printing or binding faults or damage in transit, should be reported to the proprietors promptly so that they can take up any such problems with the printer or the shipping agent. Some proprietors may be prepared to allow a more generous period for the rejection of faulty copies.

11. Reordering

It is obviously in the interests of the proprietors to continue to manufacture copies for the publishers if sales of the translation prove successful, and it will be necessary to canvass each co-edition partner regularly so that their needs can be co-ordinated, either with the proprietors' own reprint needs or so that several overseas editions can be printed together even if the proprietors do not themselves require copies of their own edition.

Provision is however included here for film to be provided to the publishers to enable them to continue printing the translation themselves if it proves impossible to reach agreement on price and delivery date for future orders. This switch of manufacturing responsibility is usually only allowed as a last resort, since it reduces the potential number of partners in the co-edition; it has also been known to lead to a situation where the publishers then offer to print for other co-edition partners. Although they could not proceed with this without permission from the proprietors, a licensee might be able to undercut the printing prices offered by the proprietors and it would then be difficult to justify maintaining control of the production. On the other hand, if the proprietors cannot

specifications listed in the Schedule to this Agreement. The Proprietors will also supply an additional   jackets free of charge.

This price is *inclusive/exclusive* of export packing as specified in the Schedule hereto and is *ex-works [location]/CIF/FOB port of*
and will hold provided that the Publishers supply all necessary material and approval of ozalids of the Translation by the dates specified in Clause 6 hereof. The Publishers agree to accept and pay for up to   per cent over or under supply of copies of the Translation.

The price per copy is based on an exchange rate of   /   as at   [*date*]. Should the exchange rate vary from this by more than 5 per cent the difference in price per copy will be divided equally between the parties hereto.

Should the Publishers wish to increase their order above the said   copies they shall inform the Proprietors by the paper cut-off date of   and such copies shall be supplied at a *price of*   *per copy/price to be agreed between the parties.*

8. (a) The Proprietors shall supply the Publishers with advance copies of the Translation by *post/courier/airfreight* as soon as production is completed. The Publishers shall confirm their approval of the Translation or notify the Proprietors of any complaints immediately on receipt of such advance copies and in advance of the date specified in Clause 8(b) hereof.

(b) The Proprietors undertake to deliver   copies of the Translation in bulk to a designated shipping agent on or around   [*date*] provided that the Publishers supply full packing, documentation and shipping instructions no later than   [*date*].

9. Payment for the said copies amounting to   is payable by the Publishers as follows: [*schedule of payment*]

10. Should the Publishers have any complaints regarding the quality or condition of the bulk shipment of copies of the Translation these must be submitted in writing to the Proprietors within one month of receipt of the shipment. In the absence of any notification within this period the Proprietors have the right to assume that the Publishers have accepted full delivery of the shipment to their satisfaction.

11. Should the Publishers require further copies of the Translation the Proprietors agree to supply such copies at a price to be mutually agreed between the parties when the order for such copies is placed. If the parties are unable to agree on the said price or delivery date for such copies, the Proprietors may agree to grant the Publishers a reprint licence for the Translation on terms to be agreed between the parties and agree to provide a quotation for duplicate film of the Translation.

***For Royalty Exclusive Deal*

offer satisfactory prices and schedules on reprints to the co-edition partners, the proprietors may on occasion be able to join a co-edition organised by a licensee.

12. Royalties

This clause should be inserted only if the price agreed in Clause 7 is royalty exclusive. A royalty inclusive price would technically require no further accounting to the proprietors, who would receive full payment whether the translation sold well or not. There is still however an argument for the proprietors being kept informed on sales of the translation, if only to keep track of when further copies might be required (see Clause 13).

If this clause is to be omitted, subsequent clauses should be renumbered to take account of this.

If royalties are to be payable, an advance should be paid; this would usually be paid in full on signature of the contract, although a larger advance could perhaps be split half on signature and half on publication or by an agreed calendar date. It is important to make it clear that this advance relates only to royalty payments and not to payment for the copies supplied under the terms of Clause 7. The royalty advance is forfeit if the publishers breach the contract in any way.

Any variation agreed between the parties (e.g. the royalty being calculated on the net amount received by the publishers rather than on the catalogue retail price) would have to be specified in this clause. The wording 'catalogue retail price' is aimed to allow for any system of pricing, whether minimum price, fixed price or not. In some countries the price on which the royalty is based will be less VAT (value added tax).

These provisions reflect the general practice of basing payment on a royalty per copy sold.

When entering into agreements with French publishers it should be remembered that it is sometimes their practice to insist on the inclusion of their *clause de passe* whereby royalties are payable on only 90 per cent of the number printed. The remaining 10 per cent is considered to be necessary to cover review copies, damaged copies and the practice of French booksellers expecting 'baker's dozens', i.e. one free copy for every 12 ordered. This 10 per cent of royalties applies not only to the first printing (when an allowance for review copies etc. would be expected) but to all printings, and applies where payment is related to the number printed but does not apply where the agreement provides for payment of royalties on all copies sold. This should be taken into account and royalties adjusted accordingly where appropriate.

Royalty rates commonly allow for the cost of translation. It is customary for the royalty rates to escalate after an agreed level of sales. The royalty percentages and the level and number of escalation points are of course open to negotiation between the parties. It is customary for different royalty rates to apply for hardback and paperback editions.

13. Accounting

The exact wording of this clause will vary depending on whether the price quoted in Clause 7 is royalty inclusive (in which case this clause is intended to secure regular sales reports) or exclusive (in which case this clause sets out payment requirements).

Accounting is commonly half-yearly in the Anglo-American tradition, although some academic publishers in these markets tend to account yearly. The Continental tradition is yearly accounting. Some countries (in particular Scandinavian) ask for three months in which to tender royalty statements and a further six months in which to pay any moneys due. This period should be resisted; three months should be adequate. It should be remembered that this clause also covers late payment of the price of the copies supplied under the terms of Clause 7, where a longer delay would be quite unacceptable.

This clause makes provision for examination of the publishers' books if required, although this is an expensive exercise and likely to be undertaken only if there is serious reason to believe that royalties are being under-reported.

12. The Publishers shall make the following payments to the Proprietors in accordance with the terms of Clause 25 hereof, namely:

(a) The sum of   which shall be in advance and on account of any royalties which may become due to the Proprietors under this Agreement, payable on signature of this Agreement by the Publishers. The said payment in advance is not recoverable in the event of any default by the Publishers in carrying out the terms of this Agreement.

(b) On the catalogue retail price excluding any VAT of all copies of the Translation sold by the Publishers:

(i) A royalty of   per cent on the first   thousand copies sold.
(ii) A royalty of   per cent on all copies sold beyond the first
     thousand.

(c) No royalties shall be payable on copies of the Translation sold at cost or less, presented to the Proprietors, presented in the interests of the sale of the Translation, lost through theft or damaged or destroyed by fire, water, in transit or otherwise.

13. Accounts/Statements for the sale of the Translation shall be made up yearly/half-yearly by the Publishers to   [*date/dates*] and the account/statement must be rendered (***together with any sums payable under the terms of Clause 12(b) hereof***) within three months of the accounting date/s. Accounts will show:

(a) the number of copies in stock if any at the beginning of the accounting period;
(b) the number of copies sold during the accounting period;
(c) the number of copies presented during the accounting period;
(d) the number of copies remaining in stock at the end of the accounting period

(*** and accounts shall be paid in accordance with the terms of Clause 25 hereof***). Should any of the payments detailed in this Agreement be three months overdue the licence herein granted shall forthwith lapse and all rights granted by it shall, without further notice, revert to the Proprietors, without prejudice to any claim which the Proprietors may have for moneys due, for damages or otherwise.

The Proprietors or their authorised representative shall have the right upon written request to examine the records of account of the Publishers in so far as they relate to the sales and receipts in respect of the Translation, which examination shall be at the cost of the Proprietors unless errors exceeding two per cent of such sales and receipts in the last two preceding accounting periods to their disadvantage shall be found, in which case the cost shall be paid by the Publishers.

14. Failure to Sign or Pay
Provision is made for the proprietors to cancel the contract if the publishers fail to sign the agreement within 60 days of the date inserted by the proprietors, if they fail to make the initial instalment of payment for the copies under Clause 9 or if they fail to pay the royalty advance specified in Clause 12(a) if this applies. It is therefore vital that the due date for payment of these amounts falls as far as possible in advance of the proprietors becoming involved in substantial production expenditure on behalf of the publishers. It may well be possible to divert paper supplies to another buyer, but if printing of the translation has already commenced, cancellation of the contract due to non-payment may result in substantial financial losses for the proprietors. This makes it all the more crucial for the proprietors to seek adequate references on licensees, and if necessary to require payment against an irrevocable letter of credit drawn on a bank in the country of the proprietors. An alternative formula would be to specify 'Failure to pay by the specified dates will render the Publishers liable to pay interest on the sums overdue equal to   per cent above the current base rate at   [name of Proprietors' bank] until such payment is made.'

15. Publication Time Limit
It should be remembered that the publishers will be receiving finished copies ready for sale and the publication time limit permitted may therefore be reasonably short, probably allowing no more than six months calculated from the expected delivery date of the books to the publishers. While there is a provision for cancellation of the contract in the case of failure to publish, in practice the interest of both parties must lie in the translation appearing. Any exceptional circumstances which might lead to delay in publication should therefore be discussed between the parties at the earliest possible stage: for example, late delivery by the proprietors might lead to the publishers wishing to hold off publication until the next appropriate selling season. A postponement of publication for a deal negotiated on a royalty exclusive basis will of course result in a delay of revenue to the proprietors.

16. Publication Date and Price
This clause provides for the publishers to confirm details of the exact publication date and price to the proprietors, and also permits the proprietors to purchase extra copies of the translation at trade discount.

NB There is no provision in this contract for the publishers to supply the proprietors with a specified number of finished copies of the translation as would be the case if the publishers had manufactured the translation themselves. This is because it is expected that the proprietors will retain the required number of copies for their own records and for the author before shipping copies to the publishers.

17. Control of Promotion and Sale of the Translation
The overall management of the publication of the translation is controlled by the publishers.

18. Remaindering
Two years is the usual period. Ten per cent of the net amounts received is the usual percentage, although for a remaindered edition the net amounts received are highly unlikely to exceed cost price. It should be remembered that no royalties will be due in the event of remaindering if the copies were supplied to the publishers on a royalty inclusive basis.

19. Sublicences
The wording of Clause 19 assumes that the proprietors have themselves exclusive authority, under their contract with the author, to handle all such forms and editions of translations of the book. That may, or may not, be so. The literary agent of the author may reserve to him/herself the handling of e.g. first serial rights, merchandising rights, electronic rights, etc. to say nothing of important film rights. Each contract must be

214

14. Should the Publishers fail to sign this Agreement within sixty (60) days of the date of this Agreement, or should the Proprietors not have received from the Publishers the payment specified in Clause 9 hereof by the due date (***or should the Proprietors not have received from the Publishers the advance specified in Clause 12(a) hereof within sixty (60) days of signature of this Agreement by the Publishers ***) then this Agreement shall be deemed not to have come into effect, and all rights granted by this Agreement may at the sole option of the Proprietors and on notice in writing from the Proprietors to the Publishers revert to the Proprietors, without prejudice to any claim which the Proprietors may have for sums due, for damages or otherwise.

15. The Publishers shall, unless prevented by circumstances outside their control, publish the Translation within   months of receipt of bulk delivery of the said copies of the Translation. If the Publishers fail to issue the Translation within that period all rights granted by this Agreement may at the sole option of the Proprietors and on notice in writing from the Proprietors to the Publishers revert to the Proprietors and on such notice any advance payments provided for in Clauses 9 and 12(a) hereof (including any outstanding unpaid portions thereof) shall be forfeited, without prejudice to any claim which the Proprietors may have for moneys due, for damages or otherwise.

16. The Publishers shall provide the Proprietors with details of the actual date of publication and the catalogue retail price of the Translation. The Proprietors shall have the right to purchase copies of the Translation at normal trade terms for personal use but not for resale.

17. The promotion, the manner and extent of advertisement, the number and distribution of free copies for the press or otherwise, pricing and terms of sale of the Translation issued by the Publishers shall be in the sole discretion of the Publishers who shall in all other respects (except only as herein provided) have the entire control of the publication.

18. If, after a period of   years from the date of first publication of the Translation hereunder, the Translation shall in the opinion of the Publishers have ceased to have a remunerative sale, the Publishers shall, on giving notice in writing to the Proprietors, be at liberty to dispose of any copies remaining on hand as a remainder or overstock (*** and shall pay to the Proprietors on such copies   per cent of the net amounts received by the Publishers, except that on any copies sold at cost price or less no royalty shall be payable***).

19. The Proprietors hereby grant to the Publishers the right to sublicense within the market specified in Clause 1 hereof the following rights, subject to the payment to the Proprietors of the specified percentages:

carefully negotiated according to the potential of the book and the specific bundle of rights held on behalf of the author by the proprietors, and the bundle granted by the one publisher to the other should be equally carefully specified.

The rights included in this sample clause do not include any licence involving the manufacturing of copies by a sublicensee, e.g. a book club or a paperback publisher in the publishers' market. This is logical since the contract presumes that all manufacture is controlled by the proprietors, at least initially. If additional copies were required for such purposes, the proprietors would expect to be asked to quote for the supply of those copies (see note to Clause 7 re increasing the order prior to the paper cut-off date).

It is important that such rights as may be granted are subject to the approval of the proprietors, such approval not to be unreasonably withheld. Swift clearance would undoubtedly be necessary for a deal with a book club or for serial rights.

The share of income to the proprietors from the sale of such rights should be agreed with the publishers in advance, but it would not be unreasonable for the proprietors to receive 80 per cent for the first serial rights and 50-60 per cent for the other rights listed. This clause requires that accounting for the income from subsidiary rights shall be made to the proprietors within an agreed number of days from the receipt of income by the publishers from their sublicensees, rather than included with the accounting arrangements for sales of the publishers' own edition (see Clause 13).

The question of book club deals for the translation is a complex one; it should be remembered that if copies have been sold to the publishers on a royalty inclusive basis, there is no justification for receiving further payment if those copies are sold on to a book club. If however copies have been supplied to the publishers on a royalty exclusive basis, payment is due and much will depend on the nature of the proposed arrangement between the publishers and the book club. If the book club buys copies from the publishers on a royalty exclusive basis, the proprietors should receive a share of the royalty paid by the club to the publishers. If the book club buys copies from the publishers on a royalty inclusive basis, the proprietors should receive a royalty on the unit price paid by the club to the publishers.

20. Out of Print

Since the only copies of the translation are those printed by the proprietors for the publishers, there need be no proviso in the contract that the licence may continue if legitimately sublicensed editions remain in the market, since no such editions exist.

A clear understanding between the parties as to exactly what 'out of print' means in the contracts they sign is important. If the translation is unavailable, no reorder has been placed with the proprietors and no arrangements have been made to supply film to the publishers to enable them to manufacture themselves (Clause 11) the contract can be cancelled.

It is important to remember that the copyright in the translated text will normally lie with the publishers, or in a limited number of cases with the translator. Unless arrangements are made for the proprietors to negotiate a transfer of the right to use that translation, any subsequent alternative arrangements made by the proprietors for an edition of the work in the same language would normally require the proprietors to refer any new licensee to the publishers (or the translator if appropriate) for the reuse of the text of the translation.

21. No Transfer

The rights cannot be transferred in any way except in the case of sublicences properly granted under the terms of Clause 19.

22. Rights Reserved

All rights not specifically granted in the contract are reserved by the proprietors. In the case of any book with potential as the basis for a film where those rights are not controlled by the proprietors, it would be advisable to add the following wording to this clause:

'The Publishers, who have no interest in or control of film rights, agree that a film company shall have the right, without compensation to the Publishers, to print and

(i) ***Book club rights where copies are supplied by the Publishers on a royalty exclusive basis: per cent of the royalty paid by the book club to the Publishers

(ii) ***Book club rights where copies of the Translation are supplied by the Publishers on a royalty inclusive basis: per cent of the price paid by the book club to the Publishers

(iii) Serial rights to newspapers and other periodicals:
    (a) First serial rights: %
    (b) Second serial rights: %

(iv) Text quotation rights: %

(v) Anthology rights: %

(vi) Digest and condensation rights: %

Any sublicences granted under this clause are subject to the prior written approval of the Proprietors, such approval not to be unreasonably withheld. Any payment due to the Proprietors under this clause shall be remitted to the Proprietors within   days of receipt by the Publishers of such sums.

20. In the event of the Translation going out of print or off the market at any time during the period of this Agreement the Proprietors shall be at liberty to terminate this Agreement on giving the Publishers six months' notice to reorder copies of the Translation or purchase a set of duplicate film as provided for in Clause 11 hereof. If on the expiration of such period of six months no such arrangements have been made all rights granted under this Agreement shall revert to the Proprietors without prejudice to any moneys paid or due to the Proprietors.

21. This Agreement and the licence hereby granted may not be assigned or transmitted in whole or in part by the Publishers (with the exception of any authorised arrangements under the terms of Clause 19 hereof), nor shall the Translation be published under any imprint other than that of the Publishers as set out in this Agreement, without the prior written consent of the Proprietors.

22. All rights in the Work whether now existing or which may hereafter come into existence which are not specifically granted to the Publishers in this Agreement are reserved by the Proprietors.

23. The Proprietors hereby warrant to the Publishers that they have the right and power to make this Agreement and that according to English law

---

publish in the   language synopses (including quotations) of not more than 10,000 words for use in promoting the film but not for resale.'

23. Warranty and Indemnity
The proprietors here warrant that they control the rights in the language in question and that the book contains nothing likely to lead to legal action in terms of defamation, libel or breach of copyright. It is important that this warranty is limited to liability under the

legislation in the country of the proprietors, since few publishers could be expected to have at their fingertips the detailed knowledge required to make such warranties under legislation worldwide.

Clause 3 already makes provision for the publishers to make changes if the contents of the book are deemed likely to lead to legal action in their own country.

24. Breach of Contract

This makes provision for cancellation following material breach of the contractual terms by the publishers or in the case of bankruptcy or cessation of business on the part of the publishers.

25. Method of Payment

This clause provides instructions on the exact method of payment to the proprietors. If the currencies required for payment for copies of the translation (Clause 7) and any advance and royalty payments (Clause 12) are different, this will have to be specified in this clause. Advance and royalty payments may be taxed at source in some countries, in which case the publishers must provide appropriate documentation to substantiate this and to enable the proprietors to recover the deduction if fiscal legislation permits.

26. Notices

This clause specifies the form in which notice must be given and requires the parties to notify each other of any change of address.

27. Arbitration

Provision is made for arbitration in the initial stages of a dispute; if the problem cannot be

the Work will in no way whatever give rise to a violation of any existing copyright or a breach of any existing agreement and that nothing in the Work is liable to give rise to a criminal prosecution or to a civil action for damages or any other remedy and the Proprietors will indemnify the Publishers against any loss, injury or expense arising out of any breach or alleged breach of this warranty by reason of publication or sale by the Publishers of the Translation pursuant to this Agreement.

24. (a) Should the Publishers at any time by themselves or anyone acting on their behalf be in material breach of any of the clauses or conditions set forth in this Agreement within months after written notice from the Proprietors to rectify such breach, or

(b) should the Publishers be declared bankrupt, or make an assignment for the benefit of their creditors, or take advantage of any insolvency law in their jurisdiction, or if a receiver or trustee is appointed for their property, or if they liquidate their business (otherwise than in a voluntary liquidation for the purpose of and followed by reconstruction within months), or if they cease their usual operation for any reason, should a petition be presented or a meeting be convened for the purpose of considering a resolution for the making of an administrative order, the winding up or dissolution of the Publishers (otherwise than a voluntary liquidation for the purpose of reconstruction)

then in such event all rights granted under this Agreement shall revert to the Proprietors forthwith and without further notice, without prejudice to all rights of the Publishers in respect of any contracts properly entered into by them with any third party prior to the date of such reversion, without prejudice to any claim which the Proprietors may have for damages or otherwise and without prejudice to any moneys already paid or then due to the Proprietors from the Publishers.

25. All sums which may become due to the Proprietors under this Agreement shall be paid by the Publishers in [*currency*], without any deduction in respect of exchange, commission or any other cause by direct bank transfer to [*details of Proprietors' bank account*]. Should the Publishers be obliged by law to deduct tax they shall send a declaration to this effect with the relevant statement of account showing the amount deducted.

26. Any and all notices given hereunder shall be in writing and sent by telex, fax, e-mail, registered or certified mail, return receipt required, to the parties at their respective addresses herein specified. The parties undertake to notify each other of any change of address within thirty (30) days of such change.

27. If any difference shall arise between the parties touching the meaning of this Agreement or the rights and liabilities of the parties hereto, the same

resolved in this way, the ideal situation would be for any legal action to take place in the jurisdiction of the country of the proprietors. This is an important consideration during the early stages of negotiations with a new customer. The legislation of some countries does not permit a contractual requirement of this kind.

An alternative (but less satisfactory) provision might read as follows:

'Any legal action brought by either party to this Agreement against the other shall be brought in the jurisdiction of the registered business offices of the party against whom the action is brought and the laws of that jurisdiction shall apply.'

28. Operation of Contract
Again, ideally the contract should specify that the contract is governed by the legislation of the country of the proprietors, but this may not always be possible.

29. Copyright Protection
This clause firmly places the responsibility for and expense of complying with any required local copyright registration procedures and the subsequent protection of rights on the shoulders of the publishers.

30. New Editions
It is recommended that the preamble limits the contract to the current edition of the work. In practice a co-edition for any subsequent edition could only be undertaken by arrangement with the proprietors since they will control the manufacturing; however, this clause reinforces the limited nature of the licence granted.

If however the relationship between the partners is good, the proprietors may wish to consider as an alternative the inclusion of an option clause which might read as follows:

'The Proprietors agree to grant to the Publishers the first option on the language rights in the next edition of the Work. The Publishers undertake to give a decision within   days of receipt of a copy of the *manuscript/proofs/adequate advance material* for the new edition from the Proprietors. The terms for any licence for the next edition are to be the subject of separate negotiations between the parties.'

shall be referred to the arbitration of two persons (one to be named by each party) or their umpire, provided that any dispute between the parties hereto not resolved by arbitration or agreement shall be submitted to the jurisdiction of the   courts.

28. This Agreement shall be governed by and interpreted and construed in accordance with the laws of

29. The Publishers agree to take all necessary steps to register the title of the Work in the name of   under any national copyright laws at the sole expense of the Publishers. The Publishers also agree to secure the benefits of copyright protection under international copyright conventions that are available for such protection, and at their own expense to pursue all relevant rights at civil and criminal law against any person who infringes such copyright.

30. This Agreement does not grant any rights with respect to subsequent editions of the Work.

AS WITNESS THE HANDS OF THE PARTIES

— — — — — —

(for the Proprietors)

— — — — — —

(for the Publishers)

Schedule

The schedule to be attached to the co-edition contract lists the quantity of copies of the translation to be supplied together with technical details. If necessary, samples of paper and binding material may be attached to the schedule. A sample schedule might read as follows:

Name of author	J. R. Jones
Title	An Illustrated Guide to Aircraft
Quantity to be supplied	5000 copies plus 250 gratis copies
Price	£4.25 per copy Run-on price £3.80 per copy
Number of pages	232 pp plus xii pages of prelims
Number of illustrations	420 colour photographs, 120 black and white line drawings
Format	234mm x 156mm
Paper	80 gsm wood-free machine finished (sample attached)
Jacket specifications	4 colour laminated
Binding	Section sewn, cased, artificial cloth, blocked on spine
Manner of printing	4/4
Packing specifications	Binder's parcels with 10 copies per parcel, stacked on pallets and crated
Paper cut-off date	September 30th 1997
Date of delivery of Publishers' text film	November 7th 1997
Date of delivery of Publishers' jacket film	November 14th 1997

Advance information/material required
by Publishers

> book information sheet (blurb and bibliographical details)
> 12 jacket proofs of the Translation
> 10 advance copies of the Translation

Schedule

Author:

Title:

Quantity to be supplied:

Price:　　　per copy　　　Run-on price:　　　per copy

Number of pages:　　　pp plus　　　prelims

Number of illustrations:

Format:

Paper:

Jacket/cover specifications:

Manner of printing:

Binding:

Packing specifications:

Paper cut-off date:

Date of delivery of Publishers' text film:

Date of delivery of Publishers' ISBN and bar code:

Advance information/material required by Publisher:

Merchandising Rights Agreement

'The world moves on, and the following precedent attempts to move with it. The exploitation of merchandising rights may stretch out to tea towels, to soft toys, to jigsaw puzzles, to coffee mugs, to T-shirts, and to many other forms of merchandising in ways which may not be familiar to all publishers, authors and artists.'

The paragraph reproduced above introduced a Precedent for Merchandising Rights in the First Edition of *Publishing Agreements*, published in 1980. Now, in 1997, the world has moved further on. Precedent One, at Clause 14(r) sets out a range (not, however, a definitive range) of ways of exploiting, through merchandising, characters, items and events in the work which the publisher is publishing in book form. Such merchandising rights may, or may not, be granted to the book publisher. The general point, made elsewhere also in *Publishing Agreements*, that if the publisher wishes to acquire a right, he/she must make sure that he/she has the skills necessary to exploit it, applies especially to merchandising rights. If the publisher is sure, then he/she will negotiate to acquire the right from the author and/or illustrator. The publisher may have his/her own merchandising division using sub-contractors to undertake the manufacturing, marketing and distribution functions while maintaining control over the merchandising programme for a particular work. Alternatively, the publisher may hand over this responsibility to a merchandising agent which has the know-how to design and develop a merchandising programme and enter into sub-licences with manufacturers of particular items or sub-contract manufacture, thus maintaining direct control over each product.

This Precedent can be adapted to cover all possibilities. It consists of the grant from the rights owner (licensor) to the licensee of the rights in all or only some aspects of a particular work to be applied to an identified category or categories of product. In many cases the licensee will need to grant sub-licences and here the chain of control, which is critical to any merchandising operation, can be put at risk. The main licensee must owe basic obligations towards the licensor in relation to the quality of the licensed products which will be backed up by its agreements with sub-licensees and manufacturers. The licensor may wish to dictate the precise terms of any sub-licence agreement entered into by the licensee as Clause 4.3 contemplates.

The length and complexity of a merchandising agreement frequently depend upon how interested the licensor is to preserve and enhance the reputation attaching to the work and secure its value in the long term or whether he simply wants a healthy short-term royalty income. Control by the licensor over the quality of merchandise is essential where there are registered trade marks concerned. It is also important simply to maintain the goodwill attached to the work. If the material is exploited in the right way, goodwill will increase and, with it, the likely royalty income.

This Precedent does not deal with detailed mechanics of quality control since they differ in every case. It should however be borne in mind that in any merchandising arrangement where the licensee is required to seek approvals from the licensor, he should be required to build into the manufacturing timetable sufficient time to secure such approvals and, if necessary, to make adjustments to the product to reflect the licensor's comments. All too frequently, the licensor is presented with a proposition on a 'take or leave it' basis and, with an eye to securing his royalty stream, the licensor may be reluctant to delay manufacture and distribution of a product with which he is unhappy.

Finally, this Precedent should be used with caution and an open mind; it will not suit all situations but applies to a relatively straightforward and typical arrangement. Legal advice should be obtained on any potential problem areas, particularly the securing of intellectual property rights (Clause 3), the vexed question of product liability and litigation (Clause 8) and competition issues generally. The Precedent is designed to be adapted and fleshed out as appropriate. It has, for this Fifth Edition, been updated by Alan Williams of Denton Hall, Solicitors with help from Rebecca Holmes-Siedle on the competition issues.

MEMORANDUM OF AGREEMENT made this   day of
        19   between   of
(hereinafter called 'the Licensor', which expression shall where the context
admits include the Licensor's executors, administrators and assigns or
successors in business as the case may be) of the one part and   of
            (hereinafter called 'the Licensee', which expression shall
where the context admits include the Licensee's executors, administrators
and successors in business) of the other part.
Whereby it is agreed as follows:

1. Definitions

In this Agreement the following definitions shall apply:

1.1 'Licensed Products' shall mean the products listed in Schedule II (as
    amended from time to time by agreement in writing between the
    parties) which are approved by the Licensor pursuant to this Agreement.

1.2 'Net Invoice Price' shall mean the price of any Licensed Products
    invoiced by the Licensee or any Sub-Licensee after deduction of
    freight, insurance, packaging costs and any value added or other sales
    tax charged thereon.

1.3 'Quarter' shall mean each consecutive three-month period that this
    Agreement remains in force the first such period beginning on the first
    day of the Term.

1.4 'Sub-Licensee' shall mean any individual, company or firm with
    whom the Licensee enters into an agreement for the manufacture or
    marketing of Licensed Products following consultation with the
    Licensor pursuant to this Agreement.

1.5 'The Term' shall mean the term of [five years] from the date of this
    Agreement which period may be extended by agreement in writing
    between the parties.

1.6 'The Territory' shall mean the territory set out in Schedule III.

---

1. Definitions

The work is to be defined in Schedule I and the licensed products or services, derived from
the work, in Schedule II. The drafting leaves scope for full details of the licensed products
to be inserted (and added to from time to time) accompanied by an indication of what
aspect of the work is going to be used in connection with each product (e.g. character,
names, illustrations). The term of the licence should initially be short but it is often
appropriate to provide for continuation of the term at the licensor's option on a year-by-
year basis. (**1.5**)

There may be registered trade marks (or service marks) already in existence or the
licensor may intend to register trade marks (or service marks) derived from the work in
respect of the goods or services licensed. Trade mark applications should only be made
where there is a genuine intention to market goods or services under the mark. Where
applications are made en bloc or as a transparent attempt to exploit the marks for all they
are worth, they may be rejected on the basis that the proprietor is trafficking in the marks.

The definition of Net Invoice Price could be amended to allow for discounts, refunds
for returns and the like. This will follow negotiations between the parties.

2. Appointment

The agreement will generally be 'exclusive' to the licensee in respect of the identified categories of licensed products. The term 'exclusive' in this context means that the licensor excludes himself and any third parties from the rights granted to the licensee. A 'sole' licence merely excludes third parties so that the licensor can undertake the licensed activities himself. Legal advice should be taken when assessing the various options.

It is important to define the scope of the rights and who owns characters, symbols and other elements, particularly those developed by the licensee during the term of the licence. See also the note to Clause 3.

It is important to note that the limitation of the appointment to the territory cannot be used (where the territory involves one or more (but not all) EEA member states) to prevent the licensee making passive sales (ie responding to unsolicited orders for the product) from customers located outside the territory although it can be used to restrict the licensee from actively marketing the products outside the territory.

3. Intellectual Property Rights

The licensor may not actually own all of the relevant intellectual property rights but rather have an exclusive licence from the author/illustrator or some intermediary which includes the merchandising rights. The precise position in respect of all aspects of the work should be checked in each case and reflected in the wording of the agreement. The moral rights of the author/illustrator may survive despite such licence or assignment. Ideally moral rights will have been expressly waived when the author/illustrator originally agreed to prepare the work. Alternatively a waiver could be obtained prior to the grant of the merchandising rights so that the author/illustrator cannot inhibit their exercise. For moral rights in general, see Appendix D.

It is usually in the licensor's interests to become the owner of the intellectual property rights in any new materials derived from the work. A new work may, though derivative, be sufficiently 'original' to enjoy its own intellectual property rights.

The 'further assurance' (**3.3**) is vital to perfect the licensor's interest in any newly generated works. But see note below.

3.2 If the agreement entered into has an effect on trade between member states it is likely to be caught by Article 85(1) of the Treaty of Rome, and would be void (unless the parties to the agreement came within the de minimis provisions). The Commission has established a principle in the patent and trade mark block exemptions (and in the new technology transfer licensing block exemption) that in an intellectual property licence, a licensee should not be required to assign back severable improvements or modifications made to the licensed works; the most it can be required to do is to grant a non-exclusive licence and this should be on a reciprocal basis so that if the licensor makes any improvements or modifications to the licensed works it would grant a non-exclusive licence to the licensee. An obligation to assign severable improvements/modifications is, therefore, unlikely to be enforceable if the scope of the licence has the potential to fall within Article 85(1).

4. Product Development

Clause 4.1 contemplates that at the date of the agreement the licensee has not put forward its proposals for a manufacturing programme and it may be superfluous in many cases. The licensor's contribution at this stage may be more than many rights owners would expect to make but it should be emphasised that quality control over every aspect of licensed merchandise is essential to maintain the value of the work in its own right, the image and reputation of the licensor and the validity of any registered trade marks.

Where the licensee is merely managing a merchandising operation and engaging sub-licensees in different areas the licensor would be advised to review, if not dictate, the terms

1.7 ['The Trade Marks' shall mean the trade marks, service marks and trade and service mark applications identified in Schedule IV.]

1.8 The 'Work' shall mean the work details of which are set out in Schedule I.

2. Appointment

The Licensor hereby appoints the Licensee as its [sole and] [exclusive] licensee in the Territory for the manufacture marketing distribution and sale of Licensed Products derived from or relating to the Work for the Term subject to the terms and conditions hereinafter appearing.

3. Intellectual Property Rights

3.1 The Licensor is the [proprietor] [exclusive licensee] of copyright in the Work [and is registered proprietor of the Trade Marks]. Any adaptation for the purposes of this Agreement of [the Trade Marks or] any material comprised in the Work shall be subject to approval in writing by the Licensor.

3.2 The Licensee hereby assigns to the Licensor (by way of present assignment of future rights) the copyright and any other intellectual property right subsisting in any material created by or for the Licensee derived from the Work or any aspect thereof. The Licensee shall not do or refrain from doing any act which may prejudice the subsistence of any relevant intellectual property rights or their ownership by the Licensor.

3.3 The Licensee shall do all such acts and execute such documents as the Licensor shall reasonably require at the Licensor's expense and request to confirm the assignment of any rights created pursuant hereto or secure the registration of the Trade Marks or the recording of the Licensee as a registered user of the Trade Marks.

4. Product Development

4.1 The Licensee shall devise a programme for the manufacture of Licensed Products and shall from time to time present to the Licensor a range of proposals for Licensed Products including details of the proposed manufacturers or any other Sub-Licensees who may be involved in their development. The Licensor shall within [14] days of receipt of such proposals indicate in writing its approval or otherwise of the said programme [and where appropriate shall require the Licensee to enter into sub-licence agreements with approved Sub-Licensees substantially in the form of the sub-licence set out in Schedule V to this Agreement].

4.2 In relation to each Sub-Licensee the Licensee shall provide such creative and technical assistance as shall be reasonably required and shall liaise between the Licensor and the Sub-Licensee with a view to securing appropriate access to any materials which may be of use to the Licensee.

4.3 The Licensee shall oversee the performance by the Sub-Licensee of its sub-licence obligations and whether or not a Sub-Licensee is involved shall ensure that the Licensor is supplied with pre-production designs and samples of the Licensed Products and the packaging therefor for approval at key stages in the development and manufacturing processes.

of the sub-licence agreement to be used and to approve the identities of any sub-licensees involved. In such a case the licensor may be less concerned to oversee the merchandising programme that Clause 4.1 contemplates.

It is also essential where registered trade marks are involved that the licensee is made a registered user of the marks in order to preserve their validity notwithstanding the licence. Professional advice is essential in this respect.

Ideally the copyright notice (**4.4**) will include an acknowledgment for the book's author/illustrator etc. but this is a matter of policy for the licensor depending both on his agreement with the author/illustrator and on the moral rights position.

5.   Packaging Marketing and Distribution

The respective contributions of the parties to these functions can vary enormously depending upon the commercial circumstances. This clause sets out a typical arrangement favourable to the licensor.

5.3 Restrictions on the customers that the licensee can supply to can also fall within Article 85(1). if the intention is a genuine protection provision to ensure that the licensed works do not get in the hands of disreputable traders and impair the quality of the mark would, it should not fall within Article 85(1). However more general attempts to control the users to whom the goods are supplied would be caught by Article 85(1) if the requisite effect on trade between member states could be established.

6.   Payment

It is usual for the licensee to make a down payment at the start of the contract which may or may not be set against future royalties. (**6.1**)

Quarterly accounting is usual in the merchandising field. Although this is inconsistent with practice in publishing it can provide the licensor with a steady income source. (**6.2**)

Royalty payments are subject to VAT.

There is scope to require more details about sales in the statements of account. This will depend on a number of factors.

Also, it is often sensible to provide that acceptance of a statement will not preclude the licensor from challenging inconsistencies or mistakes found subsequently.

Allowance could be made for withholding tax: if it has to be deducted, then a valid tax deduction certificate should be provided.

The Licensor shall within [14] days after presentation of such designs and samples communicate its approval or otherwise and the Licensee shall not proceed with the development of any Licensed Product without the relevant approval of the Licensor. Allowance for this approval period shall be built into the timetable for the manufacture of Licensed Products. Such approval shall not be unreasonably withheld.

4.4 The Licensee shall ensure that all Licensed Products [and the packaging therefor] carry a copyright notice [and trade mark notice] in a form and applied in a manner approved by the Licensor.

5. Packaging Marketing and Distribution

5.1 The Licensee shall ensure that all Licensed Products their packaging and any promotional material relating thereto shall conform with the samples thereof previously supplied to and approved by the Licensor pursuant to Clause 4 above.

5.2 The Licensee shall be responsible for advertising, distributing and marketing the Licensed Products in the Territory.

5.3 The Licensee shall not without the prior written consent of the Licensor distribute sell or authorise the distribution or sale of the Licensed Products to any third party which is not a bona fide wholesale or retail firm or company, sell or distribute to vendors or any other disreputable agent. If so required by the Licensor the Licensee shall stop trading immediately in relation to Licensed Products with any person firm or company of whom the Licensor shall disapprove on any reasonable grounds.

[5.4 The Licensee shall meet the sales targets set out in relation to the Licensed Products in Schedule VI.]

6. Payment

6.1 The Licensee shall pay to the Licensor on the signing of this Agreement the sum of [£   ] [which shall be on account of royalty payments due during the currency of this Agreement] [which shall be a non-returnable down payment in consideration for the Licensor entering into this Agreement].

6.2 The Licensee shall supply to the Licensor within [   ] days of the end of each Quarter a statement setting out details of all Licensed Products sold in the Territory during that Quarter and shall pay to the Licensor a royalty equal to [   ] per cent of the Net Invoice Price on all such sales irrespective of whether payment has been received by the Licensee [subject to deduction of the advance referred to in sub-paragraph 6.1 from the payments due in each Quarter until it is absorbed].

6.3 No royalties shall be paid in respect of Licensed Products provided for promotional purposes or otherwise delivered free of charge up to a maximum of [   ] for each of the Licensed Products.

6.4 The Licensee shall keep full and accurate accounts and records of all dealings in the Licensed Products.

6.5 The Licensor or its authorised representative shall have the right upon reasonable notice to the Licensee to enter upon the premises of the

7. The extent to which a Licensee is willing to assume liability will vary with the nature of the deal. Read this clause in conjunction with Clause 8.

7.4 A clause which prohibits the licensee from attacking the validity of the licensed marks/rights would (if the licence had the potential to fall within the scope of Article 85(1)) be caught by Article 85(1) and may or may not be capable of exemption. Up until recently it had not been possible to obtain an exemption for such a provision The case of *Moosehead v Whitbread*, however, suggested a more relaxed attitude to no challenge clauses where the licensed right/trade marks involved were not sufficiently well established in the market to create a barrier to entry. The Commission will accept a provision which provides that in the event of a challenge by the licensee to the validity of the licensed marks/rights then the licensor shall be entitled to terminate the licence and the clause has been constructed in this form.

Licensee to examine the accounts and records of the Licensee and where appropriate of any Sub-Licensees insofar as they relate to dealings in Licensed Products. Such examination shall be at the expense of the Licensor unless errors in the statement referred to in sub-paragraph 6.2 above of more than [5%] are disclosed in which case the said costs shall be met by the Licensee.

6.6 It shall be the exclusive responsibility of the Licensee to recover any money due from Sub-Licensees and purchasers of the Licensed Products and no account shall be taken by the Licensor of any bad debts incurred by the Licensee.

6.7 On the expiration or termination of this Agreement the Licensee shall for a period of [two months] be entitled to sell off any Licensed Products which have at the date of such expiration or termination been manufactured in accordance with this Agreement and all royalties in respect thereof shall be accounted for and paid to the Licensor within 15 days of the expiry of the said [two-month] period.

7. Licensee's Covenants

The Licensee covenants with the Licensor that:

7.1 **Intellectual Property Notices**: each and every one of the Licensed Products, including the packaging, labels, containers, advertisements and/or related material, shall contain such reasonable copyright and/or trade mark and/or patent notices and/or such other relevant notices as shall be required and/or approved by the Licensee;

7.2 **No Representations**: the Licensee will not make any representation or give any warranty on behalf of the Licensor;

7.3 **No Impairment**: the Licensee shall not at any time do or suffer to be done any act or thing which will in any way impair or affect any character or the symbol in the Licensed Products or the rights and interests of the Licensor therein;

7.4 **No attacks etc**: if the Licensee shall attack, question or deny the title of the Licensor in and to any such character or symbol or any copyright or trade mark pertaining to them or attack the validity of the licensed trade marks or licensed rights, the Licensor shall be entitled to terminate this Agreement forthwith by notice in writing;

7.5 **No harm etc**: it will not harm, misuse or bring into disrepute the character or the symbol;

7.6 **No expenses**: it will not create or incur any expenses chargeable to the Licensor;

7.7 **Protect**: it will protect to the best of its ability its right to manufacture, sell and distribute the Licensed Products hereunder;

7.8 **Combination Sales**: it will not use the Licensed Products for combination sales or as premiums, giveaways or for any similar method of merchandising and will ensure that its customers likewise will refrain from making such use of the Licensed Products;

7.9 **No Commercial Tie-ups etc**: it will not enter into any agreement relating to any character or symbol for commercial tie-ups or promotions

8. Liability and Litigation

The strategy for conducting litigation and the respective responsibilities of the parties can be adjusted in various different ways. This clause sets out the most traditional approach which gives each party liability and responsibility for litigation arising from matters within their control. The licensee here is expected to take out insurance to cover his liabilities. The insurance provisions could be made reciprocal.

9. Termination

The reference in Clause 9.1 (c) to s. 123 of the Insolvency Act 1986 relates to corporate insolvency: substitute s. 268 for parties who are individuals.

This clause will need to be adapted when the licensee is an individual or a partnership as opposed to a company.

with any company engaged wholly or partly in a business similar to the Licensor's business.

8. Liability and Litigation

8.1 The Licensee shall give the Licensor prompt notice of any unauthorised use of the Work or of any products or services unfairly competing with the Licensed Products which comes to its attention. The Licensor shall in its own discretion determine what action should be taken in relation to each such use subject to the full co-operation of the Licensee.

8.2 The Licensor will indemnify the Licensee in relation to any action or claim by any third party in which it is alleged that the use of the Work or any part thereof in relation to the Licensed Products pursuant to this Agreement infringes the rights of any third party provided that the Licensee gives the Licensor prompt notice of such claim or action and does nothing to prejudice the Licensor's conduct thereof.

8.3 The Licensee shall indemnify the Licensor and shall be responsible for defending or settling any claims or proceedings brought by third parties arising from any use of the Work in relation to products not approved by the Licensors or the distribution or sale of Licensed Products in any territory other than the Territory or in relation to the safety of the Licensed Products, their conformity with any statute or regulations, their design materials or method of manufacture. The Licensee shall take and maintain a policy of insurance with an insurance office of repute for a minimum of [£   ] in respect of its liabilities for the Licensed Products and shall make the same available for inspection by the Licensor at the Licensor's request from time to time.

9. Termination

9.1 The Licensor shall have the right at any time to give notice in writing to the Licensee to terminate this Agreement and any sub-licences made thereunder on the occurrence of any of the following events.

[(a) If within [12 months] of the date of this Agreement the target sales set out in Schedule VI shall not have been met by the Licensee.]

(b) If the Licensee commits any material breach of any of the terms of this Agreement which, if capable of being remedied, shall not have been remedied within 30 days of the Licensor serving written notice upon the Licensee to do so.

(c) (i) if the Licensee enters into liquidation whether compulsory or voluntary (other than for the purpose of a reconstruction or amalgamation not involving an insolvency of the Licensee);

(ii) if the licensee is deemed unable to pay its debts within the meaning of section 123 of the Insolvency Act 1986 (as amended from time to time);

(iii) if an administrator, administrative or other receiver in respect of the Licensee or any of its assets is appointed;

(iv) any steps are taken with a view to proposing or applying for any kind of composition, interim order, scheme of arrangement,

10. Partnership, Assignment, etc.
Either or both parties can be prevented from assigning rights under the contract. The formula at Clause 10.2 is the most common.

11. Governing Law, Arbitration
Individual clauses in precedents sometimes carry the particular flavour of the business with which any one precedent deals. Deliberately, therefore, as in this form of an arbitration clause, there is sometimes no attempt to harmonise different ways of approaching a very similar issue.

compromise or arrangement involving the Licensee and any of its creditors (including a voluntary arrangement under the Insolvency Act 1986);

(v) any steps are taken with a view to the dissolution of the Licensee;

(d) If the Licensor shall serve notice pursuant to Clause 7.4.

9.2 Termination of this Agreement shall not affect the rights or liabilities of the parties acquired or incurred up to the date of termination.

10. Partnership, Assignment etc.

10.1 The licence hereby granted shall not create a partnership between the parties.

10.2 This Agreement shall not be capable of assignment or transmission in whole or in part by the Licensee without the prior consent in writing of the Licensor.

11. Governing Law, Arbitration

This Agreement shall be governed by and construed in all respects in accordance with English law. If any dispute or difference arises between the parties in connection with this Agreement it shall be referred to arbitration in London before a single arbitrator. If the parties are unable to agree as to the appointment of such arbitrator within [30] days of one party serving notice on the other calling for the appointment of an arbitrator then such arbitrator shall be appointed on the application of either party to the Chairman for the time being of the [Publishers Association]. The award of the arbitrator shall be final and binding on the parties and judgment upon the award may be entered in any court having jurisdiction or application may be made to such court for judicial acceptance of the award and order for enforcement as the case may be.

Schedules

I   The Work
Title, Author/Illustrator (and description)

II Licensed Products
(Identify aspect of the Work, i.e. name/illustration etc. to be used in relation to each product)

III Territory

IV Trade Marks
Registered trade marks

Trade mark applications identifying relevant countries, use classes and goods

[V Sample Sub-licence Agreement]

[VI Targets]

Electronic Media Rights Agreements

The fourth edition of *Publishing Agreements* disappointed some readers by including a paper discussing many of the issues involved in licensing electronic rights, rather than including a precedent agreement. But the fourth edition was compiled in 1992 (and published in 1993) – almost light years ago in terms of developments in the electronic field – and there was in any case very little individual precedent material available on which to draw to form the composite 'snapshot' precedent which would have been required for this book. So the decision last time was probably right.

Now, there is far more contractual precedent material available. Of course those who draft electronic agreements are still feeling their way and are likely to continue to do so unless and until the industry reaches stability. However we feel confident enough for this edition to offer two electronic precedents – one a licence to a software developer/producer to utilise existing printed material in carrier form (e.g. as a CD-ROM) and the other a licence to an institution to make existing printed material available by local network to end users within its own site.

Why have we selected those two types of licences? The answer is that it is typically with those forms of licence that book publishers are most concerned. Some book publishers have divisions which produce electronic products, but the cost of doing so (if nothing else) precludes the vast majority of publishers even from joint ventures with electronic product producers, let alone producing their own products. So licensing is the norm for most book publishers. There are now, in any case, several books of precedents relating to all aspects of production of electronic products; fewer deal with licensing electronic rights.

All the precedents in this book require amendment, to a greater or lesser extent, to suit the circumstances of the transaction; they may also need further specialist advice. Perhaps nowhere is this more true than of electronic contracts.

This precedent is an agreement licensing a pre-existing literary work to a software producer for distribution in carrier form (e.g. as a CD-ROM), though with little alteration it could equally well apply to such licensing of works combining literary and artistic elements. It has been drafted on the premise that either the original work will form the basis for the electronic product (which would be the case for an electronic encyclopaedia, for instance – visual and audio materials being subsidiary in intellectual property terms to the main work) or that the original work will be one of a few of equal importance included in the product – for example a CD-ROM which includes a dictionary, a thesaurus and an encyclopaedia. Where the licensed material does not form a substantial part of the electronic product (measured either by volume or by importance) the licensor's ability to insist on comprehensive approval and consent provisions is likely to be considerably diminished and the contract will need to be modified accordingly. For uses of relatively insignificant portions of existing works a permissions-type agreement may be more appropriate.

Preamble
Recital 1: It is vital for licensing publishers to ensure that they *do* control electronic rights under their agreement with the copyright holder before seeking to exploit those rights in any way. It is to be hoped that head contracts being made today make the position perfectly clear; see Precedent 1 Clause 14(u). The situation may be less clear-cut with older contracts; a grant of 'mechanical reproduction rights', for instance, is unlikely to be sufficient. One criterion that must be borne in mind in interpreting contracts which are not specific over electronic rights is the intentions of the parties at the time of signature. If it is unambiguous that the contract was intended to grant rights to the publisher in future technological developments which could not have been anticipated when the contract was made then all may be well. Even if the licensing publisher has taken an assignment of the entire copyright in the work it has been held that the foregoing still applies. In any case of doubt professional advice should be sought.

Recital 2: If the licensed work is one of several to be included in the product this should be changed to something along the lines of '...based upon the Work, the X English Dictionary and the Y Encyclopaedia and the Proprietor is willing to license the Licensee to utilise the Work so as to do so ...'.

1. Licence
(a) (1) In most licensing situations it is prudent to license rights for as short a time as possible. Nowhere is this more true than in licensing electronic rights: extraordinarily rapid advances in the technology (methods of distribution, transmission, software and hardware) mean that this year's licensed products may be next year's memories. Most licensors are now aware of the need to license (particularly in terms of the platform) as narrowly as possible, since it is impossible to predict what the effect of previously-licensed products may be on the ability to license for applications as yet unknown. Platforms are dealt with in sub-clause (c) of this clause. A performance criterion (see Clause 17(a)) is worth considering, since it will enable recovery of rights if insufficient sales are being made by a licensee. A short licence term is also a desirable inclusion. Clearly the willingness of licensees to agree a licence term of perhaps three years will depend in part on their initial investment in the electronic product concerned; it would be unrealistic to expect the producer of a full multimedia product (with the attendant investment that implies) to accept a three-year licence – though a performance criterion may be more easily achievable or it may be possible to build in a three-yearly review provision. In situations involving more modest investment a licence term of three to five years is often reasonable – possibly with a provision for renewal either by mutual agreement or for automatic renewal if sales (or revenue) exceed a stipulated figure during the final year of the licence.
   (2) Whether an exclusive or non-exclusive licence is to be granted is, of course, a matter for negotiation between licensor and licensee. Much will depend on the extent of the material being licensed: if the licence is on a permission-type basis for a modest amount

MEMORANDUM OF AGREEMENT made this   day of
       19   between   (hereinafter called 'the
Proprietor', which expression shall be deemed to include the Proprietor's
assigns or successors in business as the case may be) of the one part,
and   of   (hereinafter called 'the Licensee') of
the other part, of

WHEREAS, pursuant to an agreement between the Proprietor and the
owner of the copyright, the exclusive rights of exploitation in a literary
work written by   (hereinafter called 'the Author') and
entitled   (hereinafter called 'the Work') are vested in the
Proprietor and

WHEREAS the Licensee wishes to create and develop a computer software
product at present known as   (hereinafter called 'the Product')
based upon the Work and the Proprietor is willing to license the Licensee
to do so on the terms and conditions of this Agreement

NOW IT IS HEREBY MUTUALLY AGREED as follows:

1. Licence

(a)   In consideration of the payments hereinafter mentioned and subject to the terms and conditions hereof the Proprietor hereby grants to the
Licensee for a period of   years from the date of this Agreement
(hereinafter called 'the Licence Term') the exclusive licence to develop
the Work for inclusion in the Product and to manufacture and distribute the
Work in the form in which it is included in the Product
throughout   (hereinafter called 'the Territory') for retrieval
in the   language.

---

of material non-exclusive rights are generally all that will be required. If a multimedia
work is to be developed out of an existing literary work it is likely that the licensee will
want exclusive rights. As in sub-licensing rights in print form it is important to ensure that
the contract is specific as to the actual rights being licensed, whether exclusively or non-
exclusively. For instance, an exclusive licence to utilise a dictionary for production of an
electronic product to include also a thesaurus and an encyclopaedia would not in itself
preclude the licensor from licensing rights in the same work for electronic exploitation in
a product which did not also include a thesaurus and encyclopaedia.

(3) The territory in which rights can be granted may be limited by the head contract.
Even if it is not, there may be good reasons (such as a pre-existing licence to a US publisher
which includes electronic rights) for restricting a licensee to less than world rights. Such
a restriction is practicable for carrier-based products (subject, of course, to the same EC
single market and other provisions as apply to books) and local networks, but not for
exploitation on the Internet.

(4) The language to be included here is the human language involved. Licensees of
multimedia products may intend to make them available in multi-language editions or to
issue local language editions. Again the head contract (possibly together with existing
sub-licensing agreements) will determine the availability of different languages for
licensing.

(c) It is very advisable to restrict the licensed platform. For instance, if the licensee intends to exploit only in the form of CD-ROM there is no reason to include rights to produce as a CD-I. In practice many producers are likely to wish to prevent the licensing publisher from granting electronic rights to another party for what could be an opposing platform. In these circumstances, rather than tying up other platforms by licensing them to the licensee for purely defensive reasons, a licensor can either seek to include in the contract a commitment by the licensee to exploit in such a platform or to include an option and matching rights provision for other platforms. If none of these can be agreed a time limit during which licensing others for different platforms without the licensee's consent (not to be unreasonably withheld or delayed) is precluded could be included.

At present it is often possible to license carrier-based electronic rights (e.g. CD-ROM) and on-line/satellite distribution rights separately. This is likely to become more difficult as the development of hybrid CD-ROM/on-line products proceeds.

(d) For more information on rental and lending, see the Introduction.

2. Reserved Rights
(a) A precedent for licensing on-line transmission will also be found in this Precedent Fourteen.

(b) (1) It is advisable to make any proposed 'bundling' of an electronic product (i.e. software which is included with the sale price of hardware) subject to consent. The prices paid by hardware manufacturers for software to be bundled is low in comparison with the prices paid by consumers for the same software sold separately (and is therefore likely to have an effect on royalties paid to the licensor); and there is a perception that some bundled software is bundled because it does not enjoy sufficient sales in stand-alone form. On the other hand bundled software, at whatever reward to the licensor, can promote enhanced future stand-alone sales of associated software and upgrades of the existing software. If consent to bundling is given a licensor may wish to impose restrictions over such matters as quantities and timing.

(2) Sales can also be enhanced as the result of cover disks supplied free to purchasers of computer magazines. Such disks often include only a sample of an electronic product and frequently are supplied to the magazine at a nominal price, free of charge or accompanied by payment (because of their promotional value). Depending on the nature of the work being licensed there may be no reason to prohibit such cover disks; but see note on Clause 8(b).

3. Release
(b) Before licensing exclusive rights to produce an electronic product it is necessary that the licensor should satisfy itself of the licensee's competence to develop, market and sell the product. This provision is intended to ensure that this competence is translated into actuality. Some licensees may be wary of accepting an obligation as strong as best endeavours, in which case the wording may need to be modified.

4. Alterations
(a) (1) The moral right of the author to object to derogatory treatment (the right of integrity) might be infringed by electronic (or any other) adaptation. This provision seeks to prevent such infringement. Verbatim use of an author's previously-published work in an electronic product should not cause problems but many electronic products require the original work to be adapted considerably. If that is the case then this provision will need to be amended accordingly.

(b) The licence hereby granted shall entitle the Licensee to utilise the Work only in connection with the Product.

(c) The Product shall be manufactured and distributed and made available by the Licensee only in the form of

.

(d) Before making the Product available for rental or authorising third parties to do so the Licensee shall obtain consent from the Proprietor in accordance with sub-clause (i) of Clause 5.

2. Reserved Rights

(a) All rights in the Work other than those licensed to the Licensee under sub-clauses (a) and (b) of Clause 1 are reserved by the Proprietor for exploitation by itself or in conjunction with other parties or by licence to other parties or for non-use as at its sole discretion it shall see fit. Without prejudice to the generality of the foregoing the licence hereby granted to the Licensee is solely in respect of the carrier form specified in sub-clause (c) of Clause 1 and expressly excludes any right to make the Product available to any third party by any electronic delivery service or by any means of on-line, satellite or other transmission.

(b) Save as otherwise may specifically be permitted herein the Licensee shall not without the prior consent of the Proprietor permit the Product to be included with any other work in any computer software nor without the prior consent of the Proprietor shall the Licensee permit the Product to be sold or bundled or otherwise distributed as part of a package with any other computer software or hardware or with any other material of any description.

3. Release

(a) Subject to the Licensee obtaining approvals from the Proprietor in accordance with Clause 5 the Licensee shall release and market the Product at the sole cost, expense and risk of the Licensee in all significant parts of the Territory within   from the date of this Agreement. The Licensee shall notify the Proprietor in writing of the date of release of the Product in each part of the Territory no later than two months prior to such release.

(b) The Licensee shall use its best endeavours to exploit the rights granted to the Licensee hereunder to their optimum commercial potential and shall ensure that the Product is given fair and equitable treatment and is not discriminated against in favour of any other computer software products which the Licensee may publish or distribute.

4. Alterations

(a) Save as shall be necessary for the purpose of adaptation into electronic form the Work shall not be abridged, expanded or otherwise altered

(2) Purchasers of rights for full multi-media exploitation (in particular) may seek a waiver of the author's moral rights, in the same way as do film producers. See General Proviso of Clause 14 in Precedent One and accompanying note. If a waiver of moral rights or consent for a particular application has to be obtained (from the author: the publisher has no moral rights, whether or not it controls electronic rights by way of assignment of copyright or licence) the author may wish to have the right to approve of or at least to be informed of changes and may also want the right to prevent the electronic work being credited to him/her if it is unacceptable to the author. This latter provision would require Clause 6(a) to be amended.

(b) Is an attempt to protect the author's moral right of integrity from being infringed by users of the product.

5. Consultation and Approval
The licensor should endeavour to include as many approval and consultation provisions in the contract as are reasonable in the circumstances: see the first paragraph of the notes to this Precedent and note 1 to Clause 4(a). Some of those included here are quite onerous for the licensee; but wherever an electronic product is to be based on a published work or is to utilise a substantial part the licensor should be concerned at least to have some input into the use of the original material, the quality of the product and the plans for marketing it. If the approvals and consultation provisions are sparse the licensor may wish to include in the contract the proviso that it reserves the right to require the licensee to omit the names of the proprietor and/or the author from the product, its packaging etc.

in any way for the Product without the prior consent of the Proprietor. The foregoing notwithstanding (but subject to the Proprietor's right to be consulted under sub-clause (b) of Clause 5) the Licensee shall be at liberty to include search and other apparatus in the Product so as to increase the usefulness thereof. The Licensee undertakes that the Product shall be faithful to the overall tone and character of the Work.

(b) The Licensee shall include in the Product any and all programs, methods, processes and devices as shall be available and appropriate in order to ensure (in so far as it is possible so to ensure) that users of the Product are unable to manipulate its contents so as to degrade or to subject to derogatory treatment the Work as included in the Product.

5. Consultation and Approval

(a) The Licensee shall consult the Proprietor at all times during development of the Product in respect of the Work and shall implement the reasonable requests of the Proprietor regarding use of the Work and parts of the Work and regarding preservation of the overall tone and character of the Work.

(b) The Licensee shall consult the Proprietor and shall give bona fide consideration to the views of the Proprietor regarding the proposed inclusion of apparatus and works and other materials additional to the Work in the Product. If in the opinion of the Proprietor any such additional works and/or other materials are unsuitable for inclusion with the Work the Licensee shall not include them in the Product.

(c) Within thirty days after the date of this Agreement the Licensee shall submit for the approval of the Proprietor (such approval not to be unreasonably withheld) an outline of the Licensee's marketing plans for the Product together with details of the budget therefor.

(d) The Licensee shall submit for the approval of the Proprietor (such approval not to be unreasonably withheld) the following materials as soon as they shall be available:

(i) the design and specification for the Product
(ii) the prototype of the Product
(iii)the design, labelling, inlay card, user's guide, packaging and informational and promotional materials for the Product.

(e) The Licensee shall show the final master of the Product to the Proprietor on screen (at the Proprietor's offices, the Licensee supplying all necessary equipment therefor if requested by the Proprietor so to do) for approval prior to release and such approval shall not be unreasonably withheld or delayed.

(f) No later than three months prior to the proposed release date for the Product the Licensee shall submit for the approval of the Proprietor (such approval not to be unreasonably withheld):

(i) details of the Licensee's plans for publicising and promoting the Product and of the budget therefor

(ii) a list of those persons and organisations to whom and to which the Licensee proposes to send units of the Product free of charge for the purposes of publicising and promoting the Product.

(g) The Proprietor shall notify the granting or the withholding of approval under sub-clauses (c), (d) and (f) of this Clause within fourteen days of receipt of the respective materials and under sub-clause (e) of this Clause within seven days of viewing the final master. If any such approval shall be withheld by the Proprietor the Licensee shall not proceed with further development or release of the Product unless and until it shall have re-submitted amended versions of such materials and/or shown an amended version of such final master to the Proprietor and/or re-submitted an amended list and/or outline respectively and shall have obtained the approval of the Proprietor in accordance with these provisions.

(h) If after first release of the Product the Licensee shall propose to issue a revised or new version thereof the Licensee shall obtain the Proprietor's written consent thereto (such consent not unreasonably to be withheld) and such revised or new version shall be subject to the consultations with and approvals and consents of the Proprietor as provided hereunder in respect of the original edition of the Product, in so far as such consultations, approvals and consents are capable of applying to such revised or new edition.

(i) The Licensee shall obtain the consent of the Proprietor to any proposal for renting the Product prior to implementing or agreeing such proposal and shall not proceed with such proposal unless and until such consent (which if granted shall be upon terms and conditions subject to mutual agreement) shall have been received.

(j) No consent or approval which may be given by the Proprietor to the Licensee under this Agreement shall be deemed to constitute any certification or compliance required of the Licensee pursuant to sub-clause (iii) of Clause 13.

6. Credits and Copyright Notice
(a) The Licensee shall include the name of the Author and the title of the Work and the words 'Licensed by   ' with due prominence on the inlay card and user's guide for every unit of the Product and its packaging and shall arrange for the name of the Author to appear on each occasion when the Product (or any part thereof) is displayed on screen

6. Credits and Copyright Notice

(b) (1) It may of course be a requirement of the head contract (see Precedent One, Clause 18) that the copyright notice is reproduced in sub-licensees' editions; and in any event a provision such as this should be included in all contracts for sub-licensed editions. There may be a similar provision regarding an assertion of the moral right to be identified as the author (see Precedent One, Clause 27), in which case, unless that moral right has been waived or consent has been given (see note 2 on Clause 4(a)), that too will need to be reflected in the licensing contract.

(2) In some cases the licensee will wish to use a trade mark owned or controlled by the licensor; for instance, if the title of an established printed encyclopaedia includes the name of the publishing house a licensee of CD-ROM rights is likely to wish to use the same title. Either in the contract for licensing electronic rights or elsewhere the non-exclusive right to utilise the trade mark in connection specifically and only with exploitation of the licensed electronic product will need to be granted. It is most important that such licensed use of a trade mark is confined only to the use intended and that it terminates as soon as the electronic licence ceases. Before licensing a *registered* trade mark ensure that its registration covers the relevant classes; for example electronic products fall within class 9, whereas printed books are in class 16. It is desirable, though under the Trade Marks Act 1994 no longer a requirement, for licences to be registered in the Register of Trade Marks.

7. Financial Responsibility, Production and Discounts

(b) This provision presupposes that the licensee will be responsible for manufacture of the product. Some licensees license their distributors to manufacture, in which case this provision will need to be changed accordingly (i.e. so that the licensee is to require the distributor to notify the manufactured quantities, in order that the licensor can in turn be notified). If the licensee's distributor is empowered to manufacture copies the provisions of Clause 9(a) and (d) relating to the distributor's affairs assume added importance.

8. Royalties

(a) The basis of remuneration for licensors of electronic products is by no means standardised as yet. As long as the original work constitutes a substantial part of the electronic product royalties can normally be expected. These may be based on the recommended retail price (excluding VAT) or on the dealer price; but, particularly where the licensee's distributor is responsible for manufacturing the product, there may be no recommended retail price or dealer price set. Royalties based on net receipts are therefore common. As with film contracts it is vital to establish and list what deductions, if any, are permitted to be made. It may be possible to get the licensee to agree to pay a percentage of all monies actually received by it in respect of a product, as opposed to a percentage of net receipts – in which case (subject to the proviso that the licensee has no other financial interest in the distributor's performance) the licensee's and licensor's interests in the veracity of such receipts should be identical. Royalty percentages can vary from as little as 5 per cent up to perhaps 30 per cent or 35 per cent – possibly on a rising scale. Profit-sharing is another method of remuneration sometimes encountered.

As to advances, some licensees will be willing to pay reasonable amounts in anticipation of subsequent earnings; others may be prepared to pay lump sums in advance in addition to (probably rather lower) royalties.

(b) Licensees may also wish to provide for software supplied as cover disks at cost or less to be free from royalty payments. See also note (2) on Clause 2(b).

by a user and on each occasion when the Product (or any part thereof) is printed out by a user.

(b) The Licensee shall include in some prominent place on every unit of the Product and its packaging the following copyright notice:

©

and shall arrange for such copyright notice to appear on each occasion when the Product (or any part thereof) is displayed on screen by a user and on each occasion when the Product (or any part thereof) is printed out by a user.

7. Financial Responsibility, Production and Discounts

(a) The cost of development, manufacture, marketing and promotion and all other expenses in connection with the Product and the inclusion of the Work in the Product shall be borne by the Licensee.

(b) The Licensee shall first manufacture   units of the Product unless a different quantity shall be mutually agreed between the Licensee and the Proprietor. The Licensee shall notify the Proprietor promptly of the quantities of any and all further units of the Product manufactured.

8. Royalties

(a) In consideration of the licence hereby granted the Licensee shall make the following payments to the Proprietor:

(i) the total sum of £   on account of the royalties specified in
(ii) below payable as follows:
(ii) on all units of the Product sold by the Licensee royalties as follows:

(b) No royalties shall be payable on units of the Product given away to the Proprietor or given away to publicise and promote the Product to such persons and organisations as shall have been approved by the Proprietor in accordance with sub-clauses (f) and (g) of Clause 5.

9. Accounts

(a) The Licensee shall prepare accounts showing manufactured quantities, sales and stocks of the Product and of royalties due to the Proprietor to the 31 March or 30 June or 30 September or 31 December (whichever shall occur first) following first release of the Product and thereafter quarterly to the aforementioned dates and shall deliver such accounts to the Proprietor, together with any payments thereby shown due, within thirty days of the respective accounting date. At the time of delivering such accounts to the Proprietor the Licensee shall send to the Proprietor copies of the Licensee's distributor's statements relating to the Product during the period concerned. All payments shall be remitted in pounds sterling and

9.   Accounts

(d) For a note on accounts inspection clause percentages, see note (5) on Clause 16 of Precedent One.

12. Proprietor's Warranties to Licensee

The warranties which can be extended to sub-licensees will depend on the warranties given to the licensor in the head contract. Note that this warranty specifically excludes third-party copyright materials included in the original work. Unless electronic use of such materials was envisaged from the outset it is unlikely that permissions licences will cover it. Thus if such material is required for the electronic product somebody (the author, the licensing publisher or the licensee) will need to obtain further permission to use it. As worded here, such clearance would be the responsibility of the licensee (see Clause 13(i)).

(except as otherwise specifically provided herein) shall be made without deductions in respect of exchange or taxation or otherwise.

(b) The Licensee shall not have the right to withhold any part of royalties due to the Proprietor as a reserve against returns and/or credits.

(c) If any withholding or other taxes or levies are required by law to be deducted from payments due to the Proprietor hereunder the Licensee shall provide the Proprietor with such documentary evidence of such deductions as may reasonably be required by the Proprietor.

(d) Upon reasonable written notice and during the Licensee's normal business hours the Proprietor or the Proprietor's appointed representative shall have the right to examine the Licensee's records of account at the place at which they are normally kept, in so far as such records relate to stocks, sales and receipts in respect of the Product. Such examination shall be at the expense of the Proprietor unless errors shall be found, to the Proprietor's disadvantage, in excess of   per cent of the amount due to the Proprietor in respect of the last preceding accounting period, in which event the expense of such examination shall be borne by the Licensee. Any amount thereby shown to be due to the Proprietor shall be paid on receipt by the Licensee of the Proprietor's invoice therefor. No more than one such inspection shall be made in any one twelve-month period. The Licensee shall include in its agreement with its distributor a provision similar to this provision, in order that the Licensee may examine and verify such distributor's records of account in respect of the Product.

10. VAT
All monies due to the Proprietor hereunder are exclusive of Value Added Tax, which shall be added to and paid with such monies in accordance with statutory regulations. The Proprietor's VAT registration number is   .

11. Complimentary copies
The Licensee shall send to the Proprietor on or before the day of first release   complimentary units of the Product in its packaging and the Proprietor shall be entitled to purchase further units at best trade terms. As soon as they shall be available the Licensee shall send to the Proprietor   complimentary units of each revised or new version of the Product in its packaging issued by the Licensee in accordance with the conditions hereof.

12. Proprietor's Warranties to Licensee
The Proprietor hereby warrants to the Licensee that the Proprietor is entitled to enter into this Agreement and to grant the rights in the Work hereby licensed to the Licensee and that (except in respect of other copyright works or parts thereof included in the Work) the Work neither infringes any copyright belonging to any other party nor is it defamatory.

13. Licensee's Warranties to Proprietor
The Licensee warrants to the Proprietor that

(i) in respect of other copyright works and parts thereof included in the Work which the Licensee wishes to include in or adapt for the Product, the Licensee shall obtain prior written permission from the respective copyright owners and shall pay any and all fees required by such copyright owners

(ii) the Licensee shall not by any act or omission derogate from or prejudice the copyright or any other right in the Work or infringe any moral right of the Author

(iii) the Licensee shall submit the Product for censorship certification, product certification and any other purposes for which submission shall be required and shall obtain any such certification from the appropriate authorities and shall comply with all rules, regulations and other formalities prior to exercise of the rights granted to the Licensee hereunder in each territory in which the Product is to be distributed or sold

(iv) the Licensee shall indemnify and keep the Proprietor indemnified against all actions, suits, proceedings, claims, demands and costs (including any legal costs and expenses properly incurred and any compensation costs and disbursements paid by the Proprietor on the advice of its legal advisers to compromise or settle any claim) occasioned to the Proprietor in consequence of any breach of these warranties, or arising out of any claim alleging that the Product constitutes in any way a breach of these warranties.

14. Copyright Infringement
The Licensee shall use its best endeavours to prevent the unauthorised duplicating, copying or any pirating of the Product. If at any time during the subsistence of this Agreement in the reasonable opinion of the Licensee or the Proprietor the copyright in the Product is being infringed, the party holding such opinion shall at once inform the other. If the Proprietor shall refuse or neglect to take action in respect of such infringement the Licensee may take such steps as it considers necessary for dealing with the matter; and if it so desires it shall be entitled (after providing the Proprietor with an undertaking in writing to pay all costs and expenses and to indemnify the Proprietor against all liability for further costs) to take proceedings in the joint names of the Licensee and the Proprietor. Any profits or damages which may be received in respect of any infringement of copyright in the Product shall, after the deduction of all costs and expenses, be divided equally between the Licensee and the Proprietor. The provisions of this Clause are intended to apply only to any infringement of the copyright in the Product affecting the interest in the Work licensed to the Licensee under this Agreement.

17. Termination

(a)(ii) Performance criteria may be (as here) in respect of sales or can require the licensee to pay a minimum amount to the licensor over a specified period (e.g. at least £1,000 over two consecutive accounting periods, failing which the contract terminates). The latter method gives a licensee wishing to retain a licence the opportunity to make the amount due to the licensor up to the specified minimum even though that figure may not have been earned by the number of sales made. A performance criterion is most desirable; sales of many electronic products are pathetically small at present. See also note (1) on Clause 1(a).

(iii) See note on Clause 7(b).

(viii) and (ix) These provisions are particularly important in the context of electronic licensing agreements: the casualty rate for companies in this area tends to be high.

15. Disposal of Product

The Licensee shall not dispose of or destroy the Product prior to eighteen months from its first release and then only after offering to the Proprietor the written option for sixty days to purchase units at the disposal price or to obtain units intended for destruction without charge.

16. Assignment

This Agreement is personal to the Licensee and the Licensee shall not assign, transfer, charge, license, sub-license or otherwise part with possession of the benefit or burden of this Agreement or any part of it without the prior consent of the Proprietor, nor shall the Licensee attempt to do so.

17. Termination

(a) The licence hereby granted shall terminate without further notice and all rights hereunder shall revert forthwith to the Proprietor in any of the following circumstances:

(i) on expiry of the Licence Term

(ii) if sales of the Product fall below   units in each of two successive accounting periods (as provided in Clause 9(a))

(iii) if the Licensee shall allow the Product to become unavailable to the extent that there are fewer than twenty-five units in stock (as to which the Licensee shall notify the Proprietor promptly) and to remain at or below such stock level for three months

(iv) on completion of disposal or destruction of the Product in accordance with Clause 15

(v) if any payment due hereunder to the Proprietor shall have become overdue by thirty days

(vi) if the Licensee shall at any time by itself or anyone acting on its behalf fail to fulfil or comply with any other terms or conditions accepted by it hereunder and shall not rectify such failure within thirty days of written notice from the Proprietor to do so

(vii) if the Licensee shall fail to release the Product within the period specified in Clause 3 in which case any balance of the total advance sum provided under sub-clause (a)(i) of Clause 8 then unpaid shall at once become due and payable to the Proprietor

(viii) if the Licensee shall be declared bankrupt or shall go into liquidation (other than voluntary liquidation for the purpose of reconstruction) or shall have a receiver or administrator or administrative receiver appointed of its business or shall attempt to come to arrangements with its creditors. The equivalent of any of the foregoing, though known by different terminology, shall likewise be grounds for termination under this provision

(ix) if the Licensee shall cease to carry on business as a producer and distributor of materials in the form specified in Clause 1 or if the

(b) The Proprietor may also require the licensee to destroy masters of the product on termination and to provide a certificate of such destruction.

Licensee shall otherwise cease to be in a position fully to perform its obligations hereunder.

Termination of this Agreement shall be without prejudice to the right of the Proprietor to receive any monies due from the Licensee and without prejudice to any entitlement of the Proprietor to damages and/or otherwise.

(b) Upon termination of this Agreement for any cause the Proprietor shall have the right for thirty days thereafter to purchase (at the Proprietor's discretion either for sale by the Proprietor or for any other purpose) units of the Product then remaining at a price to be subject to negotiation, which price shall not exceed cost. If this Agreement shall terminate pursuant to (i), (ii) or (iii) of sub-clause (a) of this Clause the Licensee shall have the non-exclusive right for a period of three months from the date of termination to dispose of any units of the Product manufactured by the Licensee during the Licence Term and not required by the Proprietor, subject to the terms and conditions hereof; provided that the Licensee shall not manufacture or permit to be manufactured during the three months prior to expiry of the Licence Term more units of the Product than could reasonably be anticipated as necessary to fulfil orders during the remainder of the Licence Term.

(c) After termination of this Agreement:

(i) the Licensee shall not manufacture any further units of the Product including or utilising the Work; and
(ii) the Licensee shall not attempt to delay or frustrate further exploitation of the Work by the Proprietor.

18. Relationship between Parties
This Agreement does not constitute a partnership or joint venture between the parties hereto. The Licensee is not the agent of the Proprietor and shall not hold itself out as such by advertising or otherwise to the public or to any particular third party and the Proprietor shall not be bound by any representation, act or omission whatsoever of the Licensee.

19. Confidentiality
The Licensee undertakes at all times during the subsistence of this Agreement and thereafter to keep confidential (and to ensure that its officers and employees and agents shall keep confidential) the terms of this Agreement and any and all confidential information which it may acquire in relation to the business or affairs of the Proprietor, save for any information which is publicly available or becomes publicly available through no act of the Licensee; provided that the Licensee shall be at liberty to disclose such terms and confidential information under a duty of confidence to its professional advisers and to others if and when required to do so by force of law.

257

20. Approvals, Consents and Notices

(a) No approvals or consents given to the Licensee under this Agreement shall be valid unless they are given in writing and signed by a duly authorised representative of the Proprietor.

(b) Each party shall notify the other promptly of any change of address. Any notice required hereunder shall be deemed to have been served properly if delivered personally or sent by facsimile or pre-paid first class recorded delivery post to the last-known address of the party to be served with such notice. A hard copy of any notice served by facsimile shall at once be sent by pre-paid first class post to the party to be served with such notice.

21. Waiver of Remedies

No forbearance, delay or indulgence by either party in enforcing the provisions of this Agreement shall prejudice or restrict the rights of that party nor shall any waiver of its rights operate as a waiver of any subsequent breach and no right, power or remedy herein conferred upon or reserved for either party is exclusive of any other right, power or remedy available to that party and each such right, power or remedy shall be cumulative.

22. Severability

Notwithstanding that the whole or any part of any provision of this Agreement may prove to be illegal or unenforceable the remainder (if any) of such provision and the other provisions of this Agreement shall remain in full force and effect.

23. Disputes

If any difference shall arise between the Proprietor and the Licensee concerning the meaning of this Agreement or the rights and liabilities of the parties hereto such difference shall in the first instance be referred to the Informal Disputes Settlement Scheme of the Publishers Association and, failing agreed submission by both parties to such Scheme, shall be referred to the arbitration of two persons (one to be named by each party) or to a mutually-agreed umpire in accordance with the provisions of the Arbitration Act 1996, or any amending or substituted statute for the time being in force.

24. Interpretation

References herein to Clauses are to Clauses of this Agreement. The headings to the Clauses are for ease of reference only and shall be disregarded in their interpretation or construction.

25. Governing Law

This Agreement shall be subject to and shall be interpreted in all respects in accordance with English law and the parties hereto submit and agree to the non-exclusive jurisdiction of the courts of England.

26. Entire Agreement

This Agreement is the entire and only agreement between the Proprietor and the Licensee concerning its subject matter and supersedes any and all prior agreements, arrangements and understandings (whether written or oral) relating thereto. No addition to or modification of any provision of this Agreement shall be binding upon the parties unless it is in writing and signed on behalf of the Proprietor and the Licensee.

AS WITNESS the signatures of duly authorised representatives of the parties.

For and on behalf of

For and on behalf of

. . . .

. . . .

Licensee

Proprietor

This precedent is an agreement licensing a pre-existing literary work to a licensee as a site licence for on-line distribution via a closed local area network. It could, with relatively modest changes, be adapted as a site licence for a publisher's existing electronic database. If appreciably less than a complete work is being licensed for use on such a network a permissions-type agreement may be more appropriate. On-line licensing of journals is frequently provided by journal publishers or specialist providers on a subscription basis and different criteria tend to apply.

Preamble
Recital 1: see the note to Recital 1 of the first Electronic Precedent regarding the licensing publisher's right to control electronic rights.

1. Licence
(1) Given that this is a licence to one institution for a specific site (and similar licences may be granted to other institutions) it is normal to grant non-exclusive rights.

(2) With regard to (iii), a licensing publisher may not wish end users to print out hard copies – even of modest proportions of the complete work (although see Appendix A regarding the Society of Authors/Publishers Association convention relating to fair dealing). If that is the case this sub-clause should be omitted. On the other hand a licensing publisher may be willing to permit end users to go beyond printing out extracts – for example by downloading to local hard drives. If the latter is to be permitted under the contract it will be necessary to decide (i) the maximum portion that may be downloaded; (ii) whether downloading is permitted only for research and private study; (iii) whether it must only be temporary; and (iv) whether to allow downloading in the form of text which is capable of being edited and, therefore, otherwise manipulated or whether the downloading is allowed only in the form of bitmapped images. The provision should be changed according to the circumstances, which in turn will probably result in consequential changes elsewhere in the contract.

(3) Licensors may also have to consider whether material from the licensed edition may be re-used in original documents for internal circulation within the licensed institution (only; not for sale or distribution to third parties).

2. Reserved Rights
(1) A precedent for distribution of electronic products in carrier form will be found as the first Electronic Precedent.

(2) The wording here seeks to restrict the licensee as far as possible to the usage intended. It may of course need to be amended, depending on individual circumstances.

MEMORANDUM OF AGREEMENT made this   day
of   19   between   (hereinafter called 'the
Proprietor', which expression shall be deemed to include the Proprietor's
assigns or successors in business as the case may be) of the one part, and
            of   (hereinafter called 'the Licensee') of the other
part

WHEREAS the Proprietor controls the exclusive rights of exploitation in
a literary work written by   (hereinafter called 'the Author')
entitled

(hereinafter called 'the Work') and

WHEREAS the Proprietor has issued the Work in printed book form and

WHEREAS the Proprietor wishes to make the Work available to end users
(hereinafter called 'End Users') as specified in Schedule 1 within the limits
of the site (hereinafter called 'the Site') specified in Schedule 1 and the
Proprietor is willing to license the Licensee to do so on the terms and
conditions of this Agreement

NOW IT IS HEREBY MUTUALLY AGREED as follows:

1. Licence
In consideration of the payments hereinafter mentioned and subject to the
terms and conditions hereof the Proprietor hereby grants to the Licensee a
non-exclusive licence

(i) to convert the Work into machine-readable form and to store it
electronically on the Licensee's database (hereinafter called 'the
Database', the Work as stored on the Database hereinafter being called
'the Licensed Edition'), and to make one copy of the Licensed Edition
for back-up and disaster recovery purposes
(ii) to make the Licensed Edition available for access, searching and
viewing by means of electronic data transmission to End Users within
the limits of the Site via remote terminals on the Licensee's local area
network
(iii)to permit End Users to print hard copies of extracts from the Licensed
Edition as stipulated in Clause 3.

2. Reserved Rights
(a) All rights in the Work other than those specifically licensed to the
Licensee under Clause 1 are reserved by the Proprietor for exploitation by
itself or in conjunction with other parties or by licence to other parties or
for non-use as at its sole discretion it shall see fit. Without prejudice to the
generality of the foregoing the licence hereby granted to the Licensee is
solely in respect of the uses specified in Clause 1 and expressly excludes
any right to make the Work or the Licensed Edition available by electronic

3. Hard Copying

See note (2) to Clause 1. If printing-out is to be permitted then limiting it to five per cent of the total text may be appropriate, in line with the Copyright Licensing Agency's photocopying licensing scheme. Alternatively the limit on printing could be expressed as up to a specified number of pages or screens.

Certainly if there was any question of all or substantially all of the original work being printed out as hard copy most publishers would wish the end user instead to buy a copy of the printed book.

4. Release

Although committing a licensee of on-line rights to a release date may seem to be of less importance than similarly committing a licensee of an electronic carrier product, unless there is no access use payment of any kind (see comments on Clause 9) the licensor may be at a disadvantage if the work is not released on a timely basis.

5. Alterations

Much of note (1) to Clause 4(a) of the first Electronic Precedent is relevant here, though the kind of use envisaged in the present precedent is likely to involve far less radical change (if any at all) than is the case for many carrier-based products.

6. Revisions

Especially if the period of years stipulated as the minimum duration (Clause 16) is reasonably lengthy, it is wise to provide for revisions to the work in book form to be incorporated in the licensee's on-line version. If the licensee should fail to comply with the provisions of this clause, Clause 17(a)(ii) can then be invoked.

or any other means to any party other than End Users or outside the Site or as an electronic carrier product or by any other electronic delivery service or by any other on-line, satellite or other transmission.

(b) The Licensee shall not exploit the Licensed Edition or any part of it commercially nor sell, rent, loan (with or without payment), hire out or license the Licensed Edition or any part of it to any third party nor post any of the contents of the Licensed Edition to any electronic bulletin board without the prior consent of the Proprietor.

3. Hard Copying
The Licensee may permit End Users to print hard copies of up to   per cent of the Licensed Edition (measured by wordage) for the purposes of research and private study only.

4. Release
The Licensee shall make the Licensed Edition available as stipulated in sub-clause (ii) of Clause 1, at the sole cost and expense of the Licensee, within   from the date of this Agreement.

5. Alterations
(a) The Licensee shall not abridge, expand or otherwise alter the Work in any way for the Licensed Edition without the prior consent of the Proprietor.

(b) The Licensee shall include in the Database (and elsewhere, as may be relevant) any and all programs, methods, processes and devices as shall be available and appropriate in order to ensure (in so far as it is possible so to ensure) that End Users are unable to manipulate the content of the Licensed Edition so as to degrade it or to subject it to derogatory treatment.

6. Revisions
If at any time during the currency of this Agreement the Proprietor shall issue a revised edition of the Work and shall send details of such revisions to the Licensee the Licensee shall within 30 days after receipt thereof incorporate such revisions into the Licensed Edition and shall send written confirmation thereof to the Proprietor.

7. Inspection
Upon reasonable written notice the Proprietor or the Proprietor's appointed representative shall have the right to examine the Licensed Edition at the Site so as to satisfy itself that the Licensed Edition and the uses permitted and the restrictions imposed in relation to the Licensed Edition conform to the provisions of this Agreement. If the Proprietor shall determine that they (or any of them) fail to do so the Proprietor shall be entitled to give notice to the Licensee in accordance with paragraph (ii) of sub-clause (a) of Clause 17.

8. Credits and Copyright Notice
See notes for Clause 6 of the first Electronic Precedent.

9. Payments
There are several different options available for remunerating licensors of on-line rights for local networks, including:

1. *A single outright payment.* This would be inappropriate for a licence such as this (see Clause 16) which continues, after an initial specified period, until terminated. Even where the duration is fixed it is difficult to assess how much such an outright payment should be unless there are relevant prior usage statistics available. It does of course have the advantage (possibly to both parties) of certainty; and it benefits the licensee in that it may not be necessary to render statements of usage to the licensor (see Clause 10(a)) – though a licensing publisher may require such statements anyway, for statistical purposes.

2. *An initial outright payment followed by a further outright payment for each year during which the licence continues in force.* This arrangement surmounts the first problem mentioned under 1 above but the second problem still remains.

3. *A fee for each occasion an end user accesses the work.* This can be extended to provide for separate, additional fees for each occasion an end user downloads or prints out a portion of the work (assuming those activities to be permitted under the rights granted).

4. *A fee based on the time spent by end users accessing the work.*

The clause wording as drafted combines options 2 and 3. Note that the sums due under Clause 9(i) and (ii) are outright payments and are not on account of royalties due under (iii), although they could be expressed to be. It is envisaged that if they are not on account of royalties the outright sums (representing payment to the licensor even if no on-line access occurs) may be relatively modest. Outright sums payable from the second year onwards could be expressed as related to the amount paid in the first year – e.g. the sum payable on each anniversary could be 50 per cent of the total amount paid to the licensor during the preceding year.

10. Accounts
(c) For a note on accounts inspection clause percentages, see note (5) on Clause 16 of Precedent One.

8. Credits and Copyright Notice

The Licensee shall include the name of the Author, the title of the Work, the following copyright notice:

© `

and the words 'Licensed by   ' with due prominence at the beginning and end of the Licensed Edition and shall arrange for the name of the Author and the aforesaid copyright notice to appear on each occasion when the Licensed Edition (or any part thereof) is displayed on screen by End Users and on each occasion when an extract from the Licensed Edition is printed out by End Users.

9. Payments

In consideration of the licence hereby granted the Licensee shall make the following payments to the Proprietor:

(i)   the sum of £   payable on signature of this Agreement by both parties

(ii) the sum of £   payable on each anniversary of the date of this Agreement during the continuance hereof

(iii) the sum of £   on each occasion the Licensed Edition is accessed by End Users.

10. Accounts

(a)   The Licensee shall prepare accounts showing the number of occasions on which the Licensed Edition has been accessed by End Users during the accounting period concerned and monies due to the Proprietor in respect thereof to the 30 June or 31 December (whichever shall occur first) following first release of the Licensed Edition and thereafter half-yearly to the aforementioned dates and shall deliver such accounts to the Proprietor, together with any payments thereby shown due, within thirty days of the respective accounting date. All payments shall be remitted in pounds sterling and (except as otherwise specifically provided herein) shall be made without deductions in respect of exchange or taxation or otherwise.

(b)   If any withholding or other taxes or levies are required by law to be deducted from payments due to the Proprietor hereunder the Licensee shall provide the Proprietor with such documentary evidence of such deductions as may reasonably be required by the Proprietor.

(c) Upon reasonable written notice and during the Licensee's normal business hours the Proprietor or the Proprietor's appointed representative shall have the right to examine the Licensee's records at the place at which they are normally kept, in so far as such records relate to the Licensed Edition and payments due to the Proprietor in connection therewith. Such examination shall be at the expense of the Proprietor unless errors shall be

12. Proprietor's Warranties to Licensee
See note to Clause 13 of the first Electronic Precedent.

found, to the Proprietor's disadvantage, in excess of   per cent of
the amount due to the Proprietor in respect of the last preceding accounting
period, in which event the expense of such examination shall be borne by
the Licensee. Any amount thereby shown to be due to the Proprietor shall
be paid on receipt by the Licensee of the Proprietor's invoice therefor. No
more than one such inspection shall be made in any one twelve-month
period.

11. VAT

All monies due to the Proprietor hereunder are exclusive of Value Added
Tax, which shall be added to and paid with such monies in accordance with
statutory regulations. The Proprietor's VAT registration number
i s   .

12. Proprietor's Warranties to Licensee

The Proprietor hereby warrants to the Licensee that the Proprietor is
entitled to enter into this Agreement and to grant the rights in the Work
hereby licensed to the Licensee and that (except in respect of other
copyright works or parts thereof included in the Work) the Work neither
infringes any copyright belonging to any other party nor is it defamatory.

13. Licensee's Warranties to Proprietor

The Licensee warrants to the Proprietor that

(i) in respect of other copyright works and parts thereof included in the
Work the Licensee shall obtain prior written permission for their
inclusion in the Licensed Edition from the respective copyright owners
and shall pay any and all fees required by such copyright owners

(ii) the Licensee shall not by any act or omission derogate from or
prejudice the copyright or any other right in the Work or infringe any
moral right of the Author

(iii) the Licensee shall use all reasonable endeavours to ensure that the
Licensed Edition is used in accordance with the terms and conditions
of this Agreement and shall advise all End Users of the permitted uses
and restrictions under this Agreement. In particular (and without
prejudice to the generality of the foregoing) the Licensee shall use all
reasonable endeavours to ensure that End Users keep their respective
passwords confidential and do not make such passwords available to
others

(iv) the Licensee shall indemnify and keep the Proprietor indemnified
against all actions, suits, proceedings, claims, demands, losses and
costs (including any legal costs and expenses properly incurred and
any compensation costs and disbursements paid by the Proprietor on
the advice of its legal advisers to compromise or settle any claim)
occasioned to the Proprietor in consequence of any breach of these
warranties, or arising out of any claim alleging that the Licensed
Edition constitutes in any way a breach of these warranties.

16. Duration

The licence period can of course be a fixed period of years or months, which may or may not be stipulated as being subject to renewal by mutual agreement or at the licensor's discretion; or, as here, it can continue after the initial period until one or other party wishes to terminate it.

14. Copyright Infringement

The Licensee shall use its best endeavours to prevent misuse or unauthorised duplicating, copying or any pirating of the Licensed Edition. If at any time during the subsistence of this Agreement in the reasonable opinion of the Licensee or the Proprietor the Licensed Edition is being misused or the copyright in the Licensed Edition is being infringed, the party holding such opinion shall at once inform the other. If the Proprietor shall refuse or neglect to take action in respect of such misuse or infringement the Licensee may take such steps as it considers necessary for dealing with the matter; and if it so desires it shall be entitled (after providing the Proprietor with an undertaking in writing to pay all costs and expenses and to indemnify the Proprietor against all liability for further costs) to take proceedings in the joint names of the Licensee and the Proprietor. Any profits or damages which may be received pursuant to proceedings taken in the joint names of the Licensee and the Proprietor in respect of any misuse of the Licensed Edition or any infringement of copyright in the Licensed Edition shall, after the deduction of all costs and expenses, be divided equally between the Licensee and the Proprietor. The provisions of this Clause relating to any infringement of copyright are intended to apply only to any such infringement in the Licensed Edition affecting the interest in the Work licensed to the Licensee under this Agreement.

15. Assignment

This Agreement is personal to the Licensee and the Licensee shall not assign, transfer, charge, license, sub-license or otherwise part with possession of the benefit or burden of this Agreement or any part of it without the prior consent of the Proprietor, nor shall the Licensee attempt to do so.

16. Duration

Subject to the provisions of Clause 17 the licence hereby granted shall subsist for a period of   years from the date of this Agreement and thereafter until terminated by at least ninety days' notice providing for termination at the next-following anniversary of the date of this Agreement.

17. Termination

(a)   The licence hereby granted shall terminate without further notice and all rights hereunder shall revert forthwith to the Proprietor in any of the following circumstances:

(i)   if any payment due hereunder to the Proprietor shall have become overdue by thirty days

(ii) if the Licensee shall at any time by itself or anyone acting on its behalf fail to fulfil or comply with any other terms or conditions accepted by it hereunder and shall not rectify such failure within thirty days of written notice from the Proprietor to do so

(iii) if the Licensee shall fail to release the Licensed Edition within the period specified in Clause 4

17. Termination

(a)(iv) If the site licence is to a non-commercial organisation (e.g. a university) this wording may be largely irrelevant – though if the licence is granted to a company controlled by a university it will be needed.

(a)(v) the relevant deletion must be made (and indeed something more specific could be substituted – pharmaceuticals for business, for instance.

(b) If downloading has been permitted under the licence (see comments on Clause 1, paragraph (2)) the words 'and shall arrange for any portions of the Work which have been downloaded to individual hard disks to be deleted' should be added at the end of the first sentence. To strengthen the second sentence, 'statutory declaration' could be substituted for 'written declaration'.

(iv) if the Licensee shall be declared bankrupt or shall go into liquidation (other than voluntary liquidation for the purpose of reconstruction) or shall have a receiver or administrator or administrative receiver appointed of its business or shall attempt to come to arrangements with its creditors. The equivalent of any of the foregoing, though known by different terminology, shall likewise be grounds for termination under this provision

(v) if the Licensee shall cease to operate in business/education.

Termination of this Agreement shall be without prejudice to the right of the Proprietor to receive any monies due from the Licensee and without prejudice to any entitlement of the Proprietor to damages and/or otherwise.

(b) Upon termination of this Agreement for any cause the Licensee shall cease to make the Licensed Edition available to End Users and shall delete the Work from the Database and shall destroy any copy of the Licensed Edition made pursuant to sub-clause (i) of Clause 1 for back-up and disaster recovery purposes. Within seven days of termination of this Agreement the Licensee shall send to the Proprietor a written declaration that the foregoing provisions of this Clause have been effected.

18. Relationship between Parties
This Agreement does not constitute a partnership or joint venture between the parties hereto. The Licensee is not the agent of the Proprietor and shall not hold itself out as such by advertising or otherwise to the public or to any particular third party and the Proprietor shall not be bound by any representation, act or omission whatsoever of the Licensee.

19. Confidentiality
The Licensee undertakes at all times during the subsistence of this Agreement and thereafter to keep confidential (and to ensure that its officers and employees shall keep confidential) the terms of this Agreement and any and all confidential information which it may acquire in relation to the business or affairs of the Proprietor, save for any information which is publicly available or becomes publicly available through no act of the Licensee; provided that the Licensee shall be at liberty to disclose such terms and confidential information under a duty of confidence to its professional advisers and to others if and when required to do so by force of law.

20. Approvals, Consents and Notices
(a) No approvals or consents given to the Licensee under this Agreement shall be valid unless they are given in writing and signed by a duly authorised representative of the Proprietor.

(b) Each party shall notify the other promptly of any change of address. Any notice required hereunder shall be deemed to have been served properly if delivered personally or sent by facsimile or pre-paid first class

recorded delivery post to the last-known address of the party to be served with such notice. A hard copy of any notice served by facsimile shall at once be sent by pre-paid first class post to the party to be served with such notice.

21. Waiver of Remedies

No forbearance, delay or indulgence by either party in enforcing the provisions of this Agreement shall prejudice or restrict the rights of that party nor shall any waiver of its rights operate as a waiver of any subsequent breach and no right, power or remedy herein conferred upon or reserved for either party is exclusive of any other right, power or remedy available to that party and each such right, power or remedy shall be cumulative.

22. Severability

Notwithstanding that the whole or any part of any provision of this Agreement may prove to be illegal or unenforceable the remainder (if any) of such provision and the other provisions of this Agreement shall remain in full force and effect.

23. Disputes

If any difference shall arise between the Proprietor and the Licensee concerning the meaning of this Agreement or the rights and liabilities of the parties hereto such difference shall in the first instance be referred to the Informal Disputes Settlement Scheme of the Publishers Association and, failing agreed submission by both parties to such Scheme, shall be referred to the arbitration of two persons (one to be named by each party) or to a mutually-agreed umpire in accordance with the provisions of the Arbitration Act 1996, or any amending or substituted statute for the time being in force.

24. Interpretation

References herein to Clauses are to Clauses of this Agreement. The headings to the Clauses are for ease of reference only and shall be disregarded in their interpretation or construction.

25. Governing Law

This Agreement shall be subject to and shall be interpreted in all respects in accordance with English law and the parties hereto submit and agree to the non-exclusive jurisdiction of the courts of England.

26. Entire Agreement

This Agreement is the entire and only agreement between the Proprietor and the Licensee concerning its subject matter and supersedes any and all prior agreements, arrangements and understandings (whether written or oral) relating thereto. No addition to or modification of any provision of this Agreement shall be binding upon the parties unless it is in writing and signed on behalf of the Proprietor and the Licensee.

AS WITNESS the signatures of duly authorised representatives of the parties.

For and on behalf of

For and on behalf of

. . . .

. . . .

Licensee

Proprietor

Schedule 1

End Users [e.g. 'all employees working at the Site'; or
'professional employees of the Licensee working at the Site'; or
'tutors and students of the Licensee at the Site']

The Site [e.g. 'The University of East Barsetshire, including its campus and all ancillary and associated buildings'; o r
'the offices of XYZ Limited at 33 London Road, Onetown and the factory of XYZ Limited at The Industrial Estate, Twotown']

Schedule 1
It is preferable (though at times difficult) to be as specific as possible when defining end users and the site. The information to be included here will normally originate from the institution concerned; but their requests may have to be narrowed. For instance, if end users work from home and access the licensee's network via a modem it may be advisable to specify their names and addresses and for the licensee to undertake to notify the proprietor as soon as any changes occur.

Film, Television and Allied Rights: Option and Assignment Agreements

When a publisher handles many subsidiary rights, whether volume subsidiary rights (e.g. quotation rights) or non-volume subsidiary rights (e.g. first serial rights), he/she is on, or near, home ground. He (or she) has a fairly sure sense of the extent and the value of the rights for which he is negotiating on his and his author's behalf. That sense may be conspicuously absent when the publisher deals with film rights: neither the extent nor the value of the rights may be at all clear to him, and since he acts very largely as an agent for his author there is, perhaps, a special responsibility on the publisher to understand at least the basic elements of film rights dealings.

Many agents will seek to exclude from the contract which they negotiate with the publisher on behalf of their author any dramatisation and documentary rights, as defined in Precedent One, Clause 14(p). Not all authors, however, are agented and the publisher may find himself at times in the happy but embarrassing position of having acquired 'film, TV and allied rights' (see especially the note to Clause 1 of the Assignment below), of receiving strong (and perhaps unexpected) interest in those rights from a film or television company, and of having, in truth, little idea how to proceed.

To all such publishers and equally to their authors, this Precedent is dedicated. It has, together with the Notes, been drafted by Arthur J Buck and Alan Williams of Denton Hall, Solicitors.

Introduction

Under the publishing agreement, the publisher's involvement in the film rights may come in a number of ways: the right to control; the right to negotiate; or a full grant of the rights, the author retaining no interest other than a financial one as long as the publishing agreement or a properly drawn sub-licence is in force (see for such a grant Precedent One, Clause 14(p)). The former two (that is, the right to control or the right to negotiate) are more often found than the last (a full grant of rights) and they leave the publisher in a far from satisfactory position. He does not then actually own the rights but is left to negotiate for their exploitation without either being formally appointed an agent or being able to conclude the deal himself. Film rights (and this is the important point) involve the investment of such large sums of money into the film that purchasers and their financiers look very carefully at the legal title and the publisher's right to contract.

Unless the publisher has been granted the rights (in the last of the three senses mentioned above) he should go back to the author for consent. In most cases, irrespective of whether consent is or is not required, the contract with the purchaser should actually be signed by the author (as the copyright owner) rather than by the publisher (as licensee or quasi-agent). The publisher, anyway, will not want or be able to contract as principal, not only because of the warranties usually required from the author/owner of the work, such as originality, defamation and so on, impose material potential liability, but also because the publisher will not be the copyright owner. The final, cogent, reasons for ensuring that it is the author who actually signs the option/assignment to the film or television company are first that the usual form of publishing agreement is a licence which is terminable on the happening of a number of events; not only insolvency or breach of contract can cause termination, but also the title going out of print. There should be no possibility that the ensuing reversion of rights can affect the film rights grant, particularly if that exposes the publisher to liability.

The second reason is that the Copyright, Designs and Patents Act 1988 has introduced moral rights into English law – the rights of paternity and integrity (see in general Appendix D). Those rights can be waived; not all publishers will seek such a waiver, nor all authors grant it. However, the film rights will hardly be marketable without such a waiver. At the very least, the author will have to join in the film rights grant not only as copyright owner but in order to give such a waiver.

Film and television producers rely upon a number of sources of material for their films: public domain material, copyright literary material and work specially commissioned. For present purposes, it is the second source which is relevant. Having acquired the copyright literary material, the intending film producer will then arrange for a screenplay or teleplay writer to write a screenplay or teleplay based on it, i.e. there will be an adaptation of the work. Section 21 of the Copyright, Designs and Patents Act 1988 contains a full definition of the word 'adaptation': it includes making a dramatic version of a literary work.

Because of the enormous production costs involved in making films and because of the large acquisition prices commonly paid, it is customary for a film producer to seek an option on the work for a sum usually around 10 per cent of the purchase price.

The essence of an option agreement is that the purchaser buys the sole and exclusive option to acquire certain specific, pre-negotiated rights. It is essential that the terms of the assignment of those rights are not left to the future but are settled with, and at the same time as, the option agreement. An option to buy 'rights to be negotiated' is a present ticket to future confusion, uncertainty and expense.

The option period will normally run for around a year to 18 months and is often renewable for a further six months to a year on payment of a further fee. The first fee is usually in advance and on account of the final purchase price but not returnable, whereas the second fee (about five per cent of the purchase price), whilst still not returnable, is often not on account of the purchase price. There is no reason why this extension fee should not be on account: if it is not, it is in effect a small penalty or price increase paid by the Purchaser for 'overstaying his welcome'.

The period of grace represented by the option period enables the producer to put together the other elements of the production without having committed large sums of money to the rights before he knows whether or not he can interest potential distributors and put the finance together. If he is not successful in putting his package together and finding production finance, then his loss of rights is limited to the option fee and, incidentally and not immaterially, the publisher and author are free to negotiate with third parties in the future, which they would not have been if the rights had been sold outright.

The package which the producer will want to put together before he can look for development or production finance is: an option on the literary material; a screenwriter to make an adaptation into the screenplay; a director, a budget and shooting schedule (which can only be prepared from the screenplay itself); and artists.

It is necessary at this stage to examine very briefly some of the relevant definitions contained in the Copyright, Designs and Patents Act 1988 ('the Act') and the way in which the Act approaches copyright. It extends protection to material in a number of specified categories, including literary, dramatic and musical works (defined in s 3), film and sound recordings (s 5), broadcast (s 6) and cable programme (s 7). Restricted acts are those acts in relation to a copyright work which, if done without the authorisation of the copyright owner, constitute an infringement of copyright. The restricted acts are set out in s 16. Briefly, they include copying the work, showing it in public, broadcasting it or including it in a cable programme service.

Section 5 of the Act defines a 'film' as a recording on any medium from which a moving image may by any means be produced.

Section 6 of the Act defines a 'broadcast' as a transmission by wireless telegraphy of visual images, sounds or other information which:

(a) is capable of being lawfully received by members of the public; or
(b) is transmitted for presentation to members of the public.

The agreement by which film rights are acquired should therefore ideally be expressed in the above terms and grant or exclude rights according to the rights intended to be granted or excluded. For instance, it may be intended only to grant feature film rights, or only television rights (including or excluding cable and satellite rights), and so it is possible to seek great flexibility in the contract. The financier seeks somewhat less flexible ends: he wants as much as he can get in return for his potentially large investment.

Cable, satellite and video are methods of exploitation which have revolutionised the distribution of films to the public. Further significant changes in technology and in statutory regulation are impending.

Cable started as a way of bringing broadcast reception to areas where off-air reception was poor but is now very largely used to provide a wider choice of channels and has developed most extensively in the USA and in Europe. Following the Hunt Report (Report of the Inquiry into Cable Expansion and Broadcast Policy, October 1982, Cmnd 8679), and the acceptance by the Government of the concept of commercial cable television exploitation in the UK, the Government has now granted a number of franchises for cable television networks with more to follow. The provision of cable programme services is licensed and regulated by the TIC under the Broadcasting Act 1990. The diffusion of a film over a cable network requires the consent of the copyright owner; except where diffusion is the simultaneous relay of a broadcast.

Satellite transmission has a number of advantages including a high bandwidth or spectrum of frequencies and (many will say its disadvantage) a large transmission area or 'footprint'. Satellites beam to areas larger than national boundaries, a problem with which national governments, programme and copyright licensors and talent unions (among many others), have yet fully to grapple. Transmission via satellite has so far been mainly limited to transmission to existing cable networks but broadcasting direct to individual homes on a large scale using higher-powered satellites (direct broadcast by satellite on DBS) has started and will highlight these problems.

Video cassettes (and now video discs) are beating the most immediate path to the consumer's door: the growth of the home video industry has astonished most observers. While the idea of a rental right is already covered by the Act and the concept of a *droit moral* has long been established in Europe, the issue of an author's work being released on video has been specifically dealt with in the European Directive on Rental and Lending Rights. Commercially, it is only the rental right which will be of significance as the lending right is expressed in the context of a non-exploitative situation. The aim of the rental right is to give both authors and actors a continuing remuneration from the later stages of the exploitation of their labour. This is a noble intent, but the implementation of the new law (strongly resisted by the British and American film industries) is likely to cause problems of interpretation and implementation to all those concerned in the licensing and exploitation of both the underlying and derivative works of a film released on video.

Although there is scope for each individual member state to tailor the rental right to its own vision of its entertainment industry's cultural and economic aims, the basic concept is that every 'author' (undefined, this is interpreted to include screenplay writers) shall have an unwaivable (though transferable or assignable) right to equitable remuneration. Not every member state has yet enacted this legislation. The Directive was implemented into UK law by the Copyright and Related Rights Regulations 1996 on 1 December 1996. The problems of individual interpretation of the Directive will be compounded by the staggered period of implementation. From implementation, performers, composers and authors of screenplays and underlying literary works as well as individual producers and principal directors of films all (for the sake of brevity now referred to as 'talent') have the exclusive right to prohibit the rental of copies of their work to the public (or at least to receive equitable remuneration in respect of rental).

The creation of this new right should not necessarily be regarded as an additional bargaining tool in negotiating terms of involvement in a film because, in any agreement between talent and the corporate film producer and in the absence of any intention to the contrary, talent will be presumed to have transferred their rental right in relation to the film in return for the right to receive equitable remuneration, which will be payable by the person to whom the rental right has been transferred.

There has been much discussion about how the calculation of 'equitable remuneration' will be made. The Regulations fail to offer any specific guidance. They do state that remuneration shall not be considered inequitable merely because it is paid by way of a buy-out i.e. merely because there will be no further payment there is no presumption that the remuneration paid is for less than full consideration. The Regulations go on to say that, where agreement cannot be reached, application to the Copyright Tribunal may be made to determine the amount. The Tribunal should take into account the importance of the contribution made by the author, performer or director of the film or sound recording.

The difficulty for film producers in calculating the amount of one-off payments to talent will be putting a value on their contribution. It would follow that this should be linked to the potential which the film has in the video rental market. The success of a film in one particular market may be predicted with some certainty. The real difficulties for film producers will be in assessing the unknown or unquantifiable; for example a film may be a particular success in one or two territories or the profile (and hence the profitability) of a star or writer increases during the period following production but before general release thus enhancing its box office success.

The video market is however not the only rental market. The establishment of on-line distribution systems such as video-on-demand will provide additional guidance for the calculation of equitable remuneration.

Equitable remuneration will not be payable in respect of any rental of a film before 1 January 1997. Equitable remuneration will be payable to artists and authors (or successors in title) in respect of any rental made on or after 1 January 1997 of a film made following an agreement entered into before 1 July 1994 provided that talent notify the person liable to make payment that they intend to exercise their rental right.

It is, currently, too early to assess the impact, if any, that this will have on the place of the author in the chain of exploitation of his or her material. Certainly, expert advice should be sought as to the possible ramifications not only in the short term but also in the commercial considerations over a longer period of time.

All forms of exploitation are simply another way of bringing the product to the public. The standard grant of literary film rights in the past was usually wide enough to grant to the purchaser the right to use all forms of exploitation of the original which in essence are just other ways of reproducing or copying the original film, that is by exhibiting it to the public, broadcasting it or distributing it to the public by way of video (the acts, that is, restricted by copyright in a film). Whether that traditional grant was wide enough to include exploitation using the new technologies will depend, amongst other things, on the precise wording of the grant and the date of the grant.

The Precedent offers a typical form of option agreement and, to show the essential elements, a simple form of assignment. It is not intended to be relied on without further, specialist advice. An assignment of film, TV and allied rights would normally be expected to be very much fuller and more complex, particularly if an American financier was involved or a multi-million-dollar production budget was envisaged. It would also now have to deal, head-on, with the question of the so-called electronic rights. It is not absolutely clear that all grantors will be willing to grant these rights. If they are *not* included in the grant, it will be essential (for the purchaser) to ensure that their manner and timing of exploitation are controlled in order to reduce the risk of competitive marketing; and it will be necessary to face the question of whether some forms of electronic exploitation fall within the definition of 'film' under the Act, which might give rise to complications!

Also, it should be anticipated that the warranties as to title, etc. would be fuller, the wording of the grant much expanded, and so on. A licence only of television rights takes a different form, other considerations applying.

The detailed drafting of agreements for the grant of film, TV and allied rights contains many pitfalls for the unwary. It is therefore always advisable where there is any doubt, whether about the form or the detail, to seek legal advice and preferably from a solicitor specialising in the business.

THIS OPTION AGREEMENT is made the   day of
199

BETWEEN:

(1) [   ] (the 'Owner', which expression includes his/her administrators, executors and successors in title, of [   ]; and

(2) [   ] (the 'Purchaser' which expression includes its successors in title and assigns) whose registered office is at [   ]

NOW IT IS HEREBY AGREED as follows:

1. Option
In consideration of the sum of [   ] paid by the Purchaser to the Owner (receipt whereof the Owner hereby acknowledges) the Owner grants to the Purchaser the sole and exclusive option to acquire the rights specified in the draft Assignment annexed hereto as Exhibit A (referred to as the 'Assignment' and identified by initials of the Purchaser and the Owner) on the terms therein specified in a [   ] written by [the Owner] [(the 'Author')] entitled [   ] (the 'Work').

2. Extension/Exercise
2.1 At any time before the end of [   ] from the date hereof the Purchaser may either:
    (a) exercise this option by notice in writing to the Owner; or
    (b) extend the option for a further period of [   ] by notice in writing to the Owner accompanied by payment of a further sum of [   ] and if the Purchaser so extends the option it may exercise the same by notice in writing to the Owner at any time before the end of the said further period.
2.2 Simultaneously with or as soon as practicable after exercise of the option the Purchaser shall at its expense deliver to the Owner engrossments of the documents required under Clause 4.1 below.

'**The Owner**' will be the rights-owner, the owner of the copyright in the work; as explained in the introduction to this precedent this will not usually be the publisher. It will be the author or, in some cases, the company that owns his services. There is no reason why the publisher should not be joined into the agreement, first to give his/her consent to it and secondly to ensure that all payments are channelled through him/her; but not to give the grant or warranties other than limited warranties, e.g. that he/she has not previously dealt with the rights.

1. and **2.** The initial option fee and period and extension fee and period, and the mechanics of how the period can be extended, should be clearly specified, and the rights assignment identified. There is no reason why further extensions, beyond the initial one, should not be negotiated.

3. Whether or not the option fees are on account of the purchase price is negotiable and may depend on the circumstances. Option fees are rarely, if ever, returnable. The initial fee is usually ten per cent of the final purchase price but can be any percentage. An extension fee is often five per cent and sometimes *not* on account.

4. Before getting the full payment on exercise of the option the owner will be asked to deliver an executed engrossment of the assignment, and (if the copyright is restricted in the USA or if distribution in the USA is anticipated and there is any likelihood that the US distribution may require registration) a short form assignment which will be used for registration of the assignment in the American copyright register in Washington. Registration is no longer an essential prerequisite to maintenance of copyright in America but is a sensible prerequisite to successful action against copyright infringement there. Often, for the sake of tidiness and ease of administration, the short form assignment is annexed to the main assignment when the option is signed but it is not essential that it should be. It reflects the main terms of the assignment and can therefore be prepared at any time. An example has *not* been included in this precedent.

A quitclaim is confirmation by a publisher that he/she does not maintain any claim over the film rights, i.e. that the owner is entitled, so far as that publisher is concerned, to enter into the agreement. Strictly, this is not required where the original publisher enters into the assignment as owner of the rights (since in that case the publisher *does* have an interest in the rights and signifies his/her consent by the act of entering into the agreement) but in all other cases a prudent purchaser will demand quitclaims from all English-language publishers. The form of the quitclaim is usually very standard and, provided there is authority in both the option agreement and the assignment for payment of all moneys to the publisher, there is no reason why it should not be given. Once again, it is usual (but not essential) that the wording of the quitclaim should be settled at the same time as the option.

Unusually, the purchaser does sometimes ask for quitclaims from the major foreign-language publishers also, but English-language quitclaims will more often than not be sufficient.

5. Since this is only an option and *not* a grant of rights, this clause is required by the purchaser to allow him/her to prepare a screenplay. Otherwise, technically, he/she would be in breach of copyright in making an adaptation without the owner's consent. That consent is of course implied in the whole nature of the option agreement, but why leave anything open to argument? Conversely, the publisher should ensure that sufficient authority is given only to the extent necessary; what rights are included (i.e. film or TV or both) will depend on the deal.

6. These warranties are the least that can be expected of the owner. The purchaser may require an *absolute* defamation warranty.

7.1 This clause, if included, will allow the owner to buy in all scripts or treatments if the option expires without being exercised. He/she will only want to do this if there is someone else interested in using that material. At this stage there will be two separate copyrights involved, the copyright in the underlying literary work (that is, in the published work itself) and the copyright in any script or treatment. The purchaser cannot exploit his/her

3. On Account

Sums paid to the Owner under Clauses 1 and 2 hereof shall be on account of the moneys specified in Clause 2 of the Assignment but shall not be returnable.

4. Completion

4.1 Within 7 days of receipt of the said engrossments the Owner will at his/ her/its expense:
  (a) execute and deliver to the Purchaser an engrossment of the Assignment;
  (b) procure the execution of and delivery to the Purchaser of quitclaims in [the form annexed hereto as Exhibit B or] such [other] form as the Purchaser may approve by all English language publishers of the Work.

4.2 Upon receipt of the documents specified in paragraphs (a) and (b) of Clause 4.1 above the Purchaser will:
  (a) pay the consideration specified in Clause 2 of the Assignment to the extent that it is due at that date;
  (b) at the Purchaser's expense execute and deliver to the Owner a counterpart of the Assignment.

4.3 If the Owner fails to execute and deliver the said documents in accordance with Clause 4.1 above the Purchaser is hereby authorised by the Owner to execute the same on its behalf.

5. Before Completion

During the subsistence of this option and any extension thereof:

5.1 the Purchaser shall be entitled to make adaptations of the Work in the form of film treatments and scripts and to show the same to third parties who may be interested in the production and/or exploitation of a film based on the Work;

5.2 the Owner will at the request of the Purchaser deduce its/his/her title to the rights that are the subject of this option.

6. Owner's Obligations

6.1 The warranties and undertakings set out in Clause 3 of the Assignment shall be deemed incorporated herein and shall be binding on the Owner throughout the subsistence of this option.

6.2 During the subsistence of this option the Owner shall not dispose of or encumber the said rights or do anything that would if the option is exercised prevent him/her assigning them to the Purchaser or cause the warranties in the Assignment to be untrue.

7. Exercise and Expiry of Option

7.1 If this option expires without being exercised the Owner shall have an exclusive option to purchase all the Purchaser's rights in any treatments or scripts based on the Work subject to the terms on which the Purchaser may hold such rights.

copyright in the script or treatment without acquiring the underlying copyright and the owner cannot use the script or treatment without first acquiring the rights therein. It follows that the purchase, if his/her option has expired, will usually be only too willing to sell any scripts or treatments and the only purpose of this clause is to give a contractual right to the owner (which he/she would not otherwise have) and to set a limit to the price demanded. The latter can, of course, work both ways.

7.2 The period during which this buy-in option should run is negotiable. If the principle of the option is conceded, then the period might as well be long as short. After 80 years (the maximum period to avoid offending the risk against perpetuities) the material could well be in the public domain, simply through the passage of time.

8(1) The purchaser will seek to insist on the right to assign. Under English law he/she will remain liable for his/her obligations notwithstanding the assignment; he/she cannot escape those obligations unless the contract specifically so provides, i.e. unless there is a novation – a new contract. Provision is not necessary (though it is often found) in this clause that the purchaser will remain liable.

(2) Some owners seek to limit the right to assign in an effort to control the ownership of their rights. This would be relevant where the option was being granted to a particular producer with the intention that only he/she may make the film. Even he/she will need the limited right to assign the option to his/her financiers. Sometimes the qualification 'no assignment without the owner's prior written consent, such consent not to be unreasonably withheld' is seen. That compromise rather begs the issue – there is plenty of scope for argument over 'unreasonably' in that context.

9. The agency clause is most important if, as will usually be the case, the publisher wants all moneys paid to him, so that he can deduct his share before passing the balance on to the owner (i.e. usually, the author of the original work). In the absence of the agency clause a purchaser would have to pay moneys direct to the owner. If the publisher is not a party, then he/she only has an action in damages against the owner if the moneys are not paid to the publisher. But the publisher would be able to enforce the payment if he/she were a party.

The purchaser should not be too ready to accept the agent's signature on the Assignment because that would bring the option agreement on to the purchaser's title documents to the film rights to prove valid execution of the assignment. In any event, if a US short form assignment is required (see note 4) it should be signed by the owner personally because signature by an agent may not comply with US regulations.

In practice option agreements are often varied, especially by extension, and such variations are often agreed on behalf of an owner by his agent. It may be vital for a purchaser to be able to prove that the owner is bound by an extension. The proviso permitting revocation of the agency is desirable in the interest not only of the owner but also the purchaser because otherwise the purchaser might be placed in a dilemma if the owner did revoke the agent's authority. In that case, unless the authority for payments under the next clause was expressed to be irrevocable, the purchaser would be bound to pay in accordance with the owner's new instructions but the original agent might feel aggrieved and, under some laws, e.g. USA, might claim that he had a third party interest entitling him to continued payments so that he could continue to deduct his commission before accounting to the owner.

7.2 The Owner's option under sub-clause 7.1 may be exercised by written notice at any time before the end of [   ] years from the date of this Agreement.

7.3 The price payable by the Owner upon exercise of the option under sub-clause 7.1 shall be a sum equal to all sums paid by the Purchaser in connection with the acquisition of the relevant rights plus interest thereon at [%] over the [   ] Bank base rate from time to time and the Owner shall indemnify the Purchaser against liability for any future payments that may become due in respect of such rights.

8. Assignment

The Purchaser shall be entitled to assign the benefit of this Agreement to any third party.

9. Agent

The Owner hereby appoints [the Publisher] (the 'Agent') as his agent in all matters relating to this Agreement including any variation or extension hereof [and execution and delivery to the Purchaser of the Assignment under sub-clause 4.1(a) above].

[PROVIDED THAT this appointment may be revoked or varied at any time by written notice from the Owner to the Purchaser.]

10. Payment Instructions

The Owner hereby [irrevocably] instructs the Purchaser to pay all moneys due to him hereunder to   whose receipt shall be a good discharge to the Purchaser [,unless the Purchaser has previously received written notice of revocation of such instructions].

11. Notices

Any notice to be given hereunder shall be duly given if:

11.1 delivered personally; or

11.2 mailed by first class pre-paid mail to the address stated in this Agreement of the party to be served which notices shall be deemed to have arrived in due course of post; or

11.3 sent by telex or facsimile to the addressee's number notified to the sender by the addressee or recorded in any official index of telex or facsimile numbers which notices shall be deemed to have arrived on the date of transmission if not later than one hour before close of business at the addressee on a business day or otherwise on the next business day at the addressee provided the appropriate answer back code is received by the sender of a telex and provided the sender does not receive any indication that the message is incomprehensible.

12. Governing Law

12.1 This Agreement shall be governed by and construed in all respects in accordance with English law and the parties agree to submit to the

non-exclusive jurisdiction of the English courts as regards any claim or matter arising in relation to this Agreement.

12.2 [   ]   hereby   appoints   [   ]   of
[England] (marked for the personal attention of
[   ] or [   ]) as its authorised agent for the purpose of accepting service of process for all purposes in connection with this Agreement.

SIGNED by   }
the Owner

SIGNED on behalf of the   }
Purchaser by
its director/duly authorised
representative

'**The Assignor**' will in almost all cases be the same party as the owner in the option agreement.

'**The Assignee**', however, may well be different, depending on whether the purchaser of the option has assigned his/her rights in the option to a production company, to financiers or to another entrepreneur. Options sometimes do change hands many times as producers struggle to put finance packages together.

The recitals record the legal title to the work.

Exhibit 'A'

THIS ASSIGNMENT is made on   199[   ]

BETWEEN:
(1) [   ] (the **'Assignor'**) of [   ]; and
(2) [   ] **LIMITED** (the **'Assignee'** which expression includes its successors in title, licensees and assigns) whose registered office is at [   ]

WHEREAS:
[(A) The Assignor is the sole author of the original [story][novel][play] entitled '[   ]' (the **'Work'**) and the beneficial owner of the entire copyright in the Work throughout the world [subject only to the publishing agreements of which details have been given to the Assignee]

or

(A) The Assignor is by virtue of the documents specified in Schedule A hereto the beneficial owner of the entire copyright throughout the world in the original [story][novel][play] by [   ] (the **'Author'**) entitled '[   ]' (the **'Work'**) [subject only to the publishing agreements of which details have been given to the Assignee]]

(B) Words used herein shall where appropriate have the meanings given to them by the Copyright, Designs and Patents Act 1988 save that 'films' shall not extend to:
— [any recordings made for the purpose of being broadcast or included in cable programme services as the principal or initial medium of exploitation]
— [any Video recording]
— [any recording in Interactive Formats]
— [any recording in any of Specified Formats]

(C) In the previous paragraph the following expressions shall have the following meanings:
'Video': means:
either
'Any copy of a film (other than in a Specified Format) on any medium from which the moving images of the film may be produced by any means that do not involve the projection of light through

For the consideration specified in Clause 2 hereof the assignor with full title guarantee hereby assigns to the Assignee for the full period of copyright and all renewals and extensions the whole of the film [television] and allied rights in the work throughout the world including but not by way of limitation the sole and exclusive right to do or to authorise the following acts:

1.2 The wording of the grant needs careful scrutiny; is it to be for one film only or for any number and if the latter, is there to be payment of further consideration?
If it is intended to include the right to make an original electronic version e.g. CD-ROM, such rights should be specifically included here. There is a whole question as to whether a CD-ROM is already a film (see the Introduction and the definition of a 'film'). It would also be appropriate specifically to *exclude* so-called electronic rights if they are not to be granted.

1.3 In this form, under English law, the right to present the film by 'electronic' version e.g. on CD-ROM would be included. *This* wording does not purport to grant the right to *make* an original electronic (e.g. CD-ROM) version of the original work. See 1.2 above and 1.3 below;

1.5 This specific reference is required as a result of the EC Directive on Rental and Lending Rights.

that copy [including Interactive Formats] [excluding Interactive Formats].'

or

'Any copy of a film [other than in a Specified Format] on any medium from which by the use of a reproduction apparatus the moving image of the film may be displayed in a substantially linear manner on the screen of a television receiver, home replay device or monitor.'

or

'Any copy of a film in one of the Specified Formats.'

'Interactive Format': means a format that includes presentation of a Video in combination with one or more other methods of expression, whether textual, audio, pictorial, graphical or audio visual, where a significant characteristic of the presentation is the ability of the user to manipulate the content of the presentation by means of a computing device in real time and in a non-linear fashion.

'Specified Formats': means [magnetic tape] [CD-Rom] [VHS or Beta cassette or electronic storage device] [laser or capacitance discs] [whether or not] [provided] such format is designed to be used only in conjunction with a reproduction apparatus which causes the film to be visible on the screen of a [television receiver] [home replay device].

TERMS:

1. Rights Granted

For the consideration specified in Clause 2 hereof the Assignor with full title guarantee hereby assigns to the Assignee for the full period of copyright and all renewals and extensions the whole of the film [television] and allied rights in the Work throughout the world including but not by way of limitation the sole and exclusive right to do or to authorise the following acts:

1.1 **Adapt into Screenplays etc.**: to adapt the Work into film treatments and screenplays in all languages;

1.2 **Reproduce as Films**: to make films of such screenplays recorded on any medium [Provided that the Assignee shall not without the prior written consent of the Assignor make more than one such film and the Assignor may give or withhold such consent in its absolute discretion and upon such terms including payment of further consideration as the Assignor thinks fit];

1.3 **Perform by Films**: publicly to present such films by all modes now known or hereafter to be invented;

1.4 **Broadcast**: to broadcast such films and to include them in cable programmes;

1.5 **Issue Copies**: to issue to the public copies of such films (including by way of rental or loan) and generally distribute or transmit electronic

1.7 This right can be confined to live performances because filmed performances are permitted under 1.4.

1.11 i.e. a waiver of moral rights. It was always customary to exclude *droit moral* prior to the Copyright etc Act 1988 in an effort (not always successful) to reduce the chances of argument in a jurisdiction which did not recognise the concept. It is now essential to address the problem but there remains the possibility that some jurisdictions will not accept a waiver of moral rights;

1.13 (1) Not all of the foregoing are always included in any grant of the 'film' rights. Each grant is a matter for individual negotiation and this may or may not include television, satellite, cable, video cassette, or electronic exploitation. A general exclusion of all rights not being granted should be incorporated in the draft to ensure that rights are not included by omission.

   (2) The period of the grant is invariably for the full period of copyright except in connection with films made for television where (particularly under standard BBC and ITV contracts) a licence limited to between 10 and 15 years is more common. Different rules can also apply to television in that the purchase price will be lower but the author will receive repeat fees and residuals for each transmission of the film.

or other recordings of such films by all methods now known or hereafter to be devised or invented;

1.6 **Television Spin-Offs**:
   (a)   to adapt the Work by converting it into treatments and scripts, in any languages for television programmes;
   (b)   to make audio visual recordings of such scripts on any medium or by storing performances of them by electronic means;
   (c)   to broadcast such audio visual recordings and to include them in cable programme services;

1.7 **Publicity Excerpts**: for advertising and publicity purposes only to broadcast and to include in cable programme services (whether live or by film or other recording) excerpts of the Work or any adaptations thereof (with such alteration as the Assignee may think fit) not exceeding 15 minutes in duration;

1.8 **Synopses**: to write, print, publish and sell synopses and résumés of the Work not exceeding [   ] words in length but only for the purpose of publicity and exploitation of such films [and television programmes];

1.9 **Sound Recordings**: to make sound recordings from the soundtracks of such films [or television programmes] on any medium or by any method whereby the same may be separately performed and to issue copies of such sound recordings to the public (whether by way of sale or otherwise) and by use of such sound recordings to perform the Work in public, to broadcast it and to include it in cable programme services;

1.10 **Merchandising**: to exercise all so-called 'merchandising rights' as that expression is understood in the film [and television] industries of the United Kingdom and the USA;

1.11 **Moral Rights**: to make additions to, deletions from or alterations to or adaptations of the Work or any part thereof for the purposes of or in the course of exercising the rights hereby granted and to do the acts specified above in relation to the Work or any part thereof with such additions, deletions, alterations or adaptations notwithstanding any moral right or 'droit moral' or similar right to which the Assignor may be entitled in any country;

1.12 **Customary Rights**: to do all other acts customarily comprised in grants of full film [and television] rights;

1.13 **Assigns**: to assign or license to any third party the rights specified above.

2. Payments

In consideration of the foregoing assignment the Assignee:
   (a)   **Cash**: has on or before the date hereof paid to the Assignor the sum of or sums amounting in the aggregate to [   ] (the receipt of which the Assignor hereby acknowledges);
   (b)   shall pay to the Assignor the following further sums on the dates or in the manner mentioned below:
        (i)   **Deferment**: the sum of [   ] as a deferment payable

2.   Credit will be given against the purchase price for the relevant parts of the option fee. The price may be payable in one sum on exercise of the option or in instalments; for instance, the first on exercise and the second on start of principal photography. Avoid the latter – photography may never start, so the payment would never be made. Opt instead for a period of time or the start of photography, whichever is the earlier.

Deferments are payments deferred to what would otherwise be first profits, so the payment may never be made – it is contingent on the success of the film and can be equated to profits. It is unusual for literary rights to be paid for out of deferments.

The difference between a share of profits and a deferment is that the latter is usually expressed as a quantified sum of money and is paid out before the profits actually arise. 'Profits' is an expression that is as long as the proverbial piece of string. Great care should be taken over the definition. None is included here in any detail because each definition should be tailor-made for each circumstance. Very briefly, 'profits' arise once the gross receipts from the exploitation of the film in the relevant media exceed:

(a)   the cost of production including the cost of financing;

(b)   the cost of distribution including fees, commissions and expenses;

(c)   deferments.

That simple formula can take several pages to expand in detail. Once again, great care must be taken that the definition is adequate. Gross receipts should be defined as including all income and at source rather than in the hands of a recipient, because receipts have an unfortunate habit of getting very much smaller the longer they travel. It should be *all* income, not just income from the first film but also from secondary exploitation; e.g. by way of cassette/disc, broadcast television, cable and also remakes and sequels (see the special note on page 300). The cost of production should be the actual cost as certified by the production company's auditor. Net profit definitions usually also define the recipients' right to inspect the books of account (once annually) and to receive statements (typically, quarterly for two years from the first release of the film, then half-yearly for three years, then annually). Once again, the subject is sufficiently complicated to justify taking expert advice. While it is unfortunately true that more films do not achieve profits than do, when a film is successful, it is worth having the protection of a tight definition.

As a result of the implementation of the Rental Rights Directive, it is now necessary to address this question. See the introductory notes.

3.   The purchaser will often reasonably ask for a wider range of warranties, including warranties for further assurance and for extension of copyright (in those jurisdictions where there are separate periods of copyright). The purchaser may also ask for specific authority to act in the owner's name in protecting the rights granted. He/she may also ask to inspect title documents.

4.   This is relevant where only the film rights are granted so that others such as stage or TV drama are retained; the purchaser will seek to insist that the latter rights are not exploited for a sufficient period to allow him/her to turn the film rights into profit.

only out of the 'First Profits' (as defined in Schedule A/B hereto) from the first or only film that may be made pursuant to the rights hereby granted proportionately with any other deferments that may be payable out of the First Profits;

(ii) **Profits**:

    (aa) sums from time to time equal to [   ]% of Net Profits (as defined in Schedule A/B hereto) from the first or only film that may be made pursuant to the rights hereby granted;

    (bb) if any television programme or episode (not being a film made pursuant to sub-clause 1.2 hereof) is made pursuant to sub-clause 1.6 hereof the Assignee shall pay to the Assignor not later than 28 days after the first broadcast or cable programme services transmission for each programme or episode not exceeding 30 minutes in duration an initial fee of [   ] or twice that amount for a programme exceeding 30 minutes but not exceeding 60 minutes or thrice that amount for a programme exceeding 60 minutes and a further sum equal to one quarter of such initial fee 28 days after each of up to 4 repeat broadcasts or transmissions but after 4 repeats no further fees shall be payable;

3. Warranties

The Assignor hereby warrants to and undertakes with the Assignee that:

3.1 the Work is original in [the Assignor] [the Author] and nothing therein infringes the copyright or any other rights of any third party and so far as the Assignor is aware it is not defamatory;

3.2 the Assignor is not aware of any claim that the Work infringes any right of any third party;

3.3 *he/she* will procure if and when appropriate the renewal or extension of the copyright in the Work under the laws of all countries that afford renewal or extension rights and assign to the Assignee for such renewal or extension term the rights defined by Clause 1 hereof and the Assignor hereby authorises the Assignee to execute all documents and to do all acts that may be necessary to procure such renewal or extension and assignment;

3.4 *he/she* has not granted any assignment or licence in relation to the Work [other than the publishing agreements referred to above];

3.5 the covenants implied by the Law of Property (Miscellaneous Provisions) Act 1994 shall relate to the rights hereby assigned in all countries;

3.6 the covenants implied by Section 76 of the Law of Property Act 1925 shall relate to the rights hereby assigned in all countries.

4. Embargoes

The Assignor agrees that *he/she* has not granted and will not until the [   ] day of [   ] 199[ ] grant any licence for or permit

5. It is important that the credit obligations should be fully set out.

7. The agency clause is as important here as in the option agreement.

Special Notes

Sequels and Remakes. Because a concise version of a film rights assignment has been included in this book, incorporating a comprehensive grant of rights, there is no specific reference to another aspect frequently found in a film deal: the right to make sequels and remakes. Where the main grant is for *one* film only, provision can be made for sequels and remakes which are traditionally paid for at 50 and 33 1/3 per cent of the original purchase price respectively. There are two kinds of sequels: author-written and producer-written. The purchaser will be keen to acquire such rights if he/she thinks the subject-matter will bear more than one film, as he/she will wish to be protected against the situation where his/ her film is successful and leads to a considerable increase in the value of the author's works.

Reversions. It is highly unlikely that a film-maker who is considering investing millions into a project will allow the original owner of the rights any right to rescind the agreement: actions for breach are usually specifically limited to actions for damages – after all, the concept is a sale and purchase. The position is otherwise in TV-rights-only deals where a licence for 10 to 15 years is common, all rights in the underlying material reverting at the end of the licence period.

Rarely a reversion provision is found providing for the rights to revert if a production has not commenced within 5, 10 or 15 years.

any broadcast or public performance of the Work or any adaptation thereof or inclusion thereof in a cable programme.

5. Credit
5.1 If the Assignee makes a film [or television programme] based on the Work it will give the original author credit on all copies delivered by it to its distributors or licensees [and in all major paid advertising and publicity issued by or under its control except group, list, teaser and trailer advertising and newspaper advertising of less than eight column inches] in some such form as 'Based on [   ]' mentioning the name of the Work if different from the film or programme.
5.2 No casual or inadvertent failure to afford credit as aforesaid shall constitute a breach hereof and the Assignor's remedies for a breach shall be confined to damages.

6. Moral Rights
The Assignor hereby unconditionally and irrevocably waives in favour of the Assignee the Assignor's rights under Section 80 of the Copyright, Designs and Patents Act 1988 and any moral right or 'droit moral' or similar right to which the Assignor may be entitled in any country to the extent such a waiver is permitted by the laws of such country.

7. Agents
The Assignor hereby [irrevocably] authorises *his/her* Agents, [   ], to collect and receive all moneys payable to the Assignor hereunder and declares that their receipt shall be a good discharge for such moneys [and that they shall be empowered to act in all matters arising out of this Assignment] [unless the Assignee has previously received written notice of revocation of such authority].

8. Governing Law
This Assignment shall be governed by and construed in all respects in accordance with English law and the parties agree to submit to the non-exclusive jurisdiction of the English courts as regards any claim or matter arising in relation to this Assignment.

[9. Certificate of Value
IT IS HEREBY CERTIFIED that the transaction hereby effected does not form part of a larger transaction or of a series of transactions in respect of which the amount or value or the aggregate amount or value of the consideration exceeds £60,000.]

SCHEDULE A
Title Documents of Assignor

Date	*Description of Document*	*Parties*

SCHEDULE A/B
Definitions of Receipts and Profits

SIGNED by
duly authorised for and
on behalf of the Assignor }

SIGNED by
duly authorised for and
on behalf of the Assignee }

Permission Fees

Note (1) to Precedent One, Clause 7, refers to the concept of 'fair dealing' beyond the limits of which publishers and authors may wish to charge fees for granting permission to print extracts from a book, and this particular need is sympathetically reflected in *General Practice* below. It seems useful to set out the convention which the book world has arrived at under the Copyright Acts of 1956 and 1988 which provide for such dealing 'for purposes of criticism or review'. Permission should sensibly be sought as follows:

From a copyright prose work
(a) for any extract of longer than 400 words;
(b) for a series of extracts totalling more than 800 words, of which any one extract is more than 300 words;
(c) for an extract or series of extracts comprising one-quarter of the work or more.

From a copyright work of poetry
(a) for an extract of more than 40 lines;
(b) for a series of extracts totalling more than 40 lines;
(c) for an extract comprising one-quarter or more of a complete poem;
(d) for a series of extracts comprising together one-quarter or more of a complete poem.

The above convention, arrived at by the Society of Authors and the Publishers Association, was judicially taken account of in *Sillitoe and Others v McGraw-Hill* (1981), known widely as the *Coles Notes Case*. Some publishers and authors will be happy to deem fair, and therefore make no charge for, quotation well beyond the above convention, but others may not: courtesy and common sense alike suggest that, if in any doubt, authors should ask permission.

'Fair dealing' is, however, a concept confined to the use of extracts from copyright works for purposes of criticism or review, however generously publishers interpret those two words. A publisher may feel it appropriate to charge for a short quotation used, for example, as a dedication or a chapter head. If a quotation is to be used in, say, an advertisement, the fee charged might be substantially higher, depending on whether the campaign was on a local or national level.

There are many other circumstances in which fees are paid for permission to reproduce copyright works, and this Appendix offers some guidance on the level of current practice. Finding a just balance between what is a proper return to author and publisher and what is a proper and liberal attitude to other authors and publishers is not at all easy, and individual circumstances must always affect the very general guidance set out below.

One general circumstance is the cost, which increases as staff and processing costs increase, of handling small permission fees. Some publishers, seeing that their share (often 50 per cent) of a fee of, say, £30 will not cover the cost of handling the request, may respond by setting each year a realistic level of charges and a minimum number of words chargeable. So there may in time develop, quite outside the realm of fair dealing, a modest level of reproduction of copyright work for which fees may in practice not be sought, but the following figures probably reflect current trade practice, and cover permissions granted non-exclusively throughout the world in the English language. In each case the higher figure represents major poets or authors who command top fees:

1. Poetry
1st 10 Lines: **£90–£115**
11–20 lines: **£2.00–£2.25 per line**
21+ lines: **£1.25–£1.45 per line**

2. Prose
£115–£140 per 1000 words

If world rights are not required, fees for both poetry (established poets) and prose can be adjusted as follows:

British Commonwealth (inc Canada) or US only: **one-half of world fee**
Individual countries: Canada, Australia, New Zealand, South Africa: **one-quarter of world fee**
US + Canada, EU: **two-thirds of world fee**
Australasia, Japan: **one-third of world fee**

The rate per line/poem should be reduced by one-third if the poem appears in a literary or scholarly journal or an anthology which contains more than 40 poems in copyright or in a book with a print run of fewer than 1500 copies. When assessing the fee, it is worth remembering that for **new poets** very often their only other outlet is publication in such anthologies, which therefore deserve as wide a sale as possible. Thus for subsequent editions in another format, or publication elsewhere (the US or Australasia) it is accepted practice to charge further fees of **not less than half the original fee for new poets**. Established poets may well command full fees.

Where the **prose extract** is complete in itself, (a chapter or a short story) some publishers charge an additional fee of half the applicable rate for 1000 words, depending on the scale and territory.

General Practice (poetry and prose)
Permissions are always granted non-exclusively; they normally cover the English language and one edition only. For each new edition or edition in another format (e.g. paperback), or in critical or scholarly works where the extracts used are over and above the recommended fair dealings limits, **half the original fee is normally charged**.

When the author is British, it is standard practice for the British publisher to include the open market when giving permission, and for the US publisher to do so when the author is American.

3. Performance Fees

(i) When prose extracts or poetry from the work of an individual author form a substantial part of a programme before a paying audience (e.g. a special programme at the National Theatre) it is desirable to gear the fees to a percentage of box-office takings. If it is a shorter extract or extracts it might be sensible to work out something on a time basis (so much per minute — or half minute in the case of a poem).

(ii) For competition recitals, see Precedent One, Note to Clause 14 (q).

(iii) For amateur performances of a full-length play the scale can range between £50-£75 per performance, with possible concessions depending on the seating capacity of the theatre. The scale for sketches or one-act plays generally varies between £10 and £40 per performance, depending on the eminence of the author. It is not usual to make concessions for theatre size in such cases.

4. Recipes
£80 per recipe for world rights. Pro rata as above for smaller territories.

5. Illustrations other than Photographs
The fee should be assessed in two parts, taking account of (a) the size the illustration is to be reproduced and (b) the territory required, so that the fee charged = (a) + (b). Currently (a) and (b) are each £90.

(a) *Size of Illustration as Reproduced by the Purchaser*
Quarter page or less = one-quarter of (a)
Half-page = one-half of (a)
Whole-page = (a)
Double-page spread = twice (a) basic fee.
If the illustration is in colour = twice (a)

(b) *Territory*
The same ratios apply here as those given above for prose and poetry permissions. They depend on the territories being granted.

Suggestions for Assessing Fees
(i) How the illustration is to be used: for example, if someone wants to use an inside illustration from one book on the cover or jacket of another, it is reasonable to charge a higher fee either by adjusting (a) upwards or by doubling the total fee that would normally be charged.

(ii) If the illustration is to be used in another medium (e.g. a table mat or poster) some special arrangement needs to be made — a royalty or merchandising deal (Precedent Thirteeen covers the latter). Likewise if several illustrations are to be used from a particular artist or a particular book an advance/royalty arrangement might be more appropriate.

(iii) If the illustration is to be used in more than one edition, e.g. a paperback edition, some publishers charge half the original fee for each further use.

N.B. It is advisable to set out in writing the precise title of the book in which the illustration is to appear and to stipulate that permission covers inclusion in that one book only.

(iv)   Some publishers charge 'access' fees when supplying prints or transparencies for which permission to reproduce has already been obtained. For example, if a print of an illustration is to be supplied at cost, a charge (often 10-15 per cent) is added to cover handling charges and overheads. Sometimes a lending fee is charged for film or artwork plus a penalty fee (like all fees this should be agreed and sometimes paid in advance) for every week the material is kept beyond a certain period. A written undertaking should be obtained from the borrowers that they will be responsible for and will make good any loss or damage incurred while the material is in transit or on loan to them.

(v)   Most good artists (and publishers) do not like stories equally famous for their illustrations (e.g. Winnie the Pooh) to be re-illustrated, so it is as well to stipulate that, if the purchaser is not intending to use illustrations from the source book (for which naturally a fee would be charged), he/she shall not re-illustrate the story without express written consent.

(vi) If someone wants to reproduce a colour illustration in black and white, the fee charged is nevertheless frequently that applicable to reproduction in colour.

(vii) It is desirable to obtain fees from the United States for the use of illustrations that might be in the public domain there but which are certainly in copyright in the United Kingdom. Most US publishers are prepared to pay such fees.

6. Typographical Arrangement: A Publisher's Right
UK copyright law provides for a separate copyright in the typographical arrangement (i.e. in the design and arrangement of the typeface on the printed page) which belongs to the publisher. In other words, each book carries two distinct copyright elements (in the work itself, and in the typographical arrangement). If, for example, a paperback or reprint publisher wishes to use the originating publisher's typograpical arrangement for his own edition of a book, normal practice is to charge that publisher an offset fee, which at the time of going to press is about £4.00 per page.

Copyright in the typographical arrangement of a published edition of a work lasts for 25 years from the end of the year in which it was first published.

It is worth mentioning that only a few other countries have this right (e.g.

Canada). Most notably US publishers have no similar right *and while, under the Berne Convention to which both parties are now signatories, US publishers are afforded the same copyright protection* for their typographical arrangement under UK law as British publishers, there is, unusually, no reciprocity for British publishers in the US, since there is no US typographic right. In practice UK and US publishers tend to make individual bilateral arrangements and agree fees (sometimes only nominal) on a book-by-book or publisher-by-publisher basis.

Nowadays most requests for permission to photocopy extracts from books are channelled through the CLA (Copyright Licensing Agency), which deals with both the authors' and the publishers' interests through their respective licensing bodies (see Appendix E).

7. Information to Include on a Permissions Form

1. Name and address of applicant and date of application
2. Fee required (inc VAT) and when required (on signature of form)
3. To whom fee payable
4. Details of the extract required (NB *specify that permission granted is non-exclusive and in the English language*)
5. Details of the publication in which the extract is to appear (i.e. title, author and publisher)
6. Territory granted, e.g.:
   Throughout the World including/excluding the US
   The British Commonwealth including/excluding Canada
7. List the conditions on which permission is granted, e.g.:
   (a) permission to cover one edition only unless otherwise specified;
   (b) permission does not include any extraneous copyright material which may be incorporated in the extract;
   (c) the acknowledgments required;
   (d) if the fee has not been received within one year of the above date, this agreement is cancelled and fresh application must be made;
   [(e) one copy of the book to be sent on publication].

NB: Don't give permission for territories or languages which you don't control (e.g. the US; a French translation): give name and address of the publisher/agent controlling these rights.

NB: The open market is usually understood to be included with the UK publisher's permission if the author is British or Commonwealth; with the US publisher if the author is American.

8. Fees for Published Texts Broadcast within the UK
These are governed by an overall agreement, made originally in 1947 and revised twice since then, setting out the guidelines within which the BBC may use copyright published material. The latest (1995) revision provides for two separate agreements, one for radio, the other for television. This

latter is not yet finalised but is expected to differ only slightly from the radio agreement which is printed below.

1. Radio

From the overall radio agreement depend six standard agreements detailing the fee payable and rights to be granted which are sent, as appropriate, to publishers whenever the BBC wishes to use an extract (usually small) from a published work in one of its programmes. These are:

PA1(3)	Dramatic works including extracts therefrom and shortened versions thereof;
PA2(3)	Non-dramatic prose works and extracts therefrom;
PA3(3)	Poems or extracts therefrom;
PA4(3)	Prose works required for adaptation into dramatic form;
PA(GP)(1)	**NEW:** a General Permissions Agreement covering all or some works by a particular author. Extract(s) must comprise less than 5 minutes and not more than 10% of any programme;
Radio(WS)TS2	Transcriptions.

The overall agreement provides for fees to be regularly updated and a scale of minimum fees is negotiated usually annually between the Publishers Association, the Society of Authors, and the BBC. The fees are calculated according to the type of usage (e.g. dramatisations, prose readings, poetry readings, children's or school programmes) on an airtime-occupied basis (per minute for prose and plays; per half minute for poetry).

World service (English language) rates are currently 50%, and World Service (foreign language) rates currently 10% of domestic radio rates. For translations two-thirds of the applicable rate for the original, and/or two-thirds of the applicable rate for the translation is applied (a total of four-thirds of the initial fee). Additional fees are payable in the case of repeats within a stipulated period, overseas sales (where these are permitted) and certain other conditions which are not usually negotiable. Some very well-known authors are sometimes paid at more than the minimum rates.

The basic domestic rates are used as a yardstick for calculating the fees payable by both BBC local radio and the Open University, who pay percentages based upon, and thus consequently varied by, BBC minimum standard fees.

2. Television

The overall agreement has yet to be finalised, although like the radio agreement it will provide for the minimum fees to be regularly updated. Currently there are two television agreements (Tel Lit Pubs and Tel Ed Pubs) and negotiations are currently under way to merge these into one agreement (Tel Lit 2) covering material for both general and educational use

General Note: As with all subsidiary agreements, it is up to the publisher to ensure that no rights are granted which he/she does not control.

THIS AGREEMENT IS MADE on the 17th day of January 1995 BETWEEN

THE BRITISH BROADCASTING CORPORATION of Broadcasting House London W1A 1AA ('the BBC') and

THE PUBLISHERS' ASSOCIATION of 19 Bedford Square London WC1B 3HJ ('the PA') and

THE SOCIETY OF AUTHORS of 84 Drayton Gardens London SW10 9SB ('The SoA') and

THE INDEPENDENT PUBLISHERS GUILD of 25 Cambridge Road Hampton Middlesex TW12 2JL ('the IPG')

WHEREAS:

(A) The BBC broadcasts certain copyright literary works on radio and the BBC, the PA, the SoA and the League of Dramatists made an agreement dated 15th July 1955 ('the 1955 Agreement') setting out the fees and terms which the BBC is normally prepared to offer for the use of such works (and which the PA and the SoA are prepared to recommend to their membership as reasonable) and the BBC, the PA and the SoA have from time to time agreed revisions to such fees and terms.

(B) The League of Dramatists has ceased to exist.

(C) The 1955 Agreement is now outdated and the extant parties to it desire that it should be superseded by this new agreement to which the IPG also wishes to be a party.

NOW IT IS HEREBY AGREED AS FOLLOWS:

1. The BBC, the PA and the SoA agree that on signature of this agreement the 1955 Agreement shall be terminated with immediate effect (notwithstanding the provisions of clause 11 thereof).

2. This Agreement shall commence on the date of signature and shall continue in force until terminated either by mutual agreement of all the parties hereto or by the giving of six months' notice in writing by the BBC to one or more of the PA, SoA or the IPG (hereinafter referred to together as 'the Organisations') or by one of the Organisations giving six months' notice to the BBC Provided That a notice given by any one party shall only operate to terminate this Agreement between the party giving the notice and the party receiving it and shall not affect the validity of this Agreement as between any of the other parties.

3. The Organisations agree to recommend acceptance of the terms contained in the contracts attached hereto as Schedule 1 ('the Standard Agreements') to their members (subject to their members controlling the relevant rights) being terms which the BBC agrees that it is

normally prepared to offer for the following specified types of copyright works which are listed by reference to the appropriate Standard Agreements:

Standard Agreements   Copyright Works

PA 1 (3)   Dramatic works including extracts therefrom and shortened versions thereof

PA 2 (3)   Non-dramatic prose works and extracts therefrom

PA 3 (3)   Poems or extracts therefrom

PA 4 (3)   Prose works required for adaptation into dramatic form

PA GP (1)   Poems or extracts therefrom, extracts from non-dramatic prose works and extracts from dramatic works

Radio (WS) TS2 Any works required by Transcription Service (at the percentages of the Initial Fees paid for the BBC's broadcast set out in schedule 2 to this Agreement Provided that for this purpose 'Initial Fees' shall mean fees calculated by reference to either the per minute rate specified as the Initial Fee in the Standard Agreement used to acquire broadcast rights in the Work or (after three years from first broadcast of the Work) the per minute rate agreed with the Organisations prevailing at the time of issue of the Radio (WS) TS 2)

and the BBC agrees that it will not make any substantial alteration to the Standard Agreements without notifying and consulting with the Organisations provided that the BBC shall be free to conclude agreements on different terms by mutual agreement with individual rights owners/holders.

4. This Agreement shall not apply to works specially written for broadcasting or to the use of works by the Open University, or BBC English and the fees in the Standard Agreements may not apply to copyright works based on non copyright material. For the avoidance of doubt this Agreement shall not automatically apply to works contained in programmes made by third parties for the BBC (including programmes made by independent producers commissioned by the BBC or programmes purchased from independent producers) however should third parties making programmes for the BBC offer to acquire rights in literary works on the terms of the Standard Agreements (or the BBC offer such terms on behalf of third parties) then the Organisations agree to recommend such terms to their members.

5. The fees set out in the schedules to the Standard Agreements are effective from the above date of signature and the BBC agrees to review the fees annually at the request of one or more of the Organisations unless otherwise agreed.

6. The Organisations agree that no fee shall be payable by the BBC for use of any copyright work covered by the terms of this agreement which is permitted gratuitously by law or any uses permitted gratuitously by the terms of any of the Standard Agreements.

7. The BBC shall where reasonably practicable acknowledge the titles and the authors of the copyright work covered by this Agreement which are included in its broadcast programmes.

8. The BBC shall also acknowledge the publishers of the copyright works covered by this Agreement which are included in its broadcast programmes if the BBC considers that such acknowledgement is practicable and is of general service to listeners.

Signed on behalf of the
British Broadcasting Corporation   . . . .

Signed on behalf of the
Publishers Association   . . . .

Signed on behalf of the
Society of Authors   . . . .

Signed on behalf of the
Independent Publishers Guild   . . . .

[Schedule 1 lists the standard agreements shown at Clause 3 of this Agreement]

Schedule 2

	Territory	Terrestrial %	Cable %
Permanent Rights:			
	World	125	62.5
	Commonwealth	100	50
Limited Rights:			
	World	100	50
	Commonwealth	50	25
	USA	25	12.5
	Rest of World	25	12.5
	Australia	15	7.5
	Canada	10	5
	New Zealand	10	5
	Minor Commonwealth	25	12.5
	South Africa	15	7.5

Trapped Audience Rights: 1% per sale

Side Letter

The parties hereto wish to record their thanks to the Association of Authors' Agents who, whilst not signatories to this Agreement, have been duly consulted for opinion and advice in its compilation. They hope that the AAA will continue to give them the benefit of their views in future discussions.

Signed on behalf of the
British Broadcasting Corporation   . . . .

Signed on behalf of the
Publishers Association   . . . .

Signed on behalf of the
Society of Authors   . . . .

Signed on behalf of the
Independent Publishers Guild   . . . .

Date   . . . .

Reversionary Provisions of the Copyright Act 1911

Introduction

The proviso to section 5(2) of the Copyright Act 1911 provided that, *where the author was the first owner of the copyright*, no assignment of the copyright or grant of any interest in it made by him/her (otherwise than by will), after the passing of that Act, should be valid beyond the expiration of 25 years from the death of the author. The interest in copyright was to be seen as part of the author's estate, and any agreement entered into by him/her attempting to dispose of the reversionary interest beyond the period of 25 years from his/her death should, with exceptions for collective works, be null and void.

It is thought that this limitation on an author's powers to contract was made in the interests of his/her family, but, whatever the reason, it has remained to this day, through transitional provisions of the 1956 Act, a complicated and dangerous trap which publishers need to understand at least in outline. The point is put well in paragraph 614 of the Whitford Committee Report:

> Despite the ending of the reversionary rights provision in respect of new assignments and licences, the importance of its effects in respect of old assignments and licences has recently become increasingly apparent. In fact it will take a very long time for these to disappear completely. Thus an author making an assignment in his twenties just before 1 July 1957 may not die until say 2020, in which case the life-plus-25-year period will not expire until the year 2045.

(a) The Copyright Act 1956 provided that the proviso should continue to apply to assignments and licences made before 1 July 1957, the operative date of the 1956 Act. *The proviso does not affect documents made after this date, nor does it apply if a further assignment or licence is made after this date.* In the absence of such a further assignment or licence, however, any assignments or licences made between 1 July 1912 and 1 July 1957, to which the proviso applies, will only operate until the end of the first 25-year period following the death of the author.

(b) *The proviso only applied in a case where the author was the first owner of the copyright.* It did not apply therefore in the case of an engraving, photograph or portrait 'commissioned' by some other person, or in the case of a work made by an author in the employment of some other person under a contract of service or apprenticeship. In such event the owner of the copyright was able to assign it for the full term.

(c) Since only the author him/herself was prohibited from assigning the copyright or an interest in it, the proviso does not apply to posthumous works.

The Copyright etc. Act 1988 now governs the position through para. 27 of Schedule 1 to the Act. In effect, the proviso to section 5(2) of the 1911 Act is re-enacted in respect of an assignment of copyright or a grant of interest in it made by the author, *being the first owner of copyright*, in the years between the coming into effect of the 1911 and the 1956 Acts. As stated above, therefore, the proviso does not affect documents made after 1 July 1957 but the Whitford Committee's warning, reproduced above, still stands.

This Appendix states a very general position. Any publisher or author who believes that their rights may be affected by the 1911 reversionary provisions should seek legal advice.

Non-Commercial Rights for the Print-Disabled

The growth of technology has brought many benefits to ill and disabled people. Authors and publishers will always want to allow their works to be available through new technologies either for no fee or at nominal cost for charitable purposes. At the same time, technology has a habit of running away with itself and this Appendix tries therefore to put in the balance the charitable benefit and the sensible limits which publishers should at least be aware of on their and their authors' behalf in licensing non-commercial rights for the print-disabled, defined as those who can either not read, including dyslexics, or not hold a book, temporarily or permanently.

The term 'non-commercial rights' is meant to cover the right to reproduce a book in whole or in part for the use of ill or disabled people by any of the following means: braille, recording, hospital broadcasting and possibly large type although there is a commercial market for large type editions (see Precedent One, Clause 14(k)) and also for (predominantly abridged) audio editions.

In the light of requests made internationally by organisations producing materials for the blind and print-disabled, the Council of the Publishers Association has recommended to publishers that, when they grant anthology rights, the 'anthologising' publisher should be able to pass on permission for the anthology to appear in braille, large print or closed tape where such rights are available.

Braille
Requests usually come in from the Royal National Institute for the Blind or the National Library for the Blind and other charitable agencies in the United Kingdom. By established practice publishers normally give permission for these editions free of charge but they should ensure that full acknowledgement is made to the author, the title and the publisher, together with appropriate copyright acknowledgement.

Recording
For the Print-Handicapped
Here again the vast majority of requests come from the RNIB and to a lesser extent from CALIBRE and the National Listening Library in this country, and it is established practice for publishers to give permission to these bodies subject to certain conditions:

(a) that due acknowledgement in speech is made to the author and publisher at the beginning and end of each recorded book;
(b) that the following statement in speech is recorded in each recording at the beginning of the work: 'This book is copyright. The copyright *owner/ owners has/have* allowed it to be recorded for the sole use of print-disabled people';
(c) that the recordings are in no way to be used for commercial purposes and can be sold or loaned only to print-disabled people or to agencies for them, the recipient signing a form agreeing not to resell.

The RNIB records in two formats. 'Talking Books' – full-length readings of fiction and popular non-fiction works – are recorded on non-commercial six-track cassettes from which it is extremely difficult to copy and which need special machines for playing back. The recordings are made in the RNIB's professional studios and the readers are usually actors or professional broadcasters. Works which are unlikely to be of widespread popular interest – scientific, technical and medical books, for example – are recorded in full-length form on standard (C60-type) cassettes, the readers being a team of volunteers. CALIBRE records complete, unabridged fiction and popular non-fiction on standard cassettes read by volunteer readers, often recording in their own homes. Thus there is a considerable difference between the cassettes produced for commercial sale by audio publishers and those produced by charitable organisations for the print-disabled. Commercial audio cassettes are on standard cassettes or compact discs, are predominantly abridged versions (sometimes dramatised, rather than straight readings) and are read by professionals and recorded in professional studios. It is to be noted that a leading publisher of full-length audio cassettes has said that it has no objection to non-commercial audio versions co-existing with its own commercial versions.

The RNIB has an arrangement whereby Commonwealth societies for the blind, and in some cases the US Library of Congress, can use its master tapes and record on to non-commercial tape cassettes. It is recommended that provision for this be made in individual requests from the RNIB. Alternatively, permissions given to agencies outside the UK should be subject to similar terms and conditions, although publishers may in some cases want to restrict the number of copies and stipulate a renewable licence period, and/or the right to withdraw the licence upon three months' notice in writing.

Australian societies for the blind and disabled have a central register (the National Union Catalogue) which lists all requests for permission to tape/transcribe into braille, so as to limit the number of requests made to publishers and prevent duplication. The scheme is called 'W[orks] i[n] P[rocess]' and a note about it is shown on the applications of participating societies.

Requests to make recordings for the use of those unable to hold or read a book are beginning to proliferate, but although there is as yet no central agency through which such requests can be channelled, moves are afoot to extend the RNIB's scope of activity to include the print-disabled (defined by the Royal New Zealand Federation for the Blind, as 'those unable to handle, read or comprehend printed material with ease') and thus centralise all such non-commercial requests.

Copyright law in this country makes no specific provision for recordings made for the exclusive use of the disabled. It is therefore relevant to state that once a work has been mechanically recorded the recording itself has a copyright which is separate from that in the original work, and at the same time the original work and the recording itself may lose their exclusivity since it may be legally open to others, subject to certain conditions, to record further from the recording. In the present state of knowledge and trade attitudes, it is possible only to alert the reader to this important point, not to resolve it. More work at international level is needed to enable authors and publishers to offer non-commercial rights without being in danger of losing their own original rights. Canadian and Australian copyright laws have now been amended to take care of this point.

If, therefore, publishers decide to give permission to any charitable organisation or agency, they should make clear that it is the responsibility of that organisation to ensure that copyright in the recorded work is given full protection. Publishers should also ensure that if they give permission for a work to be recorded such permission does not extend to allow the organisation to pass the permission on to any other body; that not more than, for example, 300 copies of each tape should be produced without payment of royalty; and that the other conditions which apply to recordings made for blind people should apply here, perhaps including as well a limitation of licence, subject to renewal by mutual agreement, and/or the right to withdraw the licence upon three months' notice in writing.

Blind in Business

Blind in Business is a charity, operating in a field of growing importance. Developments in technology have now made it possible for the blind who work in business, as lawyers, etc., to use combinations of equipment, e.g. a voice synthesiser which allows the blind businessman to listen to a disc on to which colleagues have stored relevant material. He can then select and store the material he needs to keep, and at any time translate it into a hard braille copy. Publishers will surely respond sympathetically to such a use of their copyright materials, but both publishers and the relevant organisations, e.g. the Society for Blind Lawyers, should be careful to ensure that a proper request for permission to copy is made, however willingly granted. A draft Application for Permission letter, and draft Permission Granted response are offered here as follows:

Application for Permission to copy for print-handicapped readers
A.

Author	Title	Edition issue date	Publisher/ imprint	ISBN/ISSN

B. Permission is sought to copy the above copyright material for my normal business use, on the following basis:

(1) I am a registered blind person with the RNIB/registered otherwise as print-handi-capped with the following:

(2) I wish to use the above material only in the following business capacity:

(3) The copied material is for my personal use only, and not for resale or circulation to others. If stored electronically, it will not be accessed or used by others without further permissions being sought.

(4) Electronic data capture will be via OCR/voice synthesiser/other (please specify).

(5) Only single braille copies will be printed out, which shall be for my personal use only, but in the process of electronic storage and retrieval [   ] back-up disks may be made, for my personal use only.

(6) If granted, this permission will constitute a non-exclusive licence to use the data and make copies only as specified above, during a period of [3 years] from the date of this letter. The licence may be revoked by you at any time on giving [3 months'] notice, and in this event all copies in hard copy or electronic format, will be surrendered to you, destroyed or wiped clean.

C.   Signed: . . . .

            Date: . . . .

● ●

D. *Permission* (to be completed by publisher or rights holder)

*(1) Permission granted on above basis.

*(2) Permission granted on above basis, with the following additional restrictions:

*(3) No fee will be charged/the following fee will be charged:

*(4) Rights not held by us, please contact:

            Signed: . . . .

            Date: . . . .

     (*Delete and complete as necessary)

Hospital Broadcasts

Some hospitals have their own private broadcasting network which normally does not extend beyond the confines of that hospital. Publishers and authors might pause before agreeing to transmission of their works over such hospital radio services to many patients who, although unwell, are fully able to read for themselves in the ordinary way. The Hospital Library Service exists exactly for such patients' needs. If a publisher does decide to give permission for a work or part of a work to be broadcast, it is recommended that at least a nominal fee be charged and that full acknowledgements be made to the author, the title and the publisher at the end of each broadcast. It is also recommended that publishers should ensure that, if the broadcast is taped, they receive an undertaking that the tapes will be destroyed once the broadcast has been made.

Hospitals with special services for the disabled may not raise such reservations. The National Listening Library is a charity which exists to provide tape recordings for print-disabled people and which runs two libraries. Library A, which by special arrangement gets most of its recordings from the RNIB, is used mostly by individual members who are supplied with special reproducers for playing the six-track cassettes. Library B is used mostly by hospitals for their print-disabled patients. There is a small annual membership fee for both hospitals and individual subscribers.

Large-Print Editions
In this country, and increasingly in the United States, such editions are produced on a commercial basis so they are not the concern of this section, but from time to time requests are received from publishers in the USA, Canada and elsewhere for permission to allow the work in question (often only a poem or an extract from a book which is being included in a school textbook) to form part of a large-print edition of which very few copies will be made. Such requests are usually tucked away in the body of the letter of inquiry which seeks blanket permission for braille, tape and large-print editions produced non-commercially, as a corollary to the main request for permission. Publishers should perhaps consider whether they are prepared to give such blanket permission without any limitation as to number of copies or length of licence.

Caveat
Charitable organisations and agencies working to provide books for disabled people should not be confused with profit and non-profit-making organisations which produce books in other media, e.g. companies which may specialise in providing 'talking books' in cassette form for motor cars.

Moral Rights

The origins of moral rights as part of copyright law lie in the historical imbalance of power between creator and entrepreneur, e.g. between the author and publisher. The nineteenth-century laissez-faire view of contractual freedom in England (and in most common-law countries) left their whole relationship at law to the terms of their contract for the transfer of economic rights of property, with such comfort for the preservation of his/her moral rights of reputation as the author might find outside contract in the field of torts, e.g. of defamation, injurious falsehood or passing off.

In continental Europe, however, creative works, seen as the expression of the personality of their creator, rather than as merely a form of property, carried in consequence a moral right, which ran alongside the economic right, developed in France through a series of nineteenth century court cases. The creator's reputation came to be protected in copyright law itself by making any purported contractual assignment of the moral right null and void. The essence of the right, in short, is that it is inalienable. (The French tend to refer to *droit moral* in the singular as a concept, and then to deal in specific rights by individual name.)

The Berne Convention did not grapple explicitly with the issue until the *Rome* text of 1928. That text incorporated into the Convention the two minimum moral rights of *paternity* and of *integrity* in this language.

Article 6 bis

Independently of the author's economic rights, and even after the transfer of the said rights, the author shall have the right to claim authorship of the work and to object to any distortion, mutilation or other modification of [or other derogatory action in relation to] the said work, which would be prejudicial to his honour or reputation.

The *Brussels* text of 1948 added to the formula the words indicated above in brackets, in order to make clear that actions other than distortion, mutilation or modification may also prejudice reputation.

To this provision *Stockholm* added in 1967 that the moral right granted under Berne should endure 'at least until the expiry of economic rights'. Since under Berne these rights (called, in the common law, simply copyright) must last, as a substantive part of the Convention, for life plus 50 years as a minimum, the *Stockholm* text (unchanged in this respect in the *Paris* text of 1971, the latest version of the Berne Convention) marked the final emergence of *droit moral* as a substantive explicit element in international copyright, for whose duration the nations *in membership* with Berne must now make explicit provision. (An escape route was provided at *Stockholm* for countries *seeking to join* Berne whereby 'those countries whose legislation, at the moment of their ratification or accession to this Act, does not provide for the protection after the death of the author of all the rights set out in the preceding paragraph may provide that some of those rights may, after his death, cease to be maintained'.)

For the UK, therefore, the question arose of how its domestic law should be amended so that the UK, a founder member of Berne, could become a signatory to the *Paris* text. On that question, and on the now irrelevant issue of whether the UK's historical treatment of the elements of *droit moral* was or was not compatible even with *Brussels*, the Government White Paper of 1986 said at Chapter 19.2 and 3:

19.2 The Berne Convention distinguishes between an author's economic rights and his moral rights, the former enabling him to earn money, the latter protecting his reputation. The moral rights specified in the Convention are:
(a) the right to claim authorship of the work, e.g. by being named as author; and
(b) the right to object to any distortions of the work which are prejudicial to his honour or reputation.

In the United Kingdom, moral rights are at present provided to some extent by copyright law, which contains certain provisions regarding false attribution of authorship, and to some extent by the common law in the form of the laws of contract, passing-off and defamation. Whitford cast some doubt on whether the law satisfied the Brussels text of Berne. Whether or not these doubts are justified, amendment of the law will be necessary to comply with the Paris text of the Berne Convention which requires Member States to protect some at least of the moral rights at least until the expiry of the copyright.

19.3 As foreshadowed in the 1981 Green Paper, the Government proposed to legislate for moral rights as follows:
(a) authors will be given the right to claim authorship and to object to distortion, but not to modification of a work to which they could not reasonably refuse consent;
(b) these moral rights will be independent of the economic rights, and will be exercisable only by the author. After his death they may be exercised by the person who inherits the copyright or, if the author no longer owns the copyright at his death, by the person to whom he had bequeathed them. An author will be able to waive his moral rights, and such waiver will override any inheritance or bequest; and
(c) moral rights will apply for the duration of the copyright.

The Copyright, Designs and Patents Act of 1988, which came into effect on 1 August 1989, carried out the basic proposals of the 1986 White Paper and now incorporates explicitly for the first time in UK law the concept of *droit moral*. It makes detailed provision for the two basic moral rights: the right of paternity (called in the Act 'right to be identified as author') and the right of integrity (called in the Act 'right to object to derogatory treatment of work'), both of which have the same period of duration, i.e. now life plus 70 years, as copyright itself.

Right to be Identified as Author

Section 77 states that the author of a copyright literary, dramatic, musical or artistic work has the right to be identified as the author of the work whenever the work is published commercially. The right is not infringed unless it has been asserted in accordance with section 78. That section provides that the right may be asserted generally, or in relation to any specified act or description of acts, either:

(a) on an assignment of copyright in the work, by including in the instrument effecting the assignment a statement that the author asserts in relation to that work his right to be identified; or
(b) by instrument in writing signed by the author.

Right to Object to Derogatory Treatment of Work

Section 80 states that the author of a copyright literary, dramatic, musical or artistic work has the right not to have his work subjected to derogatory treatment when that work is published commercially. 'Treatment' means any addition to, deletion from or alteration or adaptation (other than a translation) of the work, and treatment is derogatory if it amounts to distortion or mutilation of the work or is otherwise prejudicial to the honour or reputation of the author.

This incorporation of moral rights is sensibly qualified in three important ways:

(1) The moral right of paternity must, as set out above, be *asserted* by the author. This provision follows the sense of the Berne wording which refers to the right of the author to *claim* paternity.
(2) The moral rights are subject to *consent* (which may be oral) and to *waiver* (which must be in writing).
(3) Moral rights do not, in general, attach to employee works, to works published in a newspaper, magazine or similar periodical, or to collective works of reference. Both computer programs and computer-generated works are also exempt from moral rights.

There will, therefore, be some publishers, particularly STM (science, technical and medical) publishers who rely heavily on employee authors, or who publish largely within (a) the scope of 'a newspaper, magazine or similar periodical' and/or within (b) the scope of 'an encyclopaedia, dictionary or other collective work of reference', who will be scarcely troubled by moral rights at all. For authors are excluded by the Act from moral rights protection wherever what they write constitutes a work 'made for the purposes of such publication [i.e. at (a) and/or (b)] or made available with the consent of the author for the purposes of such publication'.

Works of Joint Authorship
Under the Act a work of joint authorship means 'a work produced by the collaboration of two or more authors in which the contribution of each author is not distinct from that of the other author or authors' (section 10). Authors of such joint works as constitute collective works of *reference* are excluded from moral rights protection (see (3) above). All other joint authors, however, have severally the two moral rights. Each joint author, for example, must assert his/her right to be identified as a joint author, and the right to object to derogatory treatment is a right of each joint author. It follows that a waiver under section 87 of either or both moral rights by one joint author does not affect the rights of the other joint authors (section 88). Particular care will, obviously, be needed to ensure that *all* authors of works of joint authorship assert or waive, as the case may be.

False Attribution of Work
This is not a true moral right, since moral rights belong to authors. The right not to have one's name falsely used as the name of the author of a literary, dramatic, musical or artistic work belongs to anyone, whether he/she is an author or not. However, the right, which was also provided under the Copyright Act 1956, is placed in Chapter IV of the Act, entitled 'Moral Rights', and is therefore noted here. The right is infringed by the issue to the public of copies of a work in or on which there is a false attribution (that is, a false statement, express or implied, as to who is the author). The right continues to subsist until 20 years after a person's death (which contrasts with the longer period of 50 years *post mortem auctoris* protection for the truly authorial moral rights of paternity and integrity).

Right to Privacy
Under the Copyright Act 1956, the commissioner of a photograph was the owner of copyright in the photograph. He was therefore in a strong position to prevent, if need be through the issue of an injunction, the subsequent publication, to the embarrassment of him and of his family, of the photograph. With the change in the Copyright etc. Act 1988 of the status of a photograph to being simply a work of art, the photographer became the author of a work of art who owns copyright in the photographs he takes.

This change of status worried both the Government and Opposition as the Bill worked its way through Parliament, because of the danger of invasion of privacy through, e.g., the sale of a wedding photograph to the tabloid press by a photographer, with the commissioner, the father of the bride perhaps, left with no remedy, since the UK has no general law of privacy.

Section 85 of the 1988 Act therefore provides that a person who for private and domestic purposes commissions the taking of a photograph, or the making of a film, has the right not to have copies of the resulting copyright work issued to the public. See, interestingly, the final note of the Note to Clause 5 of Precedent One.

Transitional Provisions

These very important provisions are set out in Schedule 1 to the Act. They provide, inter alia, that:

(a) the rights of paternity and integrity do not apply to a work the author of which died before the commencement date of the Act, 1 August 1989;

(b) the rights of paternity and integrity do not apply to things done before the commencement of the Act;

(c) the rights of paternity and integrity do not apply in respect of 'existing works' — that is, works made and completed before the commencement date of 1 August 1989 — to anything which by virtue of an assignment of copyright or a licence granted before commencement may be done without infringing copyright.

The practical upshot of the transitional provisions is that in respect of works contracted for and completed in typescript before 1 August 1989, moral rights will not apply. For works, however, contracted before 1 August 1989 but not completed (i.e. not 'existing works') at that date, moral rights will apply.

Conclusion

Most publishers will in 1997 surely have considered carefully their policy towards *droit moral*. In so far as the great majority of publishers give proper credit on title page and on jacket/binding to the author of a book, and in so far, again, as the great majority of publishers do not, without lengthy prior consultation with, followed by consent of the author, go beyond routine copy-editing of what the author writes, neither of the two moral rights of paternity or of integrity should cause concern.

The following kinds of publishing issues may well arise in the context of moral rights;

(1)   It is not so much the *author's* right of paternity which may cause trouble, as such a right alleged by a freelance editor/'ghost' writer who says that a work which he/she has substantially rewritten, or even partially written, is substantially therefore his/her work so that he/she has a right of paternity and a right to be named on the cover, the title page, etc. The publisher may in future need to build in a waiver of moral rights into contracts with all freelance writers wherever their work may earn copyright protection, and therefore, within copyright, moral rights protection.

(2)   The borderland between normal copy-editing and heavy, but in the publisher's judgment necessary, editing is obviously a grey area.

(3) In some works, e.g. series of monographs, and in works of multi-authorship, especially medical texts for practitioners, the expert general editor may well have a 'right to edit' written into his/her agreements with both publisher and contributors. How far may this contractual right

conflict with the moral right of integrity of individual specialist authors (up to and beyond 50 of them in such medical works)? See also Precedent Three.

(4)   Publishers of art books may need to consider how far indifferent reproduction of a copyright work of art (poor colour quality, cheap and unsuitable paper) may fall foul of the artist's right of integrity.

(5)   Photographers have expressed the view strongly that insensitive cropping may add up to invasion of a photographer's right of integrity.

(6)   The representatives of artists and artists' estates, e.g. DACS, the Design and Artistic Copyright Society, have made clear that the 'stamping' of the title or author of a work over their client's works of art may, again, add up, in their eyes, to invasion of the right of integrity.

Finally, it is important to bear in mind that *droit moral* is more honoured in rhetoric than in practice. The realistic stance of the UK Government should keep invocation of the right to the kind of wrongful treatment of an author which no trade association would care to defend.

It may be helpful for publishers to have for consideration possible forms of wording for the assertion of the moral right to be identified as author (attached as Schedules I and II to this Appendix).

There will certainly be occasions, most especially in dealings with freelance writers, re-writers and editors of all kinds, when neither the right of paternity nor the right of integrity may, for obvious reasons, be appropriate. In such dealings, publishers may wish to build in a 'waiver' clause, and a suggested form of wording for waiver, possibly as part of a letter, possibly as part of a short contract, is attached as Schedule III to this Appendix.

Schedules

The author is well advised to make a written general assertion of his/her right to be identified as the author of his/her work. This might sensibly be attached to the typescript of the work, and a possible form of wording follows as Schedule I.

In the author/publisher contract, whether a contract for assignment of copyright from author to publisher or a contract for grant of an exclusive licence to publish from author to publisher, a clause should be inserted on the lines suggested in Schedule II.

Schedule III sets out suggested wording for waiver of the author's moral rights to be identified as author of, and to object to derogatory treatment of, a work.

Schedule I

I, [name to be inserted], being the author of the work entitled [title, or provisional title, of work to be inserted], hereby assert generally my moral right to be identified as its author whenever it is commercially published in the United Kingdom.

Schedule II

The Author by this assignment/instrument in writing asserts his/her moral right to be identified as the Author of the work in relation to all such rights as are granted by the Author to the Publisher under the terms and conditions of this Agreement.

The Publisher hereby undertakes:

— to print on the verso title page of every copy of every edition of the work published by it in the United Kingdom the words 'the right of [the author] to be identified as author of this work has been asserted by him/her in accordance with the Copyright, Designs and Patents Act 1988'
— to make it a condition of contract with any licensee concerning any edition of the work to be published in the United Kingdom that a notice of assertion in the same terms as above shall be printed in every edition published by such licensee
— to set the name of the author in its customary form with due prominence on the title page and on the binding, jacket and/or cover of every copy of the work published by it and to make it a condition of contract that a similar undertaking is made in respect of any editions of the work licensed by it.

Notes to Schedule II
1. The distinction between a contract for assignment and a contract for an exclusive licence is of importance only to determine against whom the assertion in the contract is binding. On an assignment, the persons bound by the assertion are 'the assignee and anyone claiming through him, whether or not he has notice of the assertion' (section 78(4)(a)). On a licence, the persons bound by the assertion are 'anyone to whose notice the assertion is brought' (section 78(4)(b)).
2. Most publishers have a standard clause, of the kind reproduced above, undertaking to set the name of the author in its customary form 'with due prominence' etc. That clause may well be a sufficient *expression* of the author's moral right to be identified on the publisher's own edition. However, the author under the Act has the right in the first place to *assert* the right, and the publisher should consider both binding his/her own licensees and also printing the assertion in his/her own edition.

Schedule III

The Author hereby waives, in accordance with the Copyright, Designs and Patents Act 1988, Section 87, his/her moral rights (a) to be identified as author of and (b) to object to derogatory treatment of the work he/she is undertaking for the Publisher under the terms of this agreement with regard to such rights as are granted by the Author to the Publisher under the terms of this agreement.

Notes to Schedule III
1. Waiver of a moral right must be effected, under section 87, by an instrument in writing signed by the person giving up the right. It will therefore be important that the publisher receives back a copy of any document that includes the waiver, signed by the author.
2. This suggested waiver clause is, it must be emphasised, most likely to be relevant not so much to book authors as to freelance workers of all kinds. Even in dealings with freelance authors, it will not always be appropriate to require an author to waive both of his/her moral rights. The wording offered above can be easily varied according to individual circumstances.

APPENDIX E

Reprographic and Electronic Reproduction

Let us start with one moment of recorded history:

'We must take care to guard against two extremes equally prejudicial: the one, that men of ability who have employed their time for the service of their community, may not be deprived of their just merits, and the reward of their ingenuity and labour: the other, that the world may not be deprived of improvements, nor the progress of the arts be retarded.'

Those were the words of Lord Mansfield in a case which involved the rights and wrongs of copying, decided over 200 years ago: *Sayre v Moore* in 1785. And the task of reconciling the interests of those – authors and their business partners, publishers – who create copyright works with the interests of those – students, teachers, researchers, people in the professions and in business – who use copyright works through copying them is still with us.

Many of the current concerns of owners and users of copyright material focus on photocopying. The photocopying machine and the computer have formed an uneasy alliance, the one allowing wholesale rapid copying of complete works to the standard of the printed original, while the other does at least allow some degree of measurement of quantity, calculation of cost, and share of revenues.

Photocopying machinery has made individual control of the creators' rights of reproduction impossible, so that collective control and reward through collecting societies has become not just desirable, but necessary. And that collective control and reward depend on the capacities of the computer to absorb, record and distribute.

Now the threats to copyright works posed by photocopying have been partly overtaken by the advances in technology which allow electronic copying. Users can now scan and store works digitally; create, download and manipulate databases; and instantly transmit world-wide huge amounts of intellectual property on networks. It is hardly surprising that the speed of these developments has left most copyright communities so far unable to agree on a form of licence that satisfactorily protects the rights of owners at the same time as meeting the needs of users.

Photocopying, however, remains an enormous part of the problem, and one which will not disappear overnight. It is important to grasp the sheer size of the issue. One recent estimate put the global figure for illicit copy pages at more than 300 billion per annum. There are indications that in the advanced national economies of western Europe approximately 200 copy pages per head of population would be a reasonable estimate of the annual use of copyright works. And in the UK we know, as closely as we can know from detailed records and from a survey in 1992, that the state school system uses approximately 3.5 million copy pages of copyright works per year. In the university sector, a recent survey suggested that full-time equivalent students in British universities each took 150 copies per year during their course of study. An exploratory survey of photocopying in industry suggested that British industry copied approximately 1.7 billion pages of copyright works per annum. The role of collective agreement and administration of rights in literary works is not therefore peripheral to the copyright system. It is rapidly becoming the copyright system's central strategy for literary works in reconciling creator and user interests.

Sometimes those interests come into conflict. A number of cases have recently highlighted the wide gulf which sometimes separates the rights of owners from the needs of users. In the USA, an oil company was found liable on appeal of allowing its researchers to copy journal articles illegally. The judge cited the existence of the national collective licensing body (the Copyright Clearance Center) and pointed out that the company could have copied what it needed to legally under the terms of the CCC's business licence – a strong endorsement of the importance and effectiveness of collective licensing.

Over 20 years have passed since interest groups in the UK started to prepare in 1973 submissions to the government-appointed committee under Mr Justice Whitford about ways of regulating the copying of copyright books, journals and periodicals. These interest groups representing owners of copyright were seeking both a mechanism of control and just recompense for authors and publishers while at the same time continuing to 'satisfy the reasonable demands of a modern information-driven society'.

When it was eventually published in 1977, the Whitford Report on *Copyright and Design Law* suggested, as the best likely solution to the problem, a collective management and administration system for copying rights organised by the rights' owners themselves. This recommendation spawned first the Wolfenden Committee that brought together the representatives of authors' societies and publishers' associations, and then the de Freitas Committee that hammered out and fashioned, with these two sometimes antagonistic groups, a mutually acceptable constitution for such a licensing body.

The outcome was that in April 1982 the Authors' Licensing and Collecting Society Ltd (ALCS) together with the Publishers Licensing Society (PLS) came together to set in train the formation of the Copyright Licensing Agency (CLA) to issue licences for photocopying. CLA was incorporated in January 1983 and its first 'collective' licences became available in May 1984. The first pilot licence ran in schools during the second half of 1985.

The two rights owners groups, ALCS and PLS, have similarities of structure and purpose. Each needs members to mandate their works to become part of the licence repertoire. Both have representation on the CLA Board which reflects the views of their member associations. And on the whole each shares equally the revenue derived from licences once CLA's and their own costs have been deducted.

The Authors' Licensing and Collecting Society Ltd (ALCS), the collecting society in Britain for literary and dramatic rights, was established in 1977 by writers at the forefront of the campaign to obtain for British authors a public lending right. It is a company limited by guarantee and not having a share capital and is run by a Council of Management comprising 12 'working' writers. The interests of members of the Society of Authors and the Writers Guild are represented on the Board of CLA; which comprises six members of ALCS and six from PLS. ALCS is responsible for making payments for copying fees to writers.

The ALCS is not solely concerned with reprography. It was instrumental in setting up the Educational Recording Agency Ltd together with broadcasters and other rights owners to offer licences to educational establishments to record off-air television and radio programmes for educational purposes. Other rights administered on behalf of writers, which are best handled on a collective basis, include the foreign lending right; the cable transmission right; the private recording right; the electronic right including electrocopying; and the rental right.

ALCS is also the co-ordination partner in a consortium which has won funding for an ambitious project funded under the Fourth Framework proposals of the European Commission. The aims of the project known as IMPRIMATUR are to identify the problems arising at the interface between information technology, telecommunications and intellectual property rights and to seek to reach a measure of consensus on standards to enable interoperability of systems in the digital and global information future. At the same time, IMPRIMATUR will develop a test bed as a proving ground for new software.

The Publishers Licensing Society was established in 1981 and has now secured agreement from over 1500 mandating publishers to include their works in the repertoire offered to licensees by CLA. PLS represents the interests of a wide range of publishers from the multinationals to the single-title publisher. The three organisations that constitute the PLS Board are the Publishers Association, the Periodical Publishers Association and the Association of Learned and Professional Society Publishers.

PLS obtains non-exclusive licences from publishers that give the Copyright Licensing Agency the right to grant licences for the making of reprographic copies of copyright works. The licences cover photocopying or other methods of duplicating (excluding digital copying) plus limited paper-to-paper fax usage.

PLS is mandated by the publishers to represent them on the board of the CLA and the directors represent publishers' interests in CLA's negotiations with users.

In the 1994/5 financial year PLS paid out just over £6 million to publisher copyright holders. In 1996, the total paid out to publishers since payments began passed the £20 million mark.

CLA has six main functions and these are:

— to obtain mandates from publishers and authors via the Publishers Licensing Society (PLS) and the Authors' Licensing and Collecting Society (ALCS);
— to license users for copying extracts from copyright books, journals and periodicals;
— to collect fees from licensed users for such copying;
— to institute a system of record-keeping sufficient to provide statistically acceptable information on which to calculate a fair apportionment of the distributable income;
— to pay ALCS, PLS and foreign reproduction rights organisations (RROs) with which CLA has reciprocal agreements, their correct shares of the distributable income together with sufficient data to enable these societies to pay individual authors and publishers;
— to institute such legal proceedings as may be necessary for the enforcement of the rights entrusted to the Agency.

CLA sees its principal licensing areas in the UK as being *education*, *government* and *industry*. Each of these broad categories has several sub-groups:

Education	*Government*	*Industry*
Schools	National	Trade
Further Education	Government	Industry
Higher Education	Local Government	Commerce
Open and Distance	Public Bodies	Professions
Learning		
HM Prison Service		

In company with many other RROs around the world CLA started licensing in the schools sector. The first major development occurred in April 1986 when three-year voluntary licensing agreements with the country's local education authorities (LEAs) came into effect: these licences now cover copying in all 30,000 or so primary and secondary schools; and teacher resource centres are now also covered by such licences. Grant-maintained schools are licensed as a separate group. The Agency also licenses the private education sector through its licensing scheme for independent schools as well as language schools. Regular 30-day surveys are held in each of the schools' sectors to determine the level of copying in each sector. These surveys also form the basis on which the fees are calculated.

With the general education sector (5 to 16 years) covered, CLA next turned its attention to higher and further education (HE & FE) and during 1989, after several years of negotiating, finalised arrangements whereby the universities, the polytechnics (now also universities) and colleges of higher education became licensed from 1 January 1990. Three-year licences once again were the norm with re-negotiated renewal periods. A similar arrangement was subsequently agreed for further education colleges. The higher education licence was amended in 1993 to include CLARCS.

CLARCS is the CLA's Rapid Clearance Service. This enables university (and business) users to seek and clear permission through CLA by fax or phone for copying beyond the limits imposed by the basic terms of their collective licence. Publishers set their own rates for the cost of copying a page or chapter of a book, or journal article, and can impose limits on the number of pages copied, the number of copies taken, or the price of the transaction requested. If the copying falls within the limits imposed by the publisher, CLARCS can give permission and invoice the transaction directly. Alternatively it can refer users direct to the publisher.

The Agency is dealing with national government on a ministry-by-ministry basis starting with the Department of Trade & Industry (DTI) as the architect and guardian of the Copyright, Designs and Patents Act 1988; the Department for Education and Employment (DfEE) because educational institutions are already licensed; the Home Office which includes the Fire, Police and Prison Services; and the Inland Revenue. Negotiations are proceeding with other departments.

Public bodies, i.e. those organisations for which government ministers have some accountability, may have to be dealt with in various non-collective ways. The first public body to be licensed by CLA was the British Library, of which the British Library Document Supply Centre (BLDSC) at Boston Spa in West Yorkshire is only part. This particular licence, effective from 1 April 1991, is transactional, and was amended in 1995 to incorporate publication-specific fees determined by the rights holder.

Trade, industry, commerce and the professions because of their size and diversity presented CLA with its greatest challenge. The first step taken was the setting up of a joint task force with the Confederation of British Industry (CBI). This CBI/CLA working party, chaired by an industrialist, examined the best way forward, concentrating initially on manufacturing industry and with particular emphasis on R & D driven sectors such as pharmaceuticals, chemicals, engineering, electronics, aerospace and energy. Agreements are now in place with the Law Society and the Association of British Pharmaceutical Industry.

Basically, CLA is a banking operation with legal overtones: it collects fees from licensed users and foreign RROs for acts of photocopying from books and periodicals and other copying such as microfiche printing and, after deducting its operating costs and any reserves or provisions the Board may decide, distributes the balance to ALCS and PLS for them to pay to individual authors and publishers; and to foreign RROs for them to distribute according to local custom and practice.

Right from the outset, the authors' representatives insisted *first* that writers should benefit individually and directly from the copying of their works, rather than for the money to go to authors' societies for 'social benefit' purposes, as is the case in some parts of the world. *Secondly*, they insisted that the individual authors' shares should be paid to them directly, and not through the accounting systems of their publishers.

In order to fulfil these requirements CLA had to devise a title-based distribution system and some form of record-keeping or survey by a stratified and statistically sound sample of the licensees. CLA strives continually to improve its surveys and sampling schemes – in particular, making them simpler and cheaper to administer while maintaining statistically-valid data quality. Some form of sample, survey or information audit is a requirement of every licence issued by CLA. In addition, copying cleared through CLARCS is fully transactional with the fee allocated to a title at the time permission is granted.

On return to the Agency, the record-keeping forms and survey results, which are regarded and treated as strictly confidential documents (and some of which are deemed to be 'personal data' under the Data Protection Act of 1984) are:

— checked by the licensing office to ensure that the conditions of the licence are being adhered to;
— scrutinised by data preparation to validate the information being submitted e.g. missing ISBN/ISSNs etc. are searched for;
— keyed for computer analysis;
— subjected to a final edit for data quality;
— analysed so that print-outs can then be produced showing pages copied by ISBN or ISSN title, by author, and by publisher;
— calculated for apportionment, so that statements can be produced and cheques drawn.

A CLA licence is not a carte blanche to unrestricted copying. The conditions are clearly set down and are required to be displayed alongside every copying machine within the control of the licensee. The wording varies slightly depending on the category of the licensee. CLA also produce various user guides for retention by licensees and there is a warning notice that goes on the top of machines which acts as a reminder to copier users.

The copyright community is struggling now to find a fair means of regulating and licensing electronic copying. Much of the main use at present is in the academic world of the research student or business developer. The speed with which material can now be transmitted or exchanged has led some users to think that copyright is an outmoded concept, and merely an unreasonable obstacle to gaining rapid access to information. They ignore the fact that copyright is, rather, a mechanism which protects and values the creation of intellectual property – the so-called trading system for works of the mind. It is an irony that some of the most vociferous proponents of this dangerous argument are academic librarians, the very individuals one might hope would hold in high regard the protection of intellectual property. However, the issue is further clouded by those academics whose careers depend on publication in scholarly journals and who are used to (if not happy with) receiving no payment for their labours, or even in some cases paying for the privilege of having their work published. Putting articles on to the Internet has reinforced the misconception which confuses the free flow of information with the flow of free information.

Besides, no one can ever agree on what a 'copy', in the electronic sense, actually is. Is it merely the displaying of a piece of copyright material on a screen? Some argue that this activity is equivalent to browsing through a book or journal, and should be regarded as fair dealing, even if hundreds of users do it dozens of times a day. Downloading copyright material into your own database is clearly a form of copying, but is it a lesser activity (in the sense of what value it has) than posting material on a network so that many users can have access to it (and copy it at their will)? It may be that a licence based on contract rather than copyright law is what is required.

Despite these difficulties, a number of precedents are emerging. Electronic tagging to create unique identification of copyright material has made some progress (particularly in the music business) but the ISBN and the ISSN still do not offer enough granularity to identify sections of an anthology or individual articles in a journal. Copyright owners of print material seem reluctant to develop new standards to measure copying on a transactional basis.

Some UK publishers have offered their repertoire of journal works to the university community on a site licence basis, each site paying an annual fee (approximately equivalent to a full year's subscription to that company's print journals) entitling them to copy those works 'freely' – i.e. in all ways, including photocopying. This simple system is attractive in many ways – at least, for users and publishers. However, so far those publishers' works only are included. It may also mean that universities have to apply in the future for licences to dozens of different owners – a powerful argument, of course, for a form of collective administrative licensing. The site licence also presupposes that the works being offered belong entirely to the company offering the licence: a reasonable point of view in the case of some journal publishers, but unworkable when it comes to books or other works where the author is the main copyright holder, and where the problems of sharing income from a site licence in a proportionally fair way would become insurmountable.

It is that issue of share of income which is currently proving the biggest obstacle to a combined publisher/author agency like the CLA taking the licensing initiative for electronic copying. Authors might accept the 50/50 principle which underpinned the first photocopying licences. But some publishers argue that their role in developing electronic publications is much greater, and that their costs are much higher; and that, in consequence, the author's share should be much less. The traditional tensions of the author/publisher relationship thus look like retarding if not preventing any kind of basic joint agreement. Some kind of accord is urgently needed if other more predatory players in the field are not to pre-empt the situation and in the end deny both parties more than a token share of their rightful income.

A collecting society's best role might be to offer a repertoire of model contracts and licences. These could be based on a combination of factors: The repertoire of works offered; the size of the community covered by the licence (e.g. the number of undergraduates, the number of research students); the terms of the licence; and the likely types of use, possibly determined by the facilities available, and by using a 'hierarchy of rights', ranging from display through networking, to printing out copies for class use.

For CLA there is comfort in knowing that the UK is not alone in pioneering the collective administration of copying rights. Counterpart organisations to CLA now exist in 18 other countries – Australia, Austria, Canada, Denmark, Finland, France, Germany, Iceland, Ireland, Italy, the Netherlands, New Zealand, Norway, South Africa, Spain, Sweden, Switzerland and of course in the United States, all of them in membership with IFRRO, the International Federation for Reproduction Rights Organisations; an RRO is also presently being formed in Belgium.

Finally, the broader the repertoire an RRO can offer its licensees the better, and it is a priority of CLA to secure reciprocal agreements with similar organisations overseas, particularly those in foreign language centres where English is widely read and, of course, those in English-speaking countries where British books, journals and periodicals are being widely and extensively copied, and, equally, where much publishing in the English language takes place. CLA presently enjoys reciprocity with RROs in: USA, Canada, Australia, New Zealand, South Africa, France, Germany, Spain, Sweden, Norway, Ireland, the Netherlands, Iceland and Denmark.

CLA started to make distributions to rights holders in 1987 and, as this Fifth Edition goes to press, the Agency will have distributed by the end of 1996 over £50 million to members:

Year	Amount £
Pre-1988	1,448,264
1988/89	548,854
1989/90	1,149,931
1990/91	1,705,387
1991/92	2,679,520
1992/93	3,930,360
1993/94	4,704,484
1994/95	7,132,236
1995/96	14,460,457

The Publishers Association Code of Practice

The Code of Practice, first issued by the Publishers Association in 1982 and subtitled 'Guidelines for Publishers in their Dealings with Authors', is an important document, a milestone on the road to an equitable framework for author–publisher contracts. There are, perhaps, two tasks which face those who support the Code. The first is to find forms and styles of informal dispute settlement which are appropriate to a trade rather than a professional association. The creation of the Publishers Association's Informal Disputes Settlement Scheme has proved to have been a positive initiative, and referral to it has been built into the Precedents in this Fifth Edition. The second task is to reach out to the creators of intellectual property rights and to find ways of working with them to ensure that further milestones are passed in common purpose. Here there continues to be welcome evidence of realistic negotiation in recent texts of the Minimum Terms Agreement, to which reference is made, where appropriate, in *Publishing Agreements*, especially in Precedent One.

A constructive and co-operative relationship between authors (and the agents and representatives acting for them) and their publishers is vital to successful publishing. In the great majority of cases this relationship undoubtedly exists. Nevertheless, there can be dissatisfaction, perhaps because a title is not the success the author and publisher hoped for but also because of misunderstandings of the publishing contract, uncertainties and poor drafting, and 'customs of trade' unappreciated by the author.

The Council of the Publishers Association believes that everything possible should be done to ensure a satisfactory relationship and avoid disputes. It has therefore prepared the Code of Practice for book publishers set out below, which it recommends to members in their dealings with authors. This Code gives guidance only. It cannot deal with every variation. In general, however, failure to accept the guidance included in the Code without good reason is clearly likely to damage the standing of individual publishers and of publishing generally.

Book publishing is so varied in its scope that contracts are likely to contain many variations between, for example, different types of book with different markets, different degrees of editorial involvement by the publisher, and established or relatively new authors. Total uniformity of contract or practice is therefore impracticable. In particular, some academic, educational and reference books and works based on a variety of contributions may be subject to special considerations, though the necessity to follow the general principles of this Code remains.

NB. This Code of Practice applies only to agreements whereby an author assigns or licenses an interest in the copyright of a work to a publisher, and does not apply to agreements whereby an author invests money in the publication of a work.

1. The publishing contract must be clear, unambiguous and comprehensive, and must be honoured in both the letter and the spirit

Matters which particularly need to be defined in the contract include:

(i) a title which identifies the work or (for incomplete works) the nature and agreed length and scope of the work;
(ii) the nature of the rights conferred — the ownership of the copyright (an assignment or an exclusive licence) whether all volume rights (or part of the volume rights or more than volume rights) and the territories and languages covered;
(iii) the time scale for delivery of the manuscript and for publication;
(iv) the payments, royalties and advances (if any) to be paid, what they are in respect of and when they are due;
(v) the provisions for sub-licensing;
(vi) the responsibility for preparing the supporting materials (e.g. indexes, illustrations, etc.) in which the author holds the copyright and for obtaining permissions and paying for the supporting materials in which the copyright is held by third parties;
(vii) the termination and reversion provisions of the contract.

Should the parties subsequently agree changes to the contract, these should be recorded in writing between them.

2. The author should retain ownership of the copyright, unless there are good reasons otherwise

An exclusive licence should be sufficient to enable the publisher to exploit and protect most works effectively. In particular fields of publishing (e.g. encyclopaedic and reference works, certain types of academic works, publishers' compilations edited from many outside contributions, some translations and works particularly vulnerable to copyright infringement because of their extensive international sale) it may be appropriate for the copyright to be vested in the publisher.

3. The publisher should ensure that an author who is not professionally represented has a proper opportunity for explanation of the terms of the contract and the reasons for each provision

4. The contract must set out reasonable and precise terms for the reversion of rights

When a publisher has invested in the development of an author's work on the market, and the work is a contribution to the store of literature and knowledge, and the publisher expects to market the work actively for many years, it is reasonable to acquire volume rights for the full term of the copyright, on condition that there are safeguards providing for reversion in appropriate circumstances.

The circumstances under which the grant of rights acquired by the publisher will revert to the author (e.g. fundamental breach of contract by the publisher, or when a title has been out of print or has not been available on the market for a stipulated time) should form a part of the formal contract. In addition, a reversion of particular rights that either have never been successfully exploited by the publisher, or which are not subject to any current (or immediately anticipated) licence or edition, may, after a reasonable period from their first acquisition and after proper notice, be returned on request to the author, provided that such partial reversions do not adversely affect other retained rights (e.g. the absence of an English-language edition should not affect the licensing publisher's interest in a translated edition still in print) and provided that payments made by the publisher to or on behalf of the author have been earned.

5. The publisher must give the author a proper opportunity to share in the success of the work

In general, the publishing contract should seek to achieve a fair balance of regard for author and publisher. On occasion it may be appropriate, when the publisher is taking an exceptional risk in publishing a work, or the origination costs are unusually high, for the author to assist the publication of the work by accepting initially a low royalty return. In such cases, it is also appropriate for the publisher to agree that the author should share in success by, for example, agreeing the royalty rates should increase to reflect that success.

If under the contract the author receives an outright or single payment, but retains ownership of the copyright, the publisher should be prepared to share with the author any income derived from a use of the work not within the reasonable contemplation of the parties at the time of the contract.

6. The publisher must handle manuscripts promptly, and keep the author informed of progress

All manuscripts and synopses received by the publisher, whether solicited or unsolicited should be acknowledged as soon as received. The author may be told at that time when to expect to hear further, but in the absence of any such indication at least a progress report should be sent by the publisher to the author within six weeks of receipt. A longer time may be required in the case of certain works — e.g. those requiring a fully detailed assessment, particularly in cases where the opinion of specialist readers may not be readily available, and in planned co-editions — but the author should be informed of a likely date when a report may be expected.

Note: It is important for the publisher to know if the manuscript or synopsis is being simultaneously submitted to any other publisher.

7. The publisher must not cancel a contract without good and proper reason

It is not easy to define objectively what constitutes unsuitability for publication of a commissioned manuscript or proper cause for the cancellation of a contract, since these may depend on a variety of circumstances. In any such case, however, the publisher must give the author sufficiently detailed reasons for rejection.

When the publisher requires changes in a commissioned manuscript as a condition of publication, these should be clearly set out in writing.

Note: In the case of unsolicited manuscripts or synopses, the publisher is under no obligation to give reasons for rejection, and is entitled to ask the author for return postage.

Time
If an author fails to deliver a completed manuscript according to the contract or within the contracted period, the publisher may be entitled inter alia to a refund of moneys advanced on account. However, it is commonly accepted that (except where time is of the essence) moneys advanced are not reclaimable until the publisher has given proper notice of intent to cancel the contract within a reasonable period from the date of such notice. Where the advance is not reclaimed after the period of notice has expired, it is reasonable for the publisher to retain an option to publish the work.

Standard and Quality
If an author has produced the work in good faith and with proper care, in accordance with the terms of the contract, but the publisher decides not to publish on the grounds of quality, the publisher should not expect to reclaim on cancellation that part of any advance that has already been paid to the author. If, by contrast, the work has not been produced in good faith and with proper care, or the work does not conform to what has been commissioned, the publisher may be able to reclaim the advance.

Defamation and Illegality
The publisher is under no obligation to publish a work that there is reason to believe is defamatory or otherwise illegal.

Change of Circumstance
A change in the publisher's circumstances or policies is not a sufficient reason for declining to publish a commissioned work without compensation.

Compensation
Depending on the grounds for rejection

(i) the publisher may be liable for further advances due and an additional sum may be agreed to compensate the author, or
(ii) the author may be liable to repay the advances received.

In the former case, the agreement for compensation may include an obligation on the author to return advances and compensation paid (or part of them) if the work is subsequently placed elsewhere.

Resolution of Disputes
Ideally, terms will be agreed privately between the parties, but in cases of dispute the matter should be put to a mutually agreed informal procedure, or if this cannot be agreed, to arbitration or normal legal procedures.

8. The contract must set out the anticipated timetable for publication
The formal contract must make clear the time scale within which the author undertakes to deliver the complete manuscript, and within which the publisher undertakes to publish it. It should be recognised that in particular cases there may be valid reasons for diverging from these stated times, or for not determining strict time scales, and each party should be willing to submit detailed reasons for the agreement of the other party, if these should occur.

9. The publisher should be willing to share precautions against legal risks not arising from carelessness by the author
For example:

Libel
While it remains the primary responsibility of the author to ensure that the work is not libellous — and particularly that it cannot be arraigned as a malicious libel — the publisher may also be liable. Libel therefore demands the closest co-operation between authors and publishers, in particular in sharing the costs of reading for libel and of any insurance considered to be desirable by the parties.

10. The publisher should consider assisting the author by funding additional costs involved in preparing the work for publication
If under the contract the author is liable to pay for supporting materials, e.g. for permissions to use other copyright material, for the making and use of illustrations and maps, for costs of indexing, etc., the publisher may be willing to fund such expenses, to an agreed ceiling, that could reasonably be recovered against any such moneys as may subsequently become due to the author.

11. The publisher must ensure that the author receives a regular and clear account of sales made and moneys due
The period during which sales are to be accounted for should be defined in the contract and should be followed, after a period also to be laid down in the contract, by a royalty statement and a remittance of moneys due. Publishers should always observe these dates and obligations scrupulously. Accounts should be rendered at least annually, and in the first year of publication the author may reasonably expect an intermediate statement and settlement. The initial pattern of sales of some educational books, however, may make such intermediate payment impracticable.

The current model royalty statement (1979) issued by the Association of Authors' Agents, the Publishers Association, the Society of Authors and the Writers' Guild, or the information suggested by it, should be used as a guide, and details of the statement should be adequately explained.

343

The publisher should pay the author on request the appropriate share of any substantial advances received from major sub-licensing agreements by the end of the month following the month of receipt (providing moneys already advanced have been earned, and proper allowance made for returned stock; allowance may also need to be made if very substantial advances have been outstanding for an extended period of time).

The publisher should be prepared, on request, to disclose details of the number of copies printed, on condition that the author (and the agent) agree not to disclose the information to any other party.

Publishers should be prepared to give authors indications of sales to date, which must be realistic bearing in mind either unsold stock which may be returned by booksellers or stock supplied on consignment.

12. The publisher must ensure that the author can clearly ascertain how any payments due from sub-licensed agreements will be calculated

Agreements under which the calculation of the author's share of any earnings is dependent on the publisher's allocation of direct costs and overheads can result in dissatisfaction unless the system of accounting is clearly defined.

13. The publisher should keep the author informed of important design, promotion, marketing and sub-licensing decisions

Under the contract, final responsibility for decisions on the design, promotion and marketing of a book is normally vested in the publisher. Nevertheless, the fullest reasonable consultation with the author on such matters is generally desirable, both as a courtesy and in the interests of the success of the book itself. In particular the author should, if interested and available, be consulted about the proposed jacket, jacket copy and major promotional and review activities, be informed in advance of publication date and receive advance copies by that date. When time permits, the publisher should consult the author about the disposition of major sub-leases, and let the author have a copy of the agreement on request.

14. The integrity of the author's work should always be protected

The author is entitled to ensure that the editorial integrity of the work is maintained. No significant alterations to the work (i.e. alterations other than those which could not reasonably be objected to) should be made without the author's consent, particularly where the author has retained the copyright.

The author who has retained ownership of the copyright is entitled also to be credited with the authorship of the work, and to retain the ownership of the manuscript.

15. The publisher should inform the author clearly about opportunities for amendment of the work in the course of production

The economics of printing make the incorporation of authors' textual revisions after the book has been set extremely expensive. Publishers should always make it clear to authors, before a manuscript is put in hand, whether proofs are to be provided or not, on whom the responsibility for reading them rests and what scale of author's revisions would be acceptable to the publisher. If proofs are not being provided, the author should have the right to make final corrections to the copy-edited typescript, and the publisher should take responsibility for accurately reproducing this corrected text in type.

16. **It is essential that both the publisher and the author have a clear common understanding of the significance attaching to the option clause in a publishing contract**
The options on an author's work can be of great importance to both parties. Options should be carefully negotiated, and the obligations that they impose should be clearly stated and understood on both sides. Option clauses covering more than one work may be undesirable, and should only be entered into with particular care.

17. **The publisher should recognise that the remaindering of stock may effectively end the author's expectation of earnings**
Before a title is remaindered, the publisher should inform the author and offer all or part of the stock to the author on the terms expected from the remainder dealer. Whether any royalty, related to the price received on such sales, should be paid is a matter to be determined by the publisher and the author at the time of the contract.

18. **The publisher should endeavour to keep the author informed of changes in the ownership of the publishing rights and of any changes in the imprint under which a work appears**
Most publishers will expect to sign their contracts on behalf of their successors and assigns, just as most authors will sign on behalf of their executors, administrators and assigns. But if changes in rights ownership or of publishing imprint subsequently occur, a publisher should certainly inform and, if at all possible, accommodate an author in these new circumstances.

19. **The publisher should be willing to help the author and the author's estate in the administration of literary affairs**
For example, the publisher should agree to act as an expert witness in questions relating to the valuation of a literary estate.

20. **Above all, the publisher must recognise the importance of co-operation with the author in an enterprise in which both are essential. This relationship can be fulfilled only in an atmosphere of confidence, in which authors get the fullest possible credit for their work and achievements.**

Royalty Statements

All sums earned by the author and fee arrangements of all kinds have to be accounted for by the publisher. The amount of information provided to the author and, no less important, the clarity with which it is set out are matters which are debated intensively by representatives of publishers, authors and authors' agents.

The Association of Authors' Agents, in urging that publishers should provide sufficient information to enable themselves and their authors to review the progress of their authors' books, has stressed recently its wish to see export sales broken out into main territories, e.g. Australia, New Zealand, Canada, South Africa, possibly Europe itself (less the UK). Given that export sales may in general trade publishing add up to between 30 and 40 per cent of total sales the request does not seem unreasonable.

The introduction of Electronic Data Interchange (EDI) is likely to bring increased standardisation of the elements to be included in royalty statements. Book Industry Communication (BIC), in co-operation with representatives of the publishers', authors' and agents' associations, has produced recommendations for the information to be incorporated in publishers' royalty statements. Many of BIC's recommendations are contained in this Appendix.

Notes
1. Publisher's imprint: i.e. if different from publisher's name.

2. Dates, e.g., the VAT applicable date, and the date on which statement issued. Note, however, that if the statement is meant to be issued on or before 31 March in any year and the date of issue is in fact later than 31 March, tax problems may arise if the statement is not pre-dated to 31 March or before.

3. Royalty statements no.: i.e. 'No. 1', 'No. 2', etc., adopting consecutive numbering for statements issued in respect of each publication and, in the case of statement No. 1, stating the publication date after 'Title'. Some literary agents like to have the original publication date repeated on every statement.

4. Sales details: i.e., retail price, format, cumulative sales, specifying each relevant category — home export, special (with appropriate detail), remainder, subsidiary right — and, where relevant, stating the point at which the royalty rate changes. Where sales are reported on a 'price received' basis, the number of sales, as well as the total value, is helpful to the author.
    A separate, detailed statement may be required for subsidiary rights.

5. Royalty rate: stating the basis of calculation, e.g., '10% x **PP**' (10 per cent of published price) or $12^1/_2\%$ x Rec.' ($12^1/_2$ per cent of net amount received).

6. If the publication has gone out of print since the previous statement, it would be helpful if the tabulation were to state, above the lower horizontal line, 'Put out of print ... [date]'.

7. Printing numbers: if sheet or other stock has been transferred from one edition to another, confusion about printing numbers may arise. It would be therefore be helpful if relevant details were set out, as briefly as possible, above the lower horizontal line.

8. Deductions: only some of these items will be relevant. It may be easier not to pre-print this part of the statement but to inset by typewriter or by computer printer the required items, subtotalled and totalled. If the 'Reserve for returns' is used, then the figure should be shown separately, as here, and not simply offset against sales with only one figure showing as SALES DETAILS.

9. **VAT**: i.e. **VAT** payable on relevant items, identified by an asterisk.

Telephone no.:   PUBLISHER'S NAME, ADDRESS
Telex no.:   AND IMPRINT (*Note 1*)
VAT no.:

Our ref.:   , Royalty Manager
(Customer's a/c No.)
                  Date: (*Note 2*)

ROYALTY STATEMENT NO.   (*Note 3*)
Period covered: to
To: AGENT'S OR AUTHOR'S NAME   In respect of:
    AND ADDRESS   ISBN, AUTHOR AND TITLE
    AND VAT NO.   Printing quantity. Previous periods: 123456
                (*Note 7*)   This period: 123456

SALES DETAILS	Published price	Proceeds £	Royalty rate	Royalty £ p
(*Note 4*)			(*Note 5*)	
		(*Notes 6 & 7*)		

                                           £

Total royalties payable
Less: (*Note 8*)
    Advances paid
    Unearned balance brought forward
    Deductible corrections and contributions
    Reserve for returns
    Author's goods purchased
Sub-total

Add: (*Note 9*)
VAT @ 17¹/₂% on * items

    Balance payable/unearned

349

Territories of the World

This Appendix has over the years become more complex: firstly, because the English language is the dominant world language whose use becomes ever more widespread and more intense.

Secondly, the territories and nation states of the world keep changing.

Thirdly, an American Justice Department's anti-trust lawsuit in the mid-1970s against many major American publishers forced the British publishing industry to abandon the trade-wide British Traditional Market Agreement as such. Nothing in the Final Judgment of the District Court, however, restricts the power of American and British publishers, acting as *individual* publishing houses, of (to quote the Final Judgment itself) 'acquiring, granting, or otherwise transferring exclusive or non-exclusive copyright rights, or from exercising or authorising the exercise of such rights under the copyright law of any country' (Final Judgment in *US v Addison-Wesley*, US District Court, Southern District of New York, filed 23 November 1976). Just precisely which countries or territories are negotiated between US and UK publishers on an exclusive basis is therefore important to settle in a publishing agreement between them.

Fourthly, the territorial exclusivity of copyright dealings which underpins the exclusivity of the UK home market in publishing contracts is in conflict with the 'single market' requirements of the amended Treaty of Rome, which demand that there should be no impediments to the free flow of goods across the national boundaries of states which are members of the European Economic Area. The consequence is that, in the words of Paul Scherer, a former President of the Publishers Association, 'if you want exclusivity in the UK, you must have exclusivity in Europe'.

This Appendix tackles the issues as follows:

Schedule 1 sets out a list of the nations and territories of the world as they existed as this Fifth Edition went to press.

Schedule 2 lists the territories which a UK publisher can, in general and subject always to negotiation on individual territories, reasonably expect to be granted on an exclusive basis.

Schedule 3 offers options for publishers to explore in deciding what 'Europe' might mean in the context of 'we need exclusivity in Europe'. The notes are a statement of the position at the time that this edition goes to press and attempt to deal with the possible expansion of the European Single Market in the immediate future and beyond.

SCHEDULE 1

The Nations and Territories of the World by Continents and Regions

Africa
Algeria
Angola
Benin
Botswana
Burkina Faso
Burundi
Cameroon
Cape Verde Islands
Central African Republic
Chad
Comoros
Congo
Djibouti
Egypt
Equatorial Guinea
Eritrea
Ethiopia
Gabon
Gambia, The
Ghana
Guinea
Guinea-Bissau
Ivory Coast
Kenya
Lesotho
Liberia
Libya
Madagascar
Malawi
Mali
Mauritania
Mauritius and dependencies of Mauritius
Mayotte
Morocco
Mozambique
Namibia

Niger
Nigeria
Réunion
Rwanda
St Helena and dependencies of St Helena
São Tomé and Princípe
Senegal
Seychelles
Sierra Leone
Somalia
South Africa
Spanish Presidios
    Ceuta
    Melilla
Sudan
Swaziland
Tanzania
Togo
Tunisia
Uganda
Zaire
Zambia
Zimbabwe

North America
Canada
Greenland
Mexico
St Pierre et Miquelon
United States and its territories and possessions (including Johnston Atoll, Midway Islands and Wake Island)

Central America and West Indies
Anguilla
Antigua and Barbuda
Aruba
Bahamas
Barbados
Belize
Bermuda
Cayman Islands
Costa Rica
Cuba
Dominica
Dominican Republic
Grenada
Guadeloupe
Guatemala
Haiti
Honduras
Jamaica
Martinique
Montserrat
Netherlands Antilles
Nicaragua
Panama
Puerto Rico
St Christopher and Nevis
St Lucia
St Vincent and the Grenadines
El Salvador
Trinidad and Tobago
Turks and Caicos Islands
Virgin Islands (British)
Virgin Islands (American)

South America
Argentina
Bolivia
Brazil
Chile
Colombia
Ecuador
Falkland Islands
French Guiana
Guyana
Paraguay
Peru
South Georgia and South Sandwich
    Islands
Suriname
Uruguay
Venezuela

Asia
Afghanistan
Bahrain
Bangladesh
Bhutan
British Indian Ocean Territory
Brunei
Cambodia
China
Hong Kong
India
Indonesia
Iran
Iraq
Israel
Japan
Jordan
Kazakhstan
Korea, North
Korea, South
Kuwait
Kyrgyzstan
Laos
Lebanon
Macao
Malaysia
Maldives, The
Mongolia
Myanmar (Burma)
Nepal
Oman
Pakistan
Philippine Islands
Qatar
Saudi Arabia
Singapore
Sri Lanka
Syria
Taiwan
Tajikistan
Thailand
Turkey
Turkmenistan
United Arab Emirates
Uzbekistan
Vietnam
Yemen

Oceania
American Samoa
Australia (including territories of
    Ashmore and Cartier Islands,
    Australian Antarctic Territory,
    Christmas Island, Cocos (Keeling)
    Islands, Coral Sea Islands Territory,
    Heard and MacDonald Islands and
    Norfolk Island)
Fiji
French Polynesia
Guam
Kiribati
Marshall Islands
Micronesia, Federated States of
Nauru
New Caledonia
New Zealand (including territories of
    Tokelau (Union Islands), the Ross
    Dependency and associated states of
    the Cook Islands and Niue)
Northern Mariana Islands
Palau
Papua New Guinea
Pitcairn Islands
Solomon Islands
Tonga
Tuvalu
Vanuatu
Wallis and Futuna Islands
Western Samoa

Europe
Albania
Andorra
Armenia
Austria
Azerbaijan
Belarus
Belgium
Bosnia-Herzegovina
Bulgaria
Croatia
Cyprus
Czech Republic
Denmark (including the Faroe Islands)
Estonia

Finland
France
Georgia
Germany
Gibraltar
Greece
Hungary
Iceland
Irish Republic
Italy
Latvia
Liechtenstein
Lithuania
Luxembourg
Macedonia, Former Yugoslav Republic of
Malta
Moldova
Monaco
Netherlands
Norway (including territories of Jan
    Mayen Island, Norwegian Antarctic
    Territories and Svalbard)
Poland
Portugal (including Madeira and the
    Azores)
Romania
Russia (includes Russia in Asia)
San Marino
Serbia and Montenegro (Federal Republic
    of Yugoslavia)
Slovakia
Slovenia
Spain (including the Balearic Islands, the
    Canary Islands and the Spanish
    Overseas Territories)
Sweden
Switzerland
Ukraine
United Kingdom of Great Britain and
    Northern Ireland (including the
    Channel Islands, the Isle of Man and
    the Isles of Scilly)
Vatican City State

Antarctica
British Antarctic Territory

SCHEDULE 2

Many name changes have occurred over the years. The names below are up to date as this edition goes to press; but older names may appear in earlier schedules. The previous names are therefore indicated below, for ease of reference. The list also indicates which territories are currently British Dependencies, etc., which are currently members of the Commonwealth and which are neither. The latter remain in the list because of their past connections with Great Britain.

+ Anguilla	+ Gibraltar
* Antigua and Barbuda	* Grenada
* Australia and territories administered by Australia [See Schedule 1]	* Guyana (formerly British Guiana)
	+ Hong Kong [See Note 1]
* Bahamas	* India
* Bangladesh (formerly East Pakistan)	Iraq
* Barbados	Irish Republic
* Belize (formerly British Honduras)	Israel
+ Bermuda	* Jamaica
Bhutan	Jordan
* Botswana (formerly Bechuanaland)	* Kenya
+ British Antarctic Territory	* Kiribati (formerly the Gilbert Islands)
+ British Indian Ocean Territory	
+ British Virgin Islands	Kuwait
* Brunei	* Lesotho (formerly Basutoland)
* Cameroon (formerly the UN trusteeships of the British Southern Cameroons and the French Cameroons)	* Malawi (formerly Nyasaland)
	* Malaysia (comprising Malaya, Sabah (formerly British North Borneo) and Sarawak)
* Canada	* Maldives, The
+ Cayman Islands	* Malta
* Cyprus	* Mauritius and dependencies of Mauritius (including Rodrigues)
* Dominica	
Egypt	+ Montserrat
+ Falkland Islands	* Mozambique
Fiji	Myanmar (formerly Burma)
* Gambia, The	* Namibia (formerly South West Africa)
* Ghana (formerly the Gold Coast and British Togoland)	
	* Nauru

* New Zealand and territories administered by New Zealand [See Schedule 1]
* Nigeria (formerly Nigeria and the Cameroons)
* Pakistan
* Papua New Guinea
+ Pitcairn Islands
* St Christopher [otherwise St Kitts] and Nevis
+ St Helena and dependencies of St Helena (Ascension and Tristan da Cunha)
* St Lucia
* St Vincent and the Grenadines
* Seychelles
* Sierra Leone
* Singapore
* Solomon Islands (formerly British Solomon Islands)
  Somalia (formerly British Somaliland)
* South Africa
+ South Georgia and South Sandwich Islands (formerly administered by the Falkland Islands)

* Sri Lanka (formerly Ceylon)
  Sudan
* Swaziland
* Tanzania (formerly Tanganyika and Zanzibar)
* Tonga (or the Friendly Islands)
* Trinidad and Tobago
+ Turks and Caicos Islands
* Tuvalu (formerly the Ellice Islands)
* Uganda
* United Kingdom of Great Britain and Northern Ireland, including the Channel Islands, the Isle of Man and the Isles of Scilly
* Vanuatu (formerly the New Hebrides)
* Western Samoa
  Yemen (formerly Aden and People's Democratic Republic of Yemen)
* Zambia (formerly Northern Rhodesia)
* Zimbabwe (formerly Southern Rhodesia)

Notes

(1) +Indicates British Dependent Territories, etc. (Hong Kong will become a Special Administrative Region of the People's Republic of China on 1 July 1997 and it remains to be seen whether in practice it will be able to remain exclusive to UK publishers post that date).

(2) *Indicates member of the Commonwealth (since the last edition South Africa was invited to rejoin and did so in June 1994, Cameroon was invited to join on the basis of being a former UN mandated territory and did so in early November 1995 and Mozambique, which was the only southern African non-member, became the newest member of the Commonwealth in mid-November 1995).

(3) The following relate to territories which may be found on older schedules):
  (a) The *Leeward Islands* include the following Commonwealth members and Dependencies: Anguilla; Antigua and Barbuda; British Virgin Islands; Montserrat; St Christopher (St Kitts) and Nevis.
  (b) The *Windward Islands* include the following Commonwealth members: Dominica; Grenada, St Lucia; St Vincent and the Grenadines.

SCHEDULE 3

The European Single Market

The question 'What is Europe?' in the context of the European 'Single Market' can still be held to have a less than simple answer, but with the formation of the European Economic Area which came into effect on 1 January 1994 the position is clearer than formerly. If only today's answer, however complex, to that question was sufficient.

While the free movement of goods requirements of the Treaty of Rome applied to members of the European Union (pre-1 November 1993 the European Community) and the European Free Trade Association, the same could not be said of the 'exhaustion of rights' doctrine (i.e. that copyright owners may not by virtue of exclusive national territorial rights seek to prevent the movement within the Single Market of copyright goods put on the market anywhere within the Single Market with the consent of the copyright owner). In 1982 the European Court of Justice, in the *Polydor* decision, held that the exhaustion of rights doctrine did not apply to goods put on to the market in EFTA member states so as to override exclusive rights in the EC. The formation of the EEA has simplified this position since it is thought to supersede that ruling, subject to certain conditions relating to the origin of goods with respect to the EFTA states and without any doubt or conditions in the case of Austria, Finland and Sweden which have been members of the EU since 1 January 1995. The *Polydor* decision will of course continue to have force in respect of Switzerland which did not join the EEA. In summary, the formation of the EEA may have provided a finite Single Market of 18 states to which the rules on free movement of goods and the exhaustion doctrine apply; though those states' associations with other countries (and their various territories and dependencies) both present and potential do not equate to a finite situation in a practical sense.

The possibility of expansion of the Single Market to the Central and Eastern European states is nothing new, except that now it is a case of when it will happen rather than if it will happen. The initial question should perhaps be expanded to 'What is Europe, how big will it get and when?'

While certain territories which are not members of the EU or EFTA, such as Andorra, Cyprus, Malta, San Marino, etc., either have special arrangements with the EU which effectively make them part of the Single Market or have been considered for practical convenience to be part of the Single Market, the possible expansion of the Single Market has normally been covered in more general terms by catch-all wording similar to that in Schedule 3C below. Though catch-all wording provides comfort, the ability to include it in contracts, especially those for the licence of rights, is not a foregone conclusion and its application could well be problematical. As this edition goes to press we are in a better position than previously to predict the expansion of the Single Market with EU membership negotiations with Cyprus and Malta likely to commence in early 1998, followed by membership negotiations with Turkey and several Central European states [see Schedule 3B]. However EU trade and co-operation agreements with other Central European states, as well as Eastern European and Mediterranean states (such as Israel, Morocco and Tunisia), proliferate and that in some cases those agreements, even if not necessarily providing for consideration of future EU membership, certainly do not rule out the possibility of free trade agreements is cold comfort when it comes to predicting the future expansion of the Single Market.

Schedule 3A deals with the current position and with the addition of the catch-all wording it may be considered adequate and may serve its purpose until early in the next century – though in realistic terms the inclusion in a schedule defining Europe of those states which have applied for membership of the EU requires full consideration, irrespective of any catch-all wording. Certainly when a long-term view is a factor the inclusion of the states in Schedules 3A and 3B representing the Continent of Europe may be the simplest approach.

SCHEDULE 3A

Territories of the European Economic Area and other European territories to which the free movement of goods requirements apply (and to which the exhaustion doctrine is likely to apply in the near future).

- • Andorra
- * Austria
- * Belgium
- Cyprus
- * Denmark
- * Finland
- * France (including the Overseas Departments of French Guiana, Guadeloupe, Martinique and Réunion)
- * Germany
- • Gibraltar
- * Greece
- + Iceland
- * Irish Republic
- * Italy
- + Liechtenstein

- * Luxembourg
- Malta
- • Monaco
- * Netherlands
- + Norway (including Jan Mayen Island and Svalbard)
- * Portugal (including the Azores and Madeira)
- • San Marino
- * Spain (including the Balearic Islands and the Canary Islands)
- * Sweden
- ° Switzerland
- * United Kingdom of Great Britain and Northern Ireland, including the Channel Islands, the Isle of Man and the Isles of Scilly
- Vatican City State

*   European Union members of the European Economic Area.
+   European Free Trade Association members of the European Economic Area.
°   European Free Trade Association member not a member of the European Economic Area, though has applied for membership of the European Union; the reasons behind its failure to join the EEA may preclude EU membership.
•   Regions or countries which have special arrangements with the European Union which make them, subject in some cases to certain exceptions, part of the European Economic Area.

Other territories included in this schedule are included for practical convenience due to their geographical position. Cyprus and Malta have applied for membership of the European Union, though membership negotiations are unlikely to commence before 1998.

N.B. The details with respect to the territories of France, Norway, Portugal and Spain, which are integral parts of the countries concerned and part of the European Economic Area, should be included for the avoidance of doubt; there are territories of each of these countries which are not necessarily part of the European Economic Area and are detailed in Schedule 3D.

SCHEDULE 3B

Territories with association agreements with the European Union (or seeking such agreements) and eligible (or may be recognised as eligible) for membership of the European Union in the future.

	Albania	*	Lithuania
	Armenia		Macedonia
	Azerbaijan		Moldova
	Belarus	*	Poland
	Bosnia-Herzegovina	*	Romania
*	Bulgaria	+	Russia
	Croatia		Serbia and Montenegro
*	Czech Republic	*	Slovakia
*	Estonia	*	Slovenia
	Georgia	*	Turkey
*	Hungary		Ukraine
*	Latvia		

* Territories with association agreements which have applied for membership of the European Union. Though it is extremely unlikely that membership negotiations will commence before 1998 several of these territories have expressed a wish to become members before 2002.

+ For practical reasons it is unlikely to be possible to divide exclusivity between the European and Asian republics and regions of Russia.

SCHEDULE 3C

The following examples of catch-all wording are not without some benefit though, as previously noted, their application with respect to a particular territory may prove difficult if not impossible. The first example does fix a date for its application (though it should be noted that first publication does not apply by edition) and while this gives only one shot at the definition of the Single Market with respect to the title concerned, it is likely to be found more acceptable particularly in agreements for the licence of rights.

'Any additional territory which shall become a member of the European Union or the European Free Trade Association or the European Economic Area prior to the date of first United Kingdom publication of the Work by the Publishers shall be deemed to be included in this Schedule from the date of such territory's commencement of membership.'

'Any additional territory which shall become a member of the European Union or the European Free Trade Association or the European Economic Area during the term of this Agreement shall be deemed to be included in this Schedule from the date of such territory's commencement of membership.'

SCHEDULE 3D

Territories with connections with the European Union or member states of the European Economic Area but not thought to be territories to which the exhaustion of rights doctrine and the free movement of goods provisions apply.

Algeria
Denmark
    Faroe Islands
*   Greenland
France
*   Overseas territories: French Polynesia, French Southern and Antarctic Territories, New Caledonia and dependencies and Wallis and Futuna Islands
*   Territorial collectivities: Mayotte and St Pierre et Miquelon
Israel
Lomé Convention Countries

Netherlands
*   Aruba
*   Netherlands Antillies
Norway
    Norwegian Antarctic Territories
Portugal
    Macau
Spain
    Spanish Presidios of Cueta and Melilla
United Kingdom
*   British Dependent Territories (see Schedule 2) other than Gibraltar

*   Countries and territories which have special relations with European Union members. Member states apply to their trade with these countries and territories the same treatment as they accord other member states and each country and territory applies to its trade with member states (and the other countries and territories) the same treatment it applies to the member state with which it has special relations.

Member States of the Berne Convention and the Universal Copyright Convention

State	Berne	UCC	State	Berne	UCC
Albania	X		Estonia	X	
Algeria		X	Fiji	X	X
Andorra		X	Finland	X	X
Argentina	X	X	France	X	X
Australia	X	X	Gabon	X	
Austria	X	X	Gambia, The	X	
Bahamas	X	X	Georgia	X	
Bangladesh		X	Germany	X	X
Barbados	X	X	Ghana	X	X
Belame		X	Greece	X	X
Belgium	X	X	Guatemala		X
Belize		X	Guinea	X	X
Benin	X		Guinea-Bissau	X	
Bolivia	X	X	Guyana	X	
Bosnia-Herzegovina	X	X	Haiti	X	X
Brazil	X	X	Holy See	X	X
Bulgaria	X	X	Honduras	X	
Burkina Faso	X		Hungary	X	X
Cambodia		X	Iceland	X	X
Cameroon	X	X	India	X	X
Canada	X	X	Irish Republic	X	X
Central African			Israel	X	X
Republic	X		Italy	X	X
Chad	X		Jamaica	X	
Chile	X	X	Japan	X	X
China	X	X	Jordan	X	
Colombia	X	X	Kazakhstan		X
Congo	X		Kenya	X	X
Costa Rica	X	X	Laos		X
Cote d'Ivoire	X	X	Latvia	X	
Croatia	X	X	Lebanon	X	X
Cuba	X	X	Lesotho	X	
Cyprus	X	X	Liberia	X	X
Czech Republic	X	X	Libya	X	
Denmark	X	X	Liechtenstein	X	X
Dominican Republic		X	Lithuania	X	
Ecuador	X	X	Luxembourg	X	X
Egypt	X		Madagascar	X	
El Salvador	X	X	Malawi	X	X

Appendix I

State	Berne	UCC	State	Berne	UCC
Malaysia	X		Saudi Arabia		X
Mali	X		Senegal	X	X
Malta	X	X	Slovakia	X	X
Mauritania	X		Slovenia	X	X
Mauritius	X	X	South Africa	X	
Mexico	X	X	Spain	X	X
Monaco	X	X	Sri Lanka	X	X
Morocco	X	X	Suriname	X	
Namibia	X		Sweden	X	X
Netherlands	X	X	Switzerland	X	X
New Zealand	X	X	Tajikstan		X
Niger	X	X	Thailand	X	
Nigeria	X	X	The former Yugoslav		
Norway	X	X	Republic of		
Pakistan	X	X	Macedonia	X	
Panama	X	X	Togo	X	
Paraguay	X	X	Trinidad and Tobago	X	X
Peru	X	X	Tunisia	X	X
Philippine Islands	X	X	Turkey	X	
Poland	X	X	Ukraine	X	
Portugal	X	X	United Kingdom	X	X
Republic of Korea	X	X	United Republic of		
Republic of Moldova	X		Tanzania	X	
Romania	X		United States of		
Russian Federation	X	X	America	X	X
Rwanda	X	X	Uruguay	X	X
St Kitts & Nevis	X		Venezuela	X	X
St Lucia	X		Yugoslavia	X	X
St Vincent and			Zaire	X	
the Grenadines	X	X	Zambia	X	X
			Zimbabwe	X	

Index

Abridgement
  paperback edition, of, 109
  right to publish, 5
Acceptance
  conditions of, 6, 7
Adaptation rights
  educational works, 51
  general editor, agreement for, 77
Advance payments
  general book, for, 24, 25
Agent
  author, of, 34, 35
Anthology rights
  fees for, 18, 19, 49
  general editor, agreement for, 77
Arbitration
  contributor, disputes with, 99
  general book author-publisher
    agreement, terms of, 34, 35
  general editor, agreement for, 87
  illustration and artwork agreement,
    173
  international co-edition agreement,
    under, 218-221
  licensee, agreement licensing pre-
    existing literary work for on-line
    distribution, 275
  merchandising rights agreement,
    under, 236, 237
  packaging rights agreement, 204
  paperbacks, relating to, 111
  same language low price reprint
    agreement, 162, 163
  software producer, agreement
    licensing pre-existing literary
    work to, 259
  translation, agreement for sale of, 140,
    141
Artwork
  agreement. *See* ILLUSTRATION AND
    ARTWORK AGREEMENT
  employed illustrators, by, 166
  ownership of, 165, 166
  resale rights, 165, 166
Assignment
  individual works, of, 2

Author
  administration, help with, 345
  amendment of work, opportunities for,
    344, 345
  assisting, 343
  co-operation with, 345
  company, as, 2
  copies, entitlement to, 29
  copyright, retaining, 340
  corrections, 12, 13
  equitable remuneration of, 282, 283
  future work, option on, 32, 33
  integrity of work, protection of, 344
  letter of inducement, 2
  moral rights. *See* MORAL RIGHTS
  payments due to, ascertainment of
    calculation, 344
  publisher keeping informed, 344
  sales, account of, 343
  success of work, share in, 341
  terms of contract, explanation of, 340
  value added tax, 348, 349
**Authors' Licensing and Collecting
  Society**
  Copyright Licensing Agency,
    formation of, 332
  functions of, 333
Authorship
  multiple, 93

Book clubs
  advertising, 118
  characteristics of, 115
  club members only, supply to, 117
  Concordat, 115, 118, 19
  exclusivity, 116, 117
  international co-editions in, 216, 217
  licence, contractual issues, 116
  mail, selling by, 116
  market, 115
  Net Book Agreement, ending of, 115
  paperback rights, sale of, 108, 109
  paperbacks, offering, 115, 119
  premiums, 116, 118
  Regulations, 115, 116
  remainders, 118

Book clubs—*contd*
retail outlets, sale through, 118
rights-
    general editor, agreement for, 77
    separate royalty basis, on, 20, 21,
      51
royalty-inclusive sales, 16, 17
separate editions, 118
simultaneous publication, 115
Broadcast
definition, 281
hospital, 320, 321
rights agreements. *See* FILM, TELEVISION
    AND ALLIED RIGHTS AGREEMENTS

Cable
use of, 281, 282
Central and Eastern Europe
authors, payment of, 150, 151
copyright in, 150
literary agents, 151
private publishing in, 148
reprint licences, 149
rights purchases, 148
UK, transfer of translation rights to
    and from, 149
China
authors, payment of, 145-147
contracts in, 147, 148
copyright in, 144, 145
hard currency, shortage of, 146
literary agents, 148
publishing industry, 145
UK, transfer of translation rights to
    and from, 145-148
Co-edition
international agreement. *See*
    INTERNATIONAL CO-EDITION
    AGREEMENT
meaning, 205
Contributor
arbitration of disputes, 99
book, free copy and purchase of, 99
card, 99
contribution-
    first edition, for, 96, 97
    republication of, 95
copyright, assignment of, 97
disc form, delivery in, 94, 95
late delivery by, 94, 95
moral rights, 96-99
name, inclusion of, 97
outside sources, use of, 94, 95
payment of, 97, 99
proof corrections, 97
Copyright
assignment by general editor, 72, 73

Copyright—*contd*
Australia, in, 4
author-
    owned by, 1
    retained by, 340
Central and Eastern Europe, in, 150
China, in, 144, 145
duration, licence for, 4
educational works, notice in, 55
exclusive licence, territories within
    which
    exercised, 4
fair dealing, concept of, 303
former Soviet Union, in, 153
illustrations, in, 165, 166
infringement, 28, 29, 59
    general editor, agreement for, 84,
      85
    licensee, licensing pre-existing
      literary work for on-line
      distribution, 271
    software producer, licensing pre-
      existing literary work to, 253
material, electronic tagging, 337
moral rights. *See* MORAL RIGHTS
ownership of, 28, 29
performance fees, 305
permission fees-
    illustrations, for, 305, 306
    poetry, for, 304, 305
    prose, for, 304, 305
    recipes, for, 305
    texts broadcast within UK, 307-313
permission form, information on, 307
permissions, 303
photographs, in, 166
piracy, 28
restricted acts, 281
reversionary provisions, 315, 316
textual material, clearance for, 10, 11
typographical arrangement, in, 306,
    307
Copyright Licensing Agency
amount of distributions, 338
CBI, joint task force with, 335
fees, collection of, 334, 335
functions of, 334
general education sector, licensing in,
    334, 335
licence-
    copying under, 50, 51
    effect of, 336
    issue of, 332, 334
national government, dealing with,
    335
non-exclusive licences, grant of, 77,
    79

Copyright Licensing Agency—*contd*
Rapid Clearance Service, 335
record-keeping, 336
title-based distribution system, 336
Corrections
contributor, by, 97
educational, academic, scientific and
professional books, for, 57
general editor, by, 80, 81, 83
translation, to, 127

Delivery
disc form, in, 5, 6, 94, 95
overdue, provisions on, 6
work, of, 5-7
Digest rights
fees for, 18, 19
Documentary
rights, 20, 21
Dramatisation
rights, 20, 21

Education
reprographic reproduction licensing,
334, 335
**Educational, academic, scientific and
professional book author-publisher
agreement**
accounts, 50, 53
arbitration of disputes, 62, 63
assignment, 65
author's copies, 57
author's name, inclusion of, 55
competing works clause, 60, 61
control of publication, 53
copyright licensing, 50, 51
copyright notice, 55
corrections, 57
definitions, 63, 65
delay in publishing, 44
delivery and acceptance of work, 43-45
entire agreement, 63
general trade book agreement,
differing from, 41
headings, 63
illustrations in, 43, 44
index in, 44
infringement of copyright, 59
institutional/corporate authorship, 42
joint and multiple authorship, 42
moral rights, 55
out of print, 59, 61
publisher, rights granted to, 46, 47
remaindering, 57
revisions, 56-59
royalty clauses, 46-49
subsidiary rights, 48, 49, 51

**Educational, academic, scientific and
professional book author-publisher
agreement**—*contd*
taxation, 52, 53
termination, 61
third party sources, material from, 44,
52, 53
value added tax, 52, 53
warranties and indemnities, 55
Electronic media
forms of, 239
licensee, agreement licensing pre-
existing literary work for on-line
distribution-
accounts, 266, 267, 269
alterations, 264, 265
approvals and consents, 273
assignment, 271
confidentiality, 273
copyright infringement, 271
copyright notice, 266, 267
credits, 266, 267
disputes, 275
duration, 270, 271
end users, 277
entire agreement, 275
governing law, 275
hard copying, 264, 265
inspection, 265
interpretation, 275
licence, 262, 263
licensee's warranties, 269
notices, 273
payments, 266, 267
preamble, 262, 263
proprietor's warranties, 269
relationship between parties, 273
release, 264, 265
reserved rights, 262, 263, 265
revisions, 264, 265
severability, 275
site, 277
termination, 271-273
value added tax, 269
waiver of remedies, 275
licensing, types of contract, 239
publication through, 94, 95, 239
software producer, agreement for
licensing pre-existing literary
work to-
accounts, 249-251
alterations, 242-245
approvals and consents, 259
assignment, 255
complimentary copies, 251
confidentiality, 257
consultation and approval, 244,
245, 247

Electronic media—*contd*
software producer, agreement for
licensing pre-existing literary
work to—*contd*
copyright infringement, 253
copyright notice, 247-249
credits, 247-249
discounts, 248, 249
disposal of products, 255
disputes, 259
entire agreement, 261
financial responsibility, 248, 249
governing law, 259
interpretation, 259
licence, 240-243
licensee's warranties, 253
notices, 259
preamble, 240, 241
production, 248, 249
proprietor's warranties, 250, 251
relationship between parties, 257
release, 242, 243
reserved rights, 242, 243
royalties, 248, 249
severability, 259
termination, 254, 255, 257
value added tax, 251
waiver of remedies, 259
Electronic publishing
educational works, 51
rights, 22, 23
general editor, agreement for, 77
European Union
additional territories, 361
association agreements, territories
with, 360
exhaustion of rights doctrine and free
movement of goods provisions,
territories to which not extended,
362
Single Market, 357-362
territories of, 359

Film
definition, 281
literary rights, 283
rights agreements. *See* FILM, TELEVISION
AND ALLIED RIGHTS AGREEMENTS
Film strip
rights, 22, 23
**Film, television and allied rights
agreements**
agency clause, 288, 289
assignment-
agents, 300, 301
certificate of value, 301
completion, 286, 287
credit, 300, 301

**Film, television and allied rights
agreements**—*contd*
assignment—*contd*
definitions, 292-295
embargoes, 298, 299
entitlement to, 288, 289
governing law, 301
moral rights, 301
payments, 297-299
receipts and profits, definitions of,
302
terms of, 295-297
title documents, 302
warranties, 298, 299
author-
consent of, 280
equitable remuneration of, 282, 283
broadcast, definition, 281
drafting, detailed, 284
film, definition, 281
governing law, 289, 291
literary film rights, 283
moral rights, 280
notices, 289
option-
adaptations before completion, 286,
287
essence of, 280
exercise and expiry of, 286-289
extension or exercise of, 285
fee, initial, 285
grant of, 285
owner's obligations, 286, 287
period, 280, 281
sums on account, 286, 287
warranties, 286, 287
package for, 281
payment instructions, 289
publisher, responsibility of, 279, 280
quitclaim, 286
rental right, 283
sources of material, 280
terms of, 284

**General book author-publisher
agreement**
acceptance of work, 6, 7
advance payments, 24, 25
agency clause, 34, 35
Appendix, information in, 39
approval of work, 6, 7
arbitration, 34, 35
author's copies, 29
author's corrections, 12, 13
competing work, prohibition of, 6-8
copyright-
infringement, 28, 29

General book author-publisher agreement—*contd*
copyright—*contd*
ownership of, 28, 29
delivery of the work, 5-7, 39
entire agreement, 34, 35
future work, option on, 32, 33
governing law, 35
illustrations, supply of, 10, 11, 39
index, agreement on, 11, 39
interpretation, 35
moneys owing, 32, 33
moral rights, 32, 33, 35
preamble, 2
production and promotion
responsibility, 13
publishers' responsibility to publish,
10, 11
reversion of rights, 32, 33
revision of work, 29-31
rights and liabilities, setting out, 2
rights granted, 3-5
royalties and fees-
inclusive, book club and overseas
sales, 16, 17
own editions, payable on, 13-15
statement of sales, 26, 27
subsidiary rights-
anthology, 18, 19
book club, 20, 21
digests, 18, 19
dramatisation and documentary, 20,
21
educational reprints, 20, 21
electronic publishing, 22, 23
film strip, 22, 23
general proviso, 24, 25
generally, 16-19
hardcover reprints, 18, 19
large print, 20, 21
mechanical reproduction, 20, 21
merchandising, 20, 21
one-shot periodicals, 18, 19
picturisation, 20, 21
print-disabled, non-commercial
rights for, 24, 25
quotation and extract, 18, 19
reprographic reproduction, 22, 23
serialisation, 18, 19
single-voice readings, 20, 21
strip cartoon, 20, 21
sub-licensed paperback editions,
18, 19
translation, 20, 21
United States, publication in, 20, 21
surplus stock, remainders and disposal
of, 30, 31

General book author-publisher agreement—*contd*
termination, 30, 31, 33
textual copyright material, clearance
for, 10, 11
VAT provisions, 26, 27
warranties and indemnities, 8, 9
General editor, agreement for
accounts, 79
arbitration of disputes, 87
assignment of copyright, 72, 73
assignment, 91
competing works, 87
control of publication, 79
Copyright Licensing Agency, licences
granted by, 77, 79
copyright notice, 81
definitions, 89, 91
delivery and acceptance of work, 70,
71, 73
entire agreement, 87
free copies, 83
headings, 89
infringement of copyright, 84, 85
moral rights, 80, 81
name, inclusion of, 81
need for, 67
other sources, copyright material from,
78, 79
out of print, 85
payment, 67, 72, 73, 75
proof corrections, 80, 81, 83
remaindering, 83
responsibilities of, 68, 69
revision of work, 82, 83
subsidiary rights, 76, 77
tax, 79
termination, 87
value added tax, 79
warranties and indemnities, 80, 81

Hong Kong
Chinese licences granted in, 147
Hospital
broadcasts, 320, 321

Illustration and artwork agreement
artwork-
exhibition of, 169
loss or damage to, 168, 169
original, access to, 168, 169
ownership and copyright in, 171
release, form of, 168, 169
schedule of, 175
cancellation of commission, 170, 171
complimentary copies, 171
failure to fulfil, 171

Illustration and artwork agreement—
contd
fees, 168, 169
governing law, 173
licensing, 169
requirements, details of, 167
reversion of rights, 171
self-billing system for payment of
VAT, 173
settlement of disputes, 173
subsidiary rights, exploitation of, 168,
169
title page, illustrator's name on, 170,
171
warranties, 167
Illustrations
agreement. *See* ILLUSTRATION AND
ARTWORK AGREEMENT
copyright in, 165, 166
educational works, in, 43, 44
paperback edition, for, 106, 107
permission fees, 305, 306
supply of, 10, 11, 39
Illustrator
agreements with, nature of, 165
publisher, relationship with, 166
Indemnities
educational works, 55
general book author-publisher
agreement, in, 8, 9
general editor, agreement for, 80, 81
international co-edition agreement, in,
217-219
paperback editions, 104, 105
translation, agreement for sale of, 140,
141
Index
agreement on, 11, 39
educational works, in, 44
International co-edition agreement
accounting, 212, 213
advance copies, delivery of, 210, 211
arbitration, 218-221
assignment or transmission, not
permitted, 216, 217
author, acknowledgement of, 208, 209
book club deals, 216, 217
breach of contract, 218, 219
copies, supply of, 208-211
copyright details, 209
copyright protection, 220, 221
external permissions clearance, 208,
209
failure to sign or pay, 214, 215
governing law, 220, 221
licence period, 206, 207
new editions, 220, 221

International co-edition agreement—
contd
notice, 218, 219
operation of, 220, 221
out of print, going, 216, 217
payment, 210, 211
method of, 218, 219
production requirements, 208, 209
promotion, control of, 214, 215
publication-
date and price, 214, 215
time limit, 214, 215
quality or condition of shipment,
complaints about, 210, 211
remaindering, 214, 215
reordering, 210, 211
rights reserved, 216, 217
royalties, 212, 213
schedule, 222, 223
sublicensing, 214-217
territories, 206, 207
text, integrity of, 206, 207
translation, publication of, 214, 215
volume rights, form of, 206, 207
warranties and indemnities, 217-219

Large print right
fees for, 20, 21
print-disabled, for, 321
Libel
liability for, 343
warranty against, 8

Mechanical reproduction
rights, 20, 21
Merchandising rights
agreement-
adaptation of, 225
arbitration, 236, 237
assignment, not capable of, 234,
235
definitions, 227
governing law, 236, 237
length and complexity of, 226
liability under, 234, 235
partnership, not creating, 234, 235
payment under, 230, 231, 233
schedule, 238
termination, 234, 235
author, payment due to, 20, 21
distribution, 230, 231
exploitation of, 225
intellectual property rights, 228, 229
licensee-
appointment of, 228, 229
covenants, 233
litigation, 234, 235

Merchandising rights—*contd*
marketing, 230, 231
packaging, 230, 231
product development, 228, 229, 231
quality control, 226
Minimum Terms Agreement, 4
Moral rights
artistic works, in, 165, 173
assertion of, 32, 33, 35
author, right to be identified as, 325
written assertion of, 329, 330
Berne Convention, provisions of, 323-325
contributor, of, 96-99
Copyright, Designs and Patents Act, provisions of, 325
derogatory treatment, right to object to, 325
false attribution of work, 326
film, television and allied rights agreements, 301
general editor, agreement for, 80, 81
introduction of, 280
joint authorship, works of, 326
origin of, 323
package, in, 182, 183
policy towards, 327
privacy, right to, 326
publishing issues, 327, 328
transitional provisions, 327
translator, of, 124, 125
waiver of, 330
White Paper of 1986, in, 324

Negligent misstatement
warranty against, 8

Packages
packaging rights agreement. *See* PACKAGING RIGHTS AGREEMENT
Packaging rights agreement
advance information and material, 202-204
advance material, provision of, 194, 195
approval of material, 182, 183
arbitration, 204
assignment of, 195
author's name, display of, 183
Book Packagers Association Standard Agreement, 177
copyright clause, 180, 181
copyright notice, 181
delivery and packing requirements, 201
delivery, date of, 178, 179
force majeure, 195

Packaging rights agreement—*contd*
imperfect copies, rejection of, 184, 185
jurisdiction, 197
moral rights, 182, 183
new editions, 202
notices, 195
ownership of goods, 188, 189
penalties, 192, 193
price of copies, 178-181
proprietor-
copies, 193
warranties, 182, 183
quantities of copies, 181
remainders, 194, 195
reprints, 194, 195, 204
retention of title, 188, 189
rights and territory, 180, 181, 200, 201
sale and purchase of copies, 179
sales, accounting for, 186, 187, 189
specification, 198, 199
subsidiary rights, 186, 187
term of, 190, 191
termination, 191, 193
undertaking-
advertise and promote, to, 186, 187
publish, to, 187
Paperback editions
abridgement of, 109
advance payments for, 110, 112, 113
amendments, 109
author, display of name, 106, 107
book club rights, sale of, 108, 109
book clubs, offered by, 115, 119
copies, supply of, 104, 105
date of publication, 103
educational works, 51
hardback form, binding in, 108, 109
illustrations etc, supply of, 106, 107
joint ventures, 101
licence-
copies, supply to grantor, 106, 107
duration of, 102-105
records of account, examination of, 106, 107
reversion of rights, 111
rights being licensed, 102-105
mass market, 101
matters within discretion of publishers, 104, 105
publishers' own, 14, 15
remainders, 108, 109
returns, proviso against, 108
revisions, 104, 105
rights agreement-
disputes settlement, 111
governing law, 113

Paperback editions—*contd*
rights agreement—*contd*
options, 110-113
power to make, 105
reprint clause, 108, 109
reservation of rights, 113
termination of, 110, 111
royalties on, 106-109
copies sold below cost, on, 109
sale or disposal of copies, publishers'
right of, 110, 111
sub-licensed, 18, 19
text of work, alteration of, 109
vertical publishing, 101
warranties and indemnities, 104, 105
Paperback rights
general editor, agreement for, 77
Performance
fees, 305
Periodical rights
one-shot, 18, 19
Photographs
copyright in, 166
Picturisation
rights, 20, 21
Print-disabled
non-commercial rights for, 24, 25
Blind in Business, 319, 320
Braille, 317
caveat, 321
educational work, in, 51
general editor, agreement for, 77
hospital broadcasts, 320, 321
large-print editions, 321
meaning, 317
recording, 317-319
Production
responsibility, 13
Promotion
responsibility, 13
Proofs
period for checking, 12, 13
Publisher
author, assisting, 343
business-
possible failure of, 2
takeovers and mergers, 2
Code of Practice, obligations in, 341-
345
legal risks, sharing, 343
moneys owing, payment of, 32, 33
more than one imprint, trading
through, 2
publish, responsibility to, 10, 11
Publishers Licensing Society
Copyright Licensing Agency,
formation of, 332

Publishers Licensing Society—*contd*
functions of, 333
**Publishing Association Code of
Practice**
application of, 340
generally, 339
text of, 340-345
Publishing contract
cancellation of, 342
clear, unambiguous and
comprehensive, to be, 340
option clause, understanding of, 345
reversion of rights, terms for, 340, 341
terms, explanation to author, 340
timetable for publication in, 343

Quotation and extract rights
fees for, 18, 19, 49
general editor, agreement for, 77

Remainders
expectation of earnings, and, 345
general book, of, 30, 31
international co-edition, of, 214, 215
packaged works, of, 194, 195
paperbacks, of, 108, 109
Reprints
educational, 20, 21, 51
general editor, agreement for, 77
hardcover, 18, 19
same language low price-
accounts and statements, 160, 161
advance payment, 158, 159
agreement-
governing law, 162, 163
preamble, 157
settlement of disputes, 162, 163
terms of, 157
compulsory licensing system, 155
copyright notice, 158, 159, 161
duration of licence, 162, 163
free copies, 161
increase in requests for, 156
lump sum payment, 158, 159
name of author, display of, 158,
159
payment method, 157-159
payment of sums due, 160, 161
production of edition, 159
production quality, 158, 159
protection of copyright, 161, 163
publishers-
bankruptcy of, 163
guarantee of rights, 161
registration of work, 162, 163
reservation of rights, 163
reversion of rights, 161

Reprints—*contd*
same language low price—*contd*
rules for, 155
subsidiary rights, disposal of, 161
systematic instructional activities,
works in
connection with, 155
third party permissions, 158, 159
Reprographic reproduction
copy, meaning, 337
copying, history of, 331
Copyright Licensing Agency. *See*
COPYRIGHT LICENSINGAGENCY
fair means of licensing and copying,
336
licences, issue of, 332
means of, 331
payment for, 337
rights, 22, 23
rights of owners and needs of users,
332
rights organisations, 338
rights owners groups, 333
scale of, 332
school system, in, 332
Whitford Committee, representations
to, 332
Revision of work
educational, academic, scientific and
professional books, of, 56-59
general book, of, 29, 30
general editor, agreement for, 82, 83
paperback editions, 104, 105
Royalties
book club sales, 16, 17
general provisos, 16, 17
inclusive sales, 16, 17
international co-edition, for, 212, 213
own editions, payable on-
export hardbound sales, 14, 15
hardbound cheap editions, 14, 15
home hardbound sales, 12, 13
non-booktrade sales, 15
premium sales, 15
publishers' own paperback
editions, 14, 15
small reprints, 14, 15
paperback editions, on, 108, 109
copies lost or sold below costs, on,
109
remaindered, 108, 109
software producer, licensing pre-
existing literary
work to, 248, 249
statements, 347-349
translation rights, for, 133-135
translators, for, 122, 123, 125

Sales
statement of, 26, 27
Satellite transmission
advantages of, 282
Serialisation
sale of rights, 18, 19
Single-voice readings
rights, 20, 21
Soviet Union, former
authors, payment of, 153, 154
copyright in, 153
literary agents, 154
translation rights, payment for, 152
UK, transfer of translation rights to
and from, 152
Strip cartoons
rights, 20, 21
Subsidiary rights
sale of, 16-25
Surplus stock
disposal of, 30, 31

Television
broadcast, definition, 281
cable, use of, 281, 282
rights agreements. *See* FILM, TELEVISION
AND ALLIED RIGHTS AGREEMENTS
satellite transmission, 282
Territories
changes in, 351
continents and regions, by, 352-354
European Single Market, in, 357-362
European Union, of, 359
exclusive basis, grant on, 355, 356
issues, 351
Translation
accounts of sales, 125
agreement for sale of-
accounts of sales, 138, 139
acknowledgement, 136, 137
advance payment, 133, 134
applicable law, 142, 143
bankruptcy of publishers, 141
copies, supply of, 136, 137
copyright notice, 136, 137
copyright protection, registration
for, 142, 143
duration of, 132, 133
licence period 132, 133
notices, 143
payment of sums due, 140, 141
permissions, 134-137
preamble, 132, 133
production and promotion, 136,
137
publication, form of, 132, 133
publication time limit, 136, 137

Translation—*contd*
agreement for sale of—*contd*
publishers, responsibility of, 136, 137
records of account, examination of, 138, 139
reprinting, 139
responsibility to publish, 134, 135
rights granted, 132, 133
rights reserved, 140, 141
royalties, 133-135
settlement of disputes, 140, 141
subsidiary rights, 138, 139
territory, 132, 133
transfer of licence, 140, 141
warranties and indemnities, 140, 141
alterations to, 123
arrangement for, 134, 135
delivery of, 123
international co-edition, of, 214, 215
loss or damage to, 127
market, fitness for, 122, 123
rights in, 20, 21, 126, 127
agreement for sale. *See* agreement for sale of rights, above
failure to publish, on, 126, 127
former Soviet Union, payment in, 152
general editor, agreement for, 77
negotiation of, 131
UK and Central and Eastern Europe, transfer between, 149
UK and former Soviet Union territories, transfer between, 152
UK and People's Republic of China, transfer between, 145-148
time for publishing, 124, 125
Translator
agreement. *See also* TRANSLATION
breach of, 127
copyright, exclusive right to, 122, 123
governing law, 129
settlement of disputes, 127
author, assimilation of status to, 121, 122
free copies and terms of purchase, 125, 127
moral rights, 124, 125
objectionable or libellous matter, introduction of, 124, 125
payment to-
book club etc rights, on sale of, 125
fee, 122, 123
royalties, 122, 123, 125
US sale, on, 125

Translator—*contd*
proof corrections, 127
records of account, examination of, 125
return of rights to, 126, 127
self-billing system, details of VAT for, 129
title page and jacket, name appearing on, 124, 125
UNESCO Recommendation, 121

United States
publication rights in, 20, 21

Value added tax
author, liability of, 348, 349
contributor, payments to, 99
educational works, 52, 53
general book author-publisher agreement, in, 26, 27
general editor, agreement for, 79
licensee, agreement licensing pre-existing literary work for on-line distribution, 269
self-billing system, details for, 129, 173
software producer, agreement licensing pre-existing literary work to, 251
Video
cassettes and discs, 282

Warranties
educational works, 55
film, television and allied rights agreements, in, 286, 287, 298, 299
general book author-publisher agreement, in, 8, 9
general editor, agreement for, 80, 81
illustration and artwork agreement, in, 167
international co-edition agreement, in, 217-219
licensee, licensing pre-existing literary work for on-line distribution-
licensee's, 269
proprietor's, 269
packaging rights agreement, in, 182, 183
paperback editions, 104, 105
software producer, licensing pre-existing literary work to-
licensee's, 253
proprietor's, 250, 251
translation, agreement for sale of, 140, 141

CASSIE BROWN'S

SUGAR SENSATIONS

Six Cutting Edge Celebration Cakes!

Sugar Sensations
6 Cutting Edge Celebration Cakes © Cassie Brown

ISBN: 978-1-906316-55-6
All rights reserved.

Published in 2010 by HotHive Books
www.thehothive.com

Photography by Richie Brown
www.richiebrownphotography.com T: 07771 342 972

Book design by Mark Hobin
www.hobindesign.com T: 07836 782 000

Printed in the UK by Cambrian Printers

CONTENTS

Dedication and thanks ······· 4

Introduction ······· 5

Explanations & Questions Answered ······· 6

Sequin cake ······· 8

Rose Petal cake ······· 12

Rose Basque cake ······· 16

Swans cake ······· 22

Sea Holly cake ······· 30

Handbag cake ······· 38

Recipes ······· 44

About the Author ······· 45

Suppliers ······· 46

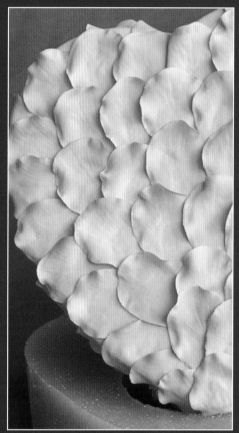

DEDICATIONS AND THANKS...

I would like to thank all my family and friends for their help and support in bringing this book together, in particular the inspirations who are:

My husband Simon – I couldn't do it without you, thank you.

My three children – Charlotte, Sam and Harry – you always keep me smiling and are my drive to be successful.

Aunty Dill – who introduced me to sugarcraft. It is the fault of this lady that I am so passionate about sugar.

Special thanks also to Michele at Lemonella who created all the edible diamanté ribbon, the edible cake stand, jewels and cake wrappers.

To Richie Brown and Margarita Vazquez for a lovely weekend of photography and for the beautiful photos that are used in the book. Also thanks to Mark Hobin for the fabulous design of the book: your creativity and vision is wonderful.

You are only as good as the team behind you!

… and a very special thank you to my Aunty Eileen.

INTRODUCTION

This book has six fabulous cake designs for you to feast you eyes on, sink your teeth into and have a go at. And yes, it's all decorated sugar.

I first got interested in sugarcraft at the age of thirteen when I was staying with my Aunty Eileen. My Aunty Dill was a member of the British Sugarcraft Guild and one night she took us to see a demonstration about how to make an orchid in sugar. I was amazed by this fascinating craft and became hooked. Luckily for me the demonstrators that night had brought some of their products for sale so I bought the orchid cutters, some flower paste and some pink petal dust, and the next day I made an orchid. Looking back now it was pretty awful, but at the time I thought it looked great!

I want this book to inspire you and open your mind to different techniques in sugar, just like that demonstration did for me, while also giving you the know-how so you too can create them.

I hope this book encourages you to experiment with your own ideas but remember, there is not a right or wrong way to create in sugar and not all techniques will work for everyone, so make sure you don't give up, just try doing it in a different way until it does work.

It's true what they say: you are only limited by your own imagination…

EXPLANATIONS & QUESTIONS ANSWERED

What is:

A celpin: these are wonderful as they come in several different sizes. Personally, I like the medium and small celpins, which are about 10mm and 5mm in diameter, excellent for rolling out nice thin ridges in the flower paste. There is a point at one end of the celpin which can be used as a veiner, and the other end is rounded which is ideal for softening the edges of the petals and leaves.

A dowelling rod: these are used to support tiered cakes. Dowelling rods are like plastic pencils which you insert into the cake and cut to size to take the weight of the upper tiers.

A posy pick: these are are like hollow, plastic pencils. They are used to hold the wire in place and stop it from going directly into the cakes.

A smoother: these are designed to smooth the icing on the cake to create a smooth texture, simply by rubbing the smoother all over the cake. You will see the difference once you have used one. Some people describe them as similar to a trowel that you plaster the walls with.

Sugar paste: There are lots of different sugar pastes on the market. Personally, I like the Cova paste which has a marshmallowy taste and texture and doesn't dry out like some pastes. Also when you cover the cake, the paste sometimes cracks at the edge and I find Cova paste easier to smooth over.

A veiner? Veiners come in all shapes and sizes and are made from lots of different materials. Personally, I like using the double-sided silicon veiner because it veins both sides of the paste and is flexible.

#wires: # means gauge, so if you have a 20# wire, this means 20 gauge wire. The higher the number on the wire the thinner it is. So 33# wire is very thin and will not hold a lot of weight, whereas a 20# wire is thicker and much stronger.

How to:

Colour the flower paste: I normally use edible dust colours to colour the flower paste as there is a wider variety of dust colours and I find it less messy than liquid colours. Simply add a little Trex to the paste and mix in the desired colour well, until the colour is evenly distributed.

Use cutters: place the cutter on the ready rolled-out flower paste and press down firmly while making circular movements around the board. Lift the cutter upside down and run your thumb over the cutter to ensure a clean cut in the paste.

Use a double-sided veiner: open the veiner out and dust with a little cornflour, as this will prevent the paste sticking. Then place the prepared petal or leaf on to the veiner, making sure that the centre of the petal or leaf is lined up with the centre of the veiner. Carefully place the second half of the veiner on top and press firmly with your hand. Open the veiner up to reveal the lovely veined petal/leaf.

Use florist tape: I like to use half-width florist tape as it makes the wire look thinner after taping. Stretch the tape to release the glue, then wrap the end of the tape around the wire as if making a flag. Then, with your finger and thumb, twist the wire between your fingers, remembering to stretch the tape to release the glue.

Decide which non-stick boards to use: again there are lots of boards on the market but I like my old faithful non-stick green board that I have had for several years. Green boards work better for me as you can see how thin you are rolling the flower paste.

▶ **TIP!** To look after your non-stick board, never clean it with water, as this may warp the board (like mine!). Simply clean by massaging Trex all over the surface of the board and wipe off with some kitchen paper. This will also prevent the flower paste getting stuck to the surface of the board.

Make a ridge: a ridge is a thicker part of the flower paste to fit the wire into. To make one, take some flower paste and roll it into a ball, then a sausage shape and push it against the board. Take the celpin and push it down into the centre of the sausage, roll to one side then go back to the centre and repeat but rolling the other way, so you create a ridge through the centre of the paste. If the ridge is too thick, simply place the celpin on top of the ridge and roll to one side, which should halve the ridge.

Soften (ball) the edges of petals and leaves: place the petal on a CelPad and using the rounded end of the celpin, place half on the petal and half on the CelPad and gently press down and push around the petal, as if writing with a pen. Don't be tempted to hold the petal as it may tear, just let it do its own thing. If the petal becomes too frilly, release the pressure as you are pushing down on it.

Recommendations:

Iced boards: I recommend using iced boards as the icing forms a barrier between the cake and the silver covered board. Roll out the sugar paste so it is a little smaller than the board you wish to cover then place the rolled-out icing on top of the board. Then finish rolling out so that the board is covered and cut the excess paste from around the edge of the board to give a neat finish.

Why white wires? I learnt the hard way when I did a competition and put a green wire into a white peace lily, thinking I could cover the wire up with dark green dust. The green wires are too dark, so can't be covered up. The judges spotted it and I lost valuable points. Even if you put a green wire into a green leaf the chances are it can still be seen, whereas white wires can be covered up with any colour.

SEQUIN CAKE

This cake is designed to be a simple yet great starter cake that is easy to put together and doesn't cost a lot to make. It's up to you how elaborate you make the decoration – maybe match the dress if you are making it for a wedding?

Materials:
- 1 x 10" fruit cake
- 1 x 8" fruit cake
- 2kg cream coloured sugar paste
- 2kg marzipan
- Apricot glaze
- Icing sugar
- Leaf gelatine
- Rice paper
- Water or white alcohol
- 10 x edible jelly roses (Lemonella, see Suppliers on page 46)
- 10 x edible jelly hearts (Lemonella, see Suppliers on page 46)

Equipment:
- Iced 8" drum board
- Iced 12" drum board
- Iced14" drum board
- 10" spare board
- Large rolling pin
- 5 Dowelling rods
- Posy pick
- Trumpet cake stand, gold (Lindy Smith, see Suppliers on page 46)
- Butterfly paper punch (optional)
- Scissors
- Hole punch (optional)
- Smoother
- Pastry brush
- 1m cream coloured ribbon
- Tracing paper
- Pin
- Gold wire

COVERING THE CAKES WITH MARZIPAN:

Place the 8" fruit cake upside down on the 8" board, then place both on the 10" spare board. If there is a little gap between the cake and the 8" board simply fill it with marzipan. Then brush the cake with apricot glaze.

Sprinkle some icing sugar on the worktop to stop the marzipan from sticking and then roll the marzipan to a thickness of ¼" (4mm). Then loosely and gently roll the marzipan around the rolling pin and lift over the cake. Unroll the marzipan over the top of the cake, smooth down the sides of the cake and cut away any excess marzipan. Use a smoother to smooth the top and sides of the cake. Repeat this on the 10" cake but place the cake on the iced 12" board. Leave to firm overnight.

▶ **TIP!** The smoother you make the marzipan the better the icing will look at the end.

ICING THE CAKES:

Sprinkle some icing sugar on the worktop to stop the sugar paste from sticking and then roll the cream-coloured sugar paste to a thickness of ¼" (4mm). Brush water or white alcohol over the marzipanned cake (this will help the sugar paste stick to the cake), then loosely and gently roll the sugar paste around the rolling pin and unroll over the cake.

With the smoother rub over the top of the cake to make sure there are no air bubbles. Then use your hands to gently work your way down the sides of the cake to remove any air bubbles from there, before using the smoother again to create a wonderfully smooth finish.

▶ **TIP!** If an air bubble does appear after the smoothing process, pop it with a sterilised pin and push the air out through the pin hole.

Repeat for the 8" cake but don't ice the spare board, just cut neatly around the bottom of the cake. The sugar paste should cover the sides of the 8" board that you have under the cake, so it looks like part of the cake.

Once dry, place the 10" cake, which should be on the 12" board, on top of the 14" iced cake board.

INSERTING THE DOWELLING RODS:

Push one rod into the middle of the 10" cake, then using a knife, mark where the sugar paste finishes on the rod at the top of the cake. Pull the dowelling rod out and cut where the mark is. Measure another four dowelling rods and cut to the same size. Place one back into the centre of the cake and push the other four around the centre; this will help support the top tier.

Place the cake stand on the centre of the 10" cake then place the 8" cake on top of the stand. You now have a wonderful wedding cake just waiting to be spruced up with a little decoration. Attach the cream ribbon around the bottom of the board with a little royal icing.

THE ARRANGEMENT:

You can buy arrangements for the centres of cakes or make your own by simply cutting out the required shapes in modelling paste about 3mm thick, then inserting a hooked gold wire into the bottom of the shape. Leave to dry, then paint the shapes with a gold food colour mixed with white alcohol, as this will help the paint to dry quicker. Alternatively you could simply buy ten jelly hearts and push them on to the gold wire.

Fill the posy pick with sugar paste then push it into the centre of the 8" cake. Push the three daisy stems into the centre of the posy pick, then gently bend the wires so they are softly curved and push them into the centre of the three daisy stems. This will give the impression that the arrangement is bursting out of the cake.

MARKING THE PATTERN:
Sketch out the pattern on some tracing paper first, then place the pattern on to the side of the cake and with a pin gently mark out the pattern on the cake.

LEAF GELATINE:
Cut squares from the leaf gelatine and paint a small amount of water around the top of the cake, then simply place the squares on to the water, overlapping slightly. Alternatively, using the hole punch, punch holes into the leaf gelatine to make edible sequins, then attach them to the cake where you have marked out the pattern using a little water.

FINISHING TOUCHES:
Using the rice paper carefully cut out two butterfly shapes (a butterfly-shaped hole punch can be used

SEQUIN CAKE

instead if you prefer), then gently bend the butterflies in half and attach them to the cake using a little royal icing. It makes all the difference!

▶ **TIP!** Adding an extra iced board at the bottom of your work of art will add grandeur to the cake and gives the impression that the cake is bigger than it actually is. I tend to make the bottom board 2" bigger than the one sat on it.

▶ **TIP!** If there are marks or imperfections in the iced cakes, simply work your pattern over the top or add an extra butterfly or two.

ROSE PETAL CAKE

This cake is a stunner, designed to impress and although it is a little time consuming it's simple to do and well worth the effort to see the reactions on people's faces when you say it's all your own work. And yes, the cake stand is edible too!

Materials:

- 1 x 8" heart-shaped cake
- ½kg white sugar paste
- 700g buttercream (see Recipes on page 44)
- 200g white flower paste (A Piece of Cake, see Suppliers on page 46)
- Cooled boiled water
- Candy pink edible food dust (Rainbow Dust, see Suppliers on page 46)
- Forsythia yellow food dust (Edable Art, see Suppliers on page 46)
- Cornflour
- Trex or petal base
- Edible cake stand, strawberry flavoured (Lemonella or Passion4Cakes, see Suppliers on page 46)

Equipment:

- Palette knife
- Medium rose petal cutter
- Large rose veiner (Passion4Cakes, see Suppliers on page 46)
- Medium celpin
- CelPad
- Non-stick board
- Flat paint brushes

INSTRUCTIONS FOR ICING THE HEART-SHAPED CAKE:

Sprinkle some icing sugar on the worktop to stop the sugar paste from sticking and then roll the white sugar paste to a thickness of ¼" (4mm).

Using a palette knife spread a thin layer of buttercream over the sponge cake (this will help the sugar paste stick) then loosely and gently roll the sugar paste around the rolling pin and lift over the cake. Unroll the sugar paste over the top of the cake and use a smoother to smooth the top and sides of the cake to make sure there are no air bubbles.

COLOURING THE FLOWER PASTE:

Mix the flower paste with your fingers, adding a little Trex or petal base and some candy pink dust colour. Continue to mix until the colour is evenly distributed and a nice pale pink.

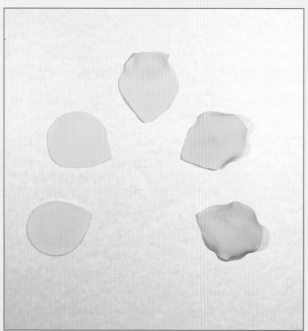

MAKING THE ROSE PETALS:

Take a small ball of pale pink flower paste and add a little Trex, this will make the paste more pliable. Roll out on a non-stick board and cut out using the rose petal cutter. Dust the rose petal veiner with a little cornflour to prevent the paste sticking then place the petal in the rose petal veiner and press down to vein. Remove the petal from the veiner and place on the CelPad. Using the rounded end of the celpin, firmly press down the edge of the petal to soften. Repeat with all the petals. Don't leave them to dry completely before putting on the cake as they may break.

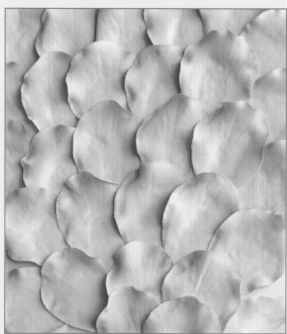

▶ **TIP!** Don't hold the petal while trying to soften the edges as it may tear; just let it do its own thing.

▶ **TIP!** You should be able to see through the flower paste when rolled out, otherwise it is too thick!

TO COLOUR:

Brush the petal with pink food dust, starting at the outer part of the petal and gently moving in towards the centre. Add a little Forsythia yellow food dust by brushing from the point of the petal with a quick stroke of the brush towards the centre.

PLACING THE PETALS ON THE CAKE:

Starting at the back of the cake, brush some water on the ready-iced cake and then start to place the petals around the base of the cake, slightly overlapping the next layer of petals, continuing until the cake is covered. Remember to start at the top and back of the heart and work your way down to the point.

CAKE STAND:

This cake stand has been specially designed for this cake and is totally edible, with a strawberry flavour. The stand is available from Lemonella Ltd (see Suppliers on page 46 for details). Take care when lifting the cake on to the cake stand, but don't be scared of it!

ROSE BASQUE CAKE

This cake is all about the wow factor – it is definitely not a traditional cake, but is fun and exciting to do. The project is simple but effective and if you are not very good at getting smooth icing this is the cake for you! Don't worry about the roses, if you haven't got time to do them you could use real or artificial ones. Have a little fun with royal icing – it's not my preferred medium to work with as it can be quite tricky to get a smooth finish, but with this cake the whole idea is texture, texture, texture! And the lights just add a little sparkle.

Equipment:
- Palette knife
- Large rolling pin
- 10" drum board
- 5" board
- Large carving knife
- Dowelling rods
- Pastry brush
- Metal ruler to smooth the royal icing
- Brush for water
- Set of 3 rose cutters, large
- Rose veiner
- 18#, 26#, 28# white wire
- Lighter or naked flame
- Non-stick board
- Large celpin
- CelPad
- Wire cutters
- Calyx cutter, large
- Bear grass 5mm cutter (Passion4Cakes, see Suppliers on page 46)
- Corn husk veiner
- Scalpel
- Posy pick
- Galaxy lights (Passion4Cakes, see Suppliers on page 46)
- Florist tape, half-width

Materials:
- 3kg royal icing
- 2 x 8" fruit cakes
- 2 x 6" fruit cakes
- 1 x 10" fruit cake
- 5kg marzipan
- Icing sugar
- Apricot glaze
- 200g white flower paste (A Piece of Cake, see Suppliers on page 46)
- Claret and autumn green coloured dusts (Rainbow Dust, see Suppliers on page 46)
- Trex
- Cooled boiled water
- 25 Claret diamonds 6mm (Passion4Cakes, see Suppliers on page 46)

CARVING THE CAKE:

Place the 10" fruit cake on to the centre of the 10" board, then place one 8" fruit cake and the two 6" cakes on top, before placing the second 8" cake on the very top.

Using the large carving knife, cut the shape of the basque into the cakes. Make sure that you have smooth edges so the cakes are blending together. Once the cake is shaped, take the top two tiers (the 6" and 8" cakes) off and place four dowelling rods into the remaining cakes. Snip the ends off so they are level with the top of the cake and place a 5" board on top. Replace the 6" and 8" cakes back on top ready for marzipanning.

MARZIPAN THE CAKES:

Brush the cakes with apricot glaze. Sprinkle some icing sugar on the worktop to stop the marzipan from sticking and then roll the marzipan to a thickness of ¼" (4mm). Then loosely and gently unroll the marzipan around the side of the cakes – don't worry about the top of the cake yet.

Firmly push the marzipan against the sides of the cake and cut away any excess marzipan, then roll out a small circle of marzipan to cover the top of the cake. Because we are covering this cake in royal icing, the marzipan is done in two sections: the sides and then the top. Don't be tempted to smooth the squared edge at the top of the cake as this is part of the design.

ROYAL ICING:

This is where the fun begins! With the palette knife take a spoonful of royal icing and then use the palette knife to paddle the icing from side to side, pressing down as you do so; this will help to get rid of any air bubbles. Then pick up some more icing with the palette knife and spread it around the bottom of the cake. Repeat this all over, working your way up the cake. Don't be tempted

to go back over the lower part of the cake once you have reached the top because royal icing dries very quickly and if you do this it will look like crumbs on the side of the cake, where the royal icing forms a crust.

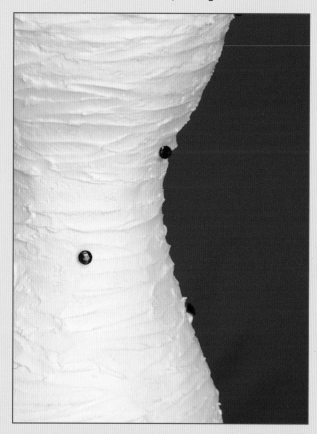

Place a desert spoonful of royal icing on the centre of the top of the cake, then start to paddle the icing until the top is covered with icing.

Using a palette knife, texture the top of the cake as you did with the sides.

Place the diamonds randomly around the side of the cake and leave to dry.

TO MAKE THE ROSES:

CONE OF THE ROSE:

Colour some white flower paste with the claret coloured dust, add Trex and mix well. Take a piece of this claret coloured flower paste, about the size of a small sprout and roll into a ball, then form a cone shape.

Bend a hook into the end of an 18# wire and hold the hook over a naked flame (this will get very hot so be careful), then push straight into the wider end of the cone shape. Leave to dry.

WARNING: *the wire gets extremely hot when doing this. If it doesn't work first time and you pull the wire out of the icing do not reheat it as any icing left on the hook will melt and drip on you or the surface and burn. If you have to pull the wire out, cut the hook off and start again.*

THE PETALS:

Roll out the claret coloured flower paste very thinly and cut out ten petals using the smallest of the rose petal set.

Place each of the petals into the rose petal veiner in turn and press down to vein. Remove each petal from the veiner, place onto the celpad and soften their edges.

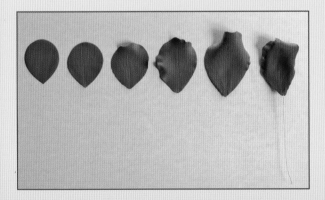

ASSEMBLING THE ROSE:

Take the first petal and cover with a thin layer of water. With the point of the petal facing down, place the cone on the centre just under the top of the petal and wrap the petal around the cone quite tightly.

Cover the second petal with water half way up and wrap around the cone on the opposite side to the first petal. From now on paint the petals with water only at the bottom of the petal in a 'v' shape, not going too far up the petal. Then place the next petal so that the end of the petal is in the centre of the previous petal and so on until all ten petals are in the rose.

Roll out the flower paste and using the medium rose cutter, cut out another five petals. Vein and soften the edges of the petals as before.

Brush a small amount of water on the bottom of the petal and continue to place on the rose, gently curving the top of the petals back and pinching them slightly to make the rose look more realistic. I recommend leaving it upside down to dry slightly while you do the larger petals, but keep looking at it and checking that it's drying in the right position.

Roll out the flower paste leaving a thin ridge through the paste, then using the large rose petal cutter cut out the petal so the ridge is going up the centre. Insert a 28# wire through the centre of the petal until it goes about half way up, vein in the rose petal veiner and soften the edges of the petal using a celpin as before.

Ball a little in the centre of the petal to cup it slightly, pinching the edges of the petals so they curl back. Leave to dry a little upside down and repeat to make five large petals.

Dust over the roses with the claret dust colour. Using the half-width florist tape, tape one petal at a time directly under the rose and then all the way down the stem. You may need to move the petals a little so that they are in the right place.

The rose is looking good but to finish you need to put a calyx on – this is the green star found at the back of the rose.

THE CALYX:
Colour some white flower paste with the autumn green coloured dust, add Trex and mix well. Roll out the green flower paste then cut out the calyx shape.

Cut little nicks all around the calyx using the scalpel or small scissors and soften the edges using the rounded end of the celpin.

Paint a little water on the calyx then push the wire of the rose into the centre and attach it to the back of the rose.

Roll a small ball of green flower paste and make it into a cone shape. Then brush a little water on the wide, top end of the cone and place the end of the wire into the centre of the top of the cone, pushing it up the wire to attach it to the back of the calyx.

Your rose is complete.

▶ **TIP!** When making the rose remember to stop and look at it from the side because if you place the petal too far down the rose it turns into a cabbage!

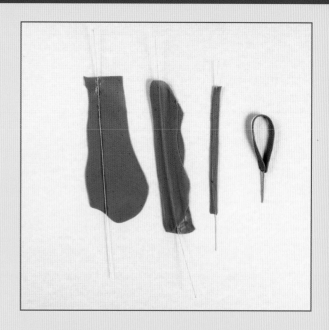

BEAR GRASS:
See instructions for straps of handbag under Handbag cake on page 41. Make the bear grass in the same way as on page 41, but while it is still damp bring the two ends of the bear grass together to create a loop and tape the two ends of the wire together.

WIRE INTO A POSY:
Hold one rose to make the centre of the posy, then place the other five around the centre rose and tape together using half-width florist tape. You may need to carefully bend the stems of the roses to help them sit in the right position. Make sure you tape all the way down the stems of the roses.

TO FINISH:
Hold the posy in one hand and place the looped bear grass between the roses, don't be scared of trying the bear grass in different places before wiring up. Once you are happy with the effect, tape them up.

Add the white lights by weaving them between the flowers in the posy. Tape down the wire but be sure not to tape up the little battery box or you will not be able to change the battery.

AMAZING!

Now push the posy pick into the top of the cake and place your beautiful flowers into the posy pick. If they stand up from the cake too much, just cut the stems down with wire cutters. I like my roses to sit quite close to the cake.

▶ **TIP!** When wiring flowers it is sometimes useful to do it in front of a large mirror so you don't have to keep turning the flowers around to see what they look like.

I first designed the swans for my daughter Charlotte's Christening cake, but added a lily flower with a little baby in it. Since then I have adapted the design to suit all sorts of cakes, with the most popular being anniversary and wedding cakes. You don't have to add the cupcakes, I just like the idea of mixing it up a bit and you can have more flavours of cake but still be quite traditional.

Equipment:

- 8" and 10" oval drum boards
- 10" and 12" oval or round spare boards
- Large rolling pin
- Pastry brush
- Smoother
- 5 Dowelling rods
- Tweezers or scissors (Passion4Cakes, see Suppliers on page 46)
- White flower paste
- Non-stick board
- Small celpin
- Scalpel
- Hosta leaf veiner (Edable Art, see Suppliers on page 46)
- 26# and 28# white wire
- Swan wing cutter (Passion4Cakes, see Suppliers on page 46)
- CelPad
- 18" iced oval board
- 000 size paint brush
- Large grass cutter (available from Passion4Cakes, see Suppliers on page 46)
- Small piping bag
- Large piping bag
- Star nozzle
- Florist tape, half-width
- Suitable wide glass bowl or dish (see illustration)

Materials:

- 1 x 8" oval fruit cake
- 1 x 10" oval fruit cake
- 2kg marzipan
- 2½kg white sugar paste
- Icing sugar
- Apricot glaze
- Autumn green coloured flower paste (made by colouring white sugar paste with the autumn green dust)
- Autumn green coloured dust (Rainbow Dust, see Suppliers on page 46)
- White modelling paste (see Recipes on page 44)
- Piping gel
- Small amount of green and brown flower pastes
- Cooled boiled water or white alcohol
- Royal icing
- Trex
- Black and yellow food colouring
- Confectioners' glaze
- Edible cake wrappers in forest green (available from Passion4Cakes, made by Lemonella, see Suppliers on page 46)
- Melted leaf gelatine
- 3 small swans (see page 24 for instructions to make the swans)
- 9 looped leaves
- 3 cup cakes
- Edible green diamanté ribbon (available from Passion4Cakes, made by Lemonella, see Suppliers on page 46)

MARZIPAN THE CAKES:

Place the 8" oval fruit cake upside down on the 8" drum board and then place this on the spare 10" board – if there is a gap between the cake and the board you can fill it with marzipan.

Brush the cake with apricot glaze. Sprinkle some icing sugar on the worktop to stop the marzipan from sticking and then roll the marzipan to a thickness of ¼" (4mm). Then loosely and gently roll the marzipan around the rolling pin and lift over the cake. Unroll the marzipan over the top of the cake, smooth down the sides of the cake and cut away any excess marzipan.

Use a smoother to smooth the top and sides of the cake. Don't forget to marzipan over the board that is the same size as the cake. Leave to firm overnight. Repeat this process with the 10" cake, placing it upside down on the 10" board and then on the spare 12" board, and then marzipan as above.

ICING THE CAKES WITH SUGAR PASTE:

Roll out the white sugar paste using a small amount of icing sugar to stop it sticking, brush the marzipanned cake with the water or white alcohol, then gently roll the sugar paste around the rolling pin and unroll over the cake. Level out the icing with your fingers then use the smoother to perfect the cake. Leave to dry.

DOWELLING RODS:

Push one of the dowelling rods into the centre of the 10" cake; allow an extra 1cm space from the top of the cake and then mark the rod to be cut. Pull out the rod and cut where you have marked, then measure and cut four other rods to the same size. Push them into the 10" cakes – one in the centre and the other four in a circle around it.

LOOPED PEACE LILY LEAVES:

Roll out the autumn green flower paste, cut out, then vein in the hosta leaf veiner.

Using the rounded end of the celpin, soften the edge of the leaf to make it more realistic. Brush a little water on to the back of the leaf at the top then simply bend in half over a paint brush handle, to meet the bottom end of the leaf.

Leave to dry, then paint with confectioners' glaze and leave to dry once again. You will need about 16 looped leaves.

TO MAKE THE SWANS:

THE NECK OF THE SWAN:

Roll a sausage of white flower paste to create the neck, slightly pinching one end of the sausage to make the beak, but be careful not to make the beak too big as you may end up with a duck!

Hold the neck about 1cm down from the beak, then roll between your fingers to create the head.

Roll the rest of the neck so it is the same thickness. Shape the neck into a question mark shape, then leave to dry on a CelPad.

TIP! Make lots of swan necks and store them in a box so when you have an urgent need for a cake, all you have to do is make the body to attach to the neck and, hey presto, instant decoration!

PAINTING THE SWAN'S FACE:

Paint the beak using yellow food colouring and add some shape to the beak using black food colouring around the edge. Then, starting at the top of the beak, paint a downward half circle and repeat on the other side (when looking head on to the swan this will look like a 'w') then make a little curve to create the eyes, and to finish, paint a diamond shape at the top of the beak between the eyes.

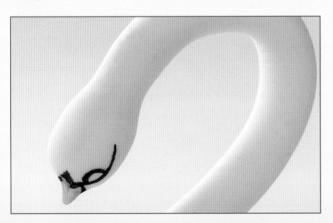

TIP! Painting the swan's face can be tricky so if you are worried or don't have a steady hand leave the face blank, it will look just as stunning.

MAKING THE BODY OF THE SWAN:

Start by taking a ball of white modelling paste about the size of a golf ball, add Trex to the ball of paste and knead until it is smooth. It is sometimes impossible to get all the cracks out of the paste but don't worry, simply knead the cracks to the bottom of the ball and make sure this part is face down to the board. Lightly press the ball into an egg shape.

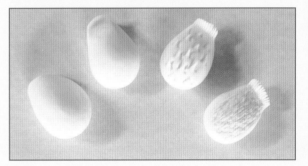

Start to shape the tail by pinching with your fingers – this should be at the top of the egg shape.

Then, using the scissors, make lots of downward cuts into the pinched part of the egg shape. It should be starting to look like a body of a swan by now.

To create the feathered look, take the small scissors and press the blade flat against the icing, making lots of little cuts across the swan's back (don't worry about the sides of the swan as your wings will cover them up). Then with the scalpel, or the pointed end of the celpin, make lots of little marks over the cuts you have just made, working your way down to the tail. Try to be messy and a bit artistic with this because if you are too regimented it will not look so effective.

CREATING THE WINGS:

Roll out some modelling paste for the wings to about 1.5mm thick. Cut out two wings with the swan wing cutter, then turn one over and place the rounded end of the wings together – this will look like a man's moustache (the reason for doing this is so you don't end up with two left or right wings, you will have one of each).

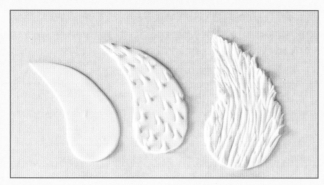

Repeat the process followed to create the feathered look across the swan's back but be careful not to cut though the wings.

Turn the wings over and brush with water, then place on the body of the swan one at a time, making sure the rounded end of the wing is to the front of the swan's body. It doesn't matter if the wings overlap slightly if they are a bit big. If there is excess paste, just fold it underneath the swan.

ATTACH THE NECK:

Once the neck is thoroughly dry, attach it to the body with a small amount of royal icing on the bottom of the neck.

Repeat the steps above to make the second swan and leave to dry. They are looking good!

BULLRUSHES:

The bullrushes are quite simple to make. Take a length of 28# wire and tape up with half-width green florist tape, then cut it into three pieces, making each of the pieces slightly longer than the previous one.

With a small amount of brown flower paste, make a sausage shape, then push the wire into the paste leaving a little of the green wire showing at the top of the bull rush, pinch at the bottom of the paste to seal on to the wire.

Repeat this process until you have nine bullrushes, three in each bunch. Then put to one side.

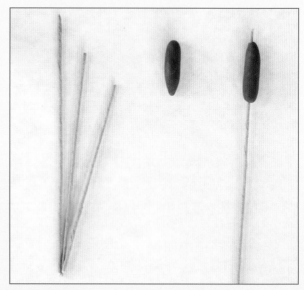

TUFTS OF GRASS:

To make the grass take a ball of green flower paste, roll it into a sausage then place it on a non-stick board. Using a small celpin hold it across the sausage lengthways and push down and roll out so you are rolling half the sausage thin and keeping the other half slightly thicker.

With the large grass cutter, place the points of the cutter on the thin part of the icing and press down to cut out. Lift the cutter up and wipe your thumb over the cutter to remove any excess paste and get a good clean cut, then push the paste out of the cutter.

Brush a little water across the thick part of the grass and roll it up, this will look strange to start with, but given a little tweak it will be fine.

Once rolled up, stand the grass on the board and with two fingers, push in and down slightly at the same time to make the tuft of grass take shape. You need three of these.

TO ASSEMBLE THE CAKE:
Place a wide glass bowl on the centre of the 18" iced oval board, then carefully remove the 10" cake from the spare board and place it on to the centre of the glass bowl.

Carefully remove the 8" iced cake from the spare board and place on to the dowelling rods, making sure the top cake is in the centre of the 10" cake. The dowelling rods will take the weight of the top cake.

▶ **TIP!** I like to use a turntable to lift the cake off the work surface and it helps to move the cake around as you are working on it.

Add the diamanté ribbon around the bottom of each tier by using a little melted gelatine on the ribbon. You will need to use one part gelatine to two parts water.

You can now start adding the leaves by putting a small amount of royal icing on the back of each one and pushing them between the two cakes. Do this all the way around the cake.

Spoon some piping gel on the centre of the top tier cake and spread it about, then pick up your wonderful swans and place in the centre. Personally I like the swans to be almost kissing because the necks make a fabulous heart shape.

Place the tufts of grass on the cake, one at the back and one either side of the swans, then gently push the bullrushes into the centre of each tuft of grass (I think three in each tuft of grass looks good). Your cake is looking wonderful, but to finish off, put some piping gel in a small piping bag and randomly pipe small dots over the cake. I think this effect looks like the swans have been splashing around, plus it adds interest to a plain cake without being too overpowering.

OPTIONAL CUP CAKES:

Put some white sugar paste into a mixer and add a small amount of water, a little at a time, until the icing goes softer.

Then place in a piping bag and pipe on to the top of the cupcakes using the star nozzle (this will look like a soft whipped ice cream).

Pipe a small amount of royal icing on the back of the three looped leaves and place on top of the cup cake, so the points of the leaves meet in the middle.

Then add a small amount of royal icing to the bottom of the swans and place into the centre of the cupcake, and, hey presto, a fabulous cake!

For the finishing touch place into the edible cake wrappers.

VARIATIONS:

In this image I have used the grass cutter to finish the edge of the cake instead of the ribbon.

Another variation of this cake would be to use just one tier on the stand:

SEA HOLLY CAKE

I have used the sea holly cutter to cut out the patterns for this cake, so carrying the theme through the cake. Using a darker colour adds to the dramatic effect, but you can adapt the colours to suit you and maybe go for pastel ones too, e.g. coffee and cream.

Equipment:

- 6" drum board
- 8" drum board
- 12" drum board
- 8" spare board
- 10" spare board
- Large rolling pin
- Smoother
- 10 dowelling rods
- Sea holly cutters: large, medium and small (Passion4Cakes, see Suppliers on page 46)
- Sea holly veiner (Passion4Cakes, see Suppliers on page 46)
- Small celpin
- Non-stick board
- Curved tweezer scissors and tweezers (Passion4Cakes, see Suppliers on page 46)
- White wires 20#, 24#, 26#, 28# and 30#
- Lighter or tealight
- Set of pointed ivy cutters (A Piece of Cake, see Suppliers on page 46)
- Ivy veiner (Edable Art, see Suppliers on page 46)
- Florist tape, half-width

Materials:

- 2 x 6" fruit cakes
- 2 x 8" fruit cakes
- 2 x 10" fruit cakes
- 5kg marzipan
- Apricot glaze
- 5kg sugar paste
- Icing sugar
- Cooled boiled water or white alcohol
- 200g white flower paste (A Piece of Cake, see Suppliers on page 46)
- Trex
- Light teal and autumn green dusts (Rainbow Dust, see Suppliers on page 46)
- Silvery moon shimmer silver hologram (Edable Art, see Suppliers on page 46)
- Royal blue dust (Edable Art, see Suppliers on page 46)
- Small amount of royal icing in a piping bag
- Silver hologram glitter (Edable Art, see Suppliers on page 46)
- 3m diamanté chain (Passion4Cakes, see Suppliers on page 46)

MARZIPAN THE CAKES:

Place one of the 10" fruit cakes on the 12" drum board. Sprinkle some icing sugar on the worktop to stop the marzipan from sticking and then roll the marzipan to a 10" (255mm) circle.

Brush a thin layer of apricot glaze on to the top of the fruit cake and place the circle of marzipan on top. Place the other 10" fruit cake upside down on top of that. If there is a gap around the middle of the cakes, fill with marzipan. Cover the 10" fruit cakes with apricot glaze.

Sprinkle some icing sugar on the worktop to stop the marzipan from sticking and then roll the marzipan to a thickness of ¼" (4mm). Then loosely and gently roll the marzipan around the rolling pin and lift over the cake. Unroll the marzipan over the top of the cake, smooth down the sides of the cake and cut away any excess marzipan. Use a smoother to smooth the top and sides of the cake.

Repeat this with the 6" cakes but place them on to the 6" board, then onto the 8" spare board. Also marzipan the 8" cakes in the same manner.

▶ **TIP!** When rolling the marzipan around the rolling pin, try to pick up using the ends of the rolling pin, don't pick up from the centre as you will squash the beautifully rolled out marzipan.

ICING THE CAKE:

Brush water or white alcohol over the marzipanned cake (this will help the sugar paste stick to the cake), then loosely and gently roll the sugar paste around the rolling pin and unroll over the cake. With the smoother rub over the top of the cake to make sure there are no air bubbles, then use your hands to gently work your way down the sides of the cake to remove any air bubbles

from there, before using the smoother again to create a wonderfully smooth finish.

Repeat with all of the cakes – don't forget to marzipan and ice down the sides of the 6" and 8" boards so the board looks like part of the cake.

INSERTING THE DOWELLING RODS:

Push one rod into the middle of the 10" cake, then using a knife mark the rod where the sugar paste finishes on the rod at the top of the cake. Pull the dowelling rod out and cut where the mark is. Measure another four dowelling rods and cut to the same size. Place one back into the centre of the cake and push the other four around the centre; this will help support the top tier. Then place the top tier on top of the 8" cake.

DECORATION:

Add some of the royal blue food dust to the white flower paste and roll it out thinly. Using the large sea holly cutter, cut out five bracts and place them with the flat bottom part of the petal facing inwards to make a snowflake shape. Then, with a little water on the underside of the bracts, place on the cake. Repeat with all five bracts. To vary the design I have used all three cutters from the sea holly set.

Pipe a small ball of royal icing into the centre of the snowflake shape, then dip a dry brush into the silver hologram glitter and brush it on to the royal icing before it dries. Repeat all over to make this pattern.

Attach the diamanté chain to the bottom of each cake with a little royal icing, to make a neat finish.

► **TIP!** Instead of using two 6" and two 10" cakes, you can put extra cake mixture into the tin before baking to make the cake deeper.

TO MAKE THE SEA HOLLY:

LARGE SEA HOLLY BRACTS:
Roll out some autumn green flower paste leaving a small ridge up the centre. Using the large sea holly cutter, press the cutter down on to the flower paste with the ridge going up the centre of the cutter and cut out the shape. Push a 28# wire into the ridge just over half way up, then vein using the sea holly veiner.

Make little nicks around the bract with scissors so it looks like a thistle or feather. Then bend it slightly at the base of the bract where the paste is on the wire, this will slightly cup the centre of the thistle. Bend the bract, then leave to rest on a piece of foam. It should look like a little man with no head, sitting by the pool dangling his feet into the water. You will need five of these.

► **TIP!** Knead Trex into the flower paste to help slow down the drying process.

MEDIUM SEA HOLLY BRACTS:
Using the medium sea holly cutter, cut out, vein and shape five bracts in the same way as you made the large ones.

SMALL SEA HOLLY BRACTS:
Roll out the green flower paste thinly leaving a small ridge up the centre, then cut out using the small cutter and snip around the edge of the bract.

Push a 30# wire into the ridge and gently curve the end of the bract over the edge of the board to dry slightly.

TO MAKE THE CENTRE OF THE SEA HOLLY:
Take a length of 20# wire and bend a small hook in one end. Take some green flower paste, slightly larger than a sprout and knead a little Trex into the paste, as this will slow down the paste drying out. Roll the paste into a neat ball, heat the hook with a naked flame (this will get very hot so be careful) and then push it into the ball of paste. Shape the ball into a large rose cone.

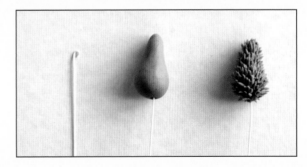

With a small pair of scissors, starting at the bottom of the cone, make small cuts, working your way up until you get to the top.

TO COLOUR THE BRACTS:

Remember I said about the man sitting by the edge of the pool? Well, dust the royal blue from the waist of the man down to his ankles, then use light teal dust where the man's head should be, to blend the two colours. I like to dust over the centre of the sea holly with royal blue dust and finish with a light dusting of the silvery moon shimmer all over the sea holly.

▶ **TIP!** You need to colour the bracts straight away – if you leave them to dry before colouring, your spikes will break off.

TO WIRE THE SEA HOLLY:

Try to do this when the bracts are still slightly damp. Hold the centre of the sea holly, then leave a gap of about half an inch down the wire and add the five large bracts.

Using half-width green florist tape, stretch the tape to release the glue and secure to the wires about half an inch under the bottom of the large bracts. Holding the taped wire pull the wires of the bracts one by one, down through the tape, so that you get a neat and tight finish to the back of the thistle. You can now put your hands into the centre of the sea holly and move the large bracts around until you are happy with where they are sitting.

Pull the centre of the sea holly down and finish taping down the wire, before attaching the florist tape under the large bracts at the top of the wire.

Start to add the medium bracts between, but behind the large bracts, and once again tape all the way down.

Then add the small bracts in the same way and tape down. Using tweezers carefully move the bracts so they look as if they are growing on the wire.

MAKING WHITE IVY LEAVES:

Roll out the white flower paste. Leave a ridge halfway up the centre of the paste and cut out the leaf using the large pointed ivy cutter. Insert a 26# white wire into the leaf. Vein in the ivy veiner and soften the edges with the rounded end of the celpin.

Leave to dry and repeat with the other two sizes of the ivy leaf to get a nice variation.

SPIKY BALLS:

Using the same method used to do the centre of the sea holly, take a length of 24# wire and bend a small hook in one end. Then take a pea-sized piece of white flower paste, knead a little Trex into it to stop it drying out and roll into a neat ball.

Heat the hook with a naked flame (this will get very hot so be careful) and then push it into the ball of flower paste.

With a small pair of scissors, starting at the bottom of the ball shape, make small cuts, working your way up until you get to the top.

You can dust the balls in any colour to suit your arrangement; I have dusted with a little brown and pink.

WIRING THE ARRANGEMENT:

Hold the sea holly in a loose bunch in front of a mirror, then add the sea holly balls and the ivy leaves in and around the arrangement.

Tape them in place using the half-width florist tape.

VARIATIONS:

You can then add lights if you wish.

There are also various ways to display the cakes to give some different looks:

1. Two-tiered stacked cake
2. Edible cake stand with a sea holly inside to raise the top tier.

2.

1.

SEA HOLLY CAKE

I first designed this cake for the table of honour at Birmingham NEC and it has since proved to be the most popular cake I have ever made. It can be adapted in several ways and looks fantastic no matter what you do with it. For an alternative look, you could leave the top of the bag as a zip, rather than putting flowers in it, and if you don't like bear grass why not cover the bag with edible sequins? Just remember to change the colour of the sugar paste to suit the final decorations.

Materials:

- 1 x sponge loaf cake
- 700g buttercream (see Recipes on page 44)
- 2kg green sugar paste (make by colouring white sugar paste with the autumn green dust)
- Icing sugar
- Autumn green coloured dust (Rainbow Dust, see Suppliers on page 46)
- 400g white flower paste (A Piece of Cake, see Suppliers on page 46)
- Confectioners' glaze
- Semolina, coloured yellow
- Forsythia yellow and red dusts (Edable Art, see Suppliers on page 46)
- Pale forsythia yellow coloured flower paste (made by colouring white sugar paste with the pale forsythia yellow dust)
- Cooled boiled water

Equipment:

- Large rolling pin
- Large knife to carve with
- Spare board to work on
- Non-stick board
- Amaryllis veiner
- Brush for water
- Tweezers
- Bear grass 15mm cutter (Passion4Cakes, see Suppliers on page 46)
- Bear grass 5mm cutter (Passion4Cakes, see Suppliers on page 46)
- Corn husk veiner
- Hosta leaf veiner (Edable Art, see Suppliers on page 46)
- Scalpel
- Rose petal veiner
- Medium celpin
- Small celpin
- Phalaenopsis orchid cutters (Passion4Cakes, see Suppliers on page 46)
- 20#, 26#, 28# white wire
- 14" mirror or 16" iced board
- Wire cutters
- CelPad
- Pale green florist tape, half-width
- Posy pick
- Arum lily cutter (Passion4Cakes, see Suppliers on page 46)

SHAPING THE CAKE:

Place the loaf cake on its side on the spare board and, with a large knife, carve each of the sides so the ends bow in slightly. Then do the same at the bottom and at the top so the corners protrude from the rest of the cake. Make sure there are no square edges and it is the shape you are trying to achieve. Use the knife to carve away a little more, if necessary.

▶ **TIP!** Have a picture of the handbag that you want to make as this will help you to create the right shape to start with. If you get the carving right, the rest will follow.

COVERING WITH SUGAR PASTE:

Sprinkle some icing sugar on the worktop to stop the sugar paste from sticking and then roll out the green sugar paste. Cover the cake with a thin layer of buttercream (this will help the sugar paste stick to the cake), then loosely and gently roll the sugar paste around the rolling pin and unroll over the cake. With the smoother rub over the top of the cake to make sure there are no air bubbles, then use your hands to gently work your way down the sides of the cake to remove any air bubbles from there. You may need to cut the icing down the sides to create a join and cut away any excess paste. This sugar paste layer doesn't have to be perfect, as it will be covered in bear grass, but the smoother it is, the better the finished result.

CREATING THE BEAR GRASS:

Roll out more green paste quite thinly, then, using the bear grass cutter (note the cutter is open ended so you can make longer stripes of grass), press down with the cutter to cut out.

Carefully line up the cutter above the last cut out strip and repeat so you have a long strip of bear grass. Place into the corn husk veiner and vein (if the veiner is not big enough for your strip of paste, open the veiner and move the flower paste over before veining).

▶ **TIP!** If you want the bear grass to look thin like mine, use flower paste instead of sugar paste, as you can roll flower paste more thinly.

▶ **TIP!** Don't be tempted to make all the bear grass first as it will start to dry and crack as you place it onto the cake, so only make as many strips as you need.

▶ **TIP!** To create darker bear grasses add some green food dust to the glaze and brush on.

COVERING THE BEAR GRASS:

Brush the cake with a small amount of water where you plan to place the first strip of paste. Then start to wrap the bag in the bear grass – you may need to cut the grass where it meets another strip of grass. To neaten the bag put a strip of grass down each side.

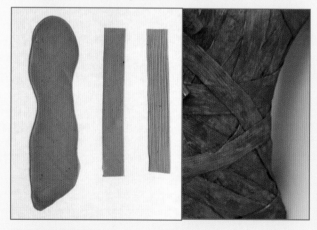

TOP OF THE BAG:

Once the bag is covered in bear grass, roll out two long strips of paste and place along the top of the bag to represent the zip. If you wish to put flowers in, like mine, this is where you can put the posy pick.

OPTIONAL: if you wish the bag to be shiny, brush with confectioners' glaze, as I have, and leave to dry. If covering the bag in sugar paste, the glaze will be absorbed, so I would suggest brushing on a shimmer dust instead.

Place the handbag on a 14" mirror or a 16" pre-iced board.

BEAR GRASS FOR THE STRAPS:

Roll out a long length of green flower paste and then brush some water along it. Place a length of 26# wire on the water and fold the flower paste over to sandwich the wire, then roll out a little on both sides of the wire to thin out. Place the 5mm bear grass cutter over the covered wire and press down, making sure that the wire is in the middle of the cutter. Cut out and then repeat this all the way along the strip, so you have a long strip of bear grass, then vein in the corn husk veiner. You will need three strips of bear grass.

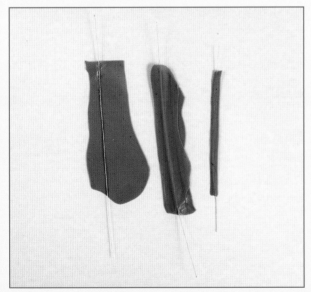

To make the bear grass shiny, brush some confectioners' glaze over the dried bear grass and leave to dry.

Tape up the three ends of the wire and then tape the other end so you create the strap. Push them into the top of the handbag.

FLOWERS AND FOLIAGE FOR HANDBAG:

TWISTED BEAR GRASS:

Roll a sausage shape of green flower paste then insert the 26# wire. Twist the flower paste on to the wire and make it as thin as you can without breaking it, roll it on a board if you find it easier. Then wrap the covered wire loosely around your medium celpin, or your finger, and stretch out the wire slightly to reveal your twisted bear grass. This is simple and quick to do but adds so much to a simple arrangement of flowers.

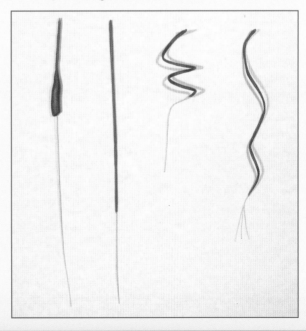

LOOPED PEACE LILY LEAVES:

Roll out the green flower paste. Leaving a ridge through the centre of the paste, cut out with a scalpel then, holding the thick end of the ridge between your finger and thumb, insert the 26# wire into the ridge with the other hand and press down, so it stays on the wire. The wire needs to be in the paste just under half way up the leaf. Place in the hosta leaf veiner and press down to make the impression of the veins on the paste then using the rounded end of the celpin, soften the edge of the leaf to make it more realistic. Brush a little water on the back of the leaf where the wire is inserted and simply loop the tip of the leaf on to the water and hang up to dry.

CURLED PEACE LILY LEAVES:

Make the leaf as above and place on the wire. Vein and ball in the same way, but when adding the water to the tip of the leaf, roll around the end of a paint brush (be careful of the wire in the central vein). Add a little water just before you stop rolling, to keep it together.

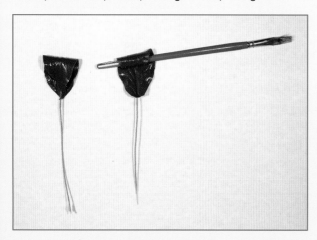

▶ **TIP!** You can make the leaves any size – try rolling the leaf around a large rolling pin rather than a paint brush. Experiment!

ARUM LILY:

Bend a small hook in the end of a 20# wire, then using a pale yellow flower paste, roll a small sausage over the hook and slightly down the wire. Thread a ball of paste on to the wire from the other end and attach to the sausage shape with a little water. The sausage shape should be just over half the length of the cutter and the ball the size of a marble. Leave to dry.

Once dry, brush the sausage shape with water, then roll in the yellow coloured semolina and leave to dry. This will give the impression of pollen. Roll out some white flower paste quite thinly, but leaving the centre part of the flower a little thicker, then cut out the petal. Vein in the amaryllis petal veiner and soften the edges using the rounded end of the celpin.

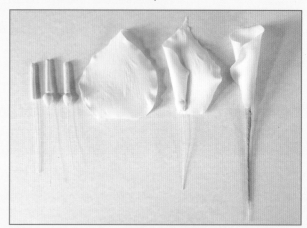

Brush a little water on the bottom edge of the petal, then place the flower centre so that the ball sits on the bottom edge of the petal. The ball of paste should be just on the water. Then roll the large petal around the centre, which should leave you with a shape similar to an ice cream cone. Mould the edges of the flower with your fingers to create a more natural shape and leave upside down to dry. Tape the base of the flower and wire several times to create a thick stem.

PHALAENOPSIS ORCHID:

THROAT OF THE ORCHID:

Make a small hook in the end of a 26# wire, then take a pea-sized piece of flower paste and attach to the hook on the wire. Mould the ball into the wider end of the tear drop shape then, using the rounded end of the medium celpin, place it against the cone shape and press the two together to form a cup-like shape in the paste. Using the tweezers, pinch the very end of the cupped shape and leave to dry.

Roll out some flower paste leaving a ridge in the centre, cut out the throat shape and attach a very small ball of paste with some water to the centre of the throat. Using the back of a scalpel press the ball almost in half and place the throat on the CelPad. Soften the edges with the rounded end of the ball tool, then from the tip of each fork to the centre, to make them curl up slightly.

Make a small hook in the end of a 26# wire and insert this down the thicker end of the throat (be careful not to put this in too far – no more than about 5mm), then leave to dry, making sure that the two wing-like pieces of the throat are raised clear of the middle part of the throat and the fork is curled up towards the throat.

Dust the centres of the throat with a little forsythia yellow dust then paint a small dot of red on to the centre of the throat where the ball of paste has been attached. Paint red lines starting from the centre of the throat and extending to the edge of the icing.

PETALS:

Roll out some white flower paste leaving a small ridge up the centre, then cut out the head of the orchid using the cutter. Insert a 28# wire into the ridge then place in a rose petal veiner and vein. Soften the edges with the celpin.

Repeat the above to make two arms and two legs, to make five petals altogether.

ASSEMBLING:

First bring the two throats together and tape using half-width florist tape. Then start at the back of the throat and wire the head and two legs, then attach the arms and wire all the way down the stem.

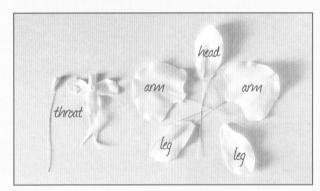

Carefully move the petals into the right place, then stand back and admire your work.

WIRING THE FLOWERS:

Holding the end of the twisted bear grass, tape together, then add the three Arum lilies and add the three Phalaenopsis orchids and tape in with the looped leaves and once again tape up the wires.

Push a posy pick into the top of the handbag and insert the wired spray.

RECIPES

Royal icing
2–3 egg whites
500g icing sugar (sifted)
5ml glycerine

Beat the egg whites in a bowl, then add the sifted icing sugar and mix until you have a soft peak.
Then add the glycerine.
If you aren't using the icing immediately, place a clean, damp cloth over the mixture to prevent it forming a crust
and store in an airtight container in the fridge.

Modelling paste: I use a JEM Petal Paste recipe
35ml or 1 egg white
140g or 1 cup icing sugar (sifted)
11g or 2 rounded tsps JEM petal powder

Lightly beat the egg white, then add the sifted icing sugar slowly until a soft peak consistency is reached.
Add the JEM petal powder – the mixture will immediately thicken.
Gradually add more icing sugar until a pliable texture is achieved.
Rub a little petal base or Trex on your hands and work the paste thoroughly.
Paste should not be sticky, nor should it be too hard.
Store in a sealed plastic bag, in a sealed plastic container.
Paste is ready to be used immediately.

Buttercream
225g butter
120g icing sugar

Weigh out the butter and put it into a bowl.
Sieve the icing sugar on top and cream the two together.
You can then add flavouring if you wish.

ABOUT THE AUTHOR

I am a sugarcraft specialist who has a passion for the sugarcraft (cake decorating) world. I was initially introduced to sugarcraft as a thirteen year old, by Aunty Eileen who took me to my first demonstration. I found out where my local Sugarcraft Guild met and joined them as an adult member as they didn't have a group for children.

The Guild encouraged me to enter competitions and I won a bronze award in my first competition, aged fourteen. I went on to study for a City & Guilds in Sugarcraft at Stratford upon Avon College, and following this I am completely self-taught.

I have entered many competitions since, in shows such as the International Cake Show at Birmingham NEC and Squires Kitchen International, winning several bronze, silver and gold awards. I have also won best in show at the British Sugarcraft Guild Competition.

When I had my first child, Charlotte, I gave up work and decided to take the plunge and go self-employed as a demonstrator and teacher of sugarcraft. I started writing for sugarcraft magazines. I now have two lovely boys, Sam and Harry, as well as the beautiful Charlotte.

I really enjoy travelling up and down the UK, demonstrating and presenting workshops. I also have my own product range, which is growing all the time.

In the future I would like to write more books, keep designing cakes and travel the world teaching and spreading the word about this wonderful craft.

I have a website and online shop at www.Passion4Cakes.com. You can also become a fan of Passion4Cakes on Facebook and follow me on twitter: http://twitter.com/Passion4Cakes

SUPPLIERS

Michele at Lemonella Ltd
www.lemonella.com
Supplier of edible cake stands and jelly roses

A Piece of Cake
18-20 Upper High Street, Thame, Oxon OX9 3EX
Tel 01844 213428
www.sugaricing.co.uk
Mail order supplier of flower paste and lots of other goodies

Lindy's Cakes Ltd
Unit 2, Station Approach, Wendover, Aylesbury, Buckinghamshire HP22 6BN
Tel 01296 622418
www.lindyscakes.co.uk
Supplied gold trumpet cake stand for Sequin Cake

Jem Cutters
www.jemcutters.com
email: jemcutters@africa.com
They supplied the recipe for modelling paste

Food dusts:

Edable Art
Tel 01388 816309
Email: edableart@mail.com

Rainbow Dust Colours Ltd
www.rainbowdust.co.uk

And me...
Cassie Brown – Passion4Cakes
Mobile: 07525 632153
Email:cassie@Passion4Cakes.com
www.Passion4Cakes.com

LEMONELLA

Bespoke hard-sugar cake stands, edible jewels, ribbons and flowers by Michele at Lemonella.

Michele believes that if a decoration is on a cake then it should be able to be eaten.

She works with over 80 colours and 50 flavours from childhood favourites to adult alcoholic indulgences to create a range of fabulous edible cake decorations and display stands to adorn your creations.

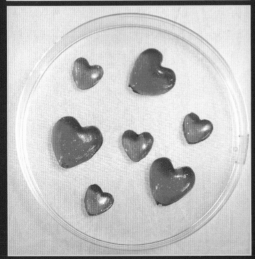

www.lemonella.com

enquiries@lemonella.com

COMING SOON...

CASSIE'S next book **SUGAR CREATIONS** will further explore cutting edge creativity with sugar!

Here's a taster of some of the flowers to come:

For future book release dates email
ceri.gautama@thehothive.com